Hindu Fundamentalism and the Spirit of Capitalism in India

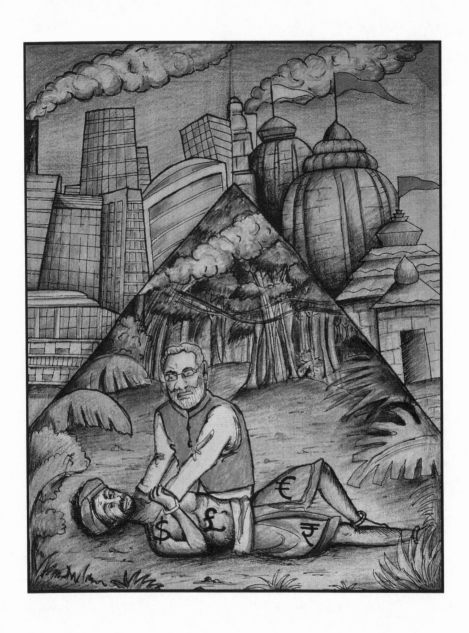

Hindu Fundamentalism and the Spirit of Capitalism in India

Hinduisation of Tribals in Kalahandi during the New Economic Reforms

Bhabani Shankar Nayak

Hamilton Books

Lanham • Boulder • New York • Toronto • Plymouth, UK

Copyright © 2018 by Hamilton Books
4501 Forbes Boulevard, Suite 200, Lanham, Maryland 20706
Hamilton Books Acquisitions Department (301) 459-3366

Unit A, Whitacre Mews, 26-34 Stannary Street,
London SE11 4AB, United Kingdom

Library of Congress Control Number: 2017947613
ISBN: 978-0-7618-6968-9 (pbk : alk. paper)—ISBN: 978-0-7618-6969-6 (electronic)

♾️™ The paper used in this publication meets the minimum requirements of American
National Standard for Information Sciences Permanence of Paper for Printed Library
Materials, ANSI/NISO Z39.48-1992.

Dedicated to my Maa, Bapa, Bou and Shreekanta Bhai
who have been crucial in the development of my inquisitive mind
and taught me to pursue and realise my dreams
by listening to the language of heart

Contents

Acknowledgments

The 'traveler self and the road' are the two witnesses of my social and academic life from a remote village of Barunadiha to Britain; a long journey inundated with the mixed feelings of pain, pleasure and excitements. I was able to finish the journey of my doctoral research with the help of a number of people. It is very difficult to name them all here but this work would remain incomplete without recognising their help and support in multifarious ways in completing this work.

This book is a product of my research for my D.Phil. I will remain indebted to Prof Jan Selby, Prof Roderick Stirrat, Dr. Ian Duncan and Dr. Vinita Damodaran for their cooperation and help during the primary stage of my research. I am thankful to Prof. John Holmwood, Dr. Ben Rogaly, Dr. Biswamoy Pati, Dr. Raju J Das, Prof. Mick Moore, Dr. Meera Warrior, Dr. Samuel Knafo, Dr. Barbara Einhorn, Prof. Richard Black, Dr. Lyla Mehta, Dr. Felix Padel, Dr. Fillipo Osella, Dr. Maya Unnithan, Julie Carr and Jenny Mooney for their inspirational and unforgettable friendship which made my stay in England meaningful and easy. Prof. Richard Grove and Clare Rogers have always extended their helping hands and encouraged me with smiling face to restore my confidence during different stages of this research. I am thankful to Dr. Pritam Singh, Dr. Meena Dhanda and Dr. Amalendu Misra for all their financial help, encouragement and love. I am thankful to Prof. Kees Van Der Pijl for all his encouragements and restoring my political commitments. I am much obliged to all my teachers especially Prof. Shantha Sinha, Prof. G.Haragopal, Prof. E.Haribabu, Dr. V.Janardhan, Dr. Sudhanshu Patnaik, Prof. Sarada Rath, Suresh Mishra, Anup Mallick, Badal Biswal and all my teachers for the strength I gathered from their encouragement and teachings. The words are not enough to acknowledge the inspiration and help of all my fellow comrades and friends inside and outside the CPI (M) who have shaped my thoughts and analytical ability.

I am much obliged to Shrijukta Naveen Pattnaik (Chief Minister of Orissa) for his financial help and friendly encouragement to carry forward my research work during an absolute crisis of my student life. My heartfelt thanks to him.

I am thankful to Pradeep bhai and Jaya bhauja for all their love and support. I am thankful to Dr. Achyut Samanta of the Kalinga Relief and Charitable Trust, Kamini Pattnaik of the Kalinga Foundation and Dr. Bansidhar Panda of the IMFA Charitable Trust, Bhubaneswar for their financial help to carry forward this research work. I am thankful to Mr Tararanjan Patnaik is Chairman-cum- Director of Falcon Marine Exports Ltd., the Managing Director of Falcon Finance Ltd. for his generous financial help and encouragement.

I will remain grateful Arun Bothra (Arun Bhai), Mohan Jena, M.P (Mohan Bhai), Matlub Ali (Ex. Minister), Panchanan Kanungo (Ex Finance Minister), Madhusmita Bhai, Dr. Sanjaya Satpathy, Sabyasachi Kar (Bhai), Susanta Bhai and Niru Bhauja for their friendship, financial support and inspiration in the crucial stage of my student life.

I am grateful to Com. Naba Pattnayak, Bhauja and Papun, Lokanath Nayak, Parameswar Bhai and Bhauja, Akhila Bhai, Prakash Pradhan, Satya Singh, Ashok Singh, Raja, Manoj Parida and Jayanta Behera for their sportive company and help during my fieldwork at Kalahandi. They have not only made my stay at Kalahandi comfortable but also accepted me as the part of their family. Maheswar Hial, Satyabahan Kumar, Munda Babu, Biranchi Bhai, Satpathy Babu, Lakhra Babu and many tribal and non tribal friends in Kalahandi helped me immensely to carry forward this work successfully by sharing the pain of underdevelopment and tribal exploitation. I am also thankful to Sarada Bhai and Surya Bhai for their inspiration.

I take this opportunity to thank all the staffs of Kalahandi District Collectorate, DRDA, all BDO's and their staffs in Kalahandi, Superintendent of Police and his Office Staff, Staffs at MADA Office, ITDA Office, District Statistical Office, District Planning Office, District Employment Office, DMO and his staffs, District Civil Supply Office, staffs of SC &ST Finance Cooperation, SBI Lead Bank, District Industries Centre and staffs of NIC at Bhawanipatna for their support and help in providing data for my research. The nature and beauty of Kalahandi, especially Thuamul Rampur and Langigarh is very much inspiring. I am thankful to the staffs of the Department of Tribal Welfare, Rural Development, Planning and Coordination, Revenue, Finance and Secretariat library at the Orissa Secretariat for their support in providing data for this research. I much obliged to the staffs of the Parija Library, department libraries of the Economics, Political Science, History and Anthropology departments at the Utkal University, Bhubaneswar. The staffs of the ST & SC Research Institute, Orissa Legislative Assembly Library, State Library and Orissa State Archives were very helpful during my literature survey for my research. I am thankful to Com. Basudev Acharya (M.P) for enabling me to access the Parliament Library which was very helpful both for data collection and literature survey. I am thankful to the library staffs of the Central library and Exim Bank library of the Jawaharlal Nehru University and Nehru National Museum and Library, Teen Murti House and New Delhi for their help. I am also thankful to the library staffs of the Indira Gandhi Library, University of Hyderabad, Centre for Economic and Social Studies, National Institute of Rural Development, Osmania University, Academic Staff College of India and M.V Foundation, Hyderabad for their help for this research.

I am sincerely thankful to all my friends here at Sussex, especially to, Narayan, Prasanta, Elamathi, 'Sagheer and Bhabi', Srikar, Jilesh, Naureen and Zuber, 'Daniel and Niki', Danny, Baba, Carry, Nagah, Jamie, Laura, Dinah, Kanwal, Nick, Nicole, Nikki, Eric, Becky, Nalu, 'Shanti Appa and Sunder', Jess and Rohit for their supportive company which made my stay comfortable. My fifth floor buddies at Sussex (Mike, Kamran, Clemens, Ishan, George, Earl, Susanna Rust, Or Raviv, Duncan, Jonathan, Yulia, Nadine, Evi, Ernesto, Andrea, Miguel, Leena, Simon, Samantha, Asma, Julie, and Siddhartha) made my stay joyful. Thanks to Susanna, Rob, Marina and Muriel for their comradeship. I am grateful to Mr.Ashoka Patel who has helped me a lot during my stay at Brighton. Prasanta, Bijaya, Baga, Tribhuban, Dilu, Badu, Mamta, and Ramesh are friends in India who are keeping my emotional strength through their imposed faith on my ability to be different. This work owes a lot to Geeta for being a constant source of emotional support.

Bipin Patel (Bhai) is a strong local guardian who never allowed me to fall behind in any sense. From the day one when he received me at the airport, allowed me to stay at his house till the submission of this work he ceaselessly supported me to finish the thesis. I will remain eternally indebted to him.

My dream for higher education came true only with the help of Dr. Shreekanta Nayak (Bhai) and Dr. Lipishree Nayak (Bhauja) without which it would be impossible for me to even think about my higher education here at Sussex. Their emotional support, financial help and elderly guidance have been the pillar of my doctoral research. Every time, I speak to Shreekanta Bhai and share my problems, he says that "nothing is going to happen to you Bhabani even on my dead body". There is no word in which I can express my sincere recognition of his love, affection, inspiration and support for my education.

I am thankful to 'Vishal Bhai and Shruti bhauja' for all their love and support. My father is my first-best friend and an organic teacher who has always been there to share my pain. He is a source of strong support and unfailing inspiration. He has given me enough freedom to dream and helping me to realise the dream to articulate creativity and taught me to understand life with a positive spirit. This thesis owes a lot to him. My grandmother, mother and brothers have never complained for the injustice of remaining far away from them all the time. Their understanding has helped me a lot to concentrate on my research and their emotional support is an important source of my pleasure in working on this book.I am thankful to all my extended family members, friends and relatives for their help and support in every step of my life.

I am grateful to Suchismita Sundaray for designing the frontispiece paint-ing for the book. I am thankful to Emma Richard, Holly Buchanan, and Beverly Shellem of Hamilton Books for all their support without which the book would not see light of the day. Finally, I take the responsibility for all the mistakes that this book may contain.

Introduction

The political economy of development and public policy making in India has experienced significant transformation during the past two decades. Especially following the 1991 new economic reforms, a substantive shift has taken place in the role of the State in India. The shift has brought new solutions and problems with the new trajectory of market over state. Minimised state action and free market and capital led economic growth have become familiar and dominant features in the landscape of Indian development planning. Distributive justice, as the basis of the post-colonial Indian state and its welfarism, has been pushed to the back seat of development thinking. The welfare state is considered to be an obstacle for economic growth and development. The consequences of such a process have led to the deinstitutionalisation of state managed development institutions and informalisation of development planning where non-state actors i.e. NGOs and COs are playing a significant role.

Such transformations have serious implications for the relationship between the Indian State and its citizens. Further, dominant development discourses in contemporary India do not represent the tribal[1] communities (*Adivasies*) that constitute eight percent of the Indian population. Rather, it highlights certain cultural drawbacks and leaves its potentialities in the dark while formulating tribal development policies. The theories highlight the different aspects of tribal development but offer different conclusions to avoid the shortcomings of dominant theories of development and their ideological agendas under the guidance of the free market. The role of the dominant ideology of the neo-liberal market, in the present paradigm of development thought, is to establish one theory that tries to answer everything and at the same time wants to suppress other available alternatives or emerging theories that would illuminate some of the many facets that it leaves in the

1

dark. In the process, sidelining other approaches, it defines itself as "mainstream economics", "development economics" and "dominant development thought". The ideas of *participation, governance and empowerment* have become the pet words in the making of development/public policies. In order to understand the process of the making and execution of public policy, under the shade of "mainstream economics" and "dominant development thought", it is imperative to be aware of the way in which the meanings of these concepts, ideas, notions and theories in it, have been constructed and used.

In India, the marginalised communities, and people like *Adivasies,* are dominated by the upper caste, upper class and feudal ruling elites. The marginalised communities like *Adivasies* are denied their right to develop as per their own needs. Thus, the right to develop and self-determination is a struggle for development. It demands a complete coverage of non-dominant analysis to the dominant elites in the national and domestic sphere to understand, explain and look for alternative ways of thinking about the development of marginalised communities like *Adivasies* in India (Mohanty, 1989). That means the debate on development and underdevelopment needs to move from the assumed dominant location to the minority social stratum of all societies in search of a creative base among the masses (Thiongo, 1996). Thus, the debate on development in India is not simply about dividing the territories, people, places and their cultures based on 'civilised urban centres and uncivilised rural peripheries', and tribal and non tribals. It is imperative to understand different dynamics and layers of development and underdevelopment which manifest different forms of alienation with the change of development policies undertaken by a market led state.

The collapse of the state command economy in the post 1991 Indian economy, and the subsequent withdrawal of welfare state from its welfare activities, caused serious disruptions in the development of marginalised groups like tribal communities. The tribal development policies, during and after the post-new economic reforms, have led to the process of transition in tribal societies from a non-monetised, forest based agrarian economic system, to a market based economic system. Does movement from an agrarian and forest based subsistence, pre-industrial economy to a market economy and from rural settings to industrial ones induce stress and adversely affect the indigenous culture and its economy and help the process of Hinduisation of tribals? How does the Hinduisation of tribals help mining-led industrial capital and its economy to grow in the tribal areas? The answer to these questions comes from historians, political scientists, economists and cultural studies. Historians like Pati (1999, 2003) consider it as a historical process of de-tribalisation whereas political scientists like Kanungo (2003) and Desai (2004a & 2004b) consider it as a political and cultural process. The economists consider it the integration of indigenous people into a larger economy as part of a worldwide phenomenon. The theoretical and methodological focus of the debates on tribal development within post-modern developmentalists and policy makers, cultural anthropologists, neo-liberal economists, cultural studies and political discourses of civil society over recent years reflects a more general and conflicting account of transition in tribal societies - as if it is a product of necessity of tribal communities or an attempt by outside forces to absorb tribals into mainstream society. Such analysis is insufficient to understand the economic, political, cultural, social and structural ideologies of economic reform programmes that marginalise tribals while formulating development policies.

The book attempts to understand and explain the impact of the new economic reforms on *Adivasies* in the Kalahandi district of Orissa. The focus of the study is on lives, livelihoods and the transition of tribal culture and economy after the implementation of the new economic reforms in India during 1991. The goal, in doing so, is to draw attention to the fact that the new economic processes in Indian economy have not only opened up its economy but also simultaneously aggravated the existing poverty and deprivation. Through these processes of marginalisation and deprivation the *Adivasies* of the Kalahandi district in Orissa, who are living in the most resourceful parts of the state, have become worst victims of this process. Although this process of development is not an accident, rather a product of the historical trajectory of tribal development planning in India in general and the challenges posed by the new economic reforms in particular. The historical development processes of the Adivasies' deprivation have been accelerated by the new economic reforms. Most importantly, it has led to a transition in the Adivasies' economy, society and culture in which they have been forced to participate, not as the primary shareholders, but as subsidiary parts from a socially and economically disadvantaged position. This has made them more vulnerable and crisis ridden. My study tries to understand this negative transition in the *Adivasies'* economy, society and culture and its interaction with the changing character of political economy of public policy at global, national, regional and local levels. However, the negative transition, and the participation of the *Adivasies* in it, still continues and this forced participation reproduces different forms of marginalisation and deprivation.

The book documents the nature of changes in the tribal culture, society and economy in the Kalahandi district, in the wake of the new economic reforms in India. How far did the reform programmes influence the social, cultural, political and economic life of the *Adivasies*? I want to find out the failures and success of the new economic reforms in providing welfare (social and economic services by the State) to the Adivasies. What is the role of reform programmes in the economic transition of the Adivasies with a particular reference to employment, agriculture and minor forest products? How are the Adivasies affected by these economic reform programmes? Is there any alternative to new economic reforms by which Adivasies in Orissa can live without the dissolution of their social, cultural and economic life and identity? How does the process of Hinduisation in the tribal areas link with capitalist market economy and de-tribalisation through Hinduisation as a cultural and political process? And how does this link with economic objectives of accessing natural resources and land in the tribal areas? My research tries to answer the above questions with an interdisciplinary language. This kind of interdisciplinary research carries an immense importance in helping to locate an alternative policy framework for the development of the *Adivasies* by using and analysing a wide range of theoretical and conceptual tools. Behind the research lies my interest in understanding how relations between culture and nature get modified when economy changes and vice versa. The interactions between nature, culture and economy have been the subject of study by social scientists, although the approaches may differ from one to another. But in my research, the idea is to understand the changing nature of tribal social, cultural and economic life due to post-economic reform led tribal development policies, in terms of development (health, education, agriculture, employment).

I argue that the transition that has taken place in the tribal society, economy and culture during the post-economic reform period is not through internal demand for change in the tribal culture and society in the Kalahandi district of Orissa, but through the requirements of external forces enforced by the public policy made by the government. This transition entails transformation of, not only the culture and social relations of production, but also many institutions in society, and a radical transformation of the world view of the tribals on individual, state, society, culture and on the issues of private property, land, market, business, social relationship, religion, government, politics and many other things. The narrative of my research establishes the link between the deinstitutionalisation of local tribal development institutions, the growth of Hindu right wing forces in tribal areas, the Hinduisation of tribals and mining-led industrial capital in the Kalahandi district. My research is intended specifically to challenge those who argue that the Hinduisation of tribals is primarily a political, cultural and religious process. It argues that Hinduisation is primarily an economic process; an unavoidable outcome of the economic reform programmes to access natural resources in the tribal areas by removing constitutional barriers - the significance of the economic outcome of such a political and cultural process that makes the political outcome secondary to the economic process. In order to justify my argument, the research has the following objectives.

The book helps us to understand and provide an institutional and historical analysis of the development of alienation and marginalisation of the *Adivasies* in the Kalahandi district of Orissa. At the same time, it will reveal how the new economic reform process is either reinforcing or sustaining this process of alienation and marginalisation and the Hinduisation that is taking the process further and deepening the capitalist social formations in the district of Kalahandi.

The study of the political economy of tribal development and transition in the tribal communities in the Kalahandi district of Orissa needs to be understood by a narrative approach along with multidisciplinary research methods, as it is impossible to replicate the realities and predicaments of tribal development policies within any particular disciplinary language. The book is based on nine months of fieldwork in Kalahandi. The first field trip was from September 2004 to October 2004 and the second field trip was from December 2004 to June 2005. The sources of my data used in this study were collected through conducting fieldwork based on ethnographic method, during which I collected two hundred thirty samples from all over the Kalahandi district. As a part of my fieldwork, I stayed, traveled extensively in all blocks of the district and participated in different social, political, governmental and cultural gatherings. The aim of my research project was to document economic and cultural transformation, to learn about their experiences, aspirations and expectations, their views about economic and political institutions and economic policies, and their perspective on the state and market that is invading their society and culture in the context of Kalahandi district in Orissa[2].

The institutional changes in the tribal societies that have occurred due to the implementation of the economic reforms at the national, state and regional level constitute market transition. This market transition has led to a wider and critical transformation involving interdependent changes in society, culture and state policy and other institutions based on informal norms and social networks that embed economic action in the tribal societies. In order to understand this interdependence of politics, economics, culture and society the study of transition societies is best pursued by an interdisciplinary research method. The interdisciplinary research method has already crystallised around the new institutionalist paradigm[3] (Cook & Levi 1990, Nee & Ingram, 1997), which has been influential in economics (North, 1990), political science (Alt & Sheplse, 1990), and economic sociology (Smelser & Swedberg, 1994). "The integrating idea of the new institutionalist paradigm is the assumption that actors identify and pursue their interests in opportunity structures shaped by custom, cultural beliefs, social norms and networks, market structures, formal organisations, and the state. The new institutionalist paradigm is well suited for studies of transitional societies because it focuses analytical attention on institutional change, its causes, and effects. Moreover, unlike the neo-classical approach, the new institutionalist paradigm does not assume efficient markets or governance structures (Nee and Matthews, 1996:403)".

In the case of my research, the institutionalist paradigm leads to fallacies as the tribals are not actors and do not pursue their interest in the given structure of power and decision making in Indian political economy of development and public policy. Rather many non-tribal and few tribal elite actors identify and pursue their interests through markets and trying to dismantle the cultural belief, social norms and networks that are incompatible with the interest of the market. Another interesting factor to note is that the power structure shaped by the customs, cultural and religious beliefs, social norms and networks in the tribal societies, most of the time works as an agency of exploitation. In order to understand these kinds of dynamics and contradictions, it is necessary to have different methodologies to study the transition of the tribal economy, culture and society in Orissa. An interdisciplinary approach to study transition in tribal society is not enough, which compels me to draw concepts and arguments from several disciplines of social sciences without any regard to particular disciplinary boundaries, leading towards post-disciplinary research methods (Jessop and Sum 2001, Sayer 2000b, 2005). However, my research work is not a post-disciplinary work as the method of post-disciplinary research has yet to develop into a fully-fledged research method. I am therefore using interdisciplinary research, while being aware of its limitations.

DEBATES ON STUDYING TRIBAL/INDIGENOUS SOCIETY

Ethnography is always preferred as a method to study tribal societies. But there is no particular research methodology to study indigenous/tribal societies. The politics of classification of knowledge (Agrawal, 2002, 1995b) is the basis of the debates on method of studying indigenous societies. The debates on the method of study of indigenous society, culture and economy arise due to characterisation of knowledge of the 'West' as scientific and 'Indigenous' as non-scientific knowledge. The classic example of this kind of analysis of 'primitive' and modern cultures and systems of knowledge can be found in the works of Levi-Strauss (1963, 1966) who suggested that 'primitive' cultures are more embedded in their environments; 'primitive' peoples are less scientific to analytic reasoning, that might question the foundations of their knowledge; and 'primitive' thought systems are more closed than scientific modes of thought. It is problematic to characterise western knowledge as modern and scientific, and indigenous knowledge as primitive and non-science. Although there is a distinction between western knowledge and indigenous knowledge the distinction, based on terms of science, is problematic while talking about sustainable development (Agrawal, 1995a). This kind of demarcation line between indigenous and Western knowledge and characterisation of knowledge gives rise to different methods of studying indigenous/tribal society, culture and economy. In terms of method, western knowledge is scientific and open which refuses to accept inquiry outside established, institutionalised science and its method (Feyerabend, 1975). In the case of indigenous knowledge, it is difficult to say now that indigenous knowledge is closed and confined. But it can be said that indigenous knowledge is bound by space and time in terms of its interaction with the outside world and its knowledge system. Methodologically speaking, a structural restraint exists in the case of indigenous knowledge that cannot question its scientific nature because indigenous knowledge is verifiable as per the positivist criteria of scientific knowledge[4]. In this way, the debate between indigenous knowledge and scientific knowledge is a product of unavailability of satisfactory methodology for distinguishing science from non-science. Hence, scientific theories based on scientific methodologies are under attack (Kulka, 1977). The methodologies that follow from the works of Levi-Strauss (1963, 1966) indicate that traditional knowledge and institutions are obstacles to development. Moreover, this kind of argument ignores people's knowledge and their institutions that play a vital role in the development process. Ignoring the role of these institutions ensures failure of development. Thus, it is necessary to document indigenous institutions and their knowledge in a systematic and coherent way to ensure development (Brokensha et al., 1980; Warren et al., 1993, Warren 1989, 1990).

In a way, this research project is trying to break away from the narrow silo of research methodology and departmentalisation of academic research. It's become somewhat sterile, almost a subset of methodological individualism[5] and moves towards a model-driven rigid disciplinary boundary, which gives certain insights, but doesn't provide full insights into the way knowledge actually operates in a society. The knowledge that operates in a society may be scientific but may not be derived through methodological research[6]. Many researchers and academicians, especially in social science, fail to understand this concept that, "we have now moved into an epoch...where truth is entirely a product of consensus values, and where 'science' itself is just the name we attach to certain modes of explanation (Norris, 1990:169)"[7]. Therefore, in my research, I am using an interdisciplinary research by covering different aspects tribal life and livelihood to start a debate over the present paradigm of development and public policy setting in India within the disciplinary language of politics and political economy[8]. Again I am using interdisciplinary research methods by borrowing language from different disciplines and am conscious about its limitations to study different aspects of tribal society.

However, I am trying to set out my methodology, deriving its strength both from deductive and indeductive analysis. But my methodological reflections and theoretical position on this particular topic prompt me to follow critical realism, which is nothing but an ontological way of studying social world. The critical realist approach recognises truth and objectivity as the adequacy of explanation and proposes a stratified ontology to distinguish between actual, real and empirical domains of the world and different powers and institutions in it. Critical realism based on the idea of materiality of the social world[9]. The critical realists look for casual explanation along with conditions and reject monolithic ontology reflected in methodological individualism practiced in social science research (Bhaskar, 1975, 1979, 1989, Sayer, 1992, 2000a). In this way, it rejects judgmental generalisations and thus produces value free and value frank research[10] in the political economy of tribal development. Further, I have followed the approach of political economy, which can unite all my methodologies used in this research work.

Although the study encompasses different shades of development debate in relation to the *Adivasies* in India, it tries to confine itself within the state of Orissa with a case study of Kalahandi district. The Kalahandi district includes thirteen blocks that can be divided into two broad categories on basis of Adivasies population concentration and the geographical locations of the area. On the basis of geographical location the district has two distinct physiographic regions i.e. the plains and the hill tracts with forests. On the basis of population concentration, the district can again divided as Adivasies-dominated areas like Langigarh block and Thuamul Rampur block[11] whereas the other eleven blocks in the district have a mixed population of Adivasies and non-Adivasies. Apart from the two predominant Adivasies blocks, the other eleven blocks have a considerable number of Adivasies who are known as dispersed tribal groups[12] according to the administrative language of the Government of Orissa. While the study has focused on two Adivasies dominated blocks i.e. Thuamul Rampur and Langigarh, it has also covered the dispersed Adivasies groups in the other eleven blocks of the Kalahandi district.

USE OF THE TERM *'TRIBE'* AND CONCEPTUAL ISSUES

It is quite a common debate on the question of the usage of the term, language, concept and contents of the research and its methodology. In my research, I faced one question from my friends, co-researchers and teachers; there are many tribal groups in India, so which tribal group or community are *you* looking at in your research? I consider the question on tribal identity and the usage of the term 'tribe' as a methodological question and justify my stand on tribal identity and usage of the term tribe in my research that reflects the methodological significance to the argument advanced in my thesis in general. I do agree with all my colleagues that there are many tribal groups in terms of their different identities based on area of residence, language, culture, religions and other social and economic practices. I have argued that the tribal identity needs to be understood and historicised in terms of tribals as individuals and as members of their communities, by taking place and cultural specifities into account. The tribal individual identity is inseparable from his or her community group identity and tribal identity in general which is under threat from cultural, religious and economic forces with the help of development policies.

While looking at this identity issue on tribal questions, I find that there is no end to the identity debate as each person carry his/her individual identity and at the same time he/she shares identity with others. Thus, the identity of an individual or a community varies. It indicates "the notion of being identical to oneself to that of sharing an identity with others of a particular group (which is the form the idea of social identity very often takes), the complexity increases further" (Sen, 2006: xii). In order to avoid this complexity of identity formation and the term 'identity' itself, I have not studied any particular tribal group while acknowledging their differences and similarities. The similarities and differences among, and between tribals, are based on tribals as individuals and as members of their community. They have their own identity as individuals and they share their identity with their fellow tribals and other tribal communities. My research is on tribals or tribal groups as a whole, which form a shared identity based on their similarities in terms of their social, cultural, linguistic and economic patterns and the problems they face in their day-to-day life. Tribals not only have individual and community identities but these individual tribals and tribal community identities are also based on social and economic inequalities. Power relationships in the tribal societies and unequal access to resources create inequality among and between tribals as individuals and as members of tribal communities. Thus any attempt to study the problems faced by tribals as whole is impossible by focusing only on tribal identities or on a particular tribal group. The density of the problems i.e. inequality and marginalisation faced by tribals due to the new economic reforms and their impact on tribals, can only be measured by equal standard by bringing their similarities and shared identity view taken from one definite side only as tribals, Adivasies, and indigenous people. This can objectify my research while looking at their problems and impact of the new economic reforms on them and their area.

However by taking communitarian claims on tribal question, one should not forget "the sense of social self at the levels of both individuality and collectivity that are informed by implicit or explicit contrast (Cohen, 1985:115)". I am trying to avoid both an implicit and explicit contrast which is again a social construction; deracinate of deconstructionist thought which neglects tribals' relationship with the natural world; their environment[13]. My research acknowledges the individual or community identities that exist among tribals and their relationship with the natural world in Kalahandi, Orissa. It can be better explained in the words of political theorist Michael

Sandel who says that "community describes not just what they have as fellow citizens but also what they are, not a relationship they choose (as in a voluntary association) but as an attachment they discover, not merely an attribute but a constituent of their identity"(Sandel, 1982:150-51). I am just using Michael Sander in the context of individual and community identities. His scheme of analysis of community identity as a natural order is completely irrelevant for India i.e. the idea of caste in India is not a natural order, rather a social construction for hierarchical domination and exploitation. Although, in the case of tribals, Michael Sandel is closer to the truth but again the problem in his conceptualiation of community identity is that when you say community identity is natural, thus the inequality and unequal power structure that exists among communities is also natural. This conceptualisation makes social change towards egalitarian social and economic order stagnant by making inequality a natural order. In this sense, I take the position of shared identity of tribals than the natural (individual and communitarian) identity of tribals by making inequality a social construct in tribal society. Another positive side of taking the shared identity among tribals is that it upholds tribal unity to fight against the common problems they face as tribals, irrespective of their individual and community identities. If there are any specificities that separate tribals from the other people in Indian society, it is their cultural narratives, oral tradition of dissemination of knowledge and non accumulative cultural life that differs them from Hindu caste system.

In India, the question of identity has a manifold connotation due to its diverse cultural social and economic system. One of the major questions of identity comes from the debate based on the difference between caste and tribe in India. The conceptualisation of caste derives its origin from endogamy (Beteille, 1991:3-28), the social hierarchy based on occupational categorisation and its past links with the labour process and its incomplete tribal fusions are documented in the Marxist historiography (Kosambi, 1956, Habib, 1995:161-189, Jaiswal, 1997:3). Many studies[14] reveal that tribals are different from caste on the basis of their social, economic, cultural and religious systems (Majumdar (1937, 1961), Dube (1977), Vidyarthi (1978, 1986), Vyas (1980), Vyas and Mann (1980), Bailey (1960), and Beteille (1984). The debates on the identity and differences based on caste and tribe is a pre-colonial Brahminical Hindu social order (Pati, 2003, Klass, 1980)[15], colonial construction[16] through the colonial policy of segregation; divide and rule policy (Quigley, 1988a, 1988b, 1993) and sustained by the post-colonial state through its ruling elites and institutionalised bureaucratic process of administration (Naregal, 2001, Pati, 2003).

The difference between caste and tribe has a long tradition of intellectual history and debate. Some scholars make the conceptual difference between caste and tribe based on endogamous and exogamous on the grounds of internal social structure (Weber, 1968:30-33, Dumont, 1972:154). The tribes "are often rigorously endogamous" and may have practised endogamy while interacting with the mainstream general society (Habib, 1995: 161-89). The Marxist historian Kosambi has viewed that caste is "class at the primitive level of production (Kosambi, 1965:50)". The means and relations of production had provided the material ground for "a new class division within each tribe (Habib, 1995: 94)". That means division in the society, based on caste and tribe, is not only a social, cultural and religious hierarchy[17] but also has its roots in class; a system of hierarchical division in the society for exploitation and perpetuation of inequality. Class division takes place in society, which traces the social origin of class. Thus, caste and tribe has its social origin as well. The present process of social and religious integration through the Hinduisation process brings back the old question of identity based on caste and tribe. In post-colonial India, the caste and tribe debate was revived, sustained and continues until today due to the politics of identity and vote bank populist politics in the contemporary Indian democracy that put the question of underdevelopment of caste and tribe to the back seat. This kind of debate at present derives its philosophical groundings from the ideas of post modernism, which is the cultural logic of capitalism[18]. The post-modern cultural logic of identity not only divides people based on their identity but also gives rise to different forms of ethnic conflicts, even in richer societies, based on their living styles and distinctiveness of their expression (Inglehart, 1997). This kind of cultural logic of identity formation is also quite popular in the anthropological works of Barth (1969), Berreman (1972), Epstein (1978), and Cohen (1985). All these works locate identity formation as a process of social interaction, which is sustained by the communities to maintain and reflect their distinct identities. In the context of caste-tribe debate in India, anthropologist Maya Unnithan-Kumar (1997:6) states that, "differences or boundaries of the caste/tribe or other inside/outside levels (such as class, religion, language etc.) are essentially maintained by members because they represent their separate and distinct identities"[19]. Historians are always at the centre of constructing identities based on history, culture and nationality (Hall, 1996), which is supported and sustained by cultural anthropologists. Post-colonial historians like; Damodaran (2006a) have extended the argument by stressing that construction of indigeneity or tribal identity to Chotanagpur; an area in the tribal state of India called Jharkhand; erstwhile Bihar. She derives her argument from the works of Dalton (1872:3 as cited in Damodaran, 2006a: 184) to link tribal identity with territory[20]. The construction of tribal identity based on any regional formation gives a narrow meaning of tribal identity and reduced tribal cosmology and put it in a regional specific sense.

The territorialisation of tribal identity is a reductionist understanding of tribal identity which reduces the tribal space, language and meaning attached to their universal world view. If the construction of tribal identity or indegenity owes its origin to one particular place then how did the same thing not happen anywhere else in India. Why do all tribal people prefer to be known as Adivasies? Why do they have similar cultural and communitarian patterns? What was the network during those days that brought all tribals under a single cultural umbrella? Without answering these questions, territorial generalisation of the construction of tribal identity still remains ambiguous. The answer to the above questions remains in the process of deterritorialisation of tribal identity, which will allow us to understand tribal identity in terms of their wider meaning systems attached to land, forest and environment. I do agree that communities and geographical region play a vital role in formulating and sustaining their identities but I find that there are two problems associated with the argument of Unnithan-Kumar (1997) and Damodaran (2006a). Firstly, it either rejects or reduces the significant role of many other factors (social, cultural interactions, state, politics, economy and environment) that shapes, reshapes and breaks the identity, its mobility and its changing notions. Secondly, by saying that only community and its members sustain their identity, means the power relations, inequalities and exploitation that exists within and among communities are also sustained by communities and its members - there is no role of the system or the environment in which community exists. Even in terms of methodology, the territorial conceptualisation of tribal identity follows the tradition of methodological individualism[21] that limits the expansion of knowledge about the social phenomenon of individual and community identity.

However, the caste and tribe debate based on identity can be located within the tribal communities. There is caste system that exists in the tribal society. But there is a difference between the caste system in Hindu social order and caste system among tribal communities. In Hindu social order the caste systems is based on the principles of segregation, untouchability and inaccessibility to different social and economic resources and are not entitled to certain privileges. However, the caste system in tribal societies, is based on the area of living, language and social and cultural practices[22]. The notions of castes among tribal communities are in the process of transition. The way Hinduisation processes are taking place in the tribal areas that incorporates mainstream Brahminical caste system into tribal communities by disintegrating their own cultural life.

The concept and usage of 'tribe'[23] in India, is very difficult to identify rather than define tribes, "and scientific or theoretical considerations were never allowed to displace administrative or political ones... the conceptions of those engaged in the listing were neither clearly formulated nor systematically applied (Beteille, 1986:299)". Those debates on the idea and the concept of 'tribe', 'native', 'indigenous', 'Adivasi', and 'Vanavasi' in the western and Indian academics as well, are nothing but different modes of analysis based on cultural formulations[24] . The meaning of these terms is fluid by nature and historically shifts its position according to the change of time and structural locations. Thus, these debates on the concept of indigenisms are somehow irrelevant to sustain the cultural identity of tribal people. Although the term 'Adivasi' is the most appropriate usage, tribal people prefer to be called and known as 'Adivasies'. But in the long run, it supports the idea of cultural nationalism[25] which is by nature dominated by the mainstream culture (culture of the majority) and suppresses minority culture; tribal or indigenous culture. The idea of India and Indian nationhood is always dominated by the mainstream culture. In the process of cultural identity formation and suppression of minority culture, it avoids the objective reality posed by economic crisis, crisis of livelihood and economic exploitation. The cultural identity formation may serve the political purposes but its contribution to end exploitation and overcome economic crisis is very minimal. Thus, those people who are using cultural categorisation to identify and protect Adivasies do not want any transformation[26]. Those who are thinking about social, political and economic transformation for liberation; the liberation of tribal people from exploitation, inequality, exploitation and crisis, need to streamline their intellectual work for resistance and opposition. As "liberation as an intellectual mission born in the resistance and opposition to the confinements and ravages of imperialism, has now shifted from the settled, established and domesticated dynamics of culture to its unhoused, decentred, and exilic energies, whose incarnation today is the migrant, and whose consciousness is that of the intellectual and artistic in exile, the political figure between domains, between forms, between homes, and between languages" (Said, 1994:332). Thus, it is important to locate Adivasies in terms of class[27] as the cultural formulations restrict social change or overcome from inequality and exploitation. The resistance for tribal liberation from all forms of exploitation and inequality can be secure through the narratives of tribal consciousness through their broad unity in terms of class based on their culture. Any idea, based on culture or on individual and community identity, creates division and weakens the tribal liberation movement. Thus, the idea of cultural nationalism, any form of identity based on consciousness and state sponsored identities, serves both the ruling elite and global capitalism. "Ethnicisation or peoplehood, resolves one of the basic contradictions of historical capitalism - its simultaneous thrust for theoretical equality and practical inequality – and it does so by utilising the mentalities of the world's working strata... Capitalism as a historical system requires constant inequality...Peoplehood is a major institutional construct of historical capitalism" (Wallerstein, 1991: 84). Through categorisation of people by identifying their identities, the capitalist social structure creates a structural hierarchy based on inequality. Thus, the identification of hierarchy based on identity (i.e. caste and tribe) serves the purpose of capitalism.

The term 'tribe' or 'tribal' is a contested term that is ethnographically imprecise and often a derogatory term in western world and even in contemporary urban centres of India, where people often use the term 'tribal' to abuse and derogate someone who is looking less stylish, shabbily dressed and, in particular 'not looking modern, in the urban sense'. But tribals constitute eighty million people in India, encompassing many tribal groups, categorised and marked, by their differences based on social, cultural, economic structure and they differ with each other in terms of language too. It is often argued that the term is historically constructed[28]. However, there are 697 tribes, as notified by the Government of India under Article 341 and 342 of the Indian Constitution, and they are known as Schedule Tribes (STs) of India based on the categorisation of tribals by the *Anthropological Survey of India* (ASI). Such categorisation is criticised as racial categorisation, as it is based on physical look and often blood groups; a legacy of colonial anthropologists and census operations (Bates, 1995). In this context, I have personal experience. While doing my fieldwork in Orissa, I interacted with Prof. P.K.Das of the Department of Anthropology, Utkal University, Orissa on the different issues faced by tribals in the country in general, and Orissa in particular. When I asked him about the basis of categorising tribals in India, he replied that many physical anthropologists like him follow the technique of anthropometry (blood sampling, measuring the head, nose and chest) despite a renewed interest amongst anthropologists in social and cultural indicators as the basis of identification. He also said that, "the social anthropologists are now using language and cultural practices as indicators, consequently influencing the notion of physical anthropologists and Government of India policies on identifying tribal population in the country"[29]. By following the criticisms made against the ASI, the Government of India set up the Lokur Committee in 1965 to fix the criteria of identifying tribal population in the country. The committee fixed qualities like; primitive traits, distinctive culture, geographical isolation, shyness of contact with the outside communities at large and backwardness as the parameters to identify tribal population in the country. There are 75 Primitive Tribal Groups (PTGs), who have been identified, based on four features i.e. a pre-agriculture level of technology, a stagnant or declining population, an extremely low literacy rate and a subsistence level of economy.

However, the word 'tribe' indicates a socially, culturally and economically cohesive unit, associated with an autonomous territory. Each tribal group associated with a particular region or territory forms their own social and cultural cohesiveness, which consists of their distinct dialect, cultural traits and other social and religious practices. This distinction makes them unique in their own ways and thus, forms their identity. There are many tribal communities in India and at the same time, they share some commonalities in terms of habitat and collective life style. The term 'primitive tribes' was often used by western anthropologists to denote "a primary aggregate of peoples living in a primitive or barbarous condition under a headman or chief"[30]. Such conceptualisation of tribes in India, or elsewhere in the world, is unwarranted and a reflection of ruling class hegemonic ideology. However, there is consensus among anthropologists about the 'tribe' as a people being at an earlier stage of evolution of society (Joshi, 1998:15). In Orissa, tribal population constitutes 22.13% of the total population of the state. The decadal growth of tribal population has declined from 1981 to 2001 by 22.43%, 22.21%, 22.13% in 1981, 1991 and 2001 respectively (Census, 2001). It is argued that the tribals were incorporated as Hindus in the 2001 census, during the BJP regime at the centre. However, the tribal populations express their cultural identity and distinctiveness in their social organisation, language, rituals and festivals and also in their dress, ornaments, art and crafts. They have retained their own way of managing the internal affairs of the village, mainly through two institutions - namely the village council and the youth dormitory. The dormitory is the core of tribal culture and it reinforces age-old traditions in Orissa (Das, 2007). But the Hinduisation process carried out by the Hindu right wing forces has endangered the tribal culture, society and their unique religion.

However, I prefer to use the term 'Adivasi' as they prefer it. I also prefer the term 'tribe' and 'indigenous people', which give a sense of internationalism to Adivasies of India, in the context of development and underdevelopment. In my research work, I use the term 'tribe'[31] as the Government of India uses the term as an administrative category for affirmative action, while formulating the development policies and institutions for tribal development. I am looking at the tribal development and cultural transition in the context of public policy or other development policy for tribals after economic reforms in India. In this context, I am using the term "tribe" as it is used in the government policy documents. But terms like; "adivasi", "native," "indigenous," "tribe", "tribal" and "aboriginal" are used interchangeably throughout this work without having any derogatory sense and interpretation.

Chapter One

Neo-liberal Lineages and Trends in the Political Economy of Development in India

This chapter analyses the historical legacies, ideological lineages and neo-liberal genesis of the political economy of development in India. Such under-standing is necessary to conceptualise several contradictory sets of events during the post-colonial era of Indian development planning and its historic legacies of colonialism. This will enable us to understand continuities and changes in different periods of development planning and the class forces and factors that determine the nature of development in India.

While doing so, the chapter aims to locate the basis of economic crises in Indian economy and its origin, development and transition of economic insti-tutions and its structures in India. It will attempt to document the domestic institutional responses to economic crises and its strategies to recover from it, without interacting with the international or external economic institutions. It intends to explain the impact of changes and development on different as-pects of society and on the lives of people. It is necessary to understand development in the path of economic history to analyse the problematique of different forms of crisis that stem from the transition that takes place in the field of public policy for development and its impact on people. Specifically, the aim of this chapter is to locate two things i.e. i) the role of Indian economic institutions during economic transition and its significance in deal-ing with economic crisis by mobilising available internal resources, and ii) the way people dependent upon local economic institutions succumb to the crisis conditions in its different forms during the transition process whenever there is an interaction between outside economic institutions and domestic, national or local economic institutions. The analysis of these two points through economic history of development can provide the genesis of the present economic crisis and neo-liberal policy response to it in an institutional and historical perspective. It would be a mistake to simply overlook or dismiss the significant historical process that has played a vital role in the structural change in the Indian economy towards the development of capitalism and the integration of the global capitalist market in India.

INTRODUCTION

The political economy[1] of development in India and its contemporary transition is passing through a neo-liberal stage which, critiques state, leads development. The transition to neo-liberal planning is taking place by using the market as an organising force for development which creates profound social, economic and cultural change and generates crisis. The institutional transformations are occurring from state to market to confront crisis and adapt to the requirements of the change in favour of market. Any attempt to document and understand such transition should be studied within the context of its historical conditions to understand the 'causes and effects' of change and crisis in the political economy of development. But most of the neo-liberal economic historians provide the causes and effects of the transition in political economy while seeking an explanatory interpretation[2] of the quantitative record of macroeconomic performances and their concluding derivations based on consensus, assumptions or a parable agreed upon when it comes to analyse economic transition and crisis involved in the transition process (Samuelson, 1962; Abramovitz et. al, 1973). The neo-liberal economists, historians and development theorists concern themselves with causality more than conditions but "lying on the border of 'theory' and 'history', economic analysis cannot escape the influence of the arbitrary initial conditions inherited from history (Bhaduri, 1999: 189)".

Therefore, the study of the political economy of development in India from a historical perspective[3] rejects the neo-classical approach that analyses economic development by analysing only the causes that led society to scarcity[4] and individuals to make choice without taking conditions into account. The study of economic history not only rejects the neo-classical approach to economic analysis, but also rejects any approach that analyses only the cause and effect without taking into account historical conditions. Moreover, the study of economic history is significant and central to the understanding of the predicaments of the political economy of development and in the making of public policy in India. This understanding is necessary to understand the ahistorical nature of neo-liberal political economy which confined itself to supply and demand without giving an answer to the question of "how supply is supplied and demand is demanded (Harris-White, 2006: 481)". Certainly the answer to the question remains within economic history which neo-liberal political economy is afraid of and attempts to ignore its significance. In this process, the neo-liberal political economy is trying to avoid the role of social, economic, cultural and religious factors in the process of production, distribution, exchange and the institutions or powers that control the process. It has not only created the conditions of supply and demand but also given an answer about the production and distribution process that provides answers to the question of the ways in which supply is supplied and demand is demanded[5]. This aspect of economic history can help us to understand the continuity, contradictions, crisis and transformations in Indian economic history and its political economy of development in India[6].

In contemporary India, politicians and economic policymakers believe that economic crisis is as natural as economic growth to any economic system and development of any country. As a result, they consider economic crisis as a crisis in the market, trade and service sector. Based on such inferences, they prescribe free market and free trade as the only alternative to recover from economic crisis. Such assumptions have paid insufficient attention to the role of other important economic institutions in different sectors of the Indian economy and their potential to recover from the crisis. Thus, it is significant to locate problems during transition periods and economic crisis in different sectors of the Indian economy i.e. industry, agriculture, trade and commerce. It is also trying to reflect upon the way the Indian economy has recovered from economic crisis in different periods of its economic growth and development and documents the impact of the transition process on people and institutional structures in India over the different period of history.

UNDERSTANDING HISTORICAL LEGACIES OF INDIAN POLITICAL ECONOMY OF DEVELOPMENT

The *growth, crisis and contradictions*[7] in the contemporary political economy of India reflect changes with continuities as part of the historical process of development. The ancient Indian economy - in terms of agriculture, trade, manufacturing and its market base - was strong in comparison to other parts of the world[8]. But the social formations in ancient India were structured in hierarchal order to impose control over resources (Thapar, 1984). The hierarchical social order and its control over resources led to the growth of feudal structures that have determined the nature of economy and institutions affiliated with it (Kosambi, 1956, 1965; Sharma, 1980, 1983, 1985; Nagarajan, 2000). However, the economic institutions during ancient India were managed by scattered feudal regimes with segmented political authority (Stein, 1985, 1989). The public institutions were managed by the despotic warrior

Chapter 1

caste and feudal class. The mercantile class streamlined the scattered feudal economic institutions and formed alliances with the political power of the warrior caste and feudal class to expand their market. The result of the process gave birth to monarchy which became the political order in ancient India (Spellman, 1964). The Muslim and Maratha rulers inherited the feudal polity and economy of ancient India during the medieval period. As a result, social and economic conditions of the masses during the early 17th century were miserable, despite this being a time when the economy was flourishing[9] under the state management (Dasgupta, 1993). This was due to "the rich, in their great superfluity and absolute power, and the utter subjection and poverty of the common people - poverty so great and miserable that the life of the people can be depicted or accurately described only as the home of stark want and the dwelling place of bitter woe . . . Their houses are built of mud with thatched roofs. Furniture, there is little or none ...bedclothes are scanty, merely a sheet or perhaps two, serving both as under- and over-sheet; this is sufficient in the hot weather, but the bitter cold nights are miserable indeed"[10]. This indicates that growth in the economy and crisis in society can go together. Such paradox increased further with the collapse of the Moghul rule, when the rise of the Maratha rule and the Indian economy was pushed into crisis as a result of political instability caused by wars and conflicts (Kumar, 1983).

The political instability helped European trade to grow in India at a time when contradictory signs were visible in the economy. On one hand, the Indian economy was largely a traditional agrarian economy often characterised as a subsistence and primitive economy in terms of production technology, while on the other there was a competitively developed network of commerce, manufacturing and credit indicating the economic tenets comparable to any other part of the world (Kumar, 1983; Frank, 1996; Maddison, 2001). Such contradiction was minimised and started declining with the growth of European trade in India. There was a steady rise in the prices of commodities like textiles, raw silk and rice. The volume of Indian indigenous trade and industry declined on a massive scale with the growth of European trade (Chaudhuri, 1978, 1985, 1990). This indicates that the interaction of Indian markets with European trade led to the decline of Indian industry, whilst simultaneously being responsible for the rise in price of essential commodities. The situation continued to worsen with the imposition of free trade on India and its legal, social and property institutions were selectively modified[11] to comply with the British colonial interest resulting in the decline of per capital income in India, whereas British per capita income grew faster than previously (Maddison, 2001).

The process of free trade was further expanded during the second half of the nineteenth century with the opening of the Suez Canal in 1869, paving the way for the integration of the Indian colonial economy with the commercial capital of the world economy. The world commerce pushed into 'the village' which encroached upon the village autonomy through different forms of administrative measures. Such changes in the economic and administrative structures jeopardised the communitarian Indian society at large and indigenous societies and their economy in particular (Bailey, 1971: 6). The commercial economy led to the growth of the land market, in turn affecting land redistribution (ibid, 1971:11). As a result of the commercial economy, the communal culture and joint family system in India got dismantled (O' Malley, 1941:384 as cited in Bailey, 1971: 10). It had a pervasive impact on the self-contained rural villages in terms of economy and the communitarian unity[12] among the village people. Colonial writers such as Hunter (1872) blamed the internal colonisation for the fragmentation of society and estates, whereas Furnivall (1948) places blame on the growth of industrial agriculture which resulted in the breaking down of communal institutions[13]. The process enlarged its scope with the growth of free trade under colonialism during the second half of the nineteenth century. The colonial free trade had a pervasive negative impact on the trade, agriculture, industry and different sectors of Indian economy (Habib, 2006).

The crisis in Indian trade during colonialism can be attributed to the British exploitation and use of unequal trade mechanisms and patterns of trade transfers (Dadachanji, 1934: 15)[14]. Further, during the world economic crisis of 1930-31, the colonial rulers manipulated Indian currency in such a way as to ensure the flow of gold to the UK (Tomlinson, 1993: 69-70). This indicates that the interaction of British commercial capital with indigenous capital in India led to the dependent growth of trade and was therefore detrimental in the growth of trade and economy[15]. The dependent growth of trade led to the crisis in the indigenous banking and credit system of India[16]. The credit structures and its functions were streamlined by dismantling the indigenous credit structures[17], resources and its operational outfit to help the imperial expansion in trade and economy which had a negative impact on the banking system in India (Bagchi, 1972; Banerji, 1963). It led to the manifestation of crisis in different sectors of the economy in eighteenth century India. In response to the economic crisis the local money lenders or the credit structure under the leadership of Bania community, formed alliances with British merchants or commercial capital with colonial protection. Such policies were adopted and pursued by the colonial administration to control the disobedient Muslim and Maratha bankers and traders (Subramanian, 1985, 1987). In this way the commercial capital of Britain took over the economy of India during 18th and 19th century. The colonial ruling class who "stimulated the development of commercial capital, were among the principal factors in the transition from feudal to capitalist production (Marx, 1894: 364)". This transition was part of mercantile capitalism created through trade which helped the growth of the world market and provided the commercially accumulated wealth for the industrial revolution (Magdoff and Magdoff, 2005). The industrial revolution led to the transition of the feudal system to capitalist production in India, which compelled the British colonial power to commercialise the agriculture and de-industrialise the Indian economy, by dismantling traditional industries in India (Dutt, 1940; Desai, 1953; Bagchi, 1976a; Roy, 2000; Clingingsmith & Williamson, 2005).

The colonial policy towards Indian agriculture was always based on the rent-seeking behaviour of the colonial state in an effort to maximise profit. The first step in this direction was to increase irrigation facilities, mechanisation and commercialisation of agriculture. The second step was to create institutional change by transforming property or land rights which resulted in agrarian, economic, and other structural changes in rural India (Cohn, 1969; Neale, 1962; Warriner, 1969; Whitcombe, 1971; Kanetkar, 1960). The Moghul warlords and landed aristocracy were transformed into bureaucratic colonial administrators and tax collectors ruling at the bottom of the Indian society. It is not that colonial administration completely transformed the landed aristocracy; rather it had increased the landlordism in a different way (Misra, 1961). Thus, the economic inequality and hierarchy of Moghul India continued and was often augmented with British patronage during the colonial period. Even social hierarchy, based on the caste system, was not destroyed by British administration; rather the higher caste and landed peasants were allowed to consolidate their traditional base (Bayly, 1988; Bailey, 1957)[18]. As a result of this there was a growth of landlessness and depeasantisation during colonialism (Kumar, 1965, 1972; Chaudhuri, 1970). In this way, British policy towards land and agriculture increased the incidence of famine in 19th century India (Dutt, 1960; Digby, 1901; Bhatia, 1963), and therefore the wider impact of colonialism on the Indian economy, society and politics can not be denied (Habib, 1975b, 1985, 2002; Kumar, 1972; Habib, 2006).

In this way, there was a historical link between the British colonial rent-seeking state and the free market economy in India, which had negative impacts on the development of the country. The foundation of liberal market economy-led development was started by the colonialism with the creation of a legal structure for the market of private property based on alienable land rights, free labour market, physical infrastructure for market, and integration into the international economy by establishing a stable exchange rate, modern management and entrepreneurship (Misra, 2003: 136). The liberal market economy was considered as the modernising force in Indian economy. Such arguments not only justified British colonialism and ignored the developed state of pre-colonial Indian economy,[19] but also considered it as a stagnant economy; a by-product of political anarchy. However, recent historical research[20] does not support the justification of colonialism and imperialism in the name of economic modernisation. In reality, the indigenous impulses towards modernisation during the late eighteenth century were halted by the British, leading to the decline of indigenous institutional structures, economic innovation and dynamism of economic development in India. Even the British incorporated some of these dynamisms into their own imperial state building, but replaced such dynamism in India by branding it as traditional. In the field of society, the colonial rulers institutionalised caste hierarchy[21] which was in an unstructured form (Dirks, 2001; Bayly, 1999; Metcalf, 1994), thus, modern historians of Indian political economy of development consider colonial intervention as the traditionalisation and travails of contemporary Indian development (Misra, 2003: 134-136). The impact of the liberal market economy on one side and traditionalisation on the other put more than half of the Indian population in absolute poverty, creating food insecurity, landlessness and debt in India at independence (Misra, 2003:138; Bayly, 1990: 118-119; Corbridge and Harriss, 2000:12-13). Thus, the current state of poverty and underdevelopment is an endemic demand constraint in both primary and intermediate demands perpetuated by colonial rule in India (Tomlinson, 1988:131). In this way, the colonial exploitation and drainage of wealth influenced all sectors of the Indian economy, which has led to the growth and institutionalisation of poverty and underdevelopment in the country (Naoroji, 1962; Roy, 1987).

IDEOLOGICAL LINEAGES OF INDIAN POLITICAL ECONOMY OF DEVELOPMENT

The characterisation of ancient Indian political economy of development and its ideological interpretation is a product of European historiography on India i.e. the work of Phillip (1961). This has influenced Indian historians to interpret ancient Indian economic history in an effort to understand the concerns of that period (Thapar, 1968). But in latter works, Thapar (1993) appears to be hesitant to characterise and interpret ancient Indian history as she mentions that it is "too distant for an ideological concern to have much meaning for contemporary society, and that the sparseness of the evidence does not provide much margin for ideological debate (ibid: 1)". But she moves on from this argument, in the latter part of the book, where she advocates an ideological interpretation of ancient Indian history in the context of glorification of ancient India's feudal and caste order by Hindu right wing forces. By looking at the state of polity and society during ancient and medieval India, it can be said that the economy was feudal. Apart from colonialism, class interests and ideologies have had a formidable impact in the shaping of Indian political economy (Kosambi, 1965; Ganguli, 1977).

Other than anti-colonial and nationalistic ideas, three things i.e. the great depression, centralised state command economy of the (then) USSR and the drives towards instant development to catch up with developed countries followed by domestic demands have shaped the economic thoughts in India during the post-war world economy (Datta, 1978). The nationalistic economic thoughts in India have followed the tradition of the German Historical School, but with a difference[22]. The anti-colonial leaders i.e. Rammohan Roy (1772-1833)[23], R. C Dutt (1940, 1960), Naoroji (1962), M.G. Ranade[24], Ranadive (1930), M.K.Gandhi[25], Ambedkar (1923), Gokhale (1962-67), Vakil (1924), Gadgil (1924), V.K.R.V. Rao (1936, 1983), Mahalanobis (1953) and their ideologies were instrumental in influencing post-colonial economic thought and development planning in India[26]. Further, the diverse culture linked with Hindu religion or Hinduism[27] has had a formative impact on the nature of the Indian political economy of development (Kapp, 1963; Cameron and Ndhlovu, 2001).

However, these factors that shaped the Indian political economy and development led to the growth of different ideological lineages and trends, which can be broadly separated into five categories i.e. nationalist, Gandhian, liberal, Marxist, cultural and religious to understand Indian political economy of development during the anti-colonial nationalist struggle[28]. The different ideological lineages of Indian political economy of development worked together towards the political and economic emancipation of the nation from British colonialism. However, the Hindu right wing political forces, whose advocates for nationalistic economy had remained with the colonial rulers, did not take part in the anti-colonial struggle in order to establish a Hindu nation with the help of the British (Sarkar and Bhattacharya, 2007). In reality when the Hindu right wing forces came to power under the Bharatiya Janata Party (BJP) led by the National Democratic Alliance, they followed in the foot prints of the Congress party and its neo-liberal economic policies. The reason for these economic similarities between the liberal Congress party and the so called Hindu nationalistic forces in the matter of economic policies is the result of the higher and dominant caste and class composition of the party and leadership which has feudal lineages[29], imposing control of resources with the help of politics and state power. In this way, there is more continuity and less change in terms of the forces that controlled state power and the productive resources in India through the pre-colonial, colonial and post-colonial periods. The post-colonial Indian capitalist class and dominant landed caste maintained the structural aspect of a colonial economy (Chandra, 1979, 1992, 1999) which has influenced post 1991 economic thinking in India, putting the economy in a perpetual crisis by forcing the Indian state to become a rent-seeking state; a legacy that can be tracked back to the Moghul and British colonial eras.

In this way, the understanding of post-colonial development trajectory in India is incomplete without connecting it with colonial history[30] and its pre-colonial genesis. During the period of British colonialism in India, the mercantile, industrial and colonial state-led capitalism and its monopoly was unable to accumulate without dismantling the pre-capitalist social relations under feudal social formations and modes of production emanating from it[31]. The necessity compelled the colonial state and capital to play a progressive role in abolishing feudalism to pave the way for an easy capitalist development[32]. Wherever British colonialism failed to abolish feudal social formations it formed an alliance with it to pursue its agenda of capitalist accumulation[33]. Many scholars like Corbridge and Harriss (2000), Sanyal (1988, 1993, 2001), Kaviraj (1988), Chakrabarti and Cullenberg (2003) have argued that such analysis of capitalist transformation in India is uncritical and deterministic, which has led to incomplete theorisation and fallacious conclusions on different dynamics of capitalist accumulation and its impact on contemporary development. It can be discussed further while looking at different trends in post-colonial political economy of development in India.

TRENDS OF POST-COLONIAL POLITICAL ECONOMY OF DEVELOPMENT IN INDIA

The post-colonial political economy of development followed a path of central planning in looking at different factors that caused underdevelopment in the Indian economy in particular and society in general. There are different views on the question of underdevelopment in the Indian economy. Scholars like Bagchi (1982) and Frank (1978) have argued that colonial exploitation and the drain of resources is responsible for 'growth dependency' as a long term result of colonialism, while scholars like Roy (2000, 2002) claim resource endowments and area characteristics are the major determinants of development and causes of underdevelopment where colonial rule has played a minor role. Meanwhile, historians like Banerjee and Iyer (2003) argue that the way institutions (land tenure system, property rights) created by colonial rule have resulted in a long term impact on the development of the country. Iyer (2004)'s study provides statistical figures to show that agricultural productivity is higher in areas which were directly under British rule than native and indirectly controlled British areas, even in the post-colonial India. It is the result of a higher proportion of irrigated area, greater fertilizer usage, faster adoption of high-yielding varieties, mechanisation of agriculture, higher percentage of rainfall and significantly lower percentage of unproductive, barren or rocky areas under the British empire compared to areas which were part of native states and indirectly controlled British areas (Iyer, 2004: 8-12). This indicates that the rent-seeking behaviour of the colonial state, the basis of the present uneven development of different regions in India, can trace its historical roots to the colonial British administration and the post-colonial rulers that followed it[34].

Iyer (2004) goes further with historical and empirical evidence arguing that "some native states were ahead of the British in the provision of public goods (ibid: 3)" which was later ruined by the British policy of right to intervene[35] in the internal affairs of the native state in the name of maintaining law and order. The nature and intentions of British colonial policy towards native states is well documented in the works of Ashton (1982). Such policy intentions inherited from colonialism can be found in the post-colonial ruling class[36].

However, by taking this historical background, the post-colonial Indian state and government followed a dual policy of development[37] after liberation from British rule. The dual policy of development has led to the growth of a mixed economy by bringing agriculture and industry together and a policy of heavy industrialisation has been followed to meet domestic consumer requirements. At the same time, it has pursued a policy of agricultural development by looking at the significant role of agriculture in the Indian economy and the needs of the people although this has been overshadowed by infrastructural development. Industrialisation (particularly mining based) is seen as the best way to stimulate accelerated economic growth and social transformation to bring backward regions into the fold of development by putting agriculture into a secondary position.

The implementation of new economic reforms during 1991 advocated the free market as the prime factor of economic growth demoting the role of state and its planning as prescribed by the 'Washington Consensus'[38]. Micro and macro economic policies need to be framed in an investment friendly way, along with laws to protect the property which makes a credible state (World Bank, 1997). The best practice of a credible state is to reform one's economy. The structural reforms in banking, tax, effective legal system to protect property and governance of law are the key components of a reform programme which has the potential for a lasting economic growth.[39] Economic growth is possible by economic liberalisation for the free play of market forces (IMF, 1997: 70-71).

In this way, the post-colonial political economy of development in India has passed through many transformations in its development planning. It has shifted from state command to market friendly development to integrate itself with the global economy by implementing the new economic policy[40]. In the process of such transformations in development planning, many religious right wing groups, reactionary and regional forces have emerged in Indian politics (Ahmad, 2000). It is a part of the global capitalist market that functions though the deterministic cultural hegemony under the support of the political process[41]. The Hindutva forces are suitable for this capitalist project in India and, as a result, the idea of Hindu ethnic nationalism has been growing with the process of liberalisation (Corbridge& Harriss, 2000). Historically, such transformations in contemporary Indian society, economy and politics are determined by the different class forces that were shaped during post-colonial development politics[42]. However, the political economy of development in India since independence is determined by the industrial bourgeoisie, rural landed elites both in terms of class, caste and bureaucracy (Bardhan, 1989b). This troika of class alliance has shaped the nature of contemporary development planning in India, which owes its historical origin to the colonial state formation. Such an alliance has pursued its interests and ideas during post-colonial planning for development in India[43] and, as a result, scholars of contemporary Indian political economy consider India's transition from colonialism as a passive revolution[44] which has failed to alter the very basis of exploitative class relations and feudal social formations based on caste.

The nationalistic ethos of post-independence India was well manipulated by the Indian capitalist class to create a single national identity rather than divergent local identities. The unitary federal polity and constitutional state were created to serve the purpose of the market mobility which can aid capital accumulation by the national capitalist class[45]. The process helped the Indian capitalist class to grow stronger leading to the changing attitude of the Indian state and its capitalist class to foreign capital during the 1970s (Patnaik, 1972). But the landed dominant classes in the agricultural sector remained opposed to the interjection of foreign capital into this sector (Varshney, 1995), although its opposition could not be sustained due to domestic industrial capitalist class pressure and international financial institutions like World Bank and IMF (Gupta, 1999). Historically, the crisis of Indian economy during the third Five Year Plan gave foreign financial institutions the opportunity to intervene in national economic matters without mobilising internal resources. Initial pressure came from the US, followed by the World Bank's Bell Mission Report[46] which put increasing pressure on India to revise its economic policies for greater involvement of American finance capital in the Indian economy (Eldrige, 1970:34-35). Further international financial institutions' prescriptions – especially the International Development Association under the leadership of American finance capital - led to the massive private investment in Indian economy during the fourth and fifth Five Year Plan period (Reddy, 1978). The private investment resulted in the private financial institutional set-up by the country in consonance with foreign capital and its affiliated institutions (Venkatasubbiah, 1961). Under such pressure and the threat of aid withdrawal from the United States, the Indian government was forced to devalue the Rupee by more than 37 per cent (Patnaik, 1972). This prompted a clear shift in government economic policies by implementing a limited programme of economic liberalisation[47].

The opposition to such economic policies followed by the centralised authoritarian regime was reflected in the general election when the Indira Gandhi led government was voted out of power. After a gap of three years,

Mrs. Indira Gandhi returned to power continuing her populist politics of development i.e. nationalisation of banks, *Garibi Hatao* (eradicate poverty) and Twenty Point Programmes. Along with her populist politics, she continued her liberalisation programmes. Scholars such as Nayar (1992) and Sridharan (1993) have argued that policy shifts towards liberalisation started during the Indira Gandhi period.

However, successive governments followed the liberalisation policy which took final shape with the implementation of the new economic reforms during 1991. The policy opened up the Indian economy to global capital and its market forces. Such policy trends were sustained by the different governments from BJP led National Democratic Alliance to the present Congress led and left-supported United Progressive Alliance. The gradual transformation of the Indian economy was possible through different political regimes as the policy of liberalisation-privatisation and globalisation received considerable support from the political and economic elites of the Indian society (Jenkins, 1999). The Indian upper classes and castes supported both BJP and Indian National Congress to follow an open door economic policy, assuming new economic reforms to be a profitable economic policy under the unquestioned superiority of global capital (Chakrabarti and Cullenberg, 2003). Thus, the post-colonial political economy of development can be divided into two. The first period of the political economy of development was under state command and planning in India. The transition of state-led development planning to the declining role of the state planning over economy led to the growth of the second period in which the political economy of development was under market command economy.

STATE LED POLITICAL ECONOMY OF DEVELOPMENT IN INDIA

The nationalist ethos of self-reliance during the course of the freedom movement in India influenced the Indian Economy after independence. Such vision was echoed in the Constituent Assembly when the first Prime Minister of India, Jawaharlal Nehru declared that independence meant the redemption of a pledge and this achievement "is but a step, an opening of opportunity, to the great triumphs and achievements that await us ... the ending of poverty and ignorance and disease and inequality of opportunity"[48]. These Nehruvian ideals led the policy makers, political leaders and economists to follow a planned and state command economic development model by establishing a central *Planning Commission of India*. State control over the economy was reinforced in Nehru's First Industrial Policy Resolution in 1948, declaring that Foreign Direct Investment (FDI) would be regulated to ensure that a majority of the ownership and effective control of the firms would remain in Indian hands. Yet there was no indication of FDI regulation in Nehru's

Foreign Investment Policy Statement in 1949. Furthermore, the necessity of hard currency, as a result of the foreign exchange crisis of 1957, prompted the Indian government to encourage FDI by lowering corporate taxes on income and royalties, signing an agreement with the USA regarding currency convertibility, sending out missions to advertise India to potential investors, and setting up foreign branches of the Indian Investment Centre[49].

In 1964, there was a devaluation of the rupee, stagnation in agriculture and industrial production and subsequently another foreign exchange crisis in 1965-66. Two successive droughts in 1965-66 and 1966-67 led to a sharp rise in prices of food and other essential commodities and sparked high inflation. Aside from these factors, the two wars in 1961 and 1962 resulted in a huge increase in defence budget expenditure leading to a fiscal deficit, and a decline in the public investment consequently jeopardising future Gross Domestic Product (GDP) growth. The crisis was visible in the Indian *third Five Year Plan (1961-66)*[50] document which suggests that "the existing social and economic institutions have . . . to be appraised from time to time in relations to their role in the nation's development. To the extent they do not adequately fulfil the social purpose or fail to secure the economic aims of the planned development, they have to be replaced and transformed".[51] The *third Five Year Plan's* concern for institutional reform was ambiguous as it did not clarify the reforms necessary for economic growth. But the 1961 Congress Party election manifesto made it clear that "a transformation of a caste and faction-ridden backward society into a unified and integrated community . . . The fundamental problem in India is not only to increase greatly the living standard of the people, but also to bring about progressively social and economic equality. Existing inequalities and disparities in the social fabric are ethically wrong and will obstruct progress on all fronts and produce considerable strains. The new social order must preserve the worth and dignity of the individual and create a sense of equality, fraternity and of cohesion".[52] Thus, historically the *third Five Year Plan* laid the basis for institutional reform for the social and economic development of the country (although it did not explicitly mention sectors needing reform and the methods of required (i.e state or market driven).

In 1973-75, there was a food shortage leading to inflation and this had serious political implications including the imposition of Emergency rule. In 1979-81 it was triggered by drought induced food shortages and reinforced by the oil crisis. Thus, the period 1967-68 to 1979-80 was characterised by a slow down in the rate of GDP growth, resulting in the decline in growth of the major sectors of the economy (agriculture and industry). Following this crisis "the Indian economy witnessed a turn around and unprecedented growth in the decade of eighties (Prasad, 2003: 111)". The Governor of RBI, Dr. Y.V. Reddy (1998: 341) claimed that during the eighties, which may be described as the pre-Reform phase, the growth in India's GDP in real terms averaged at an annual 5.9 per cent. This was better than the world average output growth of 3.3 percent; that of developing countries at 4.3 percent and of Asia (excluding India and China) at 5.1 per cent. He also described India's impressive record of maintaining an average inflation rate by controlling price rises and external sector performance record. In the genealogy of crisis and the policies enacted in order to overcome the crisis in the Indian economy, the period 1948-65 is known as "the Period of General Liberalisation (Fikkert, 1995:3-4)" and best defined as a period of short term crisis management using the state command approach. The period from 1966-1979 however, is "the period of Restrictive Phase (ibid)" in the Indian economy, characterised by complete state command of the economy that managed the crisis and performed well in terms GDP and other economic indicators (Nayak, 2009).

At different phases of time, attempts were made to liberalise the Indian economy, but these attempts became insignificant due to the command of the state in the policy process of the economic reforms. India has slowly travelled down the path of economic reform by changing its policy paradigm from the state command economy to the market command economy through the policies of liberalisation, privatisation, and globalisation and then followed by structural adjustment and stabilisation policies. The understanding of the new economic policies launched in 1991 is popularly known as the "New Economic Reforms (NER)"[53] in India which had its genesis two decades before its inception.

MARKET LED POLITICAL ECONOMY OF DEVELOPMENT IN INDIA

The real liberalisation and economic reform started in the 1980s through loosening industrial capacity licensing regulations, quantitative restrictions on import and export, flexibility in FDI and relaxation in restrictions on technology licensing agreements. However, it is widely agreed that there was a clear break in 1985, when both the pace and scope of economic liberalisation changed. In terms of scope, economic reform was on a wider canvas and more perceptible departures from previous policy were made; in terms of pace, it was sped up. In the first budget of Rajiv Gandhi premiership in 1985, foundations were laid for a new economic regime characterized by liberalisation. There was a complete paradigm shift from state command economy in India to IMF/World Bank command market economy[54]. The situation was summarised by "The Economist" (March, 23,1985); "Mr. Rajiv Gandhi's first budget tackle(d) the red tape and the draconian taxes introduced by his mother and his grandfather which have hindered the growth of Indian economy... The liberalisation is not complete...But (the changes) take India a big step away from the days when bureaucrats rather than the businessmen decided its investment plan''. ''For the first time since independence, we have in New Delhi an administration which has an unabashed allegiance to specific ideology... (Which has)... three stands: development is best left to private enterprise, taxes are evil and (the) poor are dispensable[55].'' Moreover, after adopting the above economic policy reforms, the Government of India wanted to withdraw itself from its developmental role and to free business from the state. The delivery of welfare to the people was left to the market. But the then Finance Minister, V.P Singh claimed that his priorities were to strengthen the public sector by investment in public welfare to assist the poor. Then, he was dismissed from the office, which shows the intensity of the government policy for liberalisation.

However, the economic crisis in the Indian economy continued. The problem of unsustainable expenditure from public and current accounts led to a fiscal deficit, foreign exchange crisis, internal borrowing, a steep fall in the foreign reserve and galloping inflation. The situation laid the foundation for the Narasimha Rao government to totally open up the economy to the private market. Even after the Narasimha Rao government, the left parties of the United Front Government started formulating their policies according to their pre-election manifesto and understanding on the basis of Common Minimum Programme (CMP) which also continued with the earlier component of liberalisation policy. The CMP's model of policy formulation was based on federalism, de-centralisation, accountability, equality, social justice and political and economic reforms. But before the implementation of these policies, the government ended its life span within two years with lots of conflict, compromise, uncertainty and instability. It is a matter of fact that the United Front Government also continued the policy of economic reforms that stemmed from their agenda in the Common Minimum Programme.

Subsequently the Bharatiya Janata Party (B.J.P) led National Democratic Alliance (NDA) came to power and started the Second Generation Economic Reforms by initiating Structural Adjustment Programmes (SAP) and Stabilisation Policies with other Disinvestment Policies[56] as advised by the World Bank and the IMF. The ideas behind these new economic policies were to take India from a low growth path to a higher rate of growth path by shifting from government control of the economy to a "free" market capitalist economy[57].

The economic philosophy of these programmes was to rely more on market forces, dismantle controls, reduce the role of state, liberalise prices, and replace the public with the private sector. It was based on the presumption that the public sector leads to inefficient allocation and utilisation of economic resources while looking at the impact of the new economic reforms on different sectors of the Indian economy. The same policies were followed by the UPA government after coming to power in 2004, under the Prime

Ministership of Dr. Manmohan Singh, who initiated the new economic reforms during 1991 when he was the Finance Minister of the country under
the Prime Ministership of Mr. Narasimha Rao. The vision of the reform
programme, and its objectives, were outlined in the Discussion Paper on
Economic Reforms brought out by the Ministry of Finance in July 1993
which said that "the fundamental objective of economic reforms is to bring
about rapid and sustained improvement in the quality of the people of India.
Central to this goal is the rapid growth in incomes and productive employment . . . The only durable solution to the curse of poverty is sustained
growth of incomes and employment . . . . Such growth requires investment:
in farms, in roads, in irrigation, in industry, in power and, above all, in
people. And this investment must be productive. Successful and sustained
development depends on continuing increases in the productivity of our capital, our land and our labour. Within a generation, the countries of East Asia
have transformed themselves. China, Indonesia, Korea, Thailand and Malay-
sia today have living standards much above ours . . . . What they have
achieved, we must strive for . . . "[58] The transition of Indian economy
according to the change of political regime is represented in Nayak (2009).
With the supportive political regime and pro-capital economic policies, there
was a massive growth of global capital in the form of Foreign Direct Investment in India. The pro-FDI policy increased the confidence of the global
capital market and its leaders (ibid).

However, the New Economic Reforms in India, launched during 1991,
had two components i.e.: Structural Adjustment Programmes (SAP) and Sta-
bilization Policies with other disinvestment policies as advised by the World
Bank and the IMF. The Structural Adjustment Policy was aimed at privatisation and liberalisation whereas Stabilisation Policy was aimed at the devaluation of currency, free and deregulated market, elimination and reduction of
subsidies, reduced control of the nation state over its macro economic affairs
especially in the matter of budgetary policy and monetary policy and removal of welfare policies and facilities provided by the state. These reflected the
basic features of neo-liberal economic policies, and were part of the World
Bank and IMF package that provoked criticism inside and outside India that
it was the handiwork of the Bretton Wood institutions. This deal did not
leave any space to mobilise internal resources to meet the economic crisis.
The taking of over of Indian economy by market forces could not deliver as
per the promise of the new economic reform program (Chandrasekhar and
Ghosh, 2002).

However, the entire process of new economic policies in India and their
failures can be summarised in a paragraph by the Planning Commission of
India. It was mentioned in the approach to the eleventh Five-Year Plan that,
"while the performance reflects the strength of the economy in many areas, it
is also true that large parts of our population are still to experience a decisive

improvement in their standard of living . . . . Far too many people still lack access to basic services such as health, education, clean drinking water and sanitation facilities without which they cannot be empowered to claim their share in the benefits of growth. These problems are more severe in some states than in others and in general they are especially severe in rural areas (Planning Commission 2006: 1)". The World Bank which pioneered the entire reform programme during 1991 calls the present Indian growth as "booming economy with growing gaps" and considers inclusive growth as the only measure to control regional imbalances and inequities which can sustain economic development (World Bank, 2006). Thus the Indian Ministry of Finance, talks about inclusive growth (Ministry of Finance 2007: 15-16) and focuses it in the eleventh Five-Year Plan (2007:12) by looking at the pervasive negative impact on different sectors of the Indian economy.

SECTORAL ANALYSIS OF INDIAN ECONOMY AFTER ECONOMIC REFORMS

The Indian Union Budget (1991-92), with new economic reforms, was launched with the promise of controlling inflationary pressure on the price line, tackle balance of payment crisis, reduce government expenditure, to maintain a balance between revenue collection and expenditure, accelerate industrial production, encourage FDI, create more jobs, boost export and agriculture, support rural development and help the weaker sections i.e. backward classes and improve the social services like health, education and drinking water and roads[59]. These promises of economic reforms have remained promises to this day. Launched to revive the Indian economy from the crisis, the reforms have only reinforced crisis in different sectors of the Indian economy; the opposite of the policy promise made at its launch. It can be better understood by looking at its impact on different sectors of Indian economy. Nayak (2009) argues that during the pre-economic reform period, the growth rate of three major sectors of the Indian economy was low but there was a balance between the agriculture, industry and service sectors. But during the post-economic reform period, there was a constant decline of agriculture and the agricultural sector was placed in a secondary position. The stagnancy in industrial growth and the simultaneous slow growth of the service sector is visible during the post-reform period. It also indicates that the growth disparity between agriculture, industry and service sector has increased, especially after the implementation of economic reforms during 1991, resulting in unbalanced growth (Nayak, 2009). Thus, it can be said that the economic reforms in India caused a sectoral imbalance in the Indian economy, which has led to an uneven economic growth in India. The development planning period from 1951 to 1986 was under the control of the state and government with public sector dominance. The state and government put several restrictions on the private sector, such as industrial licensing and its capacity expansion, restrictions on foreign investment, quantitative restrictions on imports and exports along with import licensing and heavy import duties with an objective of saving the domestic economy from foreign capital. This resulted in the balanced growth of three sectors of Indian economy during the pre-economic reform period, especially during 1980-1986 (Nayak, 2009). In this way, the primary sector of the Indian economy has declined during the post-reform period, whereas the secondary has remained either stagnant or has shown some growth sign. But the tertiary sector has grown rapidly (Nayak, 2009).

But the neo-liberal advocates of development planning for economic growth disagree with the state command planned economy that the Indian government instituted, despite different sectors of the Indian economy doing fairly well (Nayak, 2009). The main criticism was based on the idea that the structure within a planned economy did not allow for the free interplay of demand and supply forces in the market, leading to the emergence of a non-competitive regime, resulting in a growth of uneconomic units in different sectors, high production costs and low productivity in different sectors of the Indian economy. This has created a technological backwardness and production of low quality goods. Thus, there must be a policy shift from state command economy to market economy, as the planned economy and its state control measures has cost more than it has benefited (Mohammad and Whalley,1984:387-413) and thus change in economic policy is necessary for economic growth and development[60].

However, by following the prescriptions of the neo-liberal economist and development planners, Indian economic planning has chosen the path of transition from a state command planned economy to an open economy, by changing the restrictive economic policies which were announced during the latter part of the mid 1980s. The changes were only focused on the external sector which did not satisfy the objectives of neo-liberal political economists. They defined the changes as half hearted liberalisation which are visible in the works of Panagariya (2004) and Manor (1987). Again they advocated more comprehensive and systematic policy changes, both in the domestic and external sector, by completely removing all restrictions and policy barriers for the free play of market and global capital with an objective of greater competition and better efficiency in the economy. This paved the way towards an open door Indian economy, and the basis for liberalisation, privatisation and globalisation of the Indian economy, which took place during the 1991 economic reforms, also known as the 'New Economic Reforms'. The post-reform period growth rate of real GDP from 1992-93 to 1999-2000 was 6.46 per cent whereas the per capita income growth suffered an unprecedented decline, which increased to 3.9 percent during 2002 according to

World Bank (2003). But the per capital growth of income was confined within the urban areas and among the skilled labourers. It did not have the same impact on the rural areas of India. In this way, it had a negative impact on the different sectors of the Indian economy which can be conceptualised in Nayak (2009) and can be explained further in a sector specific context.

INDUSTRY UNDER ECONOMIC REFORMS

The industrial sector in the Indian economy has grown during the post economic reform period. For example; Bosworth and Collins (2007)'s research shows that the total factor productivity in industry grew from 0.3 per cent in 1978-93 to 1.1 per cent in 1993-2004. However, the present industrialisation process in India is moving away from its historical origin which was based on the ideas of new developmentalism for self-determination and modernisation i.e. independence of Indian industries from the foreign capital and modernisation of production (large and small scale). As a result there was a growth of state command industrialisation process, in India in which the national capitalist class have formed the industrialisation policy (Mukherjee, 2002). Industrialisation has remained largely confined to the urban centers of India (Calcutta, Bombay, Nagpur, Pune, Madras, Agra, Jaipur, Surat, Ahmadabad, Hyderabad, Delhi and Bhopal) while the rural peripheries of India have remained industrially underdeveloped. However, after the implementation of the new economic reforms, a new trend developed in the industrialisation process, in which industrial capital formed out of the combination of private and foreign capital, is now moving to the rural peripheries of India[61] where there are natural resources and raw materials. Therefore, by setting up industries in the peripheries, the industrial capital reduces transportation cost, risk and at the same time, benefits from cheap labour. Thus, the intention of such a move of industrial capital to the peripheries in India is not to industrialise peripheries, but to reduce production cost and maximise profits. In this way the rural peripheries of India, which were suffering from uneven development during pre-reform period, are now becoming more and more vulnerable to industrial capital. Thus industrialisation after economic reforms has enlarged the gap between urban centres and rural peripheries, which is a challenge before development politics. The development politics has to decide to move on a new path which can reverse underdevelopment which is "a product of worldwide capitalist expansions- and not as a backward form of capitalist development (Amin, 1994:43)" and reinforce itself through the industrialisation of the rural peripheries of India as a part of capitalist expansion[62].

However, the capitalist industrial expansion has taken a new shape during the post-economic reform period. The public sector industries faced a clear setback and industrial stagnancy reached such a level that most of the government-led industries were shut down and sold to private companies. The same public sector industries that were considered inefficient and un- profitable units were purchased cheaply by private industrialists and subse- quently benefited enormously. The industries started making profits and be- came efficient. As a result, there was a growth of industrialisation led by private companies.

AGRICULTURE UNDER ECONOMIC REFORMS

There were no specific policies on agriculture in the first phase of the eco- nomic reforms, but it affected agriculture directly and indirectly. The objec- tive of agricultural policies during the planned development was to secure food security by increasing production, availability and accessibility by the distribution of food through fair price shops. It had a strong orientation to provide support to the farmers to save them from the market exploitation, control food price and encourage production (Swaminathan, 2000). These objectives of planned agricultural development, dismantled during first phase of the economic reforms, were pushed further during the second generation economic reforms under BJP/NDA regime. The regime formed agricultural policies to integrate Indian agricultural trade with the global market which then had a negative impact on agricultural production in India.

Post-reform non-agricultural growth is accompanied by decline in agri- cultural growth (Nayak, 2009). The agricultural decline is documented by the Government of India itself which says that "the average annual growth rate of agriculture, including allied sectors declined from 4.7 percent during the Eighth Plan (1992-97) to 2.1 percent during Ninth Plan (1997-2002). As against the targeted annual growth rate of 4 percent during the Tenth Plan, growth rate in 2002-2003, the first year of the Tenth Plan (2002-07), was negative (-7.0 percent)"[63]. The Government of India was asked by the De- partment of Agriculture to give reasons for the decline of the agricultural growth rate. The Department of Agriculture, in its reply, stated that "the main reason for erratic fluctuations in annual growth rate of agriculture is attribut- able to wide fluctuations in monsoon . . . deficient or scanty rainfall"[64]. This is an apolitical and bureaucratic answer to the decline of agriculture which shifts the attention from the failure of agricultural policy during the period of post-economic reform. Followed by the prescription of the new economic reforms, trade liberalisation has led to the diversion of agriculture from food crop production to exportable cash crops. This has reinforced the crisis in agriculture in India (Patnaik, 1996, 2000, 2002, 2003a, 2003b, 2003c). The crisis in agriculture has led to the crisis in Indian peasantry (during and after the economic reforms) as a result of reduced budget expenditure on agricultural sector in terms of subsidies to farmers in the field of fertilizers, seeds and irrigation. Agricultural decline led to the decline in the food grain production in India (Nayak, 2009). The impact of economic reforms on food production and indicates the volume of crisis in Indian agriculture and peasantry created and reinforced by the new agricultural policies adopted after the launch of the new economic reform. However, the statistical data reveals that there has been a growth of area under cultivation and growth in the production of commercial crops and its areas under cultivation (Nayak, 2009). In the case of food crops, both the area under cultivation and food crop production has declined during the post-economic reform period (Nayak, 2009). This change in agriculture is a product of the new agricultural policy[65] pursued after the economic reforms. The transition from food to cash crop production has led to the commercialisation of agriculture in India. The decline in food production has led to the growth of an import based food market in which the consumers having purchasing power are eligible to access[66]. Thus the majority of the population does not have access to the market and has been placed into a situation of food insecurity[67]. The decline of production also led to the decline of food availability during the post-reform period (Nayak, 2009)[68]. The declining accessibility and availability of food has led to lowered food intake, both in the urban and rural areas, which has had an adverse impact on the poor sections of Indian society (Swaminathan, 2000). In this way post-reform agricultural growth has pushed Indian masses into food insecurity and liberalisation of trade in agriculture has reinforced it further (Ghosh, 2005, 2006).

TRADE UNDER ECONOMIC REFORMS

The problems of liberalisation and globalisation of trade have caused more problems of market volatility than of economic growth and price stability as preached by the trade theorists. The policy has led to the internationalisation of unfettered economy and growth of market fundamentalism under the guidance of the international financial institutions like the IMF which have helped the development of countries' economies and reinforced crisis in the economy of developing countries (Stiglitz, 2004). From its origin, the market fluctuation and crisis were the twin products of the capitalist system (Kindleberger, 2000) which has been reproduced again through economic policy reforms that were created to abide by the prescriptions of the international financial institutions and their lending programmes. In such a context, the economic reform in India has created a base for the liberalisation and globalisation of trade which has led to the integration of the Indian market with global market, resulting in massive growth of trade in which import is higher than the export leading to trade imbalance in the country's economy. It is

worth mentioning that the trade imbalance in the Indian economy is currently
growing (Nayak, 2009). The trade imbalance is an impediment in the convergence of the Indian economy with the stronger economies of the world.

However, the neo-liberal development planners and economic policy
makers are planning to extend and integrate the national market with international markets through trade. But inter-state trade restrictions and small regional markets within India are barriers to achieve the unification of the
market in which free flow of trade is possible. Thus, the 11th *Five Year Plan*
and *National Commission on Farmers* (2006:128-132) proposed to remove
all inter-state trade restrictions for the free flow of trade under a single Indian
market, to help the economy to grow and also help the agriculture sector and
the farmer. However, in reality, the idea is to integrate the whole country's
economy with the international market.

SERVICE SECTOR UNDER ECONOMIC REFORMS

The International Chamber of Commerce (ICC) observes that "services are
coming to dominate the economic activities of countries at virtually every
stage of development (ICC, 1999, p. 1)". The growth of the Indian economy
during recent years under liberalisation, privatisation and globalisation policies has often been regarded as having been service sector-led, as a part of
the international capitalist commercial regime. The service sector has shown
a vertical and horizontal growth during the post reform period of Indian
economy and its share grew from 43.69 per cent in 1990-91 to 51.16 per cent
in 1998-99 (Nayak, 2009). In contrast to the decline of the agricultural sector
and marginal growth of the industrial sector, the service sector grew on a
massive scale during the reform period. The total factor productivity growth
in the service sector was on an annual average of 1.4 per cent in 1978-93 to
3.9 per cent in 1993-2004 (Bardhan, 2007: 3850). The graphical representation of the sectoral average growth rates of the Indian economy during selected periods from 1980 to 2006 shows that the service sector is the only
sector which has grown rapidly during the post-economic reforms period
(Nayak, 2009). It has also shown a strong tendency to sustain growth due to
the changing structure of global capitalism that is becoming more and more
dependent on service sector industry[69]. It filters labour power and employs
highly skilled labourers, which constitutes a minimal percentage of labour
composition, whereas sectors like industrial manufacturing and agriculture,
which employ the majority of labourers in India have declined, causing unemployment and poverty. However, the growth of the service sector and the
decline of the manufacturing sector both in the field of agriculture and industry during the post-liberalisation period is a response of global capitalism
towards the declining profitability of the manufacturing sector (Beckmann

and Cooper, 2004). The declining profitability indicates the crisis in capital accumulation, as predicted by Marx and Engels (1848). The crisis in capitalist accumulation has led to the intensification of the extraction of surplus value by the expanding service sector which has led to the territorial control of labour by the ideological and repressive state apparatuses (Althusser, 1971). The entire process has created unemployment and thus poverty.

EMPLOYMENT AND POVERTY DURING ECONOMIC REFORMS

Agriculture in India still accounts for around 65 percent of all employment in the economy (Jha, 2004). However, during the enactment of economic reforms, there has been a clear decline of farming along with the mechanisation of agriculture, resulting in a rise in unemployment. A similar experience can be replicated in industrial sector as it has not shown a significant growth. At the same time, there was a decline in the rate of growth of real wages in the post-reform period of 1993-2005 compared to the pre-reform decade of 1983-93 (Bardhan, 2007). The combined effect of all these factors has caused a gloomy employment scenario in India (Nayak, 2009). Such trends in Indian economic growth are defined as 'exclusive growth' by Mody (2006) and Kannan (2006) whereas UNDP-ILO (2007) study refers to it as a 'jobless growth'. As a result of this process, there has been a growth of unemployment and poverty in India during the post- economic reform period. Recent research by scholars along the ideological spectrum, in terms of politics and in terms of research methodology, has revealed a growth of poverty, inequality and wealth disparity in both urban and rural India during the post-economic reforms period (Sen, A. & Himanshu, 2004a, 2004b; Dev & Ravi, 2007; Himanshu; 2007; and Jayadev, Motiram, & Vakulabharanam, 2007). But the official poverty ratio estimated by the NSS and Planning Commission of India shows that the poverty percentage declined from 44.5 per cent in 1983 to 27.5 per cent in 2004-05 by taking into account the consumer expenditure data. The Government of India (2003) has claimed that there was a significant reduction in poverty from around 39 per cent in the late 1980s pre-reform period to 26 per cent in 1999-2000 post-reform period. The studies by Dutt and Ravallion (2002) pointed out that the growth elasticity of poverty reduction depends on initial distribution of land and human capital, which is different from growth of income. The impact of the new economic policies does not seem to have any positive impact on the non-income Human Development Indicators like health and education (Bardhan, 2007). Such uneven development in social and economic sectors is linked with liberalisation and globalisation, which has left the poor behind in its exclusive development process (Chaudhuri, S and Ravallion, 2006; Bardhan, 2007), having a negative impact on the employment situation in India (Nay-

ak, 2009). Moreover, the overall assessment of the contribution of new economic reforms in India has failed to deliver its objectives in a positive direction. Its impact has been detrimental to the growth of different sectors of the
Indian economy, influencing its macro set up by forming an unavoidable
alliance between Hinduism, the Hindu right wing forces and neo-liberal
economy.

HINDUISM, THE HINDU RIGHT WING FORCES AND NEO-LIBERAL ECONOMY

At the outset, the Hindu religion or Hinduism looks diverse but has strong
tendencies of arbitrary and authoritarian outlook in its unstructured theology.
It is diverse in its practice as it gives more space to different cults of
thoughts, beliefs and spiritual traditions to prevail within its unstructured
philosophy. Its unstructured philosophy provides greater freedom to individuals to follow and practice their faith and beliefs in their own way[70]. But it is
arbitrary in its philosophical principles and goals. Let's take *The Bhagavad
Gita*[71] (God's Song) as an example in which the cardinal philosophical principles and goal of Hindu religion is based on the doctrine of *Karma*[72] (duty),
which is based on *Dharma* (religion or righteousness), which can provide
Artha (wealth/power/fame) and be achieved through *Bhakti* (devotion).
These four steps can provide the basis for *Gyana/Vidya* (knowledge) for the
realisation of the 'self' and the 'other' which can lead towards *Punarjanma*
(reincarnation). But the final goal is *Moksa* (deliverance or salvation) or
Nirvana (free from the cyclic process of birth and rebirth. This is the state
where human body/life unites/reunites with the supreme soul; the god). The
final goal can be achieved by following the steps of *Karma, Bhakti and
Dharma*[73].

The first four principles constitute the path of desire and the last three
principles are the path towards renunciation. One can practice and follow any
spiritual cult, belief and traditions in the Hindu religion, as there is diversity
in means, but the goal and its framework are arbitrary and autocratic. Such
philosophy influenced and justified the economic thinking and development
planning in India during the neo-liberal regime established during the 1991
economic reforms. Any attempt to question the neo-liberal economic and
development policy is considered as anti- development and economic growth
is viewed as if it is the salvation for India. Like the theory of *Karma*, the neo-
liberal development thinkers answer the questions of inequality, poverty,
marginalisation and underdevelopment as state failure, inefficiency of the
state and market failure. Like Hindu theology, the advocates of the neo-
liberal market talk about the solution of these problems in long run; there is
no time limit to achieve it (Nayak, 2007a).

However, the relationship between Hinduism and the capitalist system established by Weberian scholarship and its legacies have been criticised on several accounts (Gellner, 1982). But nevertheless, the centrality of the argument still stands and contributes to our understanding of contemporary capitalism in India and its relationship with Hindu religion. The modernisation theorists take Weber (1958)'s argument further and consider Hinduism as a "major stumbling block for modernisation" in India (Sinha, 1974: 519)[74]. In the Weberian sense, modernisation indicates rationalisation of capitalist order by removing capitalist vices from the system. Such arguments of the modernisation theorists, following Weberian legacy, can be challenged in reverse on the ground that Hinduism provides the philosophical and ideological ground, social and spiritual legitimacy to the neo-liberal market and rationalises the capitalist virtues to grow in Indian society and co-opts the tenets of resistance movements within its project[75]. This process is facilitated by the Hindu right wing forces that derive their social legitimacy and philosophical justification from Hindu religion (which is discussed later).

The post-colonial development planning is also influenced by Indian's diverse culture which provides a resistance to monolithic neo-classical economics (Cameron and Ndhlovu, 2001:61-72). Cameron and Ndhlovu (2001) have taken the example of the culture that derives from the Hinduism or Hindu religion[76] to locate the intellectual and philosophical legacy of resistance to neo-liberal policies of liberalisation and globalisation. There is no doubt that the Hindu religion has an immense influence on economic thoughts, economic policies and development planning in India (Kapp, 1963). But I think the basic fallacies in the argument put forth by Cameron and Ndhlovu (2001) remain within the contradictory and often confusing projects within Hindu religion that help the neo-liberal economy to grow in the contemporary Indian economic landscape. With the influence of neo-liberal economic ideas, there has been a declining role of state and government which has given rise to Hindu right wing forces that derive their political legitimacy and philosophical justification from the Hindu religion. The neo-liberal project has formed an alliance with the Hindu right wing forces to spread its ideas and the market, which has influenced the Indian economic planning in recent times.

Politically speaking, the nationalisation of north-Indian Hindu traditions was an interactive process in which both the colonialists and Hindu nationalists contributed to the formation of an indigenous (Hindu) cultural and political identity. This cultural and political identity of Hindu nationalists has given a political platform to the Hindu right wing forces in post-colonial Indian politics. The cultural logic of Hindu right wing politics derives its strength from three idioms i.e. i) the political culture of British colonialism, ii) the pre-colonial classical Hindu tradition. The interaction between the pre-colonial Hindu tradition and British colonial ideology produced the third idiom of nationalist modernist tradition during 19th century colonial India (Dalmia, 1999). These three idioms provide the basis for the narrow nationalistic politics of Hindu right wing forces which has influenced the development planning and economic policy of post-colonial India. There are many attempts to study the relationship between the Hindu right and neo-liberalism. The work of Deshpande (2000:211) reveals that there is a contradictory, as well as complementary, relationship between Hindutva and neo-liberal economy that may go beyond dichotomy. Thus, it is difficult to define the relationship between the two as one dimensional. In her work, Desai (2006) locates an uneasy interaction between neo-liberal economy and Hindu right wing politics. But she affirms that the Hindu right wing forces are pursuing the agendas of neo-liberal development. However, the contradictions and collaborations between Hindu right wing politics and neo-liberal economy is a part of the larger philosophy of neo-liberalism[77]. The ethics of Hindutva politics as practices by the Sangh Parivar and the economic policies followed by the BJP is concomitant with the spirit of capitalism in India (Hansen, 1998).

The dominant class and their capitalist ideologues are trying to integrate people with the market and trying to mould and convince that it is in their own interest to undermine the growing resistance to the model of free market economy under neo-liberalism (Petras & Henry, 2001:8). In this process, the integrative and absorbing role played by the religions (Geertz, 1965) often provide an ideological veil to pursue such goal and the right wing forces take it further[78]. In India, Hindu religion and its right wing forces provide a base to uphold and pursue the economic interests of the neo-liberal market of the capitalist class and mould people accordingly. The relationship between neo-liberalism[79] and Hinduism can be conceptualised from Weber (1963)'s comparative analysis of world religions, their impact on social and economic development and the origin of modern capitalist societies. It is not the starting point but a definite demarcating point to understand the relationship between religion and capitalist economy of our contemporary times. The Weberian legacies continue to dominate the discourse on religion and economic development in the works of many researchers[80]. Gradually the interaction between religion and economy[81] has created institutionalised forms of religious activities with economic motives. Over time, religious organisations and their institutions continue to exist in one form or another and continue to influence development policies and economics in general by institutionalising their right to own property, run educational and health institutions[82], serving as non-familial, non-royal, non-political social participation beyond state mechanisms (Little, 1978). This has given rise to the idea of NGOs and COs[83] affiliated with religious organisations and ideologies carrying forward their work among the people by creating a social base for these organisations with a religious motivation that sustains poverty, inequality and exploitation and works as an assuaging agency to pacify the resistance movements against the predicaments created by the capitalist market system. But capitalist market systems talk about 'participation, empowerment and democratisation'. Such language is the part of the new 'theology of development' which has its root in religion (Henkel and Stirrat, 2002:177). It provides the cultural, philosophical and ideological justification for the new development orthodoxy[84] carried out by NGOs and sponsored by both state and non-state actors.

GROWTH OF NGOS AND ITS MEANING FOR DEVELOPMENT

The growth of NGOs and the developmental process[85] during the new economic reform period has led to the decline of a state's legitimacy over its citizens. The declining legitimacy of a state over its citizens has created a gap between the people and the state. This gap has the potential to give rise to resistance movement to claim the citizenship rights. But the gap created by the minimal role of the state is covered up by the NGOs and COs (Fisher, 1997) in the process of globalisation and the resistance to the process has also declined. This new informal institutional trend created with the growth of NGOs in the development process has created volatility in culturally plural societies (Appadurai, 1991; Lash & Urry, 1994). In politics, it has increased the interdependence among political actors with the globalisation of capitalism and power (Fisher, 1997:440). The interdependence of political actors with capitalism and power has led to the formation of a troika of relationship between NGOs, the state and world capitalism (Kothari, 1986). Contrary to this view, many others see the growth of NGOs as having great potential in alleviating rural poverty (Brown & Korten 1989; Korten, 1990), creating global civil society (Sanyal, 1994; Peterson, 1992) and the ability to empower people through social movements; which can contribute to alternative development discourse which questions the dominant development paradigm and documents its flaws (Escobar, 1992, 1995; Patkar, 1995). The impact of NGOs on development is difficult to locate due to the heterogeneous nature and scope of NGO activities (Fisher, 1997). Similarly, it is difficult to generalise all NGOs as part of the development framework as they are sponsored either by the state or by national, multinational, transnational capital. Thus, the debate on the growth of NGOs and the nature of their activities and interactions with state, society and global capitalism is so diverse that it is difficult to allow a single approach to define the troika of relationship between NGOs, state and capitalism.

Further, the NGOs have become the favoured institutional set-up for the development agencies both globally and nationally (Edwards & Hulme, 1996a) which creates a process of depoliticising development. The depoliticisation of development reinforces problems which are structural and political (Ferguson 1990). Development anthropologists locate such processes as a by product of new development orthodoxy that talks about 'participation, empowerment and democratisation'. Such language is a new theology of NGO led development, with the help of local elites and government agents (Hirschman 1987; Sanyal 1994), has created a culture of consultancy reinforcing the existing power relations and inequalities within society (Stirrat, 2000; Henkel & Stirrat, 2002). Thus, NGOs prefer to maintain the status quo in the social, economic and political structure rather than to change it (Fowler, 1993; Ndegwa, 1996; Starn, 1995). Many consider it as colonisation of the masses through local elites, government agents to international agencies and donors (Reilly, 1992; Jhamtani, 1992; Fisher, 1995) encompassing local and national boundaries (Kothari, 1993). In the Indian context, Karat (1988) considers NGOs with foreign collaboration as anti-nationalist agents of capitalism that promote western political and cultural values. This is possible due to the patron-client relationship between NGOs and their donors (Mehta, 1996). There is a difference between rhetoric of NGOs and reality (Baviskar, 1995), thus, it is romantic to justify the optimism that the proponents of NGOs are doing good and unencumbered and untainted by the politics of government or the greed of the market as outlined in the work of Zivetz (1991). The process of economic reforms has expanded its base to all Indian states with the help of Indian federal polity and its centralised financial federal structure as prescribed by the Constitution[86]. It is discussed further in the context of Orissa in the next chapter.

CONCLUSION

Indian society is not only complex but also peculiar and unique in many ways, reflecting continuities and changes as determined by class forces and their institutional set-ups. It is passing through a neo-liberal stage of development in which finance and corporate capital, led by transnational capitalist class both in its local and national form, dominates the nature of state, economy and its polity in India. The transition from a state command economic planning to market led economic growth and followed by the new economic reforms has had negative impacts on the both micro and macro economic structure of India. It has led to the declining of industry and agriculture, increasing rate of trade imbalance, unemployment, poverty and disparity among different regions of the country. The growth of the service sector economy in India has remained volatile from the beginning till today.

The new economic reforms have had immense negative impacts on the macro economic structure of India. They have not only led to the declining role of state in economy but also given rise to the growth of non-state actors

(NGOs) in development planning and economy. The informalisation of development planning and declining role of state has helped to create a gap between the state and its citizens. This gap between the state and its citizens is often occupied by the religious right wing forces by their NGO networks which is a threat to the secular social fabric, democratic polity and basis of welfare state in India.

Chapter Two

Indian Federalism and the Political Economy of Neoliberal Development in Orissa

This chapter outlines the way in which Indian federalism helped new economic reforms to spread and integrate the state economy of Orissa with the larger economic set up of the country and the world. While doing so, the chapter analyses the impact of economic reforms on different sectors of the economy in Orissa. The chapter theorises contemporary development planning in Orissa by taking historical conditions into account and argues that negligence by central government, under the Indian federal structure, is a factor contributing to the economic underdevelopment of the state. It rejects the argument that considers that backwardness is the result of natural calamities in Orissa.

INTRODUCTION

The present state of Orissa was known as 'Odra', 'Kalinga' and 'Utkal' in different periods of its history[1]. Geographically, the state is situated in the eastern region of India, neighbouring the states of West Bengal on its northeast, Jharkhand on the north, Chhattisgarh on the west, Andhra Pradesh on the south and the Bay of Bengal on the east. The topography of the state can be divided into two distinct categories such as coastal plains, hilly and forest terrains (Sinha, 1971). Orissa comprises 4.74% of India's landmass with total cultivable land of 65.59 lakh hectares. Orissa's population is 36.71 million (2001 census)[2], accounting for 3.57% of the population of the country. Nearly 85% of its population lives in the rural areas and depends mostly on agriculture for its livelihood[3]. The state has abundant resources of minerals including precious and semi-precious stones[4]. The social and economic condition and its transition can be understood by looking at the history of economic development in Orissa. It can help in identifying the economic institutions and their nature and determining the political economy of development in the state in different periods of history.

Economic historians have treated the state of Orissa, during ancient and medieval periods, in a narrative manner without having any statistical facts and figures about the economy. The state's economy during the ancient period was largely feudal (Sahu, 1993). The higher caste people engaged in developed agricultural activities, even in backward areas, and helped to generate necessary surplus for the rise of regional kingdoms of ancient Orissa. The developed agriculture contributed to the marketable surplus in the villages and led to the formation of rural market institutions which were the meeting ground for economic exchanges between peasants, craftsmen and merchants (ibid:56-57). Because of the growth of agriculture, the higher castes occupied the land leading to the growth of feudalism in its institutionalised form. The institutionalisation of feudalism resulted in the diffusion of higher caste culture (i.e. Brahmanism and Kshatriyaization) leading to the collapse of tribal egalitarianism and peasantisation of tribals in the state. This process took an unambiguous shape during state formations in medieval Orissa (Sahu, 1987, 1993, 2001, 2003; Kulke, 1976).

Nevertheless there is a scarcity of quantitative literature regarding the condition of agriculture; moreover the large volume of research that has been done by economic historians on trade in pre-colonial Orissa is limited to narrative approaches. Pre-colonial Orissa, especially early-medieval Orissa, and its social and economic system was feudal by nature and was the basis for state formation (Sahu, 1993). The nature of feudalism and the role of kings, and other royal families, in the making of the state still dominates debates in the modern history of Orissa[5]. The works of economic historians, folklore, folksongs and customs on maritime trade have revealed that traditionally Orissan people had expertise in overseas trade which had a strong impact on the economy of the state[6], but there is no authoritative statistical data available to objectively reflect its volume.

However, it is interesting to note that maritime trade had a strong connection with Buddhism and Jainism. The Oriya traders harnessed religion to spread their commercial interests in places like Sri Lanka[7]. New research findings have revealed that Oriya maritime trade was extended to most of the South East Asian and European countries (Yamin, 2004; Patra, 2004, 2005; Patnaik, 1992, 1986). Oriya maritime trade enjoyed a form of monopoly over mercantile trade until the arrival and political subjugation of Orissa by Afghans in 1568 AD, Moghuls in 1591 AD, Marathas in 1751 AD and the British in 1803 AD. Political subjugation by these forces presented a formidable barrier to the indigenous maritime trade in the state and ultimately led to its decline (Sethi, 2002). The only study that gives environmental and scientific reasons for the decline of maritime trade in Orissa, Tripati and Vora (2005), claims that maritime trade declined over the period due to environmental changes (natural calamities and sea storms) as Oriya sailors were not technologically well equipped to face such environmental crises. However, the ruling class was very much part of maritime trade in Orissa and always extended their patronage to outside invaders from Afghans, Moghuls, and Marathas to the European merchants (Dutch, Portuguese, French and British) and colonial British rulers. These alliances were formed by the Oriya ruling class to ensure their safe trade and to secure other commercial interests (Sethi, 2002:13-17) during the colonial period.

Like any other parts of India, trade paved the path of colonialism in Orissa. Here the beginnings of colonialism can be seen with a team of English merchants from the East India Company who came to Orissa to establish trade relationships with the state during the rule of Shahjahan in 1633 A.D. This period in India was marked by political havoc due to internal struggles for power between the Marhattas and the Moghuls. Orissa was no exception to this political turmoil, aiding British expansion of colonial empire in the state. The second Anglo-Marhatta war of 1803-1806 put an end to this political upheaval and on 14th October 1803, the state of Orissa became a part of the British regime. The entire state of India came under the British colonialism by the end of 1855 and the British administration then divided the state into three administrative zones - Bengal Presidency, Madras Presidency and the Central Provinces. During British rule in Orissa, the state not only lost its unity in terms of administration, but people also faced economic, political and linguistic subjugation from both the British colonial rulers and Bengalis working for the British administration in the state. Internal colonisation by the Bengalis also contributed to the exploitation of the local Oriya population. In the words of Hunter (1872), "unfortunately, however, we had filled our courts and public offices with highly educated unscrupulous subordinates from Bengal, whom the Uriyas (Oriyas) regarded as foreigners just as much as if they had been Marahattas. Indeed under the Marahattas, the peasantry could always limit their miseries. The jungles afforded a safe retreat from Marhatta violence; no asylum could be found to shelter the unhappy 'Uriyas' from the dexterous extortions and chicanery of our Bengal underlings (ibid, Vo-II: 124)". The people of the state were suffering from the three forms of exploitation and subjugation under the dual colonialism of the British and Bengali officials as well as under the native feudal ruling class. John Beam describes Orissa under British rule as its darkest and most neglected period (Hunter, Stirling, Beams and Sahu, 2005). The discontent of people over the negligence and multiple forms of exploitation gave birth to the many uprisings in the state that led to the creation of a unified state of Orissa. The state became a separate province within British India with effect from 1st April 1936; however India's independence in 1949 marked the beginning of an independent Orissa. This started with six administrative districts followed by sixteen districts with twelve district magistrates in 1949. During 1933, thirty districts were formed to become the efficient and decentralised administration that continues to represent the contemporary administrative set up in Orissa (Government of Orissa, 2004).

Development in Orissa has been strongly influenced by its political history which determines post-colonial conditions of economic development. The state is now following a model of economic development on the capitalist path; a legacy of colonial capitalism supported by feudalism in the state. The entire process laid the pre-conditions that promised modernity and development for the state. Post-colonial politics of development extended promises of modernity from colonial capitalism with its colonial and feudal patterns of exploitation (Pati, 2006:38-42). The Oriya middle class is a strong supporter of projects of modernity and allows them to exploit tribals and other marginalised sections of the local population (Mohanty, 2005). The Oriya middle class, along with ruling class support, has legitimised the exploitative regime by the state of Orissa (Pati, 2006). As a result, a state with abundant natural resources is suffering from poverty and underdevelopment. Such a paradox in the development of the state owes its historical origins to class alliances formed out of landed feudal elites (including royal families) with the national and international capitalist class. The history of this post-colonial capitalist development paradox, in Orissa, is well documented in the works of Pati (2002). This paradox started unfolding with the introduction of new economic reforms, which were pursued in India from 1991, and accelerated by the Indian federal structure of economic administration.

INDIAN FEDERALISM AND NEW ECONOMIC REFORMS

The federal structure of India is reflected in the Article-1 of the Constitution of India that reads "India, that is Bharat, shall be a Union of States"[8]. The use of the term 'union' indicates the centralised tendencies of an Indian federalism designed by the Constitution of India as opposed to the idea of decentralised federalism prevalent during ancient and medieval periods[9]. The Government of India, in part one of its report of the Commission on Centre-State Relations (1988), gives a historical account that shows that during the ancient period "each province led its own life, continued its old familiar system of Government (though under the agents of the Central power) and used its own language" (Sarkar as cited in Govt. of India, 1988: 5). Even the conquered states/provinces continued to retain their own identity during ancient India (Sastri, 1987: 116). The same report (1988) goes on to document the federal features during medieval India. The provinces or the Moghul states had regional autonomy until the last Moghul ruler "made a strong bid for complete centralisation and abolition of traditional diversities and autonomy of the regions" (Govt. of India, 1988: 5). After the death of the last Moghul ruler, the states and provinces regained their regional autonomy. This came to an end with the beginning of colonial British rule and the evolution of a highly centralised administration in India.

However, the centralised administration of the British rulers resulted in inefficiency and local discontent. This compelled them to decentralise and devolve power to the states and provinces[10]. The partition of India during 1947 negatively impacted on the decentralisation project and is cited as one of the major reasons for the growth of a centralised federal system in India. The second report of the Union Powers Committee (July 5, 1947) reveals that "it would be injurious to the interests of the country to provide for a weak Central authority which will be incapable of ensuring peace, of co-coordinating vital matters of common concern…and that the soundest framework of our Constitution is a federation with a 'strong centre' (Govt. of India, 1988: 7)". The primary argument was that a strong centre could reduce regional inequality and help in the growth of balanced regional development with national unity (ibid: 8). Such a vision was reflected in the Constituent Assembly debate, and later in the Constitution of India, in support of establishing a strong centralised federalism in India (Bhattacharya, 1992; Austin 2004; Singh, 2007). The communist and socialist orientated members of the Constituent Assembly vehemently opposed the idea of centralised federalism in India and argued for decentralised federalism, although this did not generate much support (Singh, 2007:27-28). The works of Singh (2005) argue that there is a Hindu bias in the centralisation project of Indian federal system. Such a centralised federal system is echoed by the Hindu right-wing forces in post-colonial Indian politics (Singh, 2007:26). Many members of the Constituent Assembly have further argued that the strong centre in Indian federalism is a centralisation project which helped in shaping a capitalist path of development (Government of India, 1988; Bettelheim, 1968; Chattopadhyay, 1970; Desai, 1984). However, as a result of the centralised federal system of India, the central planning became a priority which gave the central government more power over the states and "shaped triangular relationships between Indian capitalism, Indian State and Indian nationalism (Singh, 2007: 29)". The troika of a centralised federal system, the Indian state and capital has established a mutually reinforcing relationship through centralised federalism and central planning in India (Singh, 1999). The Indian capitalist[11] class has played a vital role in the formation of such a troika, participating and using the Indian state for capital accumulation (Chakravarty, 1989; Chattopadhyay, 1971 & 1992; Bettelheim, 1968; Desai, 1975 & 1984; Bardhan, 1989b, Byres, 1993; Patnaik, 1975; Sen, 1982). The new economic reforms in India during 1991 were another step forward in the process of capital accumulation with the help of Indian state through a centralised federal system[12] and centralised planning for development. During the pre-reform period, Indian capitalist classes were accumulating capital with the help of the state, whereas in the post-economic reform period, both global capitalist classes and Indian capitalist classes have been accumulating with the help of the Indian state.

Moreover, the trends and patterns of the Indian federal system need to be understood in the context of the new economic reforms in India by examining their political implications, especially with reference to (i) the growth of regional politics within the federal structure, (ii) decentralised politics and (iii) centralised financial administration in India. The growth of regional politics in India demands more financial autonomy of the provincial states[13]. As former finance secretary and the present deputy chairman of the Planning Commission of India, Montek Singh Ahluwalia has argued that "liberalisation has reduced the degree of control exercised by the centre in many areas, leaving much greater scope for state level initiatives. This is particularly true as far as attracting investment…is concerned" (Ahluwalia, 2000: 1632). This indicates that for attracting foreign and private investment, internal liberalisation is necessary to reduce central control over the state governments. But when it comes to financial decision-making, the central government applies different control mechanisms to restrict states' financial autonomy which have helped the Indian economy to integrate with the global economy (Jenkins, 1999). The works of Pritam Singh go further to argue that "the balance of payment crisis of 1991, which resulted in the new regime of liberal economic reforms, has opened some avenues for de-centralisation, especially in the economic domain, but at the same time has given more power to the Centre in the process of closer integration of the national economy into the global capitalist economy than existed before 1991 (Singh, 2007: 17)". This kind of contradiction within the Indian federal system is created by the financial centralisation and political de-centralisation which is solved by the application of central rules with sub-national variations to address the divergent regional political interests that influences the national policy framework and determines the nature of Indian federalism (Sinha, 2006).

The regional autonomy of financial decision making is necessary but has far reaching consequences for the Indian federal structure. One of the major consequences of financial centralisation is the recent growth of regional movements for autonomy, based on parochial ideas. These are a threat to the Indian federal system in particular, and nation in general. The impact of new economic reforms on local politics is well documented by D.L Sheth who observed in the following words:

"The new social movements, active at the grass roots of Indian politics for over three decades now...are now also locked in conflicts with the institutions and organisations representing the global economic and political power. The global structures...have begun to penetrate local spaces without much mediation, either by way of protection or control from the State's centralised institutions of planning and bureaucracy.... The result is, local politics has become a variegated scene of conflict and collaboration with global economic structures...epitomised recently by the Cargill Food Co. winding up its operations in the face of farmers' agitation in the south of India and Pepsi Foods acquiring a durable foothold in Punjab largely due to the cooperation it received from the farmers' lobby in that state"[14]

Such collaborations and contradictions, among and between global capital and the Indian capitalist class, have far reaching consequences for the centralised economic policy project, which is a product of centralised economic and administrative policies undertaken by the Government of India during the last six decades; a colonial legacy started during British rule (Singh, 2007). The economic and administrative centralisation during the period of economic reforms is a step further. As a result, "the 1990s were characterised by the emergence of the State [level] as the effective arena of political competition (Hasan, 2002:27)". The competition is not to address the issues of poverty, inequality, corruption and exploitation but to sustain power, both at the centre and in states, and to invite more and more foreign capital. In this way, the Indian federal administrative, political and economic structure helps global and national capitalist classes to accumulate and reinforce a mutual relationship for the capital expansion without a provincial border. The central planning and economic policies have helped to integrate all states with Indian national economy. This has been further enhanced by a single national economic wave; a wave of liberalisation, privatisation and globalisation to integrate the state economy with the global capitalist economy.

SECTORAL ANALYSIS OF ORISSA'S ECONOMY AFTER THE NEW ECONOMIC REFORMS

Although the New Economic Reforms started in India from 1991, its real entry to the economy of Orissa took place and was felt during 1998 when the Government of Orissa approached the Government of India for Structural Adjustment Assistance (SAA) from World Bank/DFID for investing in social sectors i.e.; health, education, poverty eradication and improvement in infrastructure, to achieve Millennium Development Goals. The SAA was granted, under the Orissa Socio-Economic Development Credit/Loan (OSEDC), making a clear road map for the economic and structural reform process. The objectives of this reform process were outlined in the Medium Term Fiscal

Plan (MTFP) and subsequently in the Revised Medium Term Fiscal Plan (RMTFP) 2002 to 2008 (Government of Orissa, 2005:67; Government of Orissa, 2004). The process has been accelerated by the signing of a Memorandum of Understanding (MoU) as per the prescriptions made by the Eleventh Finance Commission to achieve fiscal sustainability in the state (ibid: 67).

The Government of India asked the Government of Orissa to follow the guidelines of the SAA as outlined in the RMTFP. The economic reform programmes, as advised by the Government of India and practised by the Government of Orissa, can be summarised as follows; In the industrial sector, measures were taken to reduce industrial regulations for the entry of private investment, disinvest and privatise the industries under public sector; in the agricultural sector, amendments were introduced to Orissa Agricultural Produce Act to end the state monopoly[15] and create a suitable environment for the private investment in agriculture and in its market yards and storage facilities; and in the financial sector, to reduce the ratio of salaries to the state's own revenue further to 96 percent. In order to achieve this objective, reduce the salary bill of temporary workers, either eliminate or freeze the 75 percent of vacant posts, abolish non-essential administrative posts[16] in health and education departments and follow the same policy in other government departments (Government of Orissa, 2005: 82-86). Subsequently, after implementing the policies of internal liberalisation, the Indian Government's Twelveth Finance Commission prescribed that "the central government should not act as an intermediary for future lending and allow the states to approach the market directly (as cited by the Government of Orissa, 2005:92)". This policy of the central government allowed the Orissa economy, along with other state economies, to integrate with the global and national market without any barrier.

However, the World Bank also played a major role in Orissa's economic reform process by initiating the Orissa Economic Revival Loan (OERL) programme. The programme was launched with the condition of implementing economic, fiscal and administrative reforms to liberalise the state's economy which was essential to revive economic growth and achieve rapid poverty reduction over the medium term. The policies were followed by the government of Orissa with the prescriptions of the World Bank and Government of India[17]. They not only influenced the economic policies of the state's government but also restructured the administrative set-up in Orissa. The impact of these new policies, under economic reform programmes, influenced the agriculture, trade, industry, poverty and employment sectors in the state. The negative impact of economic reform on the different sectors of the Orissa economy and its transition and development can be discussed further under separate sections.

AGRICULTURE IN ORISSA AFTER ECONOMIC REFORMS

In Orissa, 85 percent of people in the rural areas depend on agriculture, which contributes more than 50 percent to the state's economy (Kar, 1999 as cited in Das, 2005:56). Agriculture in the state consists of 29.7 percent cultivators and agricultural labourers, along with 35 percent of workers as per the 2001 Census - which is contested by Swain (2003). Her research gives more importance to agriculture as it is the most dominant economic sector in the state in terms of its workforce and output. More than 73 percent of main workers are engaged in this sector, including 44.3 percent cultivators and 28.7 percent agricultural labourers, among whom 87 percent live in the rural areas (ibid). But agriculture has been neglected during the post-reform period as a result of which food production in the state has declined. In comparison to production in the rest of India, Orissa's agricultural production has declined during the post-reform period (Nayak, 2009). Thus the contribution of agriculture to Net State Domestic Product (NSDP) declined from 67 percent in 1951 to 30 percent in 1998 although the labour force remained unchanged (Swain, 2003). This data reflects underemployment, unemployment and over concentration of labour force in Orissa's agricultural sector.

However, land ownership pattern in the state also contributed to the decline of agriculture. The per capita availability of land declined in the state from 0.39 hectare in 1950 to 0.18 hectare in 1999[18] and 0.16 hectares in 2002-03. This indicates a process of concentrated land ownership during this period of liberalisation. The concentration of land in the hands of few created more marginal and landless farmers which has had a negative impact on agricultural productivity in the state.

INDUSTRY IN ORISSA AFTER ECONOMIC REFORMS

The industrial sector constitutes only 9.1 per cent of the total workforce and the annual growth rate of industrial output for 1993-94 to 2003-04 was 1.75 per cent, which was lower than the all India average of 6.19 per cent. This indicates the minimal role of the industrial sector in the state economy. It also reveals the under-utilisation of the industrial potentiality of Orissa. The availability of natural resources, especially mineral resources, in Orissa is a key to the present process of industrialisation.

The history of mining and industrialization, both in colonial and post-colonial Orissa, is a long one, as the state is one of the richest in India in terms of mineral resource share. The process dates back to 1857 and development activities in post-colonial Orissa gained momentum in the early 1950s (Jena, 2006). According to Government of Orissa estimates (2005), the state possesses 97 percent of India's Chromite, 95 percent of Nickel, 50 percent of

Bauxite and 24 percent of coal reserves. The report reveals that Orissa has an estimated reserve of about 5, 923 million tons of 18 minerals valued at Rs. 1,674 million dollars in 1996. Thus, it has attracted both government (colonial and post-colonial) and private investment in the mining sector[19].

The present industrialisation process is part of wider industrialisation policies carried out by the Government of Orissa, driven by the 1991 industrial policy, declared by the Government of India, after the implementation of the new economic reforms. It marked a new trend in the process of industrialisation in Orissa as it was completely different from the pre-economic reform period in terms of its nature and content. During the pre-economic reform period, industrialisation in Orissa required a balance between the development of large and small scale industries whereas during post-economic reform industrialisation has focused more on large scale mining based industries and less on small scale industries[20]. However, industrialization, as such started in 1968, at the beginning of the Sixth Plan (i.e., 1980) by taking advantage of the availability of mineral resources in the state and a number of industrial policies were announced, offering to promote small scale, village and khadi industries.

However, in terms of policy formulation and implementation, these were essentially ad hoc and piece-meal measures and lacked any intelligible "vision" for future industrialisation. The present policy of mining based industrialisation derives its strength from the Industrial Policy Resolution of 1980 which was explicit in its objective to bring about rapid industrial development in the state. It was launched on a grand scale as a part of the populist politics of the State Government, and J.B. Pattnaik (the Chief Minister) announced the intention to set up "one thousand industries in one thousand days with an investment of one thousand crore of rupees"(Pattnaik, 1988:111-122). It provided for a large number of subsidies, procedural relaxations and various concessions to the intending entrepreneurs. Subsequently, the Orissa Government's 2001 Industrial Policy was a great leap forward giving a new boost for mining based industrialisation in the state. The new industrial policy promised to transfer Orissa into a vibrant industrial state, focusing on the abundance of mineral resources as an incentive for industrial investment. Further, the economic reforms and the liberalisation process initiated in 1991 provided an important opportunity to the state to leverage the natural resources to attract investment, both domestic and international[21]. In order to achieve this objective, it planned to encourage private initiatives and investments for mineral-based industries.

The policy reiterated the restriction of government intervention through the "…deregulation and simplification of rules and procedures, rationalization of Labour laws, facilitation of industrial restructuring and accelerated development of physical and social infrastructure through public-private partnership will enable a conducive business climate for attracting private investments"[22]. The policy also stated that the Government of Orissa would not provide any kind of financial support or subsidy to the Public Sectors Undertakings but it would provide tax concessions and "interest subsidy @ 5 % per annum for a period of five years from the date of commercial production on term loans availed from recognized Financial Institutions/ Banks"[23] to the private industrial investors to invest in mining and other industrial sectors of the state's economy. The pro-industrialisation policy, under the regime of liberalisation and privatisation policy, has attracted the highest foreign direct investment in the country and both national and multi-national corporations are investing in the state by looking at the availability of natural resources (Nayak, 2007b). Thus, contrary to the experience of the rest of India, industrialisation has taken a big leap in Orissa during the post-reform period as a result of which the overseas trade of Orissa has increased on a massive scale (Government of Orissa, 2003).

MICRO ECONOMIC CONDITIONS IN ORISSA AFTER THE NEW ECONOMIC REFORMS

Orissa is currently undergoing a severe financial crisis. It has moved from a revenue surplus state, in 1983-84, to a revenue deficit state now. The revenue account of the state has progressively declined over the years. This is basically due to rapid increases in revenue expenditures vis a vis revenue receipts and interest payments have also increased on the debt incurred by the state (Nayak, 2009). Orissa's revenue deficit increased from the surplus of Rs.73.74 crores in 1984-85 to a deficit of Rs. 2573.57 crores in 1999-2000. During this period of decline, the NSDP increased from 1.42% in 1984-85 to 8.46% in 1999-2000 and 4.85% in 2000-2001. In the same way, the revenue deficit and fiscal deficit of the state went up from 7.44 percent in 1984-85 to 38.76 percent in 1998-99. Nayak (2009) gives a picture of the unbalanced growth of the state economy as a result of increasing revenue deficit and fiscal deficit. In order to meet the deficit, the government of Orissa fell into the trap of borrowing, and this has increased on a massive scale during the post-reform period (ibid). However, the overall position of fiscal indicators for Orissa reveals that the reform process has had a negative impact on the micro and macro economy of the state (ibid).

Apart from the state's unbalanced economic growth during the post-reform period, there is an increasing gap between the per capital income in comparison to India (Nayak, 2009). It also reflects the declining condition of individual and state income. As a result of this Orissa has fallen behind India in different indicators of HDI (Nayak, 2009). In this way, the state is in financial crisis and economic instability reinforced by the economic reform process.

EMPLOYMENT SITUATION IN ORISSA

The employment situation is gloomy in the state of Orissa. The 'live register' of Employment Exchange Offices in the state reveals that the rate of unemployment increased from 9593 in 1956 to 7.62 lakhs by the end of 2002. The number of educated job seekers (matriculates and above) was only 1964 in 1956, and had gone up to 6.18 lakhs by the end of 2002. The government of Orissa also acknowledges the fact that there is a lack of employment both in government and non-government sectors (Government of Orissa, 2004:16). The Annual Plan of 2004-05 prepared by the Orissa government indicated that there would be a growth of unemployment. This indicates that the industrialisation process has not generated many employment opportunities in the state. However, the employment scenario[24] is almost stagnant in the state, indicating no positive impact of economic reform on employment. Unemployment during 1999-2000 was 8.34 percent in rural areas and 5.18 percent in urban areas, which indicates that the unemployment rate was higher in urban areas than in the rural areas. The incidence of unemployment among the educated was 18.3% and 15.8% in rural and urban areas respectively, whereas the incidence of unemployment in the rest of India, for the same period, was 3.8 and 8.3 per cent for rural and urban areas respectively (Planning Commission, 2005:27).

POVERTY IN ORISSA

The state is home to 45 percent of the population belonging to SC/ST communities (or some 15 million people) - a significant number in respect to the population of India's SC/ST communities (Parikh & Radhakrishna, 2005). The relative national share of the rural poor in Orissa increased from 53% in 1993–94 to 61% in 1999–2000 (Parikh & Radhakrishna, 2005: 41). The same report (Parikh & Radhakrishna, 2005: 49–50) suggests that the percentage of SCs living below the poverty line was 18.5% in 1993 and climbed to 22.4% in 1999/2000, when 47.8% of the state's rural population was living below the poverty line. The state has one of the lowest *Human Development Index (HDI)* ratings for the country, with 55% of children between the ages of 1–5 years considered as being undernourished in 2000/01, as was the case with 46% of female adults in the state in the same year (Parikh & Radhakrishna, 2005).

According to government statistics, half of the population of 32 million is below the official poverty line that indicates more than 70 percent of people are poor in the state (Kar, 1999 as cited in Das, 2005). The latest estimates of the Planning Commission of India reveal that the percentage of below poverty line population (BPL) in Orissa during 1999-2000 was 47.15 as against

26.10 at the all-India level and overall incidence of poverty was 47.2 percent which was higher than the all India average of 26.10 percent during 1999. Interestingly the incidence of poverty in the state is the highest in the country[25]. The incidence of poverty among the ST and SC population was found to be much higher, of which about 66.37 percent was in the state (Panchayati Raj Department, Government of Orissa in 1997). The data of recent years indicates that the impact of economic reform on poverty reduction is insignificant as the recent National Sample Survey shows that poverty has gone up in the state (Planning Commission, 2005).

HEALTH SITUATION IN ORISSA

The condition of health facilities and infrastructure is much lower than the all India average. During the late 1990s, the number of health centers, per lakh population, in Orissa was 3.10 as against 2.34 at the all-India level. However, the number of medical beds per lakh population was only 48.91 in Orissa, as opposed to 94.47 at the national level (CMIE, 2001). There were 180 Hospitals, 158 Community Health Centres, 184 Public Health Centres (PHCs), 1,166 PHCs (New) and 13 Mobile Health Units in the state, providing curative health services and apart from 13 established mobile health units, 84 more mobile health units were also operating in KBK Districts. In addition, there were 5 Ayurvedic Hospitals, 519 Ayurvedic Dispensaries, 9 Unani Dispensaries, 4 Homoeopathic hospitals and 460 Homoeopathic Dispensaries were operating in the state according to the latest data available from the Government of Orissa, Directorate of Health Services for the end of 2002. The health infrastructure is not enough to provide health care to the existing population in the state. As a result the child mortality rate and death rate due to other diseases is much higher than for other parts of India. The lack of government-led health care facilities has subsequently led to the growth of private nursing homes and hospitals run by the corporates or private individuals and NGOs are also involved actively in health care service delivery in the state.

EDUCATION IN ORISSA

Education is in a precarious condition as can be seen from its literacy rate and educational infrastructure. The literacy rate in the state is 63.6%, which is lower than the all India literacy average of 65.4%. There is a high density of illiteracy amongst the rural population. The gender gap in education is also higher, both in the rural and urban areas, where female literacy is much lower than male rates (Nayak, 2009). In order to solve the problem of illiteracy, there has been a growth of educational infrastructure and student enrollment in primary, upper primary and secondary schools. There were 9801 primary schools with 3.15 lakh students in 1950-51, compared to 42824 in 2002-03 with 46.08 lakh students. It shows the growth of educational infrastructure and student enrollment in primary education, although the teacher-student ratio has declined from 1:19 in 1950-51 to 1:55 in 2002-03. This is the result of the growing number of students, on one side, and the lack of recruitment of teachers on the other. This has caused the decline in the quality of primary education and resulted in a high growth in the number of student dropouts. In 2002-03, the total drop out rate was 34.2%, 36.5% for girls and, amongst SC and ST students 37.2% and 53.3% respectively (Nayak, 2009). This reflects the condition of primary education in the state.

The state had only 501 upper primary Schools with 40000 students in 1950-51, but this increased to 11,510 (with 9.54 lakh students) in 2002-03. Teacher-student ratio declined from 1.16 to 1:23 over this period and the overall dropout rate increased by 59%. The percentage of dropout rates was higher in case of SC students (47.5%), ST students (77.7%), SC girls (49.2%) and ST girls (80.3%) during 2002-03. These figures indicate the growth of gender, caste, tribal and non-tribal disparity in the field of upper primary education in recent years. In the field of secondary education, there were 172 high schools with 16,000 students during 1950-51 and this increased to 6,811 high schools with 12.88 lakh students by 2002-03. But declining teacher-student ratios and the increasing dropout rate continued - during 1950-51, the teacher-student ratio in secondary school was 1:7 which declined to 1:22 in 2002-03. The dropout rate during 2003-04 was 67.2% overall (65.9% boys and 68.5% girls), while the rate of dropouts among tribal students was much higher (78% tribal boys and 76.5% tribal girls)[26].

After analysing the above data, it could be said that there has been a decline in the quality of education in Orissa from primary to higher secondary level. The increasing rate of student dropouts and growing disparity in education indicates the failure of educational policy, even during the liberalisation period when education was pushed into the hands of the private sector and often into the informal sector under the guidance of NGOs[27].

DEBATES ON THE ECONOMIC DEVELOPMENT IN ORISSA AFTER THE NEW ECONOMIC REFORMS

Different aspects of economic development in the state reveal that the new economic reforms in India had a detrimental effect on the development and economy of the state of Orissa and put the state in a debt trap (Nayak, 2009). The economic growth rate of Orissa in terms of Net State Domestic Product (NSDP) during the pre-economic reform period was not satisfactory but there was positive growth in the state. The growth rate from 1950-51 to 1988-89 was 2.7 percent according to 1970-71 prices, whereas at 1980-81 prices the growth rate was 3.8 percent. This indicates the highest economic growth in the state while comparing it with the post-economic reform period. During the post-economic reforms period, there was growth in the mining sector from 8.7 percent to 12.7 percent, manufacturing from 2.6 percent to 8.1 percent, communication infrastructure from 7.9 percent to 13.7 percent, trade, hotel and restaurants from 5.7 percent to 6.8 percent. However, during the same period, agriculture and animal husbandry declined sharply from 3.1 percent to 1.9 percent. This indicates that while the secondary and tertiary sectors of the state's economy grew, there was decline in the primary sector as well as in employment, both in the urban and rural areas of the state. [28]

In this way, the economic development of the state during the period of new economic reforms were jeopardised and failed to achieve the desired objectives which were set during its launch. The failure of the neo-liberal development policies pursued by the Government of India and Government of Orissa led to the manifestation of underdevelopment of the region and the marginalisation of people. The ruling class in Orissa blames the negligence of central government for the failure of development policies, whereas central government blames the inefficiency of the Government of Orissa. The ruling class in India and Orissa are united in laying blame on natural calamities in the state for the underdevelopment of economy and marginalisation of its people. Therefore, the ruling class attempts to ignore the failure of neo-liberal development policies that have reinforced poverty, underdevelopment and marginalisation in the state. The truth behind the ruling class' apolitical answer to development policy failure can be scrutinised under the following sections.

NEGLIGENCE OF CENTRAL GOVERNMENT

The state politicians often blame the central government, at the national level, for its apathetic attitude to the state's development. The argument has some validity which one can find while looking at the central transfer, as percentage of GDP from 1980 to 2000, by the government of India to the Orissa government. It can be said that there was no increase in the central grant to the state government other than providing more and more loans. The relative share of Orissa under different financial commissions of the Government of India is either stagnant or showed a marginal increase whereas in the case of other states, it increased substantially (Nayak, 2009). The central transfer to Orissa has declined over the years especially after economic reform (ibid). The continuous increase of Government of India loans to the state government during the post economic reform period has made Orissa an internal rentier state, where a parasitical class of politicians and bureaucrats has often become the beneficiary of such processes.

However, the Government of India's spending on education, road and communication per person is higher in other states than Orissa. It is 43.52 times higher in Delhi, 25.9 times in Uttaranchal, 19.1 times in Assam, 8.3 times in HP, 6.9 times in West Bengal, 6.17 times in Karnataka, 4.37 times in Tamil Nadu, 4.2 times in UP, 4.2 times in Maharashtra, 3.98 times in Jharkhand, 3.94 times in AP, 3.56 times in J&K, 3.29 times in Punjab, 2.09 times in Haryana, 1.94 times in Kerala, 1.82 times in Chhattisgarh, 1.77 times in MP, and 1.2 times in Gujarat (Baral, 2006). Thus, it is valid to argue that the development policy followed by the Government of India is spreading regional disparity in development and Orissa is a victim of processes of uneven development which were widened during the process of liberalisation. As a result, Orissa ranks at the top of the deprivation index in the country (Nayak, 2009). Even the position of infrastructure in Orissa is far behind the other states of India (CMIE, 2000), and further aggravated by the social and economic hierarchy of the society in Orissa and in India (Nayak, 2009). Thus, it is clear that development of underdevelopment is a result of policy failures in the state and negligence of the central government.

NATURAL CALAMITIES AND DEVELOPMENT IN ORISSA

Natural calamities[29] in Orissa are often mentioned as the cause of the failure of development policies and underdevelopment of the state. The ruling elites, both at central and state government, unite in their belief that the factor of natural calamity is a good answer to cover the failure of development policies in the state. Even researchers have tried to link poverty in the state with the sporadic natural disasters like floods, droughts and cyclones (Pradhan, 1979), which are considered to be the cause of deplorable state of economy in Orissa. There is no doubt that natural calamities cause substantial damage to the economy of the state and loss to the people, but it appears that, during periods of natural calamity, the state's economy was performing fairly well in terms of economic growth (Nayak, 2009). Thus, natural calamities can not be taken as a major reason for the poverty and underdevelopment of the state and its economy. The natural calamities have become an apolitical and bureaucratic answer to the failure of development policies in a state that reinforces poverty and underdevelopment. The political elites at the national and at the state level find it a viable answer to avoid responsibility for the failure of neo-liberal development policies in Orissa.

CONCLUSION

In conclusion, it can be said that the unchanging mode of social and economic analysis under elite intellectual debate is fallacious in the context of Orissa due to the manifestation of dynamic feudal, social and cultural formations along with capitalist economic relations in the state. The transition of society, economy and transition of its economic institutions at different periods of its economic development takes place to incorporate the changing requirements of the ruling and non-ruling elites (Nayak, 2009). The transition in the structure of society, economy and politics is more accommodative to ruling and non-ruling elite interests than transformatory for mass emancipation from the structure of inequality and exploitation. The change of political power from the ancient to medieval period did not change the very basis of the exploitative structure in the society and economy. The medieval Muslim rulers tried to sustain it and transformed it as per their requirements. The same policy of accommodation was adopted by the colonial British administration, where even the exploitative ancient and medieval structures were reinforced wherever they were helpful to sustain colonial rule. In the post-colonial period, there have been few challenges placed by the state through the making of the constitutional law and judicial interventions. However, the very basis of the structures of hierarchy and an exploitative system have remained integral to the democratic polity in which feudal landlords, higher classes and castes continue to enjoy state power. The control of state power gives them greater mobility to control development planning in a direction which is not detrimental to their interest. The transformatory potential of society and its people is being subverted by the populist politics of welfare and development i.e. the promises of the new economic policy that follow globalisation, liberalisation and privatization. It has promised to recover the nation from economic crisis and uplift the Indian citizens by improving their economic conditions through the trickle-down effect of economic growth. It has promised to provide conditions for better agriculture, education, healthcare and other social security infrastructure that will reduce poverty and unemployment. But after one and a half decades of such promises, it has yet to yield the promised goals. Rather, the new economic policies have given a new direction to the welfare and development policies in which a few economic and political elites are the benefactors.

Moreover, the failure of these policies to achieve the desired goals has led to the growth of discontent among people. In response to this popular discontent, regional provincial states (like Orissa) and their ruling classes start blaming the central government of India and its negligence. The national ruling class blames the inefficiency of the state and its machinery for the failure of development policy. The regional and national ruling classes have united and often refer to natural calamities in the state for the failure of the development policies. Such development discourse among the ruling class has twin objectives. Firstly, it has helped to divert the masses from the failure of the neo-liberal model of development and its economic policies pursued by the state. Secondly, it has put the role of the state in the social and economic transformation into a secondary position which has helped the social and economic structure that is responsible for the sustaining inequality and exploitation. The secondary role of the state has allowed the market to play the primary role, consequently having a detrimental effect on different underdeveloped regions and marginalising people. In this context, an attempt has been made to reflect on the impact of the new economic reforms on the tribal development in India with a reference to Orissa.

Chapter Three

Tribals and the Political Economy of Tribal Development in India

A Study of Transitions in Kalahandi District of Orissa

This chapter explains the history, culture, economy and society of tribals in India with reference to Orissa and Kalahandi. It analyses the history of development of underdevelopment in the Kalahandi district and the structures of power that control the process of tribal development in the district. It focuses on the role of tribal development policies in influencing the life, livelihood and culture of tribals in Kalahandi during the post-economic reform period. It questions the general assumptions of economists, anthropologists and political scientists about the subsistence nature of tribal economy by giving empirical evidence from the Kalahandi district. This chapter argues that the tribal economy in the Kalahandi district is not a subsistence economy, rather an affluent economy in terms of productivity and availability of resources. But it is crisis ridden as a result of the power structure that controls the distribution of productive resources (land, forest and market) in the district. It also explains the way in which the new economic reform process has augmented the power structure in the district which has a negative economic, social and cultural impact on the tribals and their development process. The chapter argues that natural calamities such as flood, cyclone and drought are not the cause of tribal underdevelopment in the Kalahandi district. This chapter is divided into three parts; the first introductory part describes the social, economic, cultural and religious life of tribals in India, the second part explains the political economy of tribal development and its transition, the third part provides the case study of Kalahandi district and the history of its underdevelopment demystifying the natural calamity argument.

INTRODUCTION

The tribals of India prefer to be called 'Adivasi' and constitute 8.14% of the total population of the country, numbering 84.51 million. More than half of the tribal population is concentrated in rural areas of the states of Andhra Pradesh, Madhya Pradesh, Jharkhand, Chhattisgarh, Maharashtra, Orissa and Gujarat (Census of India, 2001)[1]. Not only in the share of population but also in the share in terms of culture, the Adivasi traditions and practices spread through all aspects of Indian culture and civilisation (Vidyarthi & Rai (1985), yet they are socially marginalised, economically exploited and branded as an underdeveloped and poor people in popular consciousness in mainland India. The popular consciousness derives images of tribal people and their social, economic and cultural life from the ideas of mainstream Indian society and its consumer modernity; an offspring of capitalism and its cultural logic (i.e. post modernism[2]). Tribals are a very distinct social group in India who live in the forest areas and hilly terrains of the country. Their societies are institutionalised in a way that acknowledges individuality; each individual's uniqueness and creativity. This form of social organisation in tribal society not only acknowledges individual uniqueness, but also nurtures it by allowing enough personal space for people to develop their creativity and, consequently, upholds the tribal communal culture in India, where each member of the tribal group contributes to their community in their respective ways without any binding principles. Nobody orders anyone to do this or do that. There is nothing called 'I', 'Me' and 'Mine'; rather the expression of 'We', 'Our' and 'Us' is reflected in all aspects of tribal life and society. The tribals are free to choose whatever they want to do in their social, cultural and economic life. The social, cultural and economic lives of the tribals have a wider meaning system where they locate their individuality in the societal life or in the life of the community. There is no place for individualism in terms of material accumulation for the self. The social, cultural and economic life of the tribals in India is based on the above ideas of individuality and society. The tribal society continues to follow communitarian culture whilst looking at the 'individual' and 'society' relationship. The principle of *Aparigrah*[3] *is* followed by both individual and society, which works as the basic structural frame to avoid conflict between individual and society. In other words, the very notions of 'individual' and 'society' that emerge in Western philosophical traditions and society are qualitatively different from those that exist in tribal societies in India which organised itself to follow a need based approach in social and individual life.

The tribals have their own social, economic, cultural, religious and political value systems based on a close relationship with their environment i.e. land and forest. They have a close and unique understanding of nature and environment as it is the source of livelihood for them. The tribal areas in

India have considerable economic potential in terms of natural resources, but the tribals of these resource rich regions rarely receive a fair share of the economic benefits occurring from mining and industrialisation in their land, which has been traditionally used by indigenous people. It is an irony of post-colonial India that the poorest people are living in the areas of richest natural resources. Such irony and paradox is an historical legacy of colonialism in which the tribals were pushed to the less valuable, barren and inaccessible areas and left with no other option than that of shifting cultivation (NAI, 1878: 30). The tribals were then pushed to plough agriculture under strict surveillance and official pressure (Elwin, 1939:118). In this way, the colonial rulers forcibly disciplined tribal culture and economy. In the process of development, such marginalisations of tribals continued even during post-colonial regimes. Though the spirit of tribal development plans and policies in India are intended to bring tribals into the fold of national development, in reality tribal development takes a back seat owing to the economic interests of various dominant groups in those processes. Thus, tribal development has only been made in a symbolic way. Only a small section of tribal elites have been able to take advantage of the development programmes, through this being co–opted within the mainstream social, cultural, economic and political power structure. The tribal development programme has more or less failed to achieve its goal, and inefficient and corrupt political bureaucracy has contributed immensely to this (Joshi, 1998:14). As a result, poverty and exploitation is abundant in the tribal areas, many of the people there constituting the poorest of the poor among the Indian population (Elwin, 1963; Goodland, 1982). Therefore, in terms of class, tribals belong to the broad class of proletariats due to their economic position in a class divided society, whilst also sharing the problem of poverty, inequality and exploitation with other poor communities and people of India.

The predicament of the tribals continues to dominate the development debates in contemporary India but the debate has yet to develop a tangible action plan for their development. The planning in India is now focusing on economic growth; the legacy of the new economic reforms during 1990s. The planning for development based on economic growth is all pervasive and motivated as "economic growth is not the natural product... and expansion of policies; it is the possible transformation of policies that have been thought through in all their dimensions." (Amin, 1997; xii). One dimensional development policy during and after the new economic reforms, with an objective of economic growth, has extended the scale of exploitation, inequality, poverty and cultural marginalisation in the tribal societies in India. The new economic policy reforms have changed the welfare notion and nature of the Indian state. As a result of this, the tribal development policies are taking a back seat in the planning and development agenda. The new development agendas based on economic growth and industrialisation left no choice of livelihood options for the tribals but compelled them to be a part of an economic system which is alien to them. Such policies added problems to the marginalisation faced by the tribals during post-colonial planning for development in India in which they were left with no options but to follow the development models imposed on them by the outside forces (Furer-Hai-mendorf, 1982). In this way, tribals have been taken for granted in the planning for development and remain as neglected partners in the history of development in India (Doshi, 1997). However, in recent years, tribals in India have suffered an additional disability of social and cultural suppression, augmented by the process of Hinduisation, which is an extension of Hindu social order, cultural and religious control over tribal religious and spiritual practices.

There is a growing debate on the religion of tribals in India, running in tandem with their Hinduisation. There is a massive conversion taking place in the tribal areas to incorporate tribals as Hindus, as a consequence of which tribals are becoming a part of mainstream Hindu society with an inferior social status. The religion of tribals has been conceptualised in many sources, including Census reports (which classify tribals and their religion as tribal, animist and primitive) and the administrative term 'Schedule Tribe' that ignores tribal religion which is different from the mainstream Hindu, Christian and other religions in India. However, the religion of tribals in India has been associated in the European imagination as predominantly a religion of nature, spirit, blind beliefs, animism etc. The European understanding of tribal religion was a product of the colonial rule and the work of the Christian missionaries in the tribal areas. The absence of regard for the material life, no greed for private property and hesitation for accumulation of wealth, lack of gender inequality, individual dishonesty and non-violent lifestyle of tribals has attracted many, and even influenced the Buddhist philosophy which is apparent and reflected in the works of Stcherbasky (1962).

However, acknowledging the unique religious practice of tribals, Indian Census reports in 1891, 1901 and 1911 classified the tribal spiritual cult as tribal religion and animist. The animist religion of tribals recognises all natural forces as powerful and thus supernatural. They also believe that their ancestral spirits guide their action. Thus, these spirits need to be appeased through animal sacrifice or any other offerings for the well being of their community and individual life. It is widely believed among the tribals that natural calamities, diseases, illness and loss of crop are the result of the displeasure of ancestral spirits. In this way, tribal religion is surrounded by nature and spirits unlike the Hindu worship of statues of gods and goddesses. Many tribal groups in Orissa still follow these practices. Those tribal groups who converted to Christianity, Hinduism or to Buddhism stop practicing such religious belief.

Majority of Hindu population believe that tribals are Hindus and they are very close to the silvan culture; the culture associated with woods which have a link with the Vedic people and their culture (Parkhill, 1995). But the image of such tribal religion has taken something of a battering in recent years. The tribal religion is under the influence and threat of majoritarianism. The gross materialism of the market and its consumer culture is spreading in the tribal areas under the leadership of the Hindu right wing organisations. The Hindu right wing organisations are working in the tribal areas in the name of improving educational and health conditions of tribals, although in reality these organisations are working with the objective of Hinduisation of tribals. This process has been given naked encouragement by the state, indigenous and foreign corporate interests, the culture of industrial and market modernity, and international finance. As a consequence of which the tribal religion and culture has all but been eroded along with the image as a land of sublime peace, fellow feeling and communitarian life. Such a process gets philosophical justification from the Hindu religion and its right wing interpretation. For example; the philosophical godfather of Hindu right wing forces, Golwalkar has written that "the tribals "can be given yajñopavîta (sacred thread ceremony of the Hindus). They should be given equal rights and footings in the matter of religious rights, in temple worship, in the study of Vedas, and in general, in all our social and religious affairs. This is the only right solution for all the problems of casteism found nowadays in our Hindu society (Golwalkar, 2000: 479)".

Many scholars have interpreted the Hinduisation project of M.S Golwalkar as a political project, but I argue that it is an economic project. It is significant to de-tribalise the tribals through Hinduisation to remove the constitutional provisions that protect tribal land and their right over other natural resources—because tribal areas are the mineral map of the country and Orissa too. Thus, any attempt to occupy and impose control over the natural resources in the tribal areas requires de-tribalisation first to eliminate legal or constitutional hurdles for the resource accumulation in their areas. The first attempt towards this project is to dismantle tribal culture through Hinduisation and the second step flows from it—to dismantle tribal economy and integrate tribals within the mainstream market. In such a context, an attempt has been made to study the features of tribal economy.

FEATURES OF TRIBAL ECONOMY IN INDIA

It is significant to study the features of tribal economy in India which will allow us to understand the nature and structure of tribal economy and its difference from the mainstream economy which can be found in the works of Dalton (1961), Majumdar & Madan (1970), Nash (1965) and Herskovits

(1952). Generally, the mainstream economists either assume[4] tribal economy as a primitive or as a non-monetised society. Such assumptions have only helped to cover the feudal and consequently capitalist features of tribal economy on one side and its uniqueness in terms of environment friendliness, self sustenance, forced subsistent and less accumulative economic system on the other. However, Majumdar and Madan (1971: 91) found nine important features of tribal economy which is noticed in almost all tribal areas of India. They branded tribal economy a primitive economy due to the following traits of tribal economy: absence of technology; barter system basis; absence of profit motive; collective endeavor in production process; slow innovation; regular market without monopoly and competition; absence of specialisation in the production process; and the notion of property among the tribals is based on expenditure rather than on accumulation. These features separate tribal economy from the mainstream economy of the rest of the country.

In general, tribal economy is self-sufficient, unstructured and non specialised (Sharma, 1985). Historically, the economy of most tribes has been subsistence agriculture or hunting and gathering. Things like cooking utensils and salt are some of the basic consumption requirements for which tribals have been dependent on the market. All these features of tribal economy can be noticed in the tribal areas of Orissa and the Kalahandi district, which indicates the commonality of tribal society and their economy in the country as a whole. It is also clear that the interaction of tribal economy with the outside economy puts tribals into a condition of marginalisation and dependency. The location of tribal habitation, constant isolation of tribals in development planning and lack of economic infrastructure keeps the features of tribal economy intact, as a consequence of which the economic marginalisation and economic exploitation continues to exist in all parts of the tribal areas of the country. Such processes of economic exploitation and marginalisation put tribals in conditions of crisis. While looking at different distinctive features of tribal economy, it is difficult to conceptualise the features on a micro level. On a macro level, the following features can be discussed to identify the differences and similarities of tribal economy with mainstream economy.

The lives, livelihoods, habitat and culture of the tribal people all over India revolve around forest, forming an indispensable part of tribal economy and its production networks. The forest provides them with vegetables, edible oil, fruits, flowers, honey, and many other food items as well as cooking wood. The works of Rai (1967) and Vidyarthi (1971) provide an account of the way tribal economy is intertwined with hills and forest. By taking note of the importance of the forest in tribal economy, the Planning Commission of India has noted that "the tribal economy revolves around forest and forest based produce, the forestry based programmes have to be so devised as to be in consonance with the socio-economic fabric of tribal culture and ethos".[5]

However, Indian governments have yet to come up with a concrete policy guideline to develop tribal economy based on forest. Rather, forest degradation through timber trade, mining and industrialisation has put constant strain on the tribal economy (Vidyarthi, 1970) and forest and wildlife protection policy has often caused problems too (Baviskar, 2003).

The land and agriculture constitutes a vital source of livelihood in the tribal areas in India. Using both hilly terrains and forest land, the tribals produce paddy, different vegetables, black grams, different lentils and now even producing different oil seeds and cash crops. Tribal agriculture is unorganized and unstructured, unlike the mainstream agriculture, due to barren and less productive lands. This has led them to follow shifting cultivation (poddu chasa) which is quite common in most parts of the tribal areas in India. The tribals use crude instruments in ploughing land, use indigenous technology and organic fertilizers and expend a considerable amount of manual labor in production. Vidyarthi (1963) has provided an account of the way tribal agriculture revolves round hill cultivation.

The economic anthropologist considers economy as a sub–system of society and thus cultural and social structure plays a formative role in the economic activities[6] of human beings (Herskovits, 1952; Firth, 1951:138; Nash, 1968:359; Nash, 1965:121–38; Dalton, 1971). In the case of the tribal economy, economic activities of tribals are determined by its culture. Every tribal and their communities have their own way of meeting their basic needs and other material wants but within their own cultural norms and values, providing the base for communitarian control over production, distribution and ownership. In mainstream society and economy every human being works as an economic unit whereas in the case of tribals, the culture of the tribals works as an economic unit (Herskovits, 1952; Dalton, 1971). In mainstream production system, individual labour works as a unit of production but in the tribal production system the family works as a unit of production system within the given cultural framework. There is no gender division of labour in agriculture, food gathering, hunting and even in the domestic household work. Tribal women often have more roles in the production system. There is the *Jajmani*[7] system which often puts community as a production unit. The tribals use simple technology for production in agriculture, hunting and food gathering. "The low level of technology, combined with small size and relative isolation, results in ingrained mutual dependence among people sharing many relationships: those with whom one is economically involved are the same as those with whom one is involved through neighborhood, religion, kinship and polity. The primitive economy in that sense is embedded in other community relationships (Dalton, 1971:91)". The production in the tribal society is not for profit but for community requirements and for instant consumption and cultural requirements. The process of distribution among tribes is based on gift and ceremonial exchanges which are reciprocal by nature in the tribal societies (Herskovits, 1952: 11; Dalton, 1971:53). However, such relationships are changing in the tribal areas with the entry of money in the form of cash into tribal society (Prasad, 1967:125–130).

There is no permanent market infrastructure or institutionalised market in the tribal areas—only a periodical market (i.e. weekly market known as *haat*) exists. The weekly market, mobile in nature, plays a vital role in tribal economy but the nature of this weekly market is mostly non-monetary. There are also special markets which are seasonal and festive by nature where monopoly and competition is absent (Majumdar & Madan (1970:91). Most of the tribals either use their products or their labor in exchange for necessary goods produced from their area, whereas they use cash to buy goods which are produced outside their area. Thus outside products are responsible for the entry of cash in the tribal market. The communitarian norms predominate over the economic norms of the market which make profit secondary in the market transactions. Though cash transactions in the tribal market are gradually increasing the barter system still dominates. Sinha (1968) considers that tribal markets and their institutions maintain the social and cultural ties among the tribals and thus work as agents of cultural change. As markets in the tribal areas are captured by the non-tribal money lenders and small local businessmen throughout India (Vidyarthi & Rai, 1985: 110–11) are responsible for the changing nature of tribal market and are paving the way for social change with mainstream market orientation.

Most political economists, policy makers and anthropologists (Karmakar, 2002; Dalton, 1971; Majumdar, 1961) have considered tribal economy as a subsistence economy. Majumdar (1961:139) goes further to argue that "a tribe uses all kinds of occupations to make out its subsistence and combines hunting with honey gathering, lumbering with chase, shifting cultivation with domestication of animals, shows the complexity of economic subsistence in the lower culture". Such arguments outline the tribal production system as less efficient, profitless and lacking in investment and thus a form of lower culture, which is not true. The tribals produce more than their necessity but, due to non-availability of the storage facilities, they sell most of their products at a low price just after harvesting it. The post-harvest marketing gives an upper hand to the local and regional traders who get tribal products at a very low price. This puts tribals at a disadvantage in generating profit from their own products, as a result of which tribals lose a lot in terms of profit. The tribals thus face a problem in reinvesting their money in their production system for its own sustenance. The existing system of marketing and lack of storage makes tribal economy vulnerable to exploitation by small regional traders and money lenders. The case of Kalahandi district in Orissa is the classic example of such a process (Nayak, 2002). There is no price system in tribal economy and social traditions among the tribals determine the tribal production, market and economy (Vidyarthi & Rai, 1985: 94). The tribals spend their surplus or borrow from local money lenders to spend in the festivals which constitute a major part of tribal expenditure. So there is no question of investment, profit and accumulation. In this way, the materiality of tribal economy embodies tribal culture. The tribal culture is the sum total of economic activities based on social and cultural relations. Thus, it is impossible to separate economy from culture and culture from economy in tribal societies in India. The transition and crisis in tribal economy started from the colonial period.

TRANSITION AND CRISIS IN TRIBAL ECONOMY DURING COLONIAL PERIOD

The tribal areas of Orissa were the last areas to be annexed by the British Empire in India due to geographical inaccessibility, and therefore tribal development received less attention and less priority in the colonial development policy[8]. The colonial government followed a policy of isolation towards tribals in the country. The policy helped the colonial rulers to divide and reduce the strength of the national liberation struggle and at the same time, keep tribals away from the benefits of colonial citizenship[9] which saved expenses from the colonial treasury. The policy also reduced the administrative costs involved in ruling inaccessible areas. Apart from these objectives, there was no attempt to uplift the social and economic base of the tribals. Such a policy of isolationism also helped the local landlords, money lenders and businessmen to exploit the tribals and the colonial ruler maintained indirect control over tribals and their areas as a result (Ghurye, 1943). Thus, the crisis in the tribal economy during the colonial period was accelerated leading to multiple forms of domination and exploitation of tribals. The appropriation of land and forest[10] by the colonial rulers led to the comprehensive sway of market institutions for the first time in the tribal areas and, as a result, the idea of private property and legal ownership of property got introduced to tribal society. This caused immense damage to the communal ownership of property and destruction of communal autonomy.

However, indirect British rule over the tribals in India resulted in tribal isolation and deprived from the privileges of the citizenship of the colonial state and at the same time increased conditions that have led to multiple forms of domination. The domination followed by multiple forms of exploitation over a population who were free from market and private property through customary laws of possession of land and other natural and forest resources. The colonial state skillfully incorporated the tribal leadership within the local hierarchy of the colonial administration to control tribal resistance to the exploitation. Thus, the indirect control of colonial rule was a single power of colonial hegemony with multiple forms of domination and exploitation. However, the impact of colonial administration and the ways of reinforcing crisis in the tribal economy was well documented by Dr. J.H Hutton, a member of the Indian Civil Service in the British administration who has used following words to describe the impact. "Far from being of immediate benefit to the primitive tribes, the establishment of British rule in India did most of them much more harm then good... It may be said that the early days of British administration did very great detriment to the economic position of tribe through ignorance of their rights and customs...many changes have been caused incidentally by the penetration of the tribal country, the opening of communications, the protection of forests and the establishment of schools to say nothing of the openings given in this way to Christian missions. Many of the results of these changes have caused acute discomfort to tribes (as cited in Taradatt, 2001:21)". These cultural changes in the process of development policies following the modernisation trend reinforced the crisis in the tribal society, culture and economy even during the post-colonial period.

LOCATING TRANSITION IN PLANNING FOR TRIBAL DEVELOPMENT IN POST-COLONIAL INDIA

The term 'development planning' can be interpreted in two ways: firstly, it indicates public policy for development; secondly it indicates planned intervention for development (Tordello, 2003). I locate both the trends of development and its meaning while looking at the tribal development planning and its transition in India. The initial development planning in India was made by ingraining the tribal population and their development needs in the consciousness of the public policy makers. Recognising the special needs and problems of the tribal population, special provisions were accorded to tribal development even in the Constitution of India. The first Five Year Plan[11] (1951–56) was designed with a special focus on tribal development, the second Five Year Plan (1956–61) adopted the principle of 'Panchsheel', the third Five Year Plan (1961–66) revamped the tribal development plan by opening of multi-purpose Tribal Development Blocks to intensify tribal development whereas the fourth (1969–74) and fifth Five Year Plans (1974–78) introduced the special strategies through the Tribal Sub Plan. Thus, from the first Five Year Plan (1951–56) to the fifth Five Year Plan (1974–78), the development policy makers followed a policy of universal development approach towards tribal development. The sixth Five Year Plan (1980–85) and seventh Five Year Plan (1985–90) stressed poverty alleviation programmes via a higher degree of devolution of funds with a particular reference to educational and economic development of the tribal population in the country. The eighth Five Year Plan (1992–97) emphasised the elimination of exploitation in terms of land alienation, regular wage payments for the tribal labourer and tribal exploitation by local money lenders. It also highlighted the development gap between the tribal population and non-tribal general population and followed sector wide approach to target vulnerability and marginalisation.

The ninth Five Year Plan (1997–2002) and the tenth Five Year Plan (2002–07) aimed at the development of tribal population through empower-ment programmes (Planning Commission, 2002: 443–445). Thus, from the sixth Five Year Plan (1980–85) to the tenth Five Year Plan (2002–07), public policy followed a targeted and sector-wide approach for tribal development in the country. However, the shift from the universal tribal development approach to targeted tribal development was exemplified by the shift in In-dian economic policy from state-command to market-orientated economy after the implementation of the new economic reforms in 1991. The transi-tion in the tribal development approach from a dedicated focus upon tribal welfare, to the concept of tribal development as 'empowerment' was a policy prescription of the neo-liberal economic reforms.

The neo-liberal economic reforms in India prescribed policies where the state has a minimal role to play in the delivery of welfare to its citizens, and in this way is broadly concomitant with the worldwide transformations in political economy that followed the collapse of the Bretton Woods agreement in 1973 and associated ideas of 'embedded liberalism' and 'welfare capital-ism' and the subsequent neo-liberal economic reform programmes that ema-nated from Great Britain and The United States (Holloway, 1995). The with-drawal of the state from welfare activities started after the sixth Five Year Plan (1980–85), in a soft way which was known as '*half hearted liberalisa-tion*' (Manor,1987). Although the economic reform programme surrendered to the neo-liberal open economy after 1991, it was not until the ninth Five Year Plan (1997–2002) and the tenth Five Year Plan (2002–07) that a new direction in the development debate in India opened up. The role of the state in the development and welfare of the tribals was reconstituted by the in-volvement of the Non Governmental Organisations (NGOs) and Self Help Groups (SHGs) in the process of tribal development. It not only reduced the role of the state in the development process by involving NGOs and SHGs but also shifted the accountability to the people and communities and their organisations, raising serious questions about the legitimacy of representa-tive government and its relation to the aspirations and needs of its citizens (tribal or non-tribal) in the world's largest democracy.

Now we are in a situation where nobody is accountable for the tribal development programmes. The NGOs involvement in the development pro-grammes dates back to the Janata government in 1978 when tax concessions for voluntary initiatives by commercial companies were introduced, and many non-governmental organisations came into being. This provided commercial institutions with opportunities to invest some of their profits in development activities, allowing them exemption from the tax structure. A change of government in 1980 and the restoration of rule by the Congress party led to the expected withdrawal of tax concessions. The Tenth Plan says that NGOs play "a very important role in sharing the responsibility of the Government in 'Reaching the Services to the Un-reached' in far-flung inaccessible areas and in developing and experimenting with alternative project models to match the needs of the local people. Voluntary Organisations are effective agents in bringing forth the most desired social change and development by virtue of their direct contact and linkages with the tribals. VOs will, therefore, be encouraged to play an effective role in improving the status of tribals in the areas of education, health, nutrition, employment and income-generation, besides sensitising the administrative machinery and concretising the tribals to realise their rights and potential, and also safeguarding them from social and economic exploitation."[12] Thus the government needed to fund these organisations for development activities and welfare delivery programmes. In the process, such NGOs remained perpetually dependent upon aid agencies and government funding, creating a class of people who were salary seeking social servants, and aimed at undermining the role of state and politics in the development of tribal population.

In such a context, an attempt has been made to study the impact of the new economic reforms in the tribals in the Kalahandi district of Orissa as a socially disadvantaged group whose culture is under threat from the NGOs, COs and VOs under the guidance of the Hindu Right wing forces through their Hinduisation process to incorporate tribals into the mainstream global market. The process being accelerated by the state and its institutions of public policy led to the manifestation of crisis in the tribal economy in Orissa during the process of economic reforms, which is responsible for the growth of market led consumer culture. In such a context, an attempt has been made to study Kalahandi district of Orissa.

KALAHANDI DISTRICT; ITS LOCATION, POPULATION AND LANDSCAPE

The Kalahandi district of Orissa is not only known for its poverty, starvation and underdevelopment but also for its paradoxes both for development thinkers and public policy makers. The availability of natural resources in terms of forest and mineral resources, highest agricultural production both in terms of rice and cash crop (in spite of natural calamities like draught, cyclone and flood) in the state and its large labour force marks the potentiality of the district for development. The availability of land and landholding size is the largest not only in the state but also in the country. It is said to be larger than the average size of landholdings in Punjab and it receives more rainfall than Punjab, and the cropped area in the district is the highest in the state of Orissa (Mahapatra & Panda, 2001). Yet, the people and different regions of the district are entrapped by backwardness in terms of income, health, education and communication in comparison to the other districts of the state. The news of hunger, starvation deaths, child selling, poverty and underdevelopment dominates in the development debate of the district reflecting the paradox and putting the challenge on the development professionals, policy makers and pressurises the democratic politics and the state as well. This paradox is not only a development challenge but also shows how massive production and availability of natural resources alone do not help in solving the problem of poverty, marginalisation and different forms of underdevelopment. This brings the question of accessibility and distribution to those available resources. The political economy of availability, accessibility and distribution depends on the structures of power and authority, thus, as long as the structure of power and authority remains unaltered, mere availability of resources is an insufficient condition to solve the problem of underdevelopment and inequality in the district of Kalahandi which is discussed in the latter part of this chapter.

GEOGRAPHICAL LOCATION OF THE KALAHANDI DISTRICT

The Kalahandi district of Orissa is located in south–western region of the state. It is situated between $19°–3`$ North to $21°–3`$ North latitude and between $82°–20`$ East to $83°–47`$ East longitude and covers an area of 8,364 square kilometers. The district shares its border in the north with the districts of Balangir and Nuapada, on the south with the districts of Rayagada, on the west with the district of Nawarangpur and Raipur (Chhattisgarh) and on the East with the district of Rayagada and Boudh. The location of the district is such that some parts of the district are inaccessible even today due to lack of road, transport and other means of communication. The people of the district, during both princely rule, colonial rule and post-colonial rule have suffered a dual domination and exploitation due its isolated location. It is described clearly in the *Report of the Orissa State's Enquiry Committee* (1939) headed by Harekrushna Mahatab, who later became the Chief Minister of Orissa. In post-colonial Kalahandi, though road, transport and other communication systems are developing now, they are being streamlined to the areas of mineral and other resource rich regions of the district. Thus, the development of communication systems is not intended to integrate inaccessible areas with the district headquarters or with areas housing health and educational infrastructures. They are not aiming towards the goal of rural development which is discussed later in the thesis (chapter 4) while looking at the role of economic reforms on the growth of the road and communication system, its objectives and impact on tribals in the district.

LAND, ITS PRODUCTIVITY AND LANDSCAPE OF THE KALAHANDI DISTRICT

On the basis of geographical locations, the district has two distinct physio-graphic regions i.e. the plains and the hill tracts with forests. The southern and western parts of the district headquarter (Bhawanipatna) are mostly pop-ulated with forests that include two tribal blocks (i.e. Langigarh and Thuamul Rampur). These two tribal blocks are the store house of natural beauty with dense forest and natural resources. It is regarded as one of the mineral rich regions of both district and state. The hill ranges of the Eastern Ghats, which cover virtually the entire eastern and southern areas of the district, and re-main largely inaccessible to this day, are where wild animals of different varieties are found in abundance. These hilly lands are known as 'Dangarla' in the local language (Das, 1962:1). The tribals in the district cultivate these lands which are again known as '*Dongar Chasa*', indicating hill slope agri-culture or hill slope farming. The hilly tracts of land cover 41 percent of the total area of the district, whereas plain covers 59 percent of land. The region with plain lands starts from the western parts of the district headquarter towards the Junagarh, Dharamgarh, Kalampur and Golamunda blocks of the district. The blocks of Bhawanipatna, Kesinga, Jaipatna, Koksara, Narla, Madanpur Rampur and Karlamunda have a mixed topography of both hilly and plain lands[13].

The cultivable lands are classified into different categories according to the geographical situation and productive capacity of the land as '*Bahal*' (bottom land of the hill), '*Berna*' (dell), '*Mal*' (terraced slopes) and '*At*' (hill top land) by the Land Settlement Office of the district (Das, 1962:6). The hilly areas are predominately inhabited by the tribal population (especially Langigarh and Thuamul Rampur), whereas the rest of the district is dominat-ed by the general population. There are, however, dispersed tribal groups in all blocks of the district. The extent to which demographic distribution of population over the land is reflected in the land ownership patterns in the district is discussed in Chapter 4 of the thesis.

The productivity of land in the district is the highest in Orissa. The pro-duction of rice can be taken as an example in which the Kalahandi district produces more than the other parts of the state, averaging higher than state production (Nayak, 2009). The district also produces cash crops like oil seeds, sugarcane, cotton and many vegetables even without using sophisticat-ed technology and high yielding varieties of seeds and fertilizers, the avail-ability of which is limited due to the absolute poverty of the farmers (Mishra,

2001:251). Still the production of food grains and cereals in the district is higher than the all-India and Orissa average (Nayak, 2009), proving the productivity of the land and productive capacity of farmers and disproving the debate on subsistence agriculture and economy of district.

DEMOGRAPHIC COMPOSITION, ADMINISTRATIVE DIVISIONS AND POPULATION IN THE DISTRICT

The district comprises of 1,334,000 people, which adds 3.64% to the state population[14]. The density of population is 168 per square km. It has 2099 inhabited and 137 uninhabited villages and out of 2236 total villages, 408 villages completely belong to the tribals in the two blocks (158, Langigarh and 250, Thuamul Rampur) of the district. These two blocks are considered to be the Integrated Tribal Development Blocks (ITDP) under the different development programmes by the Government of Orissa and Government of India. Many tribal groups live in the other eleven blocks of the district and are considered as the dispersed tribal groups in terms of administrative language for targeting development policies. The pace of urbanisation used to be very low with two sub-divisions, seven Tahasils, thirteen CD Blocks, one Municipality, two Notified Area Councils (NACs) and 273 Gram Panchayats[15]. The administrative headquarter of the district is located in Bhawanipatna. The district constitutes of 17.01 percent of SC population, 28.88 percent of ST population, and 93.09 percent rural and 6.91 percent urban population. The percentage of the marginal, semi-marginal, small and medium, landholding population is more in the district and the large landholding population in the district is very low[16]. This indicates the land ownership pattern of the district where few people have major landholdings. Traditionally, land ownership in Kalahandi district was in the hands of the few, the agrarian structure of the economy was feudal and lacking initiative to exploit the rich natural/ mineral resources, which aggravated the situation of underdevelopment of Kalahandi.

The district has twenty five small-scale industries employing 337 people. The district has a total of 37.68 percent of main workers with 35.66 percent of rural and 2.02 percent of urban workers. It has 7.39 percent of total marginal workers with 0.07 percent being urban and 7.32 percent rural workers. The unemployment situation in the district is 54.93 percent of total population with 50.11 percent in rural and 4.82 percent in urban area. The district has 7.62 Lakh hectares of cultivable land, 5.27 Lakh hectares of forest, hundreds of perennial streams and rivers, rich deposits of bauxite, graphite, and manganese, precious and semi-precious stones. Although agriculture is not developed, as only 16.97 percent of net area sown is irrigated, it is the principal occupation available and in 1991, approximately 84 percent of working population of Kalahandi was dependent on it for a living, with 45 percent of these being agricultural labourers. The per capita production and availability of food grain is higher than the other districts of Orissa[17] but still the district suffers from underdevelopment and people in poverty and starvation.

However, the state government, its politicians and bureaucrats of the state have branded the poverty and underdevelopment in the district as "the black-wash effects of development" as a result of people and their inherent disadvantageous factors like poor quality of human capital, backward and unsustainable agriculture coupled with reckless exploitation of forest resources"[18]. The available data on productivity of land, agricultural productivity and availability of natural/mineral resources shows the assumptions of the state government, politicians and bureaucrats to be myth. The underdevelopment and poverty is structural which has been reproduced in the district in the different periods of its history.

HISTORY OF DEVELOPMENT OF UNDERDEVELOPMENT IN KALAHANDI

For more than five decades now in post-colonial development politics in India, the political economy of regional, rural and tribal development in Orissa, Kalahandi has been debated for its underdevelopment and has created a hinge of development theories especially for the development of the tribals in the district. The Kalahandi district is rich in terms of natural resources, availability of land and production but the people of the district are poor and the area is underdeveloped at the same time. This dilemma is reflected in the social, economic and cultural life of the people in the district. This contradictory context in the district should be paving the way for the radical reformulation of development policies by the state and government. But instead of doing so, the state and governments are reinforcing the underdevelopment and dependency through its public policies (i.e. the new economic reforms) by following the historical legacy of underdevelopment from state formation in the district to the welfare policies and politics of 21st century India and Orissa.

The history of this dilemma can not be attributed to the geographical situation or culture of the people but must be seen as a product of the historical conditions which have reproduced underdevelopment and dependency in the present development process[19]. Thus, the notion of dependency is important to understand the tribal development in Kalahandi as it is "a framework of the analysis of development and underdevelopment" (Chilcote, 1974:21) in the district. The dependency theory is also important as it offers "a foundation for analysis of class struggle and strategies to promote class struggle...

(leading)…to the restructuring of societies, a restructuring which limits capitalism and promotes socialism in the seeking of a new and better society (Chilcote, 1974:21)". Dependency theory is criticised on various grounds, even from a Marxist perspective, in the works of Cueva (1976, 1978:19), O'Brien (1975), Myer (1975) and many other writers which has given rise to the debate between Marxism and dependency theory (Foster-Carter, 1974, 1978, 1979; Kay 1975; Taylor, 1974, 1979 and Henfrey, 1981).

In the context of Kalahandi district, the richness in mineral resources, comparatively better production and availability of land and cheap labour provides the base for capitalist accumulation[20] whereas the underdevelopment, poverty and marginalisation of the tribal people and their area is a consequence of over exploitation[21] which has led to the dependant development[22] in the district of Kalahandi. The history of development in the district will help us to understand the way economic reforms have changed the geographies and nature of production in the district. The transition in agriculture from food crop to cash crop and mining based industrialisation has put the district into a regime of export–led economy, creating a market which is alien to its people and the region. The whole process has reinforced a modern form of primitive accumulation which can be located by studying the history of the district "as a historical process situated in a particular context… [which] has its own national characteristics and is limited by the specificity of struggles which emerge from and become a part of traditions, value systems, ideas and concrete modes of organisation (Nun, 1976:51 as cited in Sofer, 1980:170)". Therefore, it is significant to follow a combined approach of dependency, historical conditions and its legacy in the contemporary tribal development policies in the district to locate the historical roots of underdevelopment and dependency of tribals in the district.

Thus, it is necessary to understand the history of formation of the Kalahandi district to understand the development of its underdevelopment and marginalisation of its people; i.e. the tribals. The history of the district reveals that the multiple forms of domination by outsiders over the native tribal people is the basis of its underdevelopment and marginalisation. There was a continuity of pre–colonial marginalisation during the colonial period which sustained and reinforced it further and was then followed up by the postcolonial ruling class in the process of district formation[23]. This can help us in understanding the changing nature of global capitalism and the nature of its local expansions by formulating an alliance between the state, development policies and Hindu right wing forces under specific historical conditions in the Kalahandi district.

The history and our knowledge of the process of formation of the present Kalahandi district comes from many sources, like ruined forts, inscriptions, paintings in the caves, temples, tribal folks, popular tales and in the writings of colonial officers. There are even myths regarding the origin of Kalahandi (meaning black pot). According to Kandh[24] myth, several centuries ago a member of the Chotanagpur Nagavamsi ruling family was installed by the Kandh community as the *Maharaja* (Superior king) of their *rajya* (kingdom) at Jugasai Patna (the present Jaipatna block). Then Jaipatna block was made up of tribals but at present the tribal population and even Kandh population is marginal and lowest in the block. This reflects how tribals are being alienated and marginalised from their own land which is now hundred percent irrigated and wetland, meaning more than double the crop can be grown after the commencement of the Indravati project. In the Jaipatna block, all the land belongs to higher caste people from coastal Orissa and some of them now from Andhra Pradesh. Another popular Kandh proverb says that the present Kalahandi is known as '*Karonda*' and '*Kandhadesh*' (kingdom of Kandh)[25]. A tradition that persists today is that during the coronation of the king of the Kalahandi, the king had to marry a Kandh girl before getting the royal throne[26]. The name 'Karonda' as '*Kharonde*' was found in the writings of the colonial officers like Lieutenant Elliot, Deputy Commissioner of Raipur (1856). He mentioned that Kalahandi is "known only on the Nagpur side as Kharonde (Karond), the Oriya name being Kalahandi, and as there is no place or village corresponding to the former name it would appear to be a corruption of the latter, though it has been originally entered in the accounts" (Elliot, 1856:11)[27].

According to a popular belief documented in the District Gazetteers of Kalahandi by Senapati and Kuanr (1980:2), a powerful man of Rajaputana named Kalahambir came to this part and ruled for many years and after his name, the name of the area become 'Kalahandi'. There are prehistoric paintings which the district gazetteers reveal as another source of the origin of the district and its name Kalahandi derived from the '*Gudahandi*' a hilly track located close to Koksara block. It is said that the present Kalahandi was an extension of Hati and Tel[28] valley civilisation which is proved by various archaeological excavations and findings of prehistoric, neolithic and paleolithic tools, coins and potteries indicative of the stone-age culture in the district (Mohanty & Mishra, 2000:68–74, Deo, 2000: 63, Deo, 2006: 89–94, Panda, 2000: 56–62, Panda, 1993:51, Senapati, N. & Kuanr D.C., 1980; 35–58). The history of Kalahandi and its origin reveals that an early civilization existed in the district. However, politically speaking according to the *Kalahandi Rajdarbar (palace) records*[29], the Kalahandi district and the then Karonda was a part of the Gangavamsi Empire of Orissa up to the 13th century, followed by the Nagavamsi dynasty from the Chotanagpur royal family[30]. It is said that this period was the beginning of entry of outsiders to the district by deliberate policy, as tribals were considered as lazy and unproductive people. This process of isolating tribals was the beginning of tribal land alienation in the district (Pati, 1999:348). The patronage of non-tribals over the tribals, especially to Brahmins, on the issue of land ownership was followed by concessions to Kulta/ Khshetriya caste people for agriculture led to the pauperisation of tribals in the district (Pati, 1999; Mishra & Acharya, 2004). This system of dual domination over tribals in the district continued even during Moghul rule as "the rule of Nagas" (Nagavamsi) was practically independent. This was mostly due to the geographical location of the territory and the impenetrable forests and hills with which the region was covered (Senapati & Kuanr, 1980:57)". This indicates that the geographical location of the district also helped the local feudal ruling class to continue their uninterrupted exploitative rule over the tribals. The local Nagavamsi rule was disrupted by the occupation of Kalahandi by the Bhansla Raja of Nagpur and the district became a part of Nagpur Kingdom till the Maratha domination during 1766 to 1788. The three Anglo-Maratha wars led to the fall of Nagpur Kingdom before it lapsed to the British, suzerainty naturally extended to Kalahandi in 1863 when the district came under the direct control of the British.

The district under colonial rule led to the integration of the region[31] with the colonial administrative system of the Central provinces associated with market, money and power (Pati, 1999). The imposition of a different administrative system and extraction of high taxes[32] led to the further marginalisation of tribal people in the district. For example, the land settlements led to the abolition of the traditional land management system[33] and, along with higher taxes, had a detrimental effect on the economic position of the tribals. It also reinforced social stratification by spreading the idea of legal and private ownership of land, which were alien to tribals in the district. This gave special space to local rulers to exploit tribals due to their ignorance about the new system. The local rulers were responsible for collecting tax from the cultivators of the village on behalf of the king. And the people who migrated from outside the district or coastal belt to assist the king added to the exploitation. During colonial rule this coastal elite continued its presence in the district to help British rule and exploited the tribals as well. British colonialism did not interfere in the local administration much, other than collecting revenues from land and forest while keeping an eye on the tribal resistance movements[34] opposed to this exploitative system being maintained by the combined forces of British colonialism, royal king, feudal landlords and middlemen.

However, the British government started interfering with the power and privileges of the local kings and landlords of Central Provinces during the last decades of the 19th century. The district being a part of the Central Province, the king and his landlords in the district had to suffer, as their power was being curtailed by the deployment of police forces in the district, directly controlled by the British government (Senapati & Kuanr, 1980:68). The deployment of a police force in the district during the last decades of the 19th century was part of the policy of the Empire to control and suppress the nationalist liberation movement in the district in which tribals were at the forefront. The tribal movement in the district had twin intertwined objectives i.e. to fight against British colonialism and feudal aristocracy and protect their culture and economy from outsiders. British colonialism had defeated them, but it was the feudal aristocracy and their allied elites that remained as a force in the district and continued to invade tribal culture and exploit the tribal economy. The objectives of tribal movement in the district remained as bygone dreams of tribals even after independence and now they suffer from internal colonialism[35] of feudal aristocracy (the king and landlords), money lenders and businessmen who have formed a coalition of elites in the district; to control the state power through democratic politics and determine the direction of development planning in post-colonial Kalahandi.

Like other parts of the Indian subcontinent, the people of Kalahandi celebrated the victory of the Indian freedom struggle and passed a resolution on the eve of Independence Day with national spirit. The resolution declared that "the people of Kalahandi state rejoice at India's attainment of full independent powers consequent on the transfer of power from the British to Dominion of India…will remain ever memorable in the history of India, nay, in the history of the world, and hope that this country will play an important role to contribute towards the preservation and promotion of peace and prosperity of the world (as cited in Senapati & Kuanr, 1980:62–63)". After independence, the district merged with the state of Orissa on the 1st of January 1948 but remained underdeveloped as a result of the transition of politics and power from British colonial rulers to the kings and landlords of the district during post-colonial democracy in Kalahandi; marking a new beginning of pre-existing internal colonialism.

The district also experienced its own political history where the elected candidates belonged to Ganatantra Parisad and its ideological successor, the Swatantra Party[36] under the leadership of the Kalahandi royal family. In this respect, until the 1980s, there was a convergence between the factors of voting in the state of Orissa as a whole and in Kalahandi, where the latter consistently voted against the political current of the state as a whole. The Maha Raja (king) of the district became the member of the Indian Parliament successively from the district. The king became the elected politician and feudal rule changed into democracy without any vital change within the power structure in the district. Such transition in the district did not have any impact on the social and economic relations that existed during colonial and pre-colonial periods. The royal family from the Naga dynasty still plays a crucial role in democratic politics in the district, thus sharing a powerful role in the political economy of development and planning in the district. One member of the royal family has represented the district successively from the first Lok Sabha election (1951) to sixth Lok Sabha election (1977). Only during the elections from seventh Lok Sabha election (1980) to eleventh Lok

Sabha election (1996), was the royal family out of power, but it returned during 12th Lok Sabha election (1998) and continued to represent the district uninterruptedly till 14th Lok Sabha election (2004)[37]. The Hindu right wing forces played a vital role in bringing the royal family back to power in the district by reviving the relationship of the royal family with local landlords and forging an alliance with local elites, businessmen and contractors in the district. As a result, internal colonialism and feudal aristocracy still persists in different forms within the democratic norms of the parliamentary politics in the district. This led to the changing composition in the political power structure in the district. Nayak (2009) reveals the paradox of Indian democracy in which the majority tribal populations of the district have been denied the right to have their representative in the Orissa State Assembly[38]. Nayak (2009) also indicates that there is no change in the political power structure of the general population of the district as their representation in the state assembly has remained the same. This reflects the attempts to curb the political representation of the tribals. While such a decision was taken by the Delimitation Commission of India (2006), the tribal representatives were the silent spectators of this process of disenfranchisement[39]. This indicates that despite the reservation of seats in State legislature and in Parliament for the Scheduled Tribes who are the largest population in the district, the Schedule Tribe members, both in State assembly and Parliament are passive participants[40] in the political process and have been content to have only a minor say in the distribution of development resources (Jayal, 2001).

However, the political power in the district is controlled by a regional political party called BJD and a right wing Hindu political outfit called BJP, who are in power. Although the Congress party (INC) has some support base in the district it has not been able to transform its support base to the ballot box in order to capture power. In the case of the BJP, it has consolidated its base by forming alliances with the regional party (BJD), local royal family and other elites in the district. The composition of political power and its representation reflects on the way the Hindu right wing politics of the BJP not only consolidated its base but also improved its position in the district with the help of the royal family in different elections from 1991 to 2004(Nayak, 2009)[41]. The alliance of the BJP with the royal family indicates that after more than the five decades of Indian independence from British colonialism and end of kingship, the power of the royal family hasn't declined in terms of control over politics and state power; although control over social, economic and individual life of the district and its people has declined. But still the social legitimacy and political power of the royal family provides its members enough power to control the planning for development in such a direction which will not be detrimental to the interests of royal family in particular nor their local allies in the district i.e. local elites (both tribals and non-tribals), landlords, businessmen and contractors in general.

Thus, such an alliance is playing a vital role and exploiting the development projects which are meant for the masses i.e. tribals in the district.

In this way, the fruits of development policies are controlled and enjoyed by a few people in the district. The coastal elites and higher caste people of the district have continued their monopoly over society and dominated the economy of the district. The middle men among local tribal people and the coastal elite have a decisive voice in the district and have exploited the development programmes and resources for their personal benefit. Thus historically, like the pre-independence era, the people of Kalahandi, especially the tribals, have faced the same multiple forms of domination and exploitation since independence. These middle men and coastal elite provide the social and political base for both the major parties of Orissa like the Congress, Janata Dal, Biju Janata Dal and now Bharatiya Janata Party. The passivity of the tribal politicians of Orissa in general, and Kalahandi in particular, is attributed to several factors, including the sharp divide between the coastal, developed eastern region and the hilly backward western part of Orissa. The subservient position to which tribal politicians have been relegated by all major mainstream political parties and the absence of education and political consciousness add to the problem.

In this way the paternalistic parliamentary politics controlled by dominant classes and castes has reinforced a process of disenfranchising the tribals in the district and thus denied them the benefits of citizenship, such as affirmative action and delivery of welfares provided by the state led development.

SOCIETY, CULTURE AND ECONOMY IN KALAHANDI WITH REFERENCE TO TRIBALS IN THE DISTRICT

The present society in the district is formed out of a peculiar alliance between the majority of poverty stricken tribals living in the interior hilly terrains and forest on one side, and on the other side the few members of royal family forging an alliance with established costal elites outside and inside the district, tribal and non-tribal elites, businessmen and higher caste rich contractors within the district continuing to hegemonize their power over masses. In this way, it is easy for anyone to find such divided society in terms of social and economic classes that co-exists within the district. With such social formations of landed aristocracy with royal family, businessmen, elites and contractors in the district control the productive resources, development planning and thus the economy of the district.

The development and political economy of the district is well expressed in the following Oriya poem which can be translated as "you are right sir, poverty, starvation, illiteracy, hunger in Kalahandi are big lies of the planning and frustration. All these things are strategies against the district as money is there in the air of Kalahandi; money is flying in the sky of Kalahandi. The political leaders in Kalahandi have their bank accounts in Swiss banks, government officials in Kalahandi are building unidentified big mansions in the state's capital city of Bhubaneswar, contractors of the district are replacing their cars with updated Scorpios and other new model cars, the social workers of different NGOs in the district are flying to Delhi in search of national and international funding. The local journalists in the district are changing their bikes twice in a year and some have got cars now. Without any aid, Kalahandi can survive and can sing the song of self esteem. But these political leaders, government officials, NGO workers and journalists will die without any aid; they will be bankrupt and die in poverty in search of money, money and money"[42]. The poem is a reflection of the political economy of development planning in the district which is controlled and manipulated by a few elites in the district where the masses continue to suffer in poverty, underdevelopment and marginalisation. The regional elite formation in the district is an alliance of the dominant castes (Karan and Brahmins coalition) in the state which have been controlling the development planning and sharing the fruits of development like patron-client, reinforcing underdevelopment and poverty by multiple forms of exclusions in the district (Mohanty, 1990; Jayal, 2001).

However, the predicament of development of the district in general and tribal people in particular remains within the trap of the unholy alliance of landed aristocracy with politics and business, which is nothing but a part of the larger strategy of capitalist accumulation through internal colonialism in the district. As Rodolfo Stavenhagen has noted, "capitalist accumulation requires unequal development and social and economic polarisation. . . the system of stratified interethnic relations plays a crucial role. Because more often than not, the pattern of capitalist domination/subordination involves not only economic classes and geographic regions, but also ethnic groups, particularly when in the post-colonial ethnocratic state social class divisions happen to coincide or overlap with ethnic (linguistic, cultural, religious, racial) distinctions. Of course this does not just "happen" accidentally but is the outcome of a particular colonial and post-colonial history. Thus, the pattern of ethnic stratification that we encounter in so many countries today is the expression of a deeper structural relationship that we may call internal colonialism (Stavenhagen, 1996)"[43]. This process has been rampant after the new economic reforms and is expedited by the development policies that follow the norms of the reform programmes.

ECONOMIC REFORMS AND LOCATING TRANSITIONS IN SOCIAL AND ECONOMIC LIFE OF TRIBALS

This part of my analysis, although it covers the meaning of consumer culture and its relationship with modern market, is more concerned with how certain modern market experiences and dilemmas have been formulated, the rise of market led society in tribal areas of India, Orissa and Kalahandi, the relationship between tribal needs and their social structures, the power of market systems to create desire based society and tribal people's freedom of choice, the nature of identity formation based on the new market system and reproducing Hindu social order and the mainstream idea of happiness, social and economic status in the individual and community life of tribals in the district. It has also changed the gender relations in the tribal areas. The idea of this discussion is to locate the Hinduisation process as not only a religious process that dismantles tribal culture but also an incorporation of market led consumer culture into tribal society. This incorporation of consumer culture into tribal society redesigns itself by establishing a relationship with right wing Hindu fundamentalist organisations.

However, since the advent of the new economic reforms in India in 1991, a significant social and cultural transformation has taken place within the tribal societies. The public policy for tribal development has continued to shift from a 'needs' based development approach to a 'desires' based development approach that is having a colossal impact on the tribal society, culture and economy. The Freudian idea[44] is being implemented through economic reform which has reinforced the market as the focal point in the discourses surrounding development. The penetration of modern and mainstream market into tribal society through Hinduisation is the root cause of the current process of dismantling tribal communitarian culture. In such a context, an attempt has been made to study social and cultural transformation in tribal societies in the Kalahandi district of Orissa which has undergone massive transformations following the post 1991 economic reforms, aiding the growth of Hindu right wing organisations in the tribal areas. This transformation is taking place under the genesis of a Hinduisation process that helps the global market to penetrate into tribal areas,[45] which is the basis of growth of consumerism and deepening of capitalism through the mainstream market.

CONSUMPTION CULTURE VS. CULTURE OF CONSUMPTION IN THE CONTEXT OF MARKET

Consumption as a process and consumers as human beings are not the same throughout the world. Differing from place to place and time to time and with the change of social and cultural practices, the pattern of consumption and consumer behavior changes. This makes consumption a social and cultural process (Slater, 1997). Thus consumption requirements or needs of consumers are determined by the social and cultural process which again determines the institutions or agencies providing consumption requirements or needs of consumers i.e. state and market. When people say, we or I need something; it indicates their, his or her claim on the social or economic resources or their, his or her right or share in the resources for the fulfillment of their needs. The necessary requirement for the fulfillment of consumer needs is to mobilise resources for the production of those goods and services to satisfy consumer needs. The resource mobilisation and institutions involved in it, takes place in the society under a particular cultural set up. Thus the production process and the agencies or institutions (i.e. state and market) involved in the process to satisfy the consumer requirements should ultimately be accountable to social and cultural values and need not forget the individual and group claim in the production process[46].

The entire process of interaction between consumption, consumer and their needs and the modes of production process forms the consumer culture within a given social, economic, political and cultural set-up that gives the social basis of the market. "The market system can only be understood when it is replaced within the context of an economic life, and no less a social life...And this complex is itself constantly evolving and changing; it never has the same meaning from one era to the next"[47]. But the present growth of the neo-liberal market is a powerful ideological trend of contemporary capitalism that tends to avoid the social origin and social history of the market[48]; thus it tries to make the concept of the market more invisible and ambiguous. "Towards the end of the nineteenth century the concept of the market in the economic theory underwent a dramatic change...the market became an abstract concept that acquired tremendous analytical interest as a price making and resource allocating mechanism. Historical and social approaches were firmly rejected during this period... The concept of the market was thinned to such a degree that John Neville Keynes Sr spoke of the 'hypothetical market...This, however, was a price worth paying, according to the marginalist thinkers since many difficult problems...could be solved...In particular, it became possible to conceptualise and model the whole economy as a system of markets (Swedberg, 1994:259)". By creating such a situation of transformation in the conceptualisation of the market, the neo-liberal theorists were trying to avoid getting the blame for market failure and at the same time were able to put the market at the forefront to lead the society where 'people were considered as consumers' and 'needs as desires'.

However, this transformation has resulted often in consumer needs being seen as consumer desires. Needs are being redefined as desires; the shift is unique and took place in a specific condition of dominant mode of cultural reproduction under the market led capitalist social system in the West (Slater,

2004). This shift has created a culture of consumption and made it a natural order. "Consumer culture is not the only way in which consumption is carried out and everyday life reproduced; but it is certainly the dominant way and possesses a practical scope and ideological depth which allows it to structure and subsume all others to a very great extent. Nor is consumer culture a purely western affair. It arose in the west, from about the eighteenth century onwards, as part of the west's assertion of its own difference from the rest of the world as modern, progressive, free, rational. But in the idea of consumer culture there was an assumption of dominance and denigration, of western sense of itself as civilised and righteously affluent, as possessing values that have a universal character. Consumer culture has been a flagship for the advance of western business, western markets and a western way of life. As an aspect of the universalising project of the western modernity, consumer culture has both global pretensions and global extension (Slater, 2004: 7–9)". This idea of western consumer culture has been reproduced through the neo-liberal economic reforms in India where market conscious mainstream Hindu society is trying to dominate the tribal society under the pretension of superior culture to spread the market and incorporate tribals as consumers of the global market. The consumerism of the global market spread through several interlocking developments through rationalisation of market-led modernity project in the form and organisation of mass production (Aglietta, 1979; Boorstin, 1973; Fraser 1981; Pope, 1983) and mass participation in consumption (Miller, 1981, 1987, 1994; Williams, 1982; Richards, 1991). This idea of consumerism as modernity was spread through the market and foregrounds radical individualism that derives its philosophical logic in post modernism[49]. Radical individualism promotes self seeking individual interests that break the social, cultural and communitarian norms and the basis of interaction between consumer, consumption needs and production process. It has been replicated in the social and cultural breakdown of relationships among individuals and communities in the tribal society.

On the other hand, consumerism is helping to spread the idea of feudal aristocracy through the idea of luxury, decadence and superficiality as modern life. It also diverts the working class consciousness through alcohol and sports and controls the power of transformation by the idea of public morality (Rosa, 1992a). The idea of consumer culture has not only influenced consumption in terms of commodity but also in terms of time. It is trying to control the leisure time through public orders (Cross, 1993; Cunningham, 1980; Berry, 1994), in fear of creative thoughts and transformative action which may upsurge from the leisure time. Again, through controlling leisure time, consumer culture keeps persuading people not to stop working once their needs are satisfied, rather to continue to work to fulfill their desires, which is the basis of the shift from the need based society to desire based consumer society where work is a never ending process, allowing no time to think creatively about the day to day problems that people face in society—everything from inequality to exploitation takes a back seat in a market led consumer society and gratification of material desires becomes top priority[50]. The gratification of unlimited material desires puts people in a situation where they forget about their own position in an exploitative and unequal system and never get any time to think about it. On the other side, in order to satisfy the material desires of the consumers, there is mass production and at the same time to increase the material desire there is advertisement of consumer goods before their production, preparing the ground for mass production (Mukerji, 1983; Pope, 1983; Schudson, 1981, 1984). The mass production needs the expansion of the market and creates a desire for mass consumption which is both the objective and subjective trend of capitalism and its market institutions. The incorporation of indigenous people into the mainstream market can open up a wide arena for the market and increase its consumer base. In this process of incorporation the capitalist market finds difficulty in penetrating the indigenous and tribal society as its communitarian norms and culture is an obstacle in the expansion process of market and consumer ideas. Thus the capitalist market needs the help of Hindu right wing forces to dismantle the communitarian culture by bringing tribals into the mainstream society through the Hinduisation process and then spread the idea of consumerism and market.

MARKET, INDIVIDUAL AND SOCIETY IN TRIBAL AREAS

After the initiation of the new economic reforms under the genesis of neo-liberal policies in India during the 1990s, a shift took place in 'society' and 'individual' relationships. The central crystallisation of neo-liberal political economy is the unregulated free market and social and political institutions suitable to it, particularly private property and its definition and application by rule of law. Free market social relations place special emphasis on the individual self-interest and consequently social and economic institutions are shaped to facilitate the pursuit of this interest. At the centre of this individual world is a system of self accumulation which more than anything satisfies not only individual *needs* but also individual *desires* or *wants*. The individual's desire overrules the individual's need. Such broad ideas are influencing tribal society and culture in a way that gives rise to a new conflict between individual and social interest, one that was hitherto non-existent due to the intrinsic and peculiar relationship between the individual and society amongst tribal groups. This conflict between individual and society is the basis of the dismantling of the tribal communitarian culture. The fragmentation of tribal life has led to the augmentation of conflicts between individuals for their own interests. These conflicts are contributing to the growth of vulnerability, marginalisation and poverty. The disunity among the tribals also presents an opportunity to non-tribals and other ruling elites to exploit tribals on a paramount scale.

Markets do not have a uniform influence on the tribal population in India. The impact of the market on tribal populations varies according to their social and geographical location. Although few tribals live in the urban centres in mainstream society, they integrate with the market relatively easy, and again a few among them might even become beneficiaries of the market, the majority of the tribal population who live in the hilly terrains and forests areas, face real difficulties in integrating themselves with the market and inevitably suffer negative consequences to their traditional cultural life. Thus, to assess the variation in the effects of markets on outcomes one must identify an exogenous source of variation in market participation The economists and anthropologist have developed and put together five complementary hypotheses to explain what pulls or pushes indigenous peoples toward or away from markets: (*a*) the allure of foreign goods (Orlove, 1997, Bauer, 2001), (*b*) encroachment by outsiders (Gross et al. 1979), (*c*) resource scarcity from internal population pressure (Diamond, 1995), (*d*) taxation (Cooper, 2000), (*e*) the desire to improve individual well-being by capitalising on one's comparative advantage and gains from trade (Henrich 1997, Godoy 2001), and (*f*) distaste for markets (Hirschman 1984). All these factors are important to understand the way the market influences tribal societies in India and influences negatively. The factors seem irrelevant for the tribal or indigenous societies in India as they do not have any desire for foreign goods[51], no indication of resource scarcity, no desire for individual well being at the cost of their community. They do not need the modern market for their primary or secondary needs, so the modern market is quite distasteful for the tribals. They call their market as *haat or bazaar (market)* which has a wider social and cultural meaning attached to it that serves the interest of tribal communities in terms of their basic needs. The buyer and seller relationship in *haat* is much more communitarian than consumerist. The communitarian interest carries more importance in such kind of *haats* than profit making. The second factor is very important to understand the intervention of mainstream market that not only intrude *haat* but also brings outsiders to take over tribal land, market, culture and invade their economy. In this way, the market in its contemporary, consumer-specific manifestation engenders a collision between the tribal individual and society and exhausts their resources. This conflict between individual and society is being further enhanced by the state policies in the tribal community which are supposed to deliver development and welfare to the tribal population in the country. This is discussed further in the latter part of this chapter.

THE PROBLEMS WITH MAINSTREAM MARKET IN TRIBAL AREAS IN KALAHANDI DISTRICT

The tribals markets are known as haat (weekly market) which is not only a place of buyer and seller but also a place of communitarian network. They talk about festivals, marriages and availability of forest products in different areas. This can be better understood from the following example. During my fieldwork, I was listening to a conversation between a tribal shopkeeper (tribal man) and buyer (tribal woman) in a tribal haat in the Gunupur of Kalahandi district, which can be translated as follows;

> "My daughter got her first menstruation today, I am arranging a party (Toki Parab means virgin girl's festival for her first menstruation)[52] tonight, and if you are free then why don't you join us. Ask all your family members to come, it will be nice to get together and have all of you in this festive occasion of my family. You should all come and give blessings to my daughter and make all of us happy (Gunupur, 18/04/2005)", the tribal woman said to the shopkeeper.

In reply to the tribal woman's invitation, the shopkeeper replied:

> "The haat will be over at 3pm or 4pm then I'll go back to my home, take a bit of rest and try to come, but do not wait for me. You may need more mahua (a kind of flower from which tribals prepare wine by boiling in water—the botanical name of mahua is bassia latifia) for tonight. Take more, I will make a low price for you and give you two kilograms of mahua free of cost as my gift (ibid)".

Then the conversation followed with a kind of colloquial joke on the shopkeeper and buyer relationship. The above chat indicates the wider meaning of a market in tribal areas and it has a different place in the tribal social and cultural life. I found the same form of relationship among buyers and sellers in tribals markets in different places of the district which indicates that the non-monetised relationship is the dominant mode of market interaction in tribal societies in the district. The interaction between the buyer and seller sounds like the talk of an embedded relationship which is unlikely in non-tribal areas of the state. In sum, accumulation of profit is not the central objective of tribal markets.

The non-monetary exchange in the tribal market for material and non material items such as food, oil, alcohol, labor and other services, not only underpin and affirm relationships of amicability, communal sharing, fellow feeling, and cooperation but also marks a uniqueness in their social life where market has a wider meaning. But the entry of money into tribal society through the market has spoiled the individual and community relationship. Money "as a visible object, money is the substance that embodies abstract economic value... If the economic values of the objects are constituted by their mutual relationship of exchangeability, then money is the autonomous expression of this relationship. Money is the representative of abstract value. (It) is a specific realisation of what is common to economic objects (Simmel, 1978 (1900):120). He goes further to say that money "is conducive to the removal of the personal element from the human relationships through its indifferent and objective nature (Simmel, 1978 (1900):297). In this way money has objectified the relationships in the tribal society. And through money it has become much easier for the market-led capitalist system to facilitate the accumulation process through generating more and more profit (Altman, 1987:168). The accumulation process and objectification of rela-tionships in the tribal society has made a visible and lasting impact upon the tribal culture[53]. However, the transition of tribal society from a pre-market, non-monetised society to the contemporary money–led consumerist market society in the Kalahandi district incorporated within the economically and culturally dominant society has seen profound changes. However, it would be incorrect to portray tribals in the Kalahandi district as simply victims of forces (money and market) beyond their control; they have passively ac-cepted what the dominant Hindu mainstream society has imposed on them through state and public policy for tribal development.

Another aspect of tribal market is that tribals as consumers are conscious about the seasonal availabilities of different things that are very close to their day-to-day life. They are also well aware of the price of those commodities and different producers and their products. This indicates that the tribal mar-kets are informative or tribals are informed about the market that operates in their area which helps them in decision making. The availability of informa-tion is central for the efficient decision making by citizens and consumers (Stigler 1961, Stiglitz 2000). However, in the case of the new market, created by the new economic policy of reforms to integrate the tribal market into the mainstream market, tribals become vulnerable due to lack of knowledge about it and the ways it operates, as they do not have any information about the new market and its price structure, availability of goods and about the product and producer. The new market undervalued the information and is blind towards openness to information; the political system that follows the market becomes less informative and more regulatory to save the interests of the market. The works of Farber (1991:554–83) argue that speech—or "in-formation," as he puts it—is a public good, and is, therefore, likely to be undervalued by both the market and the political system. According to Farber (1991), this is the reason behind a special constitutional protection by the state for information-related activities both in the field of the market and of politics. This indicates that state regulation over the market is essential for the fair functioning of the market. However, the new market simply made tribals individually objectified consumers who needed to remain as unconscious consumers as per the structure of the mainstream market. In this way the state and government policy has aggravated the problem in tribal society by helping the mainstream market to spread in the tribal society. Another problem with the mainstream market is that it has placed money as the focal point of tribal life and society, which is discussed below.

TRANSFORMATION DUE TO THE INCORPORATION OF CASH (MONEY) INTO TRIBAL SOCIETIES

The modern capitalist market does not enter into tribal society alone. It enters with its ideas and institutions. The growth of the idea of money in the form of cash and more and more acquisition is the reflection of such an idea embedded in the spirit of the capitalist market. Money is documented by Weber (1905, 1998:53) as the principal feature of modern capitalism while he has written about "the acquisition of more and more money, combined with the strict avoidance of all spontaneous enjoyment…is thought of purely as an end in itself, that vis-à-vis the happiness of, or utility to, the particular individual, it appears as quite transcendental and whole irrational. Man is dominated by acquisition as the purpose of his life; acquisition is no longer a means to the end of satisfying his material needs. This reversal of what we might call the 'natural' situation, completely senseless from an unprejudiced standpoint, is evidently a leading principle of capitalism as it is foreign to all people not under capitalistic influence". The tribal societies in the Kalahandi district are not only alien to modern capitalism in its all forms but also alien to the idea of money in the form of cash. The new economic reforms have created a new market situation through the change in agriculture from food crop production to cash crop production. The new market is based on money transaction in the form of cash in all its interactions, whereas in the tribal market money, in the form of cash, plays a secondary role. During my fieldwork in the Kalahandi district, I found that few tribal people use cash in the tribal market (haat), and many people even buy things without paying anything. I asked many tribal women, who bought cooking oil without paying any money to the shopkeeper, about this, and they all replied in a similar way; "Last week, I gave him (the shopkeeper) vegetables from my field, he has also taken mahua[54] (a kind of drink made out of a flower) many times from me, so I am not paying him any money". I asked the same question to the shopkeeper who replied; "It happens between us as I used to get many things from her field without paying her anything, so it is ok between us". This mode of transaction is quite common in the tribal weekly markets of Thuamul Rampur, Langigarh, Risida and even in the markets of the district headquarter; Bhawanipatna. It reflects that the actors in the tribal market don't have acquisitive intention to make more and more money and accumu-

late more profit. Seven months after my visit, I went to the same place again
and saw a different kind of transaction where there was a rise in the number
of people using money in the form of cash for their market interaction (buy-
ing and selling). After observing the difference, I went back to a school
where I was staying during my fieldwork. I talked to a school teacher[55] and
shared my different experiences with him. He told me that "tribals are becoming more and more conscious about money these days due to more and
more weekly markets in the tribal areas. This has been happening for the last
ten years". The teacher's reply clearly reflected the relationship between
economic reforms and the penetration of the market, and its culture, into
tribal society. This is the way money is pervading into the tribal societies in
the district through the market, playing a major role in the growth of economic underdevelopment of tribals in the district. But the neo-liberal development policy makers blame natural calamities for the cause of underdevelopment of the region and tribals in the district.

THE MYTH OF NATURAL CALAMITIES AND
UNDERDEVELOPMENT DEBATE IN KALAHANDI

Orissa has twice experienced acute famine in 1865–66 and 1888–89 and
Kalahandi was among the most affected areas, but little is known about the
impact of famine there, except that relief centres were opened to supply
cooked food[56]. The 1888–89 scarcity occurred due to crop failure in general.
During this famine, it is said that the rate of death was 81 persons per mile
and the severity of famine was indicated by the suspension of land revenue
(Bhatia, 1967:79). After independence, Kalahandi suffered drought in
1954–55, 1965–56 and 1974–75. It has been estimated that during the
965–66 drought, 55 percent of the population depended on free kitchens, but
during 1974–75 drought the Drought Prone Areas Programme was launched
by the Government of India to mitigate the drought problem in the country.
The District Gazetteer informed that the landless agricultural labourers were
the worst sufferers. The landowners were also suffering, as they could neither
reap a harvest nor could they do the manual labour[57]. From the mid-eighties,
the Kalahandi district has become a news column in local, regional, national
and international news and print media and is known for its droughts, starvation deaths, poverty and other natural calamities and human made maladies.
The human made maladies have made the district more vulnerable than the
natural calamities. The failure of development policies often gets less attention through citing the causes of natural calamity and poverty and underdevelopment in the district, which is a myth for the following factors. The first
myth is that drought is the cause of poverty, vulnerability, starvation and
underdevelopment in the district. This is not true as the average annual

rainfall in the district is higher than the average rainfall in the state (Pradhan, 1993; Kar, 1988) and often the actual rainfall is more than normal (Government of Orissa, 1999, 2002). Thus, the cause of drought in the district does not fit into the argument of crop or agricultural failure due to natural calamity caused by less, or lack of, rainfall. The average production of food grains and cereals in the district is higher than other districts in the state and in the country as well. Nayak (2009) provides a strong base to refute the logic of drought for the cause of poverty and underdevelopment in the district. This is also a befitting answer to those who blame the traditional cropping patterns in the district for its low productivity. The second myth is that the people of the district in general and tribals in general, are basically lazy people and depend on post-natural calamities relief and they are not productive[58]. The farmers of the district use less technology, fertilizer, pesticides and less hybrid seeds but produce better than the rest of the state and in the country (Mallick, 1974). The abundance of production of food in the district can be found in the historical records, for example the land revenue settlement records which have revealed that "during the last 20 years there was no failure of crops except in the years 1938–39, 1946–47, 1947–48 and 1950–51 when there was partial failure. There was, however, sufficient reserve stock to meet the requirement of the people"[59]. On the other hand, the land question provides the answer to the distressed conditions in the district as the ownership is in the hands of few though the per capita availability of land and per capita cropped area in the district is highest in the state (Government of Orissa, 1999, 2002; Pradhan, 1993:298). But the fertile land, or for that matter land in general, is in the hands of the few people who are the major owners of land whereas the majority of people are small landowners or landless (Das, 1962; Government of Orissa, 1999, 2002). That means the agricultural and food production is controlled by a few which causes food scarcity, poverty and starvation deaths. The natural calamities in the district can not be blamed exclusively. However, according to a recent study by Swain and Swain (2005) the natural calamities, like super-cyclones, had no impact on tribal population in the district.

However, the miserable condition of people in general, and tribals in particular, continues to dominate the development debate based on the idea that natural calamities are the cause of underdevelopment and poverty in the district. The ruling class in the Kalahandi district is from the landed aristocracy in alliance with the coastal elites in the state. As a result, the landed aristocracy and costal elites formed a new class of traders and money lenders in the district who control political, economic power and control the production and distribution system which has caused poverty, starvation and underdevelopment in the district. The state politico-bureaucracy has helped such a formation to grow in the district by making development policies in which the above class has remained as the stakeholders in the district. The success of development policies depends on the breaking down of such a nexus in the district which gives natural calamities as the cause of underdevelopment to conceal their role in the failure of the development policies in the district. The natural calamities in the district have become a fabled answer to the poverty and underdevelopment of the district. This has helped the liberalisation, privatisation and globalisation policies to spread in the district without taking any accountability for the failure of the development policies. The process has placed poverty, underdevelopment and drought in the folklore of the district. The impact and the failure of the development policies under the guidance of new economic reforms (liberalisation, privatisation and globalisation) on the tribals in the Kalahandi district are discussed in the next two chapters.

CONCLUSION

The new economic reforms have not only led to the transformation of tribal development policies but also restructured local development in such a way that they have weakened the government led institutions of welfare delivery and development in the district of Kalahandi. The weakening of the local development institutions and welfare mechanism has not only influenced the rural development in the district but also had a precarious impact on the economy, society and culture of the tribals in the district as they are the most marginalised social and economic groups in the district and in the state as well. The segregation based on the rural and urban areas, tribal and non-tribal areas has led to social and cultural segregation among the people in the district. In the terrain of social and cultural life, the people started locating the people of the rural areas, mostly tribal people, as underdeveloped and their culture as responsible for their poverty and other forms of marginalisation, indicating integration of tribals into the mainstream society is the only solution for development. Such a process is the reflection of unequal development in the economy in terms of region and people, polarisation in politics based on tribal and non tribal, and stratification of inter-ethnic relations in the district, the domination of outsiders over the region's resources, and subordination of tribal society, culture and language by mainstream Hindu right wing forces as part of larger project of capitalist accumulation. This entire process of deinstitutionalisation in the district has helped in reinforcing the unequal class relations and given the opportunity to the elite class and caste people to continue their hegemony over the masses by controlling the production and development planning process. Thus, underdevelopment of tribals in Kalahandi district reveals historical continuity, even during post-colonial planning and state-led development, and has been accelerated further during the post-economic reform period. In such a context an attempt has been made to study the impact of economic reforms on tribals in the Kalahandi district both from social, economic and cultural point of view in the next two chapters.

Chapter Four

Impact of the New Economic Reforms on Tribals as a Poor Economic Class in Kalahandi

Locating Economic Transition of Tribals

This chapter documents the impact of economic reforms on tribals in Kalahandi district by taking different sectors i.e. agriculture, food security, mining based industrialisation, displacement and land alienation, unemployment and poverty into account. While explaining the impact of economic reforms on different sectors of the tribal economy, it outlines the economic transition of tribals in Kalahandi district during the post-economic reform period. The chapter argues that the new economic reforms have had a negative impact on the tribal economy. The process of economic transition and its impacts have made tribals more vulnerable and enlarged processes of marginalisation in the district.

INTRODUCTION

Any attempt to locate transitions in the tribal economy, as a consequence of economic reforms, is impossible without understanding the structural basis and conditions of tribal economy in the district of Kalahandi. Many existing studies (e.g. Mishra, 2001) locate the underdevelopment of Kalahandi district and its tribal population as a product of local conditions i.e. work culture (laziness), disadvantaged geography (inaccessibility), economic position (poverty and underdevelopment) and natural calamities. This kind of analysis is not only reductionist but also fails to understand the gamut of development processes and their historical legacies in the district. Firstly, it helps neo-liberal development policy makers to overcome crises in tribal development policies and failures without being accountable. Further, such analysis either ignores the role of institutions (state, government and public policy), or gives minimal importance to structures within and outside the district in which economic and development activities take place. Other studies on the other hand, (e.g. Joshi, 1998) consider tribal economy as independent from the mainstream economy and at the same time, blame the state and its policies for the cause of underdevelopment of tribals and their area. In order to avoid and reject this kind of contradictory and reductionist analysis, my research starts with an understanding of the general aspect of economic analysis of tribal development before and after economic reforms by depicting the structure and conditions in which agriculture and forest products play a vital role. The study of these two aspects indicates how the tribal economy differs from the mainstream economy even in an environment clearly dominated by (the structures of mainstream economy) and within institutional structures that are predominantly capitalist and feudal by nature. Thus, the tribal economy can be treated as different from the mainstream economy but not as independent. It remains dominated by a combination of pre-capitalist, feudal and capitalist tenets in its economic structure. Such analysis can reveal that "the underdeveloped economy was not a backward local economy but a limb of the dominant economy (Amin, 1994:57)".

In the context of Kalahandi district, the study of Currie (2000) has taken the argument further by arguing that poverty, underdevelopment and hunger is the result of failures of democratic politics, and state and development policies to address the predicaments of tribal people in the area. His study highlights the role of collective action by civil society groups and the media which has played a major role in protecting and asserting the right of the people to access public welfare. In a way, his study depicts the role of the state in perpetuating poverty, hunger and underdevelopment in the district. Jayal (1999) makes a similar kind of argument by criticising the failure of democratic politics and state in the context of Kalahandi but asserts "the use of institutions of parliamentary democracy, such as adversarial politics in the legislature, a vigilant press, and a judiciary receptive to public interest litigation, in order to bring the issue to public notice and to demand government accountability (Jayal, 1999: 238)". Both the works of Jayal (1999) and Currie (2000) romanticise the role of judicial activism and collective actions of the civil society while reflecting on the failure of democratic politics and the state.

There are two problems in this type of analysis. Firstly, it ignores the role of democratic space and the conditions that allow such activism. It is impossible to think about collective action in an undemocratic or dictatorial state and judicial activism in the absence of operational and active constitutional laws. Secondly, it promotes the neo-liberal agenda by reducing the role of the welfare state and democratic politics and by projecting civil society and collective actions as being against the state.[1] The anti-state projection of COs and NGOs is an attempt to fix alliances and simultaneously bargain with the state to create their operational social space for their existence without a state. There is a strong connection between state and different civil society organisations. It is ironic that most of the civil society organisations and NGOs in the district are funded by the state government of Orissa and the central government in Delhi. The projection of civil society organisations and NGOs, as opposed to the state, is a veil that co-opts and neutralises resistance movements against the failure of tribal development policies in the district.

The predicaments of tribals in Kalahandi state, and its tribal development policy failure, are quite apparent, but the question of what led to the failure of the state's tribal development policy remains unexplored. Thus, it is important to study tribal development and economy from below – that is the operational logic of the tribal society and economy in the district along with its relationship with state, national, international economy or the economy outside tribal society. It needs to depict the relationship of the tribal economy with the outside world. The introduction of cash crops, floriculture and other agro-businesses in tribal agriculture and economy is the result of such a complex interaction and relationship between tribal economy and dominant mainstream economy. In such an interaction, the tribal economy suffers due to the withdrawal of tribal agriculture from food and other agricultural production. John Harriss (1982) and H. Friedmann (1978) have documented the growth and tendency of agro-businesses to withdraw from agricultural production and focus on their profit making activities while leaving farming to small-holders and scheme them rather than replacing them. This is not the result of a coincidental response to and/or penetration and influence by the dominant mainstream economy, but rather by systematic design that puts the tribals in an exploitative situation and keeps the tribal economy as dependent on market. This mode of production[2] can be called a "tribal mode of production", incorporating theoretically the logic of contemporary transitions in tribal economy and agricultural production within a dominant economy based on the market.

The penetration of the mainstream market into the tribal economy in Kalahandi has taken place as a result of economic reforms which have led to a transition in tribal agriculture from food crops to cash crops. The PDS (Public Distribution System of food) declined during the era of economic reforms as part of its structural adjustment policy in the district. The transition in food production and food distribution as a consequence of economic reforms saw food insecurity increase in tribal areas (Nayak, 2002). The reform program has also put mining based industrialisation at the top of devel-

opment priorities, causing displacement, cultural disintegration and livelihood vulnerability for tribals across the district. There has been a growth in
transport and communication during this period for mining based industrialization, for the drainage of natural resources from the district in the name of
development. This process has caused environmental degradation and landlessness as a consequence of which livelihood insecurity, poverty, unemployment and migration has become rampant in the district. The whole process
has taken place in such a way to have led to the corrosion of the constitutional provisions for the tribal development during the post-economic reform
period. The scenario of transition is taking place by eroding affirmative
action as enshrined by the Constitution of India. This reverse trend is well
documented by the Ministry of Tribal Affairs: "The last decade has witnessed a reversal of this philosophy and the economic policies and reforms
being taken up are leading towards a negative approach to the disadvantaged
classes, especially the tribal communities. There has been a clear shift from
the strong protection role of the state towards these communities to one of
justification for their exploitation in the name of economic development. The
laws and protective safeguards as laid down in the constitution for the tribal
people are facing severe changes and amendments"[3]. Such reverse trends in
development policies, during and after the reform process, have had a negative impact on different sectors of economy for tribals in Kalahandi district,
which is discussed in detail in the following section.

SECTORAL ANALYSIS OF THE POST-ECONOMIC REFORM SCENARIO AND ITS CONSEQUENCES FOR TRIBALS IN THE KALAHANDI DISTRICT OF ORISSA

The transition of tribal economy in the Kalahandi took place as a result of
shifts in the agricultural and industrial policy of the government of Orissa in
the aftermath of the new economic reforms. The shift in agricultural policy
has paved the way for a shift in agricultural production and its commercialisation, whereas the shift in industrial policy has launched the process of
mining based industrialisation in the district by putting small scale industries
into the secondary sector. Simultaneously, industrialisation has led to pressure on tribal land, agriculture and forest products which are the basis of
tribal livelihood in the region. The pull-out of the state from welfare and
other development activities for tribals has added to problems in the district
which will be discussed in the following separate sections.

TRANSITION IN AGRICULTURE

The agricultural production in the Kalahandi district is mainly based on the staple food requirements of the region. The general populations (non-tribals) of the district eat rice as their staple food along with maize and millet as their supplementary dietary requirement, while the tribal population in the district uses maize and millet as their staple food along with rice as supplementary food. Agricultural production in Kalahandi took place using simple local technology and local seeds. The use of fertilizers and modern technology for agricultural production was minimal, even amongst big farmers in the district. Thus, agricultural production was independent of a market based on seed, fertilizers and other agricultural technologies. In terms of market, agriculture in the district was focused on the internal demands of the region while exporting the surplus of foodgrains to other parts of the state and the country. In this way, a kind of rational agriculture[4] was taking place in the district. The new agricultural policy adopted for Kalahandi during 1993, followed by the new economic reforms, was based on four main objectives; i) reduce paddy (rice) production by reducing the paddy coverage from the existing 3,18,000 hectares to 2,70,000 hectares by the year 2002–2003, ii) substitute food crop production by increasing production of sugarcane, cotton and pulses like red gram, green gram black gram and oil seeds like sun flower, groundnuts and other commercial crops, iii) replace unremunerative local varieties of seeds and production technology with high yielding and hybrid varieties of seeds, modern technology and fertilizers to emphasize efficiency in increasing production, iv) focus on export-oriented agricultural production.[5] While looking at the objectives of the new agricultural policy, one can say that there is a clear direction of the government to shift the district's agriculture from food production to cash crop production. Such transitions in the agricultural sector have overlooked the food requirements of the people of the region and their internal demands while focusing on the external requirements of the market[6].

In this way, the new agricultural policy in the district has laid the basis for the promotion of export oriented agriculture and its market in the district. The policy of export-oriented agriculture has led to further demands for the transition of agricultural production in the district from food crops to cash crops. The tribal farmers used to produce rice, vegetables and a few other crops with some oil. However, government officials of the agriculture department in the district were directed to promote the new agricultural policy and encourage tribals to cultivate cash crops like; sugarcane, cotton, oil seeds, coffee, onion, vegetables, ginger, turmeric and other spices[7]. Other than these crops, the government also encouraged the growth of floriculture and fruit orchards.

Such agricultural policy transition also promoted the mechanisation of agriculture with the use of modern technology, pesticides, fertilizers and use of high yielding varieties of seeds[8]. Traditionally, tribal communities did not use chemical fertilizers, hybrid seeds and pesticides for their agriculture (Das, 1980: 710–11) and members of agricultural tribal communities in the district neither had knowledge nor had the expertise to use them. This has led to the dependency of agriculture in Kalahandi in terms of production, demand and supply. Thus, the new policy directions of agriculture during the post-reform period has opened up a new market for fertilizers, seeds, agricultural equipment and other accessories necessary for the new production regime. Such a transition in the agricultural production system has had huge social implications in the tribal society and the wider meaning systems attached to their production process and weekly markets. The tribals in the district consider that a good harvest is a product of the blessing of the *Penu or Dharani devata (earth god, mother earth)*, rain and water god. During the failure of agriculture, they consider that it is their fate and a result of earth, rain and water gods' anger on them.

The implementation of the Upper Indravati Multipurpose Project for hydro-electricity and irrigation started in 1999. The command areas of the project have become the most irrigated land areas of the district. The irrigation facilities have encouraged multi-crop farming and given a new impetus to the agricultural production in the district. The transition in agricultural production in the district has changed this cosmic causation to the commercialisation and concrete economic analysis of the social and cultural life of the tribals[9] as the demand for agricultural production is no more dependent on internal demands but on supply determined by external requirements through market. However, the products of the new production regime neither fulfilled direct consumption requirements of the people nor had the market for it in the district. Thus, it paved the way for the outside market to interact with the district economy. Simultaneously the production regime in the district has become dependent on the outside market. The artificial demand control by the new market has led to lower prices of cash crops which have become beneficial to the actors in the new market, and the producers or the farmers in the district have become more and more vulnerable to the process of growth in the new market. There were not even any industries[10], other than rice mills, in the district to absorb the produced sugar, oil and cotton. Thus, the cash crop produced by the tribals and other farmers led to the distress sale of their products to the local money lenders and businessmen who have become the beneficiaries of the transition. In this way the new agricultural policy of the post-economic reform period has changed the nature of agricultural production and the scope of its market, which has ultimately determined the nature of demand and supply in the district. The different aspects of agricultural transition and its problems can be discussed separately while looking at the changes in agricultural production, horticulture and floriculture, sericulture and mulberry cultivation and its impact on food security among tribals in particular and tribal economy in general.

Agricultural Production

The change in the cropping pattern, brought about by the new economic reform policies, has led to changes in the district's agricultural production. Cropping patterns in the district depend on soil quality, rain and irrigation facilities, climate and food requirements of the region and its people, as well as government agricultural policy. The Government of Orissa also reduced funding by 50 percent for tribal agriculture during the post-reform period. The tribals in Kalahandi district used to get Rs. 7167466 for agriculture during the pre-reform period of 1980–1991 and this was reduced to Rs. 3871016 during 1991–2003. Similarly, there was a decline in funding for irrigation in the tribal areas. There was a marginal increase in government expenditure for horticulture, business and agro-forestry in the tribal areas as well as an average increase of 30 percent in funding, but the focus of funding was on cash crop production (Nayak, 2009)[11]. This has led to the stagnancy and decline trend in tribal agriculture in the district.

The data on area wise crop production and yield in Kalahandi, from 1985–2000 reveals that the production of paddy marginally increased from 38.31 percent of total production during 1985–90 to 48 percent and 61 percent during 1995–2000, due to the double cropping in a year (Nayak, 2009). But wheat production declined marginally from 0.25 percent during 1985–90 to 0.21 percent during 1995–2000. The food crops on which tribals depend on their daily food declined on a massive scale during the post-reform period. Maize production declined from 2.26 percent during 1985 to 0.98 during 1995–2000. Similarly, food crops like Jawar declined from 0.72 to 0.06 percent, Ragi declined from 4.03 percent to 0.64 percent and Kulthi declined from 5.20 percent to 2.66 percent during the post-reform period of 1995–2000. However, the production of cash crops, oil seeds and other commercial crops increased its ratio in comparison to food crops. The production of crops increased in the district during the post-reform period (Blackgram from 5.25 percent to 6.58 percent, Mung from 6.71 percent to 9.87 percent and Arhar from 2.82 percent to 4.58 percent during 1995–2000). Similarly, cash crops such as til, mustard, groundnut, onion, potato, sugarcane and cotton seem to have averaged a 50 percent increase in production (Nayak, 2009)[12]. In this way transition in agriculture took place with the changing cropping pattern in the district during the post-economic reform period, in which the primary food requirements of tribals became secondary and commercial crops became primary in agricultural production in the district. The change in the cropping pattern and shift of focus to cash crops has also changed the nature of agricultural production in the district from its local need orientation to the export orientated market.

Horticulture and Floriculture

Horticultural production was given more importance during the post-economic reform period than the production of food crops which are primary food requirements of the tribals in the district. The *Integrated Prospective Plan on Land and Water use for Kalahandi district (1993 to 2003)* which was developed during the post-economic reform period stressed increases in fruit and vegetable cultivation on a commercial basis by keeping the demands of the external market in mind (p.61–70). In particular, the policy encouraged the production of banana, pineapple, papaya, ber, guava, custard, apple and pomegranate etc. The *Integrated Rural Development Programme (IRDP), Drought Prone Area Programme (DPAP), JRY/Social Forestry* schemes and *Integrated Tribal Development Agency (ITDA)* in the district were diverted to develop fruit orchards and encouraged both tribal and non-tribal farmers to enter into such a production regime which had no market nor internal demand in the district and no place in tribal daily dietary food requirements. The Training of Rural Youth for Self Employment (TRYSEM) programme was used for gardening and mushroom cultivation in the district. In this way, the new agricultural policy has followed an integrated approach to combine agricultural production in Kalahandi with the outside market. The Government of Orissa has encouraged tribal farmers through different agricultural income generating programmes to produce more and grow more mixed orchards with a focus on exportable mango, pineapple and banana. The funding for such horticultural programmes increased from Rs. 206325 during 1980–1991 to Rs. 2159864 during 1991–2003. The funding for vegetable production declined from Rs. 103345 in 1980–90 to Rs. 15250 in 1991–2003. Similarly the funding for potato production was completely abolished. The funding to grow mixed orchards increased from Rs.2500 in 1980–90 to Rs. 11091 in 1991–2003. The increasing trend of funding continues for producing more pineapple and banana which has increased 120 times during the post economic reform period. The funding for Pisciculture was also seen as a priority in the district, which is mountainous and often faces drought. Tribals were encouraged to involve themselves in Pisciculture for which government funding increased from Rs.28500 in 1980–1990 to Rs.52300 in 1991–2003 (Nayak, 2009).

Sericulture and Mulberry Cultivation

The tribal blocks i.e Langigarh and Thuamul Rampur were chosen for sericulture and mulberry cultivation by the Government of Orissa, with the help of the Kalahandi district administration. This led to a complete shift in tribal agriculture and made tribals dependent on the market for their food. The District Rural Development Agency (DRDA), Kalahandi took up different programmes to encourage sericulture and mulberry cultivation. The DRDA transferred Rs.33.02 lakh from JRY and DPAP funds to the Assistant Director, Sericulture (ADS), Kalahandi for taking up mulberry plantations on the lands of the 447 identified tribal beneficiaries during 1991–1996. However, the sericulture and Mulberry experimentation in the tribal areas failed badly by the end of 1999, as bank loans were not sanctioned. Rs.29.08 lakh invested out of JRY on the plantation became wasteful. Even after the failure of experimentation, the government of Orissa has not abandoned the idea of sericulture and mulberry cultivation in Kalahandi. The funding for such a programme continued to grow over the period of 2003 to 2006 and declined slowly during 2006–07 (Nayak, 2009)[13]. In this way, the new economic-led agricultural policies failed in the district by creating desires among the tribal farmers and pushed the tribals in the Kalahandi district into a position of food insecurity.

FOOD SECURITY AND PDS IN KALAHANDI

Food Security means the availability of food at all the times, access to all persons—in terms of quantity and quality (nutritionally adequate)—and acceptable within the given culture and food habit. It is indicated by physical and economic accessibility of food. The physical access to food depends on production, procurement, storage, buffer stock and supply of food, whereas the economic accessibility to food depends on the purchasing power of the consumer. The Public Distribution System (PDS), as a food policy, covers all the above items necessary for food security. The policy of PDS has been made primarily with the objective of providing food security to the poor and simultaneously fixing remunerative prices to the producers. In fact the latter function was better served in the course of the implementation of the PDS. This was done in order to prevent farmers from resorting to distress sales due to weak bargaining power and monopoly market functionaries. The government, through procurement operations, provided a Minimum Support Price to the producer to save the producer from market exploitation and boost production. It also helped build buffer stocks to secure against the scarcity situation. However, consumers suffered from food insecurity due to lack of purchasing power (Nayak, 2007: 71–72). The PDS[14], as a food security policy, took a new turn after the implementation of the new economic reforms, with a detrimental effect on both producer and consumers. The decline in food subsidies, limit on procurement, targeting and revamping of the

PDS has subsequently led to the collapse of food security and its policy (Swaminathan, 2000).

In case of Kalahandi district, food production and procurement increased after the commissioning of the Indravati Irrigation project, which allowed farmers to grow multiple crops in a single year. In terms of production, the district was given a target of 150,000 tonnes of rice for procurement as well as 65,000 tonnes fixed by the government for procurement from the district[15]. In terms of procurement, the district comes under the Titilagarh division of the Food Corporation of India (FCI)[16] which has sub-centres in Kesinga, Junagarh, Bhawanipatna, and Narla Road to procure foodgrains from farmers. There is no sub-centre of FCI in the tribal areas of Kalahandi as a result of the nexus between rice millers and FCI agents[17]. Thus, production and procurement of food in the district are higher than in other parts of Orissa, but the district has received more attention for death by starvation than anywhere else in Orissa and India. The public action and judicial activism pushed the state to step into the issue of food insecurity among tribals in Kalahandi district (Currie, 1998a & 1998 b). The question of starvation deaths and hunger has remained as a question in the district in general and among tribals in particular. The district that produced most food suffers from food insecurity. Such a paradox indicates that higher production of food cannot provide food security to the people. Thus, availability and accessibility of food through the distribution mechanisms of the PDS is significant for food security among the tribals in the district (Nayak, 2002, 2007).

However, after the implementation of the new economic reforms, the PDS declined on a massive scale due to a shift away from universal orientation[18] to targeted and revamped orientation which led to the failure of food security policy in the district. The District Manager, Orissa State Civil Supplies Corporation Ltd., (OSCSC) of Kalahandi district stated in April, 1999 that due to non-receipt of the release of orders in time and non-cooperation of FCI authorities, full quantities of food grains could not be lifted for distribution under the PDS. He had also stated in May 1998 that FCI and Orissa State Warehousing Corporation (OSWC) authorities were not giving the stock on 100% weight and this fact had been intimated to the concerned quarters but the shortage could not be realised. Apart from all these problems, the price of food items available under the PDS also increased during the period of post-economic reforms and price rise led to the economic inaccessibility of food by the poor and tribal consumers in the district. Three price mechanisms were followed in the district during the post-economic reform period. All rural families (ration card holders) and Below Poverty Line population in the district, whose names were recorded in DRDA/Block B.P.L Register, were supplied monthly with 16 kg of rice per BPL family with a price of Rs.4.75 per kg. Families staying in the non-ITDP and non-DPAP blocks, along with those living in urban areas, were supplied with the same quantity of rice supplied at the rate of Rs.6.30 per a kg. There was a different price for the APL families which was closer to the market price[19]. The reduction of the price gap between market food price and PDS food price led to the declining of food intake from the PDS-run FPS in the district. In this way the poor tribals have become the victims of price rise as poor and tribal people spend more on food items as a percentage of their consumption expenditure. The problem of dual price mechanism, one for APL families and another for BPL families also became redundant and consumers discouraged to buy from PDS outlets, while the delivery system added problems for the distribution of food grains under PDS in the district.

The entire process led to the collapse of PDS in the district, particularly in terms of food off take from the PDS run fair price shops. The data collected from the Orissa State Civil Supplies Corporation Ltd., (OSCSC) at Bhawanipatna reveals that food off take from the PDS declined on a massive scale in the tribal areas of the district over one decade. During the pre-economic reform period of 1980 to 1990, the food allocation for tribals in the district was 78 percent, which increased to 84 percent during the post-economic reform period of 1995 to 2005. But food off take of tribals from the PDS run shops declined from 63 percent in 1980–1990 to 41 percent in 1995–2005. In the case of non-tribals there was also a marginal increase in food allocation under PDS in the district and the off take also showed a marginal growth. In this way, post-economic reform food policy led by PDS failed to provide food security to the tribals in the district. In general, the objective of PDS has failed in the district in terms of its distribution mechanism.

Apart from the failure of food security policy in the district, the PDS failed to understand the food practices of tribals and food culture. A recent ethno-botanical survey of food practices among Kandha tribes in Kalahandi district by Panda and Padhy (2007) revealed that tribals use many types of naturally occurring unusual additional food items such as carnal of mango, several types of tubers of the genus *Dioscorea*, wild bean *Mucuna utilis, Madhuca indica, Caryota urens* pith*, Tamarindus indica* seeds, young limbs of bamboo (*Dendrocalamus strictus*) and wild mushrooms. They process these items in a unique way by boiling repeatedly and discarding the boiled water each time to clean the bitter tasting chemicals (alkaloids) from the food items. These food items are used to supplement during a crisis period or lean season when conventional food items i.e. rice, finger millet and a few popular pulses are not available. Another study by Sinha and Lakra (2005, 2007) has identified 43 species of weeds belonging to 36 genera and 26 families of plants, 50 types of leaves, 46 types of fruits, 11 types of flowers, 14 types of tubers and 5 types of gums are commonly consumed by tribals as per the seasonal availability. The research by Panda, Panigraphy and Padhy (2005) studied the plants used by the Kandha tribe of the Mantriguda valley in the Kalahandi district. The study found that they cultivate thirteen plant species of millets, pulses, oil seeds and paddy and collect wild edible fruits, tubers, leaves, roots, mushrooms and youngling shoots of bamboo, to supplement their diet. By taking this into account, the interim report of the Orissa State Legislative House Committee on Drought and Other Natural Calamities (1987) opined long back that food relief through PDS has to take the food habits of the region into consideration. However, the post-economic reform food security policy has overlooked the food habits and food requirements of the tribals in the district. The rice and wheat distributed by the PDS network is not eaten by the tribals in the district, rather consumed by the affluent section of society. The tribals eat rice and wheat during the festive season only. The rice eaten by tribals is also different from PDS rice which is unfamiliar to the food habits of tribals in the district. In this way the new economic reforms have reinforced food insecurity among tribals in the district.

INDUSTRIALISATION IN THE DISTRICT

The Kalahandi district was one of the most industrially backward districts of Orissa and in India. There was debate in India's parliament during the 1990s over declaring the district as a no-industry zone due to its lack of industrial infrastructure. It is often argued that lack of industrialisation, even after more than four decades of Indian independence, has contributed to the under development of the district. Therefore, it is argued that industrialisation is an unavoidable leverage for the development of the people and different regions of the district (Rao and Misra, 2005). There were no major industries in the district other than few rice mills which increased to more than 150 in the year 2004–05. More than 70% were built in the five years after the commissioning of the Indravati project during 1999, and the location of most of these is in the command areas of the Indravati Irrigation project which are non-tribal areas of the district. The first large scale industry was set up when the IPICOL signed an MoU with the Western Orissa Sugar and Chemical Industries Ltd for the establishment of a 2500 TCR capacity sugar project in Dharamgarh Sub-division with an estimated project cost of Rs.32.00 crores. This industry put Kalahandi on the path of industrialisation and was augmented by the set up of two large scale industries—the Kornark Growers Cooperative Spinning Mills Ltd, Kesinga and Orissa Regional Cooperative Oil Seed Growers Union Ltd. at Bhawanipatna—by the Western Orissa Sugar and Chemical Industries Ltd. Attempts were made to industrialise the district at different periods of time but large scale industrial set-ups were invisible during the pre-reform period. However, the Kornark Growers Cooperative Spinning Mills Ltd and Orissa Regional Cooperative Oil Seed Growers Union Ltd have become ineffective in running the management of these two industries due to lack of government funding and governance. The Western Orissa Sugar and Chemical Industries Ltd has completely shut down due to making loss as a result of mismanagement, corruption and government apathy towards its recovery during the post-economic reform period. The industry has collapsed completely leaving the broken building in the Dharamgarh area symbolising the failure of government led industrialisation in the district.

The new economic reforms have led to the transition of industrial policies by both the Government of Orissa and the Government of India[20]. The post-economic reform industrial policies have given a new boost to the industrial development in the district. As a result of which there are twenty eight agro and food based industries, fifteen electronics and mechanical based industries, five chemical based industries, fourteen forest and mineral based industries, nine paper, plastic, glass and ceramic industries with fourteen repair and servicing industries[21]. The major boost to industrialisation in Kalahandi took place when the Vedanta Alumina Ltd (VAL)[22] signed a MoU with the Government of Orissa on 7th of June 2003 to set up a large scale Alumina refinery in the tribal block of Langigarh. As per the MoU, the VAL is setting up a one million tonnes per annum alumina refinery along with associated 75 MW Captive Power Plant and three million tonnes per annum bauxite mining facilities at Lanjigarh in the district with an approximate investment of Rs.4000/-crore. The company requires 723.343 ha of land for its refinery and another 721.323 ha of land for the bauxite mining on top of the Niyamgiri Hill which is categorized as Reserved Forest Area. This industrial project has raised many issues in terms of its impact on environment, tribal lives and livelihoods.

Issues of Environment

The VAL industrial project first raises the issue of environment. The Niyamagiri hill and its surrounding areas are ecologically sensitive, where eight distinct types of plants are found in different seasons, and *Terminalia tomentosa* and *Shorea robusta* are among the most dominant species. It is also home to many other species i.e. Dhaura (*Anogeisses*), Jamun (*Eugenia jambolana*), Tangan (*Xylia xylocarpa*), Kasi (*Bridelia*), Bandhana (*Ougeinia dalbergioides*), Sisu (*Dalbergia latifolia*), Bija (*Pterocarpus marsupium*), Kuruma (*Adina cordifolia*), Gambhari (*Gmelina arborea*), Kusum (*Schleichra trijuga*), Mohua (*Bassia latifolia*), Kendu (*Diospyros melanxylon*), Amla (*Phyllonthus emblica*), Harida *(Terminalia chebula)*, Karda (*Claistanthus colinus*), Bel (*Aegle marmelos*), Champa (*Michelia champaca*), Dhaura (*Anogeissus latifolia*), Amba (*Mangifera indica*), Arjun (*Terminalia arjun*) and Karanj (*Pongamia pinnata*).

The Niyamgiri hill is also source to many perennial streams—Tel, Naga-bali and the Bansadhara River which is the main source of drinking water and irrigation in the area. The working plan of the Kalahandi Forest Division has proposed the Niyamagiri areas as a wildlife sanctuary and the State Wildlife organisation has proposed to declare this area as the South Orissa Elephant Reserve (as mentioned in the vide–memo no. 4643/3WL(Cons) 34/ 04 dated 20.08.2004 and cited in EPG, 2007: 8). By looking at the biodiversity in Langigarh area in general and ecological importance in Niyamgiri hill in particular, the Central Empowered Committee (CEC) of the Supreme Court Report (2005) has recommended that the use of the forest land in an ecologically sensitive area like the Niyamgiri Hills should not be permitted. The CEC further observes that the area is rich in wildlife, has dense forest cover and has been proposed to be notified as a Wildlife Sanctuary in the Working Plan of the area duly approved by the MoEF under the Forest Conservation Act, 1980. It again mentions that mining is proposed on Niyamgiri Hill "*which is an important wildlife habitat, part of elephant corridor, a proposed wildlife sanctuary, having dense and virgin forest, residence of an endangered Dongaria Kandha tribe and source of many rivers/rivulets.*"[23] The Langigarh areas and surroundings were once a place of natural beauty which was destroyed by the VAL.

The proposed bauxite mining of the Niyamgiri hill by the VAL would destroy the area's biodiversity and also have a negative impact on local water resources. As Aluminum refineries are water intensive industries, which require gallons of water to clean bauxite, this could compound water scarcity in the area, affecting irrigation and drinking water supplies. In this way, the VAL project will not only destroy the flora and fauna of region but also the lives and livelihoods of many primitive tribals groups in the area (EPG, 2007).

Tribal Lives and Livelihoods

The impact of the VAL project goes beyond the biodiversity argument of conservationists and environmentalists and the livelihood argument of economists. The *Niyamgiri* (Law Mountain) is known as a sacred hill for a primitive tribal group like Dongria Kondhs who consider it as Niyama Raja (king of law). The Dongaria Kondhs believe themselves to be the descendants of Niyama Raja and the land in the forest areas of Niyamgiri is given to them by the Niyama Raja. They feel that being the descendants of Niyama Raja, it is not dignified to work as a wage labourers. They consider wage labour as derogatory to their culture and thus do not work for outsiders. However, they do work for fellow community members for a minimal wage or with an exchange of labour where there is no employee and employer relationship. The cultivation of Niyamagiri hill slope is the inalienable right of Dongaria

Kondhs and very central to their identity. One can be only called a Dongaria Kondh by virtue of cultivating *Dongar* (hill slope land) since each plot of *Dongar* is haunted by an ancestral spirit that helps provide bumper crops. The Dongaria Kondhs consider hill plots (haru), roof of the house (temberi) and fruit orchards immovable property and one must possess them anywhere in the Niyamgiri hills to lay claim to being a Dongria (Daspattnaik, 1984: 39). The Dongaria Kondhas economy and its major sources of livelihood are directly related to Niyamgiri hill and its adjacent forest areas. Nearly 40 to 50% of their annual income is derived from selling forest products like pineapples, Siali leaves, Myrobalans and Amla etc. They grow fruit crops like pineapple under the thick forests (EPG, 2007). The Dongaria Kondhs have not been known for hunting at any point in their history. Cultivation of hill slops and collecting fruits and other forest products are central to their livelihood.

The proposed opencast mining area of the VAL falls on the top of Niyamgiri hills close to the Khambesi village. This is one of the most sacred places for Dongaria Kondhas; "from the vantage point of this elevated location, it is easy for their highest regarded god 'Niyama Penu' to observe their activities and protect them from all odds. Hence hunting, cutting and felling of trees, slashing and etc., on Niyamraja range continues to be a taboo, owing to long standing belief in his sovereignty and omnipresence...thus Niyamgiri hill holds the highest rank owing not only to its physical characteristics but also on account of the religious lore associated with it (Jena et al. 2002:319). In this way, Niyamgiri is not only central to the lives, livelihood and economy but also to the social, spiritual and cultural lives of primitive tribal groups[24] in the area.

The post-economic reform period has accelerated the process of interaction between the tribal communities in Kalahandi and multinational capital led mining based industrialisation[25] and different institutions of state, government and non governmental agencies involved. In such a context, it is important for development planners to locate different factors that influence the extent to which indigenous interests can achieve benefits from such interactions. The first is the bargaining power available to them and associated, for example, with land ownership. The second is the political power to enforce control over decision making. The third is the ability of tribal communities to both mobilise such leverage and extend it. The experience shows that the tribal communities are far from the above three factors to achieve benefits from the present industrialisation process in the Kalahandi district. The above three factors can be discussed in detail which can reflect how tribals are vulnerable to present industrialisation.

The first factor depends on the legal inheritance of land ownership and control over natural resources. But most of the time tribals are not conscious of legal land ownership and do not have the legal documents to prove that they are the owners of the land. During my field work when I asked a group of tribal people why they did not have any legal land document they replied to me in a single voice, "The land does not belong to us, we belong to the land". This single statement reveals the relationship between land and tribal people. They never consider land as a form of private property, so community owns the land. Again they said that "it takes a long time and we do not have the money to bribe revenue department officials who will prepare legal documents of land ownership for us". The official complexity and bureaucratic method of land administration in Orissa, which takes a long time to prepare land ownership documents, along with tribal illiteracy and corruption, makes the issue of legality a major problem for tribals.

The realisation of political power to enforce controls over decision making is far from the tribals. Though there are provisions under the Indian constitution and under the three tier administrative structure of Orissa to realise and enforce political power to exercise controls over land and other natural resources, the politics in tribal areas are based on caste and the distribution of money or alcohol. Most tribal leaders are controlled by businessmen and coastal elites and do not have any say in the decision making. Most of the time, they remain either silent or follow whatever they are asked to say. Most of their interest is in making money and not looking after the interests of their fellow tribals. During the tribal masses, communities are often mobilised based on their caste affiliations rather than on development politics. So, there is no space for the third factor to work effectively to obtain benefit from the industrialisation.

The displacement of tribals from their own land and the disintegration of their culture through industrialisation creates consciousness amongst tribals and brings development politics back to the agenda. This consciousness has led to many tribal resistance movements, opposing industrialisation and displacement, for rehabilitation and resettlement and a secure livelihood. The industrialisation of Kalahandi with the opening of the Vedanta Alumina Ltd. at Langigarh is quite fresh in the narratives of tribal people of the area. Many people narrate their experience in the following words:

> "First, we heard that Sarkar (government) is going to open the Vedanta factory in our area i.e. Langigarh. Secondly, we heard that we will get jobs in the company (Vedanta) and our area will get more facilities from water to electricity, schools for children and health for all; collector sahib (district collector) and sarakari babus (government officials) came and convinced us. But during that time, we never thought that we would be asked to leave our vitamati (birth place/land) for this. We never thought that our Niyama raja would be destroyed by the Vedanta. Where do we get our fruits, firewood and food? Where do we get water if the Niyamagiri is destroyed? Where would we pray and where would our Niyama raja live if the Vedanta conducts mining in the Niyamagiri hill? Eventually Vedanta came, the construction of industry started

and we started to see the impact of such a company on our daily life, liveli-hood and environment. We do not feel the same any more in our own land. Many outsiders are around; we do not get any jobs in the Vedanta as promised. We lost our land, forest and culture together (Anonymous, 12/02/2005)".

These words and feelings can be substantiated while looking at the reha-bilitation and resettlement colony called Vedanta Nagar constructed by the VAL for the instantly displaced tribals. The houses in the rehabilitation colo-ny look like urban slums. The childcare centre, community hall and health-care centre constructed by the VAL for 108 tribal families is nothing but a mockery of the childcare, health and community leisure. These houses for the childcare centre, community hall and healthcare centre are just one or two room buildings that are rarely opened. They are defunct before use, and symbolise the denial of health, community leisure and childcare to the tribals in the area. The rehabilitation colony has taken away the freedom of the tribals in terms of their physical movement, the cosmological territory of forests and the bigger meanings attached to leisure–time beyond that which is institutionalised in a community hall.

In this way, the post-economic reform industrialisation process in Kala-handi not only indicates the establishment of large scale mining based indus-tries of mass production for other industrial requirements. The culture of such mass production does not directly create a mass consumption society as the industry does not produce anything that the tribals or the general people in the area need for their direct consumption requirements. But the growth of the market associated with the industrialisation creates a consumer society based on desire. The tribals work as unskilled industrial labourers in the industry like Vedanta and the wages they get from their day long work directly goes to the market as they are no longer producing food for their consumption. They have to depend on the market for food. In this way industrialisation has not only changed the landscape of production for direct consumer requirements but also helped to direct industrial wages towards the market. Desire based consumer society has created a consumer culture that underpins the growth of the market. The growth of the market creates new social and economic processes based on economic exchange which leads to the commodification of social relationships among the tribals and their com-munities. The dynamic social and economic life of the tribals comes to an end with the growth of a culture often associated with industrialisation which is automated, repetitive and spiritually alienating for the tribals from their environment and nature of their production as well.

TRANSPORT, COMMUNICATION AND NATURAL RESOURCE EXTRACTION

The development of road, communication and transportation systems during the post-economic reform period are selective and focused on tribal areas which are the maps of abundant natural and mineral resources. There has been massive construction of road and other modern communication systems to the Langigarh and Thuamul Rampur blocks of Kalahandi district. Langigarh and Thuamul Rampur are home to many primitive tribal groups, medicinal plants, rivers and tributaries. The Langigarh block is also known for its Niyamagiri Hill which is the storehouse of bauxites where as the Thuamul block is known for its rich mine stones and bauxite deposits. Thus, the two blocks are under the eye of metal and mining multinational companies. The Vedanta Alumina Company has already set up its Alumina plant in the block even after huge opposition to it from civil society groups, NGOs, political parties, tribals, environmental groups, intellectuals, activists and judiciary. In order to accelerate the process of natural and mineral expropriation from these two tribal areas, funding of road and transport in the tribal areas of the district increased 98% during the post-economic reform period of 1991–2005 in comparison to the pre-reform period of 1980–1991. Besides funds flowing to develop road and communication systems in the tribal areas during the post-economic reform period, the Integrated Tribal Development Agency (ITDA), Kalahandi has diverted funds of Rs.149, 20468 from the different tribal development programmes for the construction of road and communication systems in two tribal blocks during 2004–2005[26]. However, 152 villages out of total 294 tribal villages in Thuamul Rampur and 38 villages out of total 471 total tribal villages in Langigarh block are yet to be connected by road and transport systems. These villages remain inaccessible today, despite mass construction of roads and improvement in communication systems in the district (Nayak, 2009)[27]. These 190 villages in two tribal villages are still inaccessible due to the fact that these areas do not fall under the mining and other natural resource map for instant extraction.

Thus, the massive investment in the construction of road, transportation system and communication in Kalahandi district is neither facilitating positive change in the standard of life of tribals in terms of communication, nor their economic development. Rather it increases the connectivity to different mining areas of the district. It also promotes market unification by bringing various tribal *haats* (weekly local market in the tribal areas of Kalahandi) together with the mainstream market in the district. It has facilitated the faster movement of people and goods which has extended the market and its integration[28] with the local market. The speedy integration of the market by modern roads and transportation system reduced the time which made time as money. The person who can use his/her time more meaningfully can develop. The tribals in Kalahandi do not know how to use time as they do not have the capacity and avenues to access, use the infrastructure or institutions which can made them enable to use time productively. Each new method and mode of transportation and communication system destroys the rents of its predecessor, but in time raises prices so high in its own rent seeking that it undermines its long run welfare activities by encouraging competitive new entry (Girard, 1965: 212–73). The tribals were conscious about the tribal *haats* which are informative in terms of price of goods, its supply and demand in the district. However, market integration, growth of road, communication and transportation has led to the growth of a market in which tribals are not conscious of factors such as price, availability of goods as per their need, and its demand and supply logic as opposed to their traditional weekly market based system. Now tribals do not know the price, availability or origin of goods. In this way the new market is less informative to tribals and makes them prone to being victims of market exploitation. Thus, the development of road, transport and modern communication systems serves the purpose of tribal development less while helping to spread the idea of time-value and competitive spirit to mobilise rent. This reflects the rent seeking behaviour of the state at the cost of tribal welfare programmes. The process enhances further dismantling of tribal communitarian culture and making tribals more vulnerable to the open market and its ideology of consumerism. Further, the industry and mining-led growth in road, transport and communication has also caused tribal displacement and land alienation in the tribal areas of the district.

LAND ALIENATION AND DISPLACEMENT

The relationship between land and tribals is documented in various studies. The UN (2001) study on indigenous land rights, for instance, found that " (i) a profound relationship exists between indigenous peoples and their lands, territories and resources; (ii) this relationship has various social, cultural, spiritual, economic and political dimensions and responsibilities; (iii) the collective dimension of this relationship is significant; and (iv) the intergenerational aspect of such a relationship is also crucial to indigenous peoples' identity, survival and cultural viability. There may be additional elements relating to indigenous peoples and their relationship to their lands, territories and resources which have not been captured by these examples"[29]. There is an intrinsic relationship between land and the tribal population in the district which is central to the economic, social and cultural existence of tribals in Kalahandi. A recent study, conducted by the Planning Commission of India (2004: 208), reveals that 89 percent of poor tribals are landless, which constitutes 25 percent of the population in the district. This indicates that more than

50 percent of tribals are landless and there is a link between poverty and landlessness among tribals. Thus, any attempt to displace tribals from their land is suicidal for tribal lives, livelihood, society and culture in the district. Thus, special legal measures were ascribed in the Constitution of India which directs the national and the state governments to ensure tribal rights over land and other natural resources[30].

However, displacement of tribals from their land and the problems of tribal land alienation[31] in Kalahandi go back to the history of state formation in the district[32]. The ruling and non ruling elites in the tribal areas i.e. the local chiefs and rajahs, who were earlier dependent on tribal goodwill and compliance for the legitimacy of their rule, were able to shift their dependency to colonial rulers and their military force and became the rent extracting agents of British rulers in tribal areas (Padel, 1995). Similarly, during the post-colonial state formation in Kalahandi and after its annexation with the state of Orissa, the tribal and non-tribal elites shifted their allegiance to the costal Orissa elites and have remained as rent seeking elites within the district with the help of the state power. The shift of such allegiances helped the influx of non-tribals who were helping local elites for different profit seeking activities including land occupation. Such a process faced stiff resistance from the people of Kalahandi, which was suppressed by the state power both during the colonial and post-colonial period (Senapati and Kuanr, 1980, Padel, 1995). Historically, this shift of alliance and influx of non-tribals to tribal areas has a strong correlation and formed the basis of land alienation in the district (Pati, 1993).

In order to understand the problem of land alienation during economic reforms, it is significant to understand the land ownership and distribution pattern in the district. This was well documented in the *Final Report of the Land Revenue Settlement in Kalahandi District 1946–56,* the first land document compiled by J .Das, the Settlement Officer of the Kalahandi district. According to the report; "good lands and most of the villages are held by Brahmins and Kulthas[33]. The Kulthas predominate in the North–east areas and Brahmins in the South-west areas of the district. They are good agriculturists and are reported to have been brought from Sambalpur side during the time of the Raja Udit Pratap Deo near about the year 1867 (who married a daughter of the Raja of Sambalpur[34]). They have excavated big tanks and improved the land considerably. The Kulthas and Brahmin Gountias are well to-do persons of the locality and have erected good pucca buildings in their villages and own fertile land but the condition of the tenants under them is generally poor who live from hand to mouth and are in debt. Besides having larger areas of land under them, they also do money and paddy lending business. The uprising of Kandhas in Kalahandi in 1882 was due to their discontent at being ousted from their land by the Kulthas, a large number of whom were slaughtered and besieged in the uprising. The oppression of the tenants by Kulthas and Brahmin Gountias was a common feature in Kalahandi (Das, 1962: 3)." The report has clearly reflected how tribals were being dominated as tenants in their own land whereas ownership remained in the hands of the higher caste Brahmin giving them a higher class position in the social life of the Kalahandi.

After more than five decades of merger of the district with the province of Orissa and with the post-colonial Indian state, the condition of tribal tenants and the land ownership pattern has not changed. The landlessness in tribals is very high which was documented in a study conducted by the *Tribal and Harijan Research and Training Institute (THRTI)* during 1978–80 in all tribal areas. The data from the study showed 22.84% of tribal households to be landless whereas 40.46% owned less than 2.5 acres each (THRTI, 1987). The process of land alienation is the product of a dual domination (money lenders and higher caste Brahmin Gountia landlords) over the tribals and over their land, and continues today, as identified from the land holding and operational pattern in the district.

The operational pattern of land in the district was highly centralised between 1971 and 2001. The percentage of marginal farmers owning less than one hectare of land increased over the years from 17.40 percent in 1971 to 39.94 in 1991 and increased further to 43.2 percent during 2001. But the average land area operated by the marginal farmers declined from 0.63 percent in 1971 to 0.43 percent in 2001. Such marginalisation took place during the economic reform period which was 0.20 percent higher than the pre-reform period. Similar trends can be found among the farmers owning one hectare to ten hectares of land in the district. In the case of big land owners who owned ten hectares of land to more than ten hectares of land, their percentage increased to 1.02 percent in 2001. Similarly, the average land area operated by big farmers increased marginally during the post-economic reform period (Nayak, 2009)[35]. The operational land holding pattern indicates that there was a concentration of land in the hands of a few big land owners and landlordism continued to exist in the district. The data also reveals that there was a growth in land ownership among households who owned less than one hectare or between one hectare and five hectares of land. Most of the tribals do not have legal land ownership documents, so it was difficult to calculate the number of land ownership pattern and alienation of land among tribals in the district. But most of the tribals fall into the category of marginal farmers who are the worst victims of land alienation processes during the post-economic reform period.

However, the concentration and consolidation of landholding in terms of ownership indicates that the land reform policy is either a failure or less effective or has not been implemented properly both in terms of ceiling on land holding and on the consolidation of landholding. The land ownership and distribution pattern in the district is creating a class polarisation among the people of the district by creating a structure where few people own a vast array of land, making many either landless or small farmers. Nayak (2009) reveals that small landholders-operated land areas are comparatively less than the people owning higher landholding because of the fact that small land landholding size is less productive. This has forced small farmers or land-owner tribals to either sell their land or leave the land uncultivated which creates landlessness again. Bhaduri (1983) calls it the 'forced commercialisa-tion of land' which has led to the indebtedness of poor farmers in the district. This forced commercialisation of land has not only created a situation of landlessness but also has led to a condition of depeasantisation and poverty which establishes a link between land, poverty and depeasantisation. This linkage helps to understand the exploitation in the rural agrarian societies (Basu; 1990, Bardhan; 1989). The situation is gloomy in case of tribals as they do not have the legal documents of their land ownership and even they do not know about the legal ownership of land. It can be better understood from the following interviews which I had during my fieldwork in the dis-trict.

Do you have any land? How many acres of land you and your family have own? Do you have any legal documents of the land you cultivate? I asked these questions to a tribal couple in the Perumanji village of Thuamul Ram-pur block. Both husband and wife took me to the backyard of their house, showed me a huge area of plain and hilly tracts of land with less dense forest and told me that "our land starts from here till you can see but we do not know what a legal land document is. We do not have that document. We have been cultivating this land for generations together" (Interviewed on date 13/03/05). I asked the same questions to a tribal who was cultivating 'Don-gar' in the near by village of the Biswanathpur (the block headquarter of the Langigarh block). He replied that "all these areas are mine but I am unable to cultivate all the land as I do not require much. I can manage by cultivating a small plot of land here" (Interview date 29/04/05). During my interaction, I found out that he neither knew about legal ownership of land nor about the amount of land he owned. I asked the same questions in many other parts of the district but the answer was always the same. In the tribal areas of Thua-mul Rampur and Langigarh, the landlessness among the tribals is higher than the other parts of the district. More than 77 percent of tribals in Thuamul Rampur and 78 percent of tribals in Langigarh block do not have legal land documents to assert their legal right over land. Only 7 percent of tribals in Thuamul Rampur and 12 percent in Langigarh have legal land ownership documents leaving 11 and 15 percent tribal landless in the respective areas. In case of the district as a whole 53 percent tribals have legal land docu-ments, 39 percent tribals do not have legal land documents and 8 percent of tribals are landless in the district (Nayak, 2009)[36].

However, the displacement and land alienation of tribals in the district has taken a new turn during the post-reform period which has pushed the district towards reckless mining based industrialisation. In the entire tribal areas of the district, the tribal block of Langigarh at the centre of mining based industrialisation led by Sterlite and Vedanta Resources' which is setting up the Vedanta Alumina Ltd in an area of 85 percent reserved forest area. The project has displaced and caused land alienation among the most primitive tribal groups (PTGs) i.e. Dongria Kondhs and Kutia Kondhs in the block. There are nearly 108 tribal families including PTGs that have already been ousted and 360 more are in danger of losing their lands. More than 90 villages in and around Niyamgiri hill are facing the danger of industrial displacement and most of them are tribals. It is difficult for Dongria and Kutia Kondhs to claim rehabilitation and resettlement package from the Government of Orissa as they do not have legal land documents. Traditionally these two tribal groups have resided in the Niyamgiri hills and possessed land of their own, and passed it on to their descendants, which has been overlooked by different land settlement and land ownership surveys conducted by the different governments in Orissa (Daspattnaik, 1984: 26). It has had a colossal impact on tribals of Langigarh, which is at the centre of industrial and mining led displacement causing land alienation among tribals. The rehabilitation package provided by the Vedanta Aluminum Ltd and the Government of Orissa to the displaced tribal families of Langigarh has been very minimal. The rehabilitation colony called the *Vedanta Nagar* at Langigarh has 105 houses where 104 tribal families live. However, the colony has taken away the cosmological environment and freedom of the tribals. A tribal female resident in the rehabilitation colony says that "in the name of development and rehabilitation, they have given us this house where we are unable to sleep and breathe as there is no proper ventilation in the house. They have provided us with childcare and a health centre, but they have taken away our *Niyama Raja* (god of law), forest, ancestral land, forests...fruits, flowers, and trees. I do not feel like I belong to this place anymore. I am forced to stay here as there is no other option for me (Anonymous, Interview date; 30/04/05). The same feeling was expressed by many tribal residents of the rehabilitation colony.

However, industry and mining-led displacement land alienation has caused enough damage to the life and livelihood of the tribals in Langigarh area. The land used for agriculture and the forest used for collecting different forest products is no longer available to the tribals to sustain their livelihood, making them vulnerable to unemployment and destitution.

EMPLOYMENT, UNEMPLOYMENT AND MIGRATION IN THE DISTRICT

The workforce in the district has 5–6 lakh people composed of the age group of 15 to 40 in a total population of over 13 lakhs. This indicates that nearly 50 percent of the population is available for employment to contribute in different sectors of economy in the district (Nayak, 2009)[37]. The availability of the workforce in all age groups indicates a lower number of dependent people in the district, other than the aged and children. Nayak (2009) reveals that even the aged and children are involved and constitute a part of the district's work force. The categorisation of the workforce in the district reveals that most of the marginal workers are tribals seeking employment. There are 22682 marginal workers seeking instant employment in rural areas of the district whereas only 111 marginal workers looking for employment in the urban areas of district. This data also reveals the rural and urban divide in the composition of workforce in the district as the majority of marginal workers belong to rural tribal areas of the district, whereas only less than 0.1 percent marginal workers are seeking employment in the urban areas of the district (Nayak, 2009). The main workers are involved in agricultural activities or employed in different government and private offices in the district. And the marginal workers are composed of landless agricultural workers to domestic servants. The classification of labour in Kalahandi reveals that 12.29 percent workers are small farmers, 15.03 percent workers are marginal farmers, 26.03 percent are agricultural labourers, 1.13 percent are rural artisans and 62 percent are BPL families (Nayak, 2009).

Amongst all these categories, tribal population constitutes 78 percent in the district. This indicates that tribals constitute a higher percentage of the workforce in Kalahandi[38]. However, the Government of Orissa claims that there has been a 3283 percent growth of the mining area in the Kalahandi district as a result of which the mining-led industrialisation increased employment by 200 percent in Kalahandi during the reform period. By taking the ratio of mining area and employment into consideration, it can be said that only 1.6 workers were employed for every one hectare of mined area in the district. (Khatua & Stanley, 2006: 142). The entire mining-led industrial growth has taken place in the tribal block of Langigarh, but most of the tribals are unemployed—which constitutes of 95 percent of the population in the area. The tribal unemployment ratio in the Langigarh block is gloomy while comparing it with the employment situation of tribals in the entire district.

Further, the data available from the *District Employment Office and District Statistical Office* at Bhawanipatna reveals that out of 21 percent of tribals registered in the district employment office for employment, only 12 percent of tribals got employment during 1980 to 1990. During the post-economic reform period of 1995–2005, the number of registered tribals increased to 32 percent but employment declined to 3 percent. A similar trend could be found among the non-tribals as well. But in case of non-tribal population, registrations in the district employment office increased 10 percent although there was a 21 percent decline in the number of people getting employment. In the district as a whole, there was a rise of unemployment as more and more people registered themselves but less people found a job (Nayak, 2009)[39]. This indicates that there was a general declining trend of employment scenario and a growth of unemployment in the district during the period of economic reforms.

An impact assessment study on the rural development programmes in Kalahandi district from 1998–2001 was conducted by Sen et al. (2002a), claiming that 93% of beneficiaries under different employment schemes i.e. JGSY and EAS found adequate funds, 84.5% under SGSY and 82.4% under IAY beneficiaries confirmed the adequacy of funds. As a result of which the average unemployment level per year per household declined by 3.9% in the district in total. Moreover, the study reveals that none of the sample villagers were found to be fully aware of all aspects of the various employment generating rural development programmes in the district. Agriculture provides the highest employment in the district but its mechanisation and the changing focus of government from agriculture led to the increase in the number of unemployed people in the district. There was nearly a 50 percent decline in agriculture based income generating activities among the tribals during 1991–2005. Government investment in agriculture based income generating activities has declined from Rs. 7167466 in 1980–91 to Rs. 3871016 in 1991–2005 (Nayak, 2009).

Further, the ban on recruitment by the Government of Orissa during the post-economic reform period completely closed the door for tribals' recruitment to various vacant posts reserved for tribals as part of the affirmative policy of the government, as per the directives of the Indian Constitution. So, employment of tribals in the government sector has become virtually nil. There are few private players in the district where affirmative policy of job reservation for tribals is not applicable. The industries like rice mills or VAL do not employ tribals as they do not have skills to work in those places although sometimes the tribals work as manual labourers. This process of labour demand in the district creates seasonal and shadow employment for tribals but, in effect, tribals are unemployed.

In this way, there has been a massive growth of unemployment in the district due to the changing patterns of agriculture, displacement for industrialisation and mining and land alienation which has led to migration of tribals in search of livelihood and a place for habitation. During the pre-reform period (1980–1990) tribal migration from rural areas to urban areas of the district was confined to 9 percent, which increased to 21 percent during the post-economic reform period. Similarly the migration of tribals to outside the district increased from 5 percent to 12 percent. In the case of non-tribals, and the district as a whole, migration also increased during the reform period (Nayak, 2009)[40]. The inner district migration has taken place from rural tribal areas to the urban centres like Bhawanipatna, Kesinga and Dharamgarh, whereas inner district migration has taken place to Orissa's urban areas, like Bhubaneswar, Cuttack, Berhampur and Sambalpur. The outside destinations for tribal migration from the district are to the city of Raipur in the neighboring state of Chhattisgarh and to the city of Vijayanagaram and Visakhapatnam in the state of Andhra Pradesh.

The migration of tribals breaks down the territorial segregation imposed on them for a long time by living in the hilly terrains and interior forests. But when the whole family migrates from their own natural habitat and its jurisdictions, to a farm, factory, town, which is non-tribal to its core, the tribal communitarian culture is shattered, and their traditional lifestyle along with their livelihood falls into a system of decay and caused cultural disintegration. Thus I consider migration of tribals as a process of de-tribalisation that puts tribals under double danger i.e. loss of livelihood and cultural disintegration. The migration of tribals to urban areas not only causes cultural disintegration but also results in the weakening of their claim over natural resources and land[41]. The majority of people migrating from the district are poor and landless tribal labourers who are unemployed (Planning Commission, 2004: 216). Thus, it is clear that there is a link between landlessness, poverty and migration among the tribals in the district, which increased over the years of reform period.

POVERTY IN KALAHANDI AFTER THE NEW ECONOMIC REFORMS

The debate on Kalahandi's poverty continues to echo in different rural and tribal development plans but the question remains: why does poverty exists among tribals in an area of high biodiversity like Kalahandi. Gupta (1991) tries to answer the question by blaming the nature of production (mono crop) and fallacies in technology use. His work tries to argue that the changing nature of production has given rise to the markets for mass consumption of external manufactured products. Such transformation in the production regime in the tribal areas has reinforced poverty and the capitalist state has sustained it in an area of biodiversity. However, the history of poverty in the district in general, and amongst tribals in particular, dates back to the very basis of state formation in Kalahandi during the colonial and post-colonial period. A different survey report by the Government of Orissa, Kalahandi states the district is the fourth largest home to the poor people in the state.

More than 87 percent people in the district are poor (Samal, 1996). Further, a recent study reveals that 25 percent of people are landless and the majority of them constitute tribals and 89 percent of landless tribal people live in abject poverty in the district (Planning Commission, 2004: 208). This indicates links between landlessness and poverty in the district in general and tribals in particular. However, the poverty in the district during the post-colonial period can be attributed to the failure of democratic politics and state (Currie, 2000) which has led to multiple forms of exclusion and deprivation of tribals. The inaccessibility and non-availability of development infrastructure to deliver welfare to tribal communities has led to economic marginalisation and poverty.

The welfare-led tribal development policies have failed to address the predicament of tribal poverty due to the indifferent state and its myopic development policies. As a result, poverty increased in the district after the reform period. In the district, 2.42 lakh[42] families were listed as being under the below poverty line during 1992 which increased to 3.08 lakh in 1997[43]. This indicates that poverty has increased at a household level during the post-reform period. There were 85. 77 percent of non-tribals listed in the below poverty line survey during 1992, declining to 62.71 percent in 1997. It indicates that within five years of post-economic reform period from 1992–1997, poverty declined amongst the non-tribal population in the district at the rate of 23.06 percent.

The impact of economic reforms on the reduction of poverty among tribals is minimal in comparison to non-tribals in the district. For example, 87.05 percent of tribals in Langigarh were below the poverty line during 1992 and declined to 80.23 percent in 1997. Similarly, there were 93. 09 percent of tribals in Thuamul Rampur block under below poverty line in 1992, declining to 88.76 percent in 1997. This indicates that both in Langigarh and Thuamul Rampur block poverty declined at the rate of 6.82 percent and 4.33 percent respectively (Nayak, 2009)[44]. This gives a dismal picture of the impact of new economic reforms on the poverty of tribals in the district.

A research (through unstructured and random sample surveys) conducted on the economic condition of tribals in the district during January to March 2005 in the two tribal blocks, provides a different picture of poverty among tribals in Kalahandi district. More than 230 samples were collected from different villages of Thuamul Rampur and Langigarh block in which tribals were interviewed about their economic conditions, looking at life issues. The sample is proportionally classified by taking different parts of the block into consideration and the percentage is calculated by taking 158 complete household samples. The survey revealed that only one percent of tribals lived a middle class life, upper class tribal population was non-existent, whereas 57 percent of tribals were very poor, with a per capita monthly income of below Rs. 300, and 30 percent of tribals were poor in the Thuamul Rampur block.

In Langigarh block, 53 percent of tribals were very poor, 43 percent tribals were poor, 9 percent of tribals lived a lower class life and only 4 percent of tribals belonged to the middle class. Upper class tribals were non-existent in the block. The analysis of per capital monthly expenditure revealed that most of the tribal people in Langigarh and Thuamul Rampur block spent less than 4 GBP in a month. The majority of tribal populations in both the blocks were composed of unskilled, agricultural and landless workers and the percentage of skilled and semi-skilled workers was quite low. More than 77 percent of tribals in Thuamul Rampur lived in their forest huts and only 8 percent tribals had houses with two to three bedrooms, and a similar trend was visible in the Langigarh block with an increasing number of homeless tribals which consti- tuted 11 percent of the tribal population. However, tribals in both the blocks did not desire a very luxurious life. The research survey revealed that 67 percent of tribals in the Thuamul Rampur areas desired to earn a monthly income of twenty dollars, only 18 percent wanted to earn more than twenty dollars, whereas only 11 percent wanted to earn more than 100 dollars and no one wanted to earn more than 200 dollars in a month. A similar trend can be found in Langigarh block while looking at the desired monthly income of tribals in the area (Nayak, 2009)[45]. This indicates that the incidence of pover- ty is higher in the tribal areas of the district but the tribals have limited desire in terms of their income and economic necessity. Nevertheless, most of the poverty eradication programmes have failed to address even the minimal desires of tribals in terms of their economic necessity.

However, an impact assessment study on the rural development pro- grammes in Kalahandi district from 1998–2001, conducted by Sen et al. (2002a), claimed that the average household income increased from Rs.10210 to Rs.12,791, implying an increase of 25.3%. It was also found that 14.6% of the sample households in the aggregate had crossed the poverty line in the district. It also claimed that there had been some improvement in the living status of the village population in the district indicating the improved condition of tribal lives. This study was conducted to monitor rural develop- ment programmes by the Ministry of Rural Development, Government of India.

Thus, both the government of India and the Government of Orissa, while claiming the positive impact of economic reforms on the reduction of pover- ty among the tribals in Kalahandi, have been unable to provide the causes of poverty reduction among the tribals in the district. The Government of Orissa and the Kalahandi district administration has yet to provide a detailed analy- sis of why poverty has declined faster among the non-tribals than the tribals in the district. The recent study by World Bank (2008) claimed that the geographical seclusion has significantly affected the tribals to access new opportunities generated by the reform programmes, meaning a minimal de- cline of poverty amongst the tribals in the district. But the World Bank

(2008) analysis lacks a coherent understanding of poverty amongst tribals and does not provide any alternative for poverty eradication among tribals through geographical inclusion. Rather the study is unable to acknowledge the geographical seclusion has increased during the post-economic reform period in terms of declining base of local and rural development institutions. Such processes have enlarged poverty due to the failure of anti-poverty and other development programmes to eradicate poverty among tribals. This is also supported by the findings of impact assessment studies, conducted in Kalahandi on rural development programmes, which reveal the institutional deficiencies in the implementation of anti–poverty programmes. The study goes further to locate other lacunas, i.e: lack of awareness about the programme, lack of participation in the decision making process and ineffective institutional infrastructure for the failure of poverty eradication programmes in the district (Sen et al. 2002a, 2002b; Shylendra and Bhirdikar, 2005). The following sections analyse the way that local and rural development institutions, which were meant for inclusive development and poverty eradication, were ruined during the period of economic reforms. The collapse of local tribal development institutions has led to a condition of sustained poverty and underdevelopment among tribals in Kalahandi district.

THE CONDITION OF LOCAL AND TRIBAL DEVELOPMENT INSTITUTIONS IN THE DISTRICT DURING POST-ECONOMIC REFORMS

The downsizing of government-led development infrastructure was part of a policy package of reforms as it was considered to be inefficient to deliver welfare to the people as desired. Thus, the downsizing of development institutions became an imperative to follow as per the norms of the reform programmes and its successful implementation from state level to district and local level. As a result, the local development institution i.e Block Development Offices (BDOs)[46] which plays a vital role in the implementation of all development policies at a local level, including tribal development, had to be downsized for efficiency. Thus, the development institutions in the Kalahandi started declining after the implementation of the new economic reforms (Nayak, 2009). The total BDO staff strength in the district was 426 during 1980–85 which increased to 458 during 1985–90. The declining trend of staff strength of BDOs in the district started after the implementation of the reform programmes, as a result of which, the number of staff in the BDOs declined to 450 during 1990–95, 438 in 1995–2000 and further to 428 during 2000–2005 (Nayak, 2009)[47]. A comparative analysis of the local development institutions in terms of staff strength in the Kalahandi district shows that there was a strong existence of the local development institutions during

the pre-reform period, whereas it declined on a large scale after the implementation of the new economic reforms. A sense of this decline is outlined in
Nayak (2009). The two decades of data analysis from 1980 to 2005 reveals
that there was a growth of local development institutions during the pre-
reform period of 1980 to 1990. The post-reform period of 1995–2005 shows
a decline as a result of the new economic policies which were intended to
dismantle the local development institutions. It paved the way for the neo-
liberals to blame the government and lack of institutional efficiency (Nayak,
2009).

    In order to establish the idea that privatisation is the only best alternative
for development, the neo-liberal policy makers and ruling class, both at national and state level, provided massive funds to the local development institutions for tribal development in Kalahandi after the implementation of the
new economic reforms. During 1979–80 total funds flow, by taking all tribal
development schemes into account, was Rs. 20, 9900, which was increased
to Rs. 91, 07118 in 1988–89. It declined on a massive scale during the
beginning of the new economic reforms and the declining trend continued
until 1994–95. During 1990–91, the funds flow for tribal development in the
district was Rs.28, 11328 which declined to Rs. 21, 89584 in 1991–92. But
from 1992–93, funds flow for tribal development in the district showed an
upward trend and reached its peak during 1999–2000, when the funding was
Rs. 274, 05462, increasing further to Rs. 391, 07024 in 2002–2003 (Nayak,
2009)[48]. But by the time there was a funds flow for tribal development in the
district, there was a decline in the institutional infrastructure to implement
the tribal development policies and utilize the tribal development funds.
Thus, the massive funds flow both from the Government of India and state
Governments of Orissa under different schemes for the tribal development in
the district of Kalahandi did not contribute in the process of tribal development. Nayak (2009) explains that there was a growth of funding for tribal
development in the district during the pre-reform period especially from year
1985 to 1990. But there was a decline just after the economic reforms during
1991 to 1995. This was the half decade period when the local development
institutions started declining, but there was a funds flow for the tribal development in the district when there was minimal institutional infrastructure to
utilize the funds. Thus, the funds from different projects remained unspent
and returned to the central and state government's treasury again.[49] The tribal
development funds remained unutilized and kept growing during the period
of post-economic reforms as evidenced in reviews of financial and physical
achievements under different anti-poverty schemes for tribals from 1992 to
1999. Nearly 13.5 percent of funds remained unutilized during 1992 which
increased to 28. 66 percent in 1993 and 30 to 37 percent in 1997 and further
to 33. 1 percent in 1999 in the district (Nayak, 2009)[50]. It clearly shows the

growing trend of the ineffectiveness of the local development institutions even to utilize the target expenditure.

It is ironic to note that there was massive funding and yet the funds were remaining under utilized or unutilized. Such a paradox created by the new economic policy has had a detrimental effect on tribal development by first reducing funds for tribal development which put the local tribal development institutions in the resource crunch. Then the advocates of the new economic reforms prescribed policies that capped recruitment and put bans on new employment that weakened the local development institutions in the district. When the local development institutions became weak, there was a flow of funds to project that the state and government-led development institutions were inefficient for welfare delivery. This paradox can be projected by taking the example of the Kalahandi district. Such paradoxical policy of the New Economic Reforms policy package[51] has had a detrimental effect on the development of the Kalahandi people, and the tribals in particular. After the implementation of the new economic reforms, the development institutions in the district declined on a massive scale which caused and added to the problem of underdevelopment of the district. There was a decline of staff strength in the district due to restrictions put on new recruitments to reduce public expenditure. Vacant posts caused by retirement and death remained un-filled, and many people were asked to take voluntary retirement after 1991. The process of restrictions on new employment and retrenchment policies resulted in the decline of development institutions which led to the mismanagement and consequently closing down of some sections in the local institutions, adding to the failure of development policies and creating mistrust of the masses regarding public institutions in the district. Thus, the neo-liberal policy prescriptions efficiency argument is nothing but a means to dismantle public institutional infrastructure and the Kalahandi district is an example of this process.

However, a comparative analysis of local development institutions, in terms of staff strength in the Kalahandi district, shows that there was a strong existence of local and tribal development institutions during the pre-reform period, whereas it declined on a large scale after the implementation of the new economic reforms. The comparison of staff strength in local tribal development institutions during the pre-reform and post-reform periods data[52] analysis from 1980 to 2005 (Nayak, 2009) shows that the staff strength of local development institutions was higher during the pre-reform period (1980 to 1990) and declined during the post-reform period (1995–2005). The economic policies of the post-reform period have caused damage to the BDOs in terms of strength and effectiveness to implement development policies due to the lack of personnel. They have paved the way for the neo-liberals to blame the government and its lack of institutional efficiency which is a product of their own policy. Further, the analysis on the declining trend of the local development institutions shows that the rate of decline is lower in urban and non-tribal areas, whereas higher in rural and tribal areas of the district. In this way the new economic reforms have created a tribal- non-tribal and urban-rural divide in terms of base of the local development institutions in the district (Nayak, 2009).

Tribal-Non-tribal Divides

The analysis of the declining trend of staff strength (Nayak, 2009)[53] in local development institutions (BDOs) reveals that the declining rate of local development institutions in tribal areas were higher than the local development institutions in non-tribal areas during the post-economic reform period (ibid)[54]. There were 398 local development employees working in different tribal dominated blocks in the district during 1980 to 1990 which declined to 320 during the post-reform period of 1995 to 2005. In non-tribal blocks, there used to be 492 local development staff during 1980 to 1990, declining to 425 during 1995–2005. Thus, the local development institutions declined in non-tribal areas but the rate was lower than the tribal areas of the district (ibid)[55]. The weakening of local development institutions in tribal areas through a higher rate of decline led to the failure of tribal development policies to deliver tribal welfare in the district. In this way, the new economic reforms have created a tribal-non-tribal divide in terms of infrastructure base by weakening local development institutions in tribal areas and strengthening the local development institutions in the urban and non-tribal areas of the district.

Rural–Urban Divide

There was a growth in the rural and urban divide in the district during the post-economic reform period. The infrastructure in the urban area developed rapidly during the reform periods, whereas the rural infrastructure declined in the district. As per the administrative division of district, Bhawanipatna, Kesinga, Dharamgarh, Junagarh and Jaipatna blocks can be considered urban in the regional context of the Kalahandi district. In the same way, Thuamul Rampur, Madanpur Rampur, Narla, Langigarh, Karlamunda, Kalampur, Golamunda and Koksara can be considered as rural areas of the district. The development gap, in terms of local development infrastructure, increased in urban areas while it declined in the rural areas. In urban centres, like Bhawanipatna, the local development staff strength was 86 during 1980–1990 and increased to 93 during 1995–2005. In a similar way, another major urban centre of the district is Kesinga had 95 staff in its different local development institutions during 1980–1990 which increased to 100 during 1995–2005. The urban centres like Dharamgarh also showed a rise in local development institutions and staff strength, whereas urban areas like Junagarh showed stagnancy in the growth of local development institutions. In most of the other areas of the district, the local development institution declined in terms of its staff strength. The way in which the process of economic reforms caused a rural-urban divide is argued in Nayak (2009)[56]. The Langigarh block is the only tribal block and rural area which showed a growth of local development staff during the post-reform period; there were 46 personnel during 1980 to 1990 which increased to 50 during 1995–2005 (Nayak, 2009). Thus, the Langigarh block is the only tribal dominated block where the local development infrastructure has grown during post-economic reform period with the intention of pushing through the industrialisation process of the government of Orissa. As the Langigarh block is the storehouse of Bauxite mines and the Vedanta Alumina Company is setting up a mega industry in the block, so the government employees were increased in the block to speed up the mining based industrialisation to help the Vedanta Aluminum Ltd. This indicates that the growth of local development infrastructure in the Langigarh block was not necessarily meant for welfare delivery.

However, post-reform development policies have put rural and tribal development in the district in the back seat, whereas during the pre-reform period, tribal and rural development was the prime focus of the development policy as 93% of the people live in the rural areas of the district and most of them are tribals. And local development infrastructure, available to 93 % of rural-tribal people is equivalent to the (and often more) infrastructure available to the 7% of the urban population in the district during the post-economic reform period (Nayak, 2009). It is quite clear that the economic reforms have not only created urban-rural divides but also increased and concentrated the development infrastructure within the few urban centres in the district in which few people are the beneficiaries of the development policies. The block-wise analysis of distribution of local development infrastructure reflects it more clearly in (Nayak, 2009) which also reveals that during the pre-reform period, both urban and rural areas showed a growth tendency in terms of local development infrastructure in both urban and rural blocks of the district, whereas during the post-reform period local development infrastructure has only grown in the urban blocks and declining in the tribal dominated blocks. Thus, the economic reforms have resulted in spreading and widening the disparities of local development institutions in tribal, rural and urban areas of the district. Such polarisation[57] between urban and rural areas of the district is often the source of confrontations among people and regions. Further, such polarisation of local development infrastructural base explains clearly the way in which uneven regional development has taken place under the period of economic reforms. The widening of the gap between the urban non-tribal areas and remote tribal areas in the district is reinforcing underdevelopment in the tribal areas. The segregation of areas created by the reform-led neo-liberal development policies have created a sense of segregation felt in the social and cultural lives of people and are often the root cause of hatred and violence in the Kalahandi district.

However, the urban-rural and tribal-non-tribal divide aftermath of the new economic reforms has placed the Kalahandi district in a new regime of enormous polarisation in which there is a development of marginalisation of tribal welfare which has led to the underdevelopment of tribal people and their areas in the district. Thus, underdevelopment[58] of tribals in the district is not a backward stage of development, due to geographical position or cultural traits of region and its people, but a product of the development process followed as a result of economic reforms. Such polarisation is being created along with paradoxical development policies in which massive funds flow to the region for the development of infrastructure while at the same time quick redundancies in the local development institutions occur. This has led to the failure of development policies in the district and funds remain unutilized or underutilized and then return back to the same government or donors' treasury.

Exposing the Paradox

It seems that this is a paradox of the ideas of the new economic policy. It has not only created the urban-rural and tribal-non-tribal divide, but also resulted in a complete collapse of tribal development policy in Kalahandi district. The new economic policy advocated for the reduction in the welfare activities of the state, leading institutions to reduce expenditure. At the same time it advocated the reduction in the welfare expenditures, but in reverse, there was a massive funds flow for tribal development in the Kalahandi district during the period of economic reforms which is projected in the work of Nayak (2009)[59].

The comparative analysis of funds flowing for tribal development in the Kalahandi district during the pre-economic reform and post-economic reform periods show that there was an extraordinary growth of funding for tribal development which was quite opposed to the idea of economic reforms agenda. But the funds were remaining unutilized due to lack of institutional infrastructure. During the post-reform period there was a massive decline in the infrastructure (Nayak, 2009) which was a conscious decision by the neo-liberal policy makers to defame the state-led development institutions after weakening their ability to perform. The comparison of data shows that there was a massive gap between funds allocation and availability of local development institutions to utilize the funds to carry out development policies for the development of tribals. There was a growth of funds allocation but decline in the local development institutions. Thus, it is a myth to argue that during liberalisation, there was a reduction in the budget allocation for tribal development. Rather there was a massive funding for tribal development after liberalisation to prove that the government institutions were inefficient. The inefficiency of government led-local development institutions are the products of the structural adjustment policies, and bans on new recruitment and conservative employment policies have weakened the government-led development institutions.

The reduction in social sector expenditure is likely to hit the tribals hard as they are the most marginalised social group in the country in terms of limited availability and accessibility to education and health facilities[60]. Thus, it is necessary to address to the problem of tribals while formulating plans and policies for tribal development by incorporating tribals into it through their participation in development decision making (Joshi, 1998). The failure of development policies in such a direction, under the aegis of the new economic reforms to uplift the tribal from poverty and the region from underdevelopment, has led the policy makers, politicians and bureacrats to lay the blame on the natural calamities in the district. The natural calamities in terms of flood, cyclone and drought[61] are the most apolitical and bureaucratic answer to the failure of the neo-liberal model of development. The crisis in the tribal development policy, declining role of state-led local development institutions in the district created a space for NGOs and COs which started taking advantage of the situation by reducing the faith of the people over state, government and its institutions. Even the financial institutions which were created during the pre-reform period to carry out anti-poverty policies, income generation and debt relief programmes, collapsed in the district during the post-economic reform period.

Failure of Financial Institutions i.e. Agricultural Cooperatives and Marketing Societies

The Government of India (1971) created Large Sized Agricultural Multi Purpose Cooperative Societies (LAMPS) in tribal areas, designed to provide production and consumption credit and undertake the marketing of agricultural and minor forest products. The necessity of cooperatives and marketing societies were reiterated further by the Government of India (1973) to stop indebtedness and land alienation among tribals. The Government of Orissa followed these national tribal development policies and implemented it in different parts of the tribal areas in the state during 1975–76. The Government of Orissa was far ahead of the national government in understanding the significance of a cooperative system in the tribal economy and society. It created the Tribal Development Cooperative of Orissa in 1967 under the Orissa Cooperative Societies Act 1962. The Government of Orissa also created the Orissa State Schedule Caste and Schedule Tribe Development Finance Cooperative Corporation Ltd in 1979 to provide institutional credit

for the various income generating activities of tribals and Primary Agricultural Credit Cooperative Societies were formed to provide specific loan for
agricultural development. These institutions were created at local level, block
level, district level and state level to ensure efficiency in its activities and to
deliver twin institutional objectives of eradicating poverty and underdevelopment and ensure sustainable livelihood for poor, tribal and rural population.
In this way, the agricultural credit cooperatives and marketing societies were
developed in the district during the pre-reform period of 1974–79, as a part of
the policy which was aimed at enabling institutional access to credit facilities
for the poor and tribal population in the district. The specific objectives of
these institutional set-ups was to provide minimum support price to the producers, encourage production and a market safety net to the producers in
general and save tribal farmers, in particular, from the local money lenders
and middle businessmen in the area.

   However, the post-economic review of different cooperatives and marketing societies in Kalahandi district reveals that most of the institutions are
either defunct or have been completely shut down due to various reasons. All
the six LAMPS in the district, started during the pre-reform period have been
"running on losses due to a low level of business coupled with low recover,
contributory loss from PDS business and inadequate margins relating to input
distributing business"[62] during the post-economic reform period. Further,
detailed analysis of cooperative societies in the district reveals that the
growth of different cooperative societies was stagnant from 1960 to 1980 and
declined considerably from 1991 to 2001. The classification of different
cooperatives and marketing societies in the district reveals that credit and
multi-purpose cooperatives declined from 270 in 1980 and 89 in 1991 to 72
in 2001. The agricultural cooperatives also declined from 27 in 1980 and 12
in 1991 to 8 in 2001. The growth of housing cooperatives was stagnant in the
district, whereas the industrial, marketing, banking and other cooperatives
showed a growth tendency during the post-economic reform period. The
industrial cooperatives showed a marginal growth from 21 in 1980 and 23 in
1991 to 28 in 2001. The marketing cooperatives also increased from four in
1980, six in 1991 to eight in 2001. Similarly the banking and other cooperative institutions grew from 44 in 1991 to 53 in 2001. This indicates that
economic reform has had negative impact on the agricultural, housing, credit
and multipurpose cooperatives, whereas it has had a positive impact on the
industrial, marketing and banking cooperatives in the district (Nayak,
2009)[63].

   The study of membership of six LAMPS in the district from 1985 to 1997
reveals that there was a considerable growth of both tribal and non-tribal
members in the district. There was no sign of a declining trend in the membership of cooperatives in the post-economic reform period in the district.
The only difference between the pre-economic reform period and the post-

economic reform period was a change in the composition and pattern of memberships in the cooperatives. It reveals that the non-tribal members grew faster than the tribal members during the post-economic reform period (Nayak, 2009)[64]. The growth of tribal membership in the cooperatives reveals that there is a marginal decline of tribal membership in the Thuamul Rampur block from 62.47 percent in 1985 to 56. 83 percent in 1997, whereas in the Langigarh block the membership increased from 47.51 percent in 1985 to 48.79 percent in 1997, at a time when the membership in total in the district has shown a marginal decline (Nayak, 2009)[65].

The performance of cooperatives in the district during the post-economic reform period reveals that the membership increased from 10,000 in 1991 to 13,000 in 1997. The share capital increased from Rs. 14 lakhs in 1991 to Rs. 19 lakh in 1997. The working capital and deposits increased during and after the reform period, whereas borrowings, outstanding loans and overdue loans declined due to repayment of loans. These were very positive signs for the efficient and successful working of the cooperatives in the district. Thus, it is difficult to understand the growing loss of cooperatives in the district from Rs. 3.10 lakh in 1986 to Rs. 5.96 lakhs in 1997. One of the reasons is related with the growing management and administrative costs, which doubled during the post-economic reform period. Another negative aspect of cooperatives in the district is that marketing of tribal products declined from Rs. 3.2 lakh in 1989 to Rs. 1.8 lakh in 1997. It indicates that post-economic reform policies on cooperatives and marketing societies had a negative impact on tribal economy and failed to increase its procurement from the tribals. Similarly the cooperatives and marketing societies in the Kalahandi district failed to increase the distribution of consumer goods during the period of post-economic reforms. It declined from Rs. 66 lakhs in 1988 to Rs 16 lakh in 1997. Without looking at the above lacunas in the cooperative systems, the Government of Orissa started withdrawing its role from the management and running of cooperative societies in the district during the post-reform period. The idea was to reduce the financial burden of the loss made by the cooperatives in the district. The government of Orissa gave a clear direction for the involvement of NGOs, COs and SHGs to carry out the role of cooperative and marketing societies in the tribal and non-tribal areas of the district. Even a recent research survey, conducted by the Planning Commission (2004), reveals that 25 percent of households had been beneficiaries of NGOs, mostly in securing loans in the district. The Self Help Groups (SHGs) are also playing a major role in this process and expanding their base in the district by undertaking different activities including income generating activities such as broom, jute rope, leaf-plate making and bamboo work besides the collection of minor forest produces from the tribal areas (ibid). Such romanticisation of NGOs, COs and

SHGs successes in dealing with cooperative institutions not only proves government inefficiency and inability but also its intention to encourage the role of non-state, private actors to deal with the issues of most vulnerable sections i.e. poor tribals in the district.

CONCLUSION

The findings of the analysis in this chapter show that during and after the implementation of the economic reform period, the tribals in the district have faced a trivalent of dangers; i) negative transition of agriculture from food crops to cash crops, ii) growth of industrialisation and pressure on tribal land and their natural resources, iii) declining role of state and informalisation of its tribal development policies with urban and non-tribal focus.

The tribals and their economy in the district are based on land, forest and agriculture. The tribals of the Kalahandi district have two types of economic activities; i.e. one is based on economic activities that fulfill the immediate food requirements, which are available from the forest and agriculture. The second type of economic activity involves storage of seasonal agricultural and other forest products for the future consumption requirements. In both economic activities, the tribals in the district try to limit their needs as per their consumption requirements. The efficient food availability in the forest, abundant natural resources, and higher agricultural production leads to surplus that paves its way to the local market. But before it goes to the local market the local money lenders and businessmen buy the surplus from the tribals at a cheap cost as the agricultural cooperatives declined and became defunct during the post-reform period. The money transaction in the tribal areas of the district paves the market to flourish without any institutional framework for the rural markets, as the regional marketing societies have closed down during the post-reform period. Further, the development policies of the post-reform period have focused on mining based industrialisation in the district which has increased the pressure on land, forest, agriculture and natural resources; thereby putting the livelihoods of the tribals in danger.

However, the success of any tribal development policy depends on institutional arrangements to pursue and implement those policies. Thus, institutional arrangements, by taking the economic and cultural requirements of the tribals in different regions of the district are necessary preconditions without which tribal development policies can not produce automatic results and are bound to fail. The tribal development policies envisaged by the new economic reforms were based on one major argument which portrayed state-led development institutions as inefficient and responsible for the failure of development policies in the district. It costs a huge public expenditure which needs to be capped through restrictions on government employment and cuts in welfare spending. This has led to the collapse of public institutions, followed by the failure of development policies. The collapse of local development institutions run by the state and government is a product of the liberalisation and structural adjustment policies of the new economic reform policy package which put an end to the functioning of these institutions in the district. The process has taken two major ways to achieve its objectives. The first attempt was made by the neo-liberal policy makers to weaken it by putting restrictions on the new recruitments which made local development institutions stagnant and inefficient in welfare delivery to pave the way for privatisation. When the privatisation process failed to provide the alternative, then neo-liberal policy makers made the second attempt to create a mass consciousness in the minds of the people by providing visible signs of inefficiency and the failure of the state-led local development institutions. The second policy attempt aimed at rejecting social and mass base of state-led local tribal development institutions and to create a social base for privatisation and its institutions without facing any competition from public institutions. As a result of which, tribals are becoming more and more victim to such a process in which economic marginalisation is the only outcome.

However, economic marginalisation is not possible without changing the social and cultural set up of tribal society. The change in the social, cultural and religious set up of tribal society is imperative to overcome the constitutional and legal barriers that protect tribal rights over their land, forest and other natural resources from the market and corporate expropriation. Thus, de-tribalisation of tribals in terms of their social, spiritual and cultural life is an attempt to remove the legal and constitutional barrier which can only allow the mining based industrial capital to enter into the tribal areas. Thus, Hinduisation of tribals is the easiest way of de-tribalisation in which the constitutional protections get removed without any obstacles. The accumulation process is not possible in the tribal areas by only dismantling the tribal economy. The tribal culture often reminds and alienates one's right over resources but the tribal culture in Kalahandi reminds them of their rights over land, forest and natural resources based on customary inheritance. Thus, it is important to dismantle tribal culture and de-tribalise tribals in the district to reduce the tribal claim for their right over land, forest and natural resources. The economic reform process has been able to dismantle tribal economy through changes in agricultural policy and by focusing to industrialise the tribal area, to exploit the natural resources. Such processes could not destroy the very foundation of tribal culture and their social identity. Thus, all the protective measures and affirmative actions enshrined in the Constitution of India came to the rescue of tribals to protect their economy and culture. Therefore, social and cultural transition of tribals through de-tribalisation, or Hinduisation of tribals, is the only way to occupy tribal land and other resources by removing legal measures. Once the tribals are Hindus then the Constitutional affirmative actions and protective measures will not be applicable to the tribals. This argument is further clarified in the concluding chapter.

Chapter Five

Impact of the New Economic Reforms on Tribals as Socially Disadvantaged Groups in Kalahandi

Locating Social and Cultural Transition of Tribals

This chapter will look at the social and cultural impacts of the new economic reform policies on the tribals in Kalahandi district. It is important to locate the impact of economic reforms on the tribal culture due to two reasons. Firstly, it is a reductionist approach to conduct an impact study based on economic analysis without studying cultural impacts. The second reason is more important, stressing the tribal culture as it embodies the materiality of economic, cultural and social relations in tribal society. Thus an understanding of tribal culture and its transition is imperative to understand the predicaments of tribal lives and society due to cultural disintegration and loss of livelihood. By doing so, I argue that the post-economic reform period tribal development policies have helped the growth of Hinduisation of tribals in the district. The Hinduisation of tribals is a process to ensure the necessary conditions with one objective and two outputs. The objective is to enlarge a Hindu social and cultural order, which has lost its social base over the years. Such a process has both a political and an economic output. Politically, it helps the Hindu right wing forces[1] to expand and consolidate their vote bank politics to capture state power in order to achieve the Hindu nationalist project of making India a Hindu nation. The economic output of the Hinduisation process is having a devastating effect on the tribals. It is not only ruining the cultural identities of tribals but also helps in removing all the constitutional affirmative measures that protects tribal right over land and other natural resources. Such processes help the mining-led industrial capital, allowing it to enter into the tribal areas without any constitutional and legal barriers. The disintegration of tribal culture through Hinduisation is also helpful to incorporate tribals into the mainstream market as consumers, helping market forces to spread their networks for the deepening of capitalism in tribal areas.

My argument is based on systematic analysis of the post-economic reform-led social development policies for tribals on health and education in the Kalahandi district. The withdrawal of the state and collapse of its institutions during the post-economic reform period in Kalahandi has led to the informalisation of tribal welfare policies i.e. health and education. This informalisation process has helped for the growth of NGOs and COs in the district which are either directly or indirectly affiliated with different Hindu and Christian religious institutions. I am focusing on Hindu religious affiliations of NGOs in this chapter, whilst also referring to Christian religious affiliations. In this way, this chapter documents the cultural hegemony of Hindu right wing forces over tribal lives, society and culture during the post-economic reforms Kalahandi.

INTRODUCTION

The tribals and their communities in Kalahandi are very distinct social groups and in terms of class, they belong to the class of 'have-nots'; in addition they suffer from social oppression and fall within the lower rank of the Hindu caste order. Thus, the tribals in the district suffer from manifold problems of isolation, marginalisation and disadvantageous situations, both in the social and economic life of the Hindu social order. The tribals in the district have faced multiple forms of domination at different stages of their history that have continued even during the post-colonial process of development. The process has accelerated itself with the tribal development policies followed after the new economic reforms, which have invaded their economic life and livelihood, and put them in a perpetual condition of crisis.

The neo-liberal development model, followed for tribal development in Kalahandi after the implementation of economic reforms, has led to the economic marginalisation and de-peasantisation of tribals through the collapse of traditional sources of income and livelihood i.e. land, agriculture and forest. The de-peasantisation of tribals was started with the beginning of peasantisation of tribals in the district. The first attempt to Hinduise the tribals in Kalahandi was made through the process of social stratification and peasantisation of tribal societies during the pre-colonial period. The process of peasantisation of tribals and social stratification provided the base for securing social legitimacy for the growth of feudalism in the tribal areas of the district. Thus, peasantisation of tribals in Kalahandi was the first attempt to Hinduise the tribals' access to land and control over other natural resources in the district (Pati, 1999, 2001). But the outcome of peasantisation and Hinduisation of tribals during the pre-colonial period was not intended to de-tribalise tribals, rather to grab land and natural resources in the district. As a result, tribals became peasants but remained as tribals in terms of their culture. The post-economic reform de-peasantisation of tribals has both the economic and cultural logic of de-tribalisation in the district. The tribal culture and traditions have become more significant than ever before in giving meaning to the lives of tribals after the collapse of their traditional occupational base in the district through the process of economic marginalisation and de-tribalisation. The welfare state and its parliamentary democracy, based on elections at regular intervals, came to the rescue of tribals during economic marginalisation as a part of its obligations to the idea of citizenship. On the other hand, the Constitutional laws in India[2] direct the states and governments to take affirmative actions to protect and promote the social, economic, political and cultural interests of marginalised groups and communities, including the tribals. The constitutional and legal provisions in particular, and tribal culture in general, are two impediments for the growth of market and its agencies to expropriate natural resources from the tribal areas.

However, it is difficult to change the constitutional and legal provisions for the tribals. Any attempt to change the constitutional structure that protects tribals will question the very basis of relationship between the state and citizenship of marginalised communities i.e. tribals in the country. Thus, it is important to de-tribalise the tribals in Kalahandi in such a way by which the problems of constitutional and legal provisions for tribals can be revoked naturally. Economic marginalisation and de-peasantisation is a necessary condition but not a sufficient condition to de-tribalise the tribals. The dismantling of tribal culture is the only alternative for de-tribalisation, which can serve the twin objectives of capital (local, national and international). Firstly, it can give a free hand to mining-based industrial capital to enter into tribal areas to exploit the mineral resources without any legal and constitutional barriers. The mining-led industrialisation and transition in agriculture has ruined the traditional income and livelihood source of tribals, as discussed in the earlier chapter. Industrial labour is the only livelihood option available to the tribals in the district. It is easy to transfer tribal industrial labour into economic being to incorporate tribals as consumers and expand the mainstream market in the tribal areas, which is the second objective. These two objectives can fulfill the requirements for the naturalisation of capitalist social relations in the tribal areas to overcome the cultural contradictions of capitalism[3], leaving the outcomes entirely contingent on tribals in the district.

However, the process of the naturalisation of capitalist social relations, through de-tribalisation, started with the implementation of social development programmes for tribals during the post-economic reform period. Social development is only possible through the expansion of the health and educational infrastructures (Sen, 2005). As health and education are two necessary tenets to determine one's own self and understand the 'others' forming the basis of social development and wellbeing (Ryan and Deci, 2000). Thus, health and education are two important means for the self-determination and social development of tribals in the Kalahandi district. The post-colonial state has promised social development via its constitutional commitments to provide universal heath care and universal education to the tribals as marginalised citizens and uplifts their situation through welfare-led tribal development policies. The constitutional commitments of the post-colonial state for social development have become secondary to the ideas of efficiency, profit and economic growth promoted during and after the post-economic reform period. The tribals are the victims of such a policy shift of the state as a result of which the condition of health and education in the tribal areas of Kalahandi is in a dismal condition. The social development of tribals in terms of health and education is no more a state obligation; rather it is the voluntary responsibility of Non Governmental Organisations (NGOs) and Civil Society Organisations (CSOs) in the district. Such transitions of state and government towards tribal social development has helped the NGOs and CSOs affiliated with the Hindu right wing forces to expand their base in the tribal areas and Hinduise tribals in Kalahandi district. The Hinduisation of tribals in the district has had an immensely negative impact on the tribal society, culture and their economy. The process of Hinduisation has pushed tribals toward a situation of de-tribalisation through cultural pauperisation and alienation of legal rights during the post-economic reform period.

IMPACT OF NEW ECONOMIC REFORMS ON TRIBALS AND THEIR SOCIAL DEVELOPMENT IN KALAHANDI

Social development in the Kalahandi district has been declining over the years. A comparative study of the Composite Development Index (CDI)[4] of 1991 and 2001 in Orissa by Meher (1999) reveals that the tribal districts are falling far behind the non-tribal districts in the state. And the deprivation in the tribal districts of the state has increased over the years. The CDI rank of Kalahandi was ninth among thirteen undivided districts of Orissa during 1970s, declining to eleventh in CDI rank during 1980s and remaining in eleventh rank during 1990s. But during and after the period of new economic reforms, the CDI rank of the district fell to thirteen in 1991 and continued to be in that rank in 2001. The CDI rank therefore places the district in the lowest order of the development in the state (Nayak, 2009)[5]. The decline and stagnancy in CDI rank of the district indicates the failure of development policies and a crisis in social development during the post-economic reform period. Health and education are two important indices in CDI (or in any development index) to measure social and human development. Thus, a crisis in social development in Kalahandi district indicates crises in the health and education sectors in the district. The composite variation[6] between 1991 and 2001 in the health and education sector shows the negative impact of the new economic reforms in the district. In the field of education, the composite variation was -5.19 percent in 1991 which increased to -5.76 percent during 2001. The increase of composite variation of education between the two periods indicates that there was a growth of marginalisation and deprivation in the field of education in the district. In a similar way, the composite variation of heath was -4.22 percent in 1991 and increased to -5.91 percent in 2001 (Nayak, 2009)[7]. It shows that the composite variation was higher in health than education while looking at two base years of post-economic reform period, which indicates that marginalisation and deprivation of health was higher than the educational sector in the district.

However, the condition of health and education among tribals in the district became more vulnerable during the post-reform period; making the social development of tribals miserable - which is discussed in detail later. There are two predominant views on the prevailing crisis in the social development of tribals and their society in the Kalahandi. The first view is the official view of the central and state governments, politicians, bureaucrats and their institutional agencies including the NGO's and other civil society organisations. The official view is that the crisis in tribal social and cultural life is not an issue of underdevelopment, poverty, inequality and exploitation but a result of a stagnant and exclusive tribal culture in the district. The incompatibility of tribal culture with modern educational and health systems has contributed to the dismal condition of health and education among tribal people in the district. The other view comes from the social and cultural anthropologists[8] who locate the crisis in tribal society and culture as outside cultural interventions, so the tribals need to be protected from outside intervention, which is the only role the state has to play. In a way, the cultural anthropologists who are studying tribal underdevelopment, are trying to promote a zoo for the tribals with the help of a police state to control outside intervention in the tribal society and regulate the tribal society itself. The official approach and the approaches of anthropologists' understanding of the cultural transition and crisis in tribal societies are therefore mired in the neo-liberal justification, through the cultural logic of tribal underdevelopment. Both the views neglect the role of different actors and institutions in the pauperisation of tribal life and livelihood and disintegration of their culture. These two views have taken a wider space in the systematic withdrawal of the Indian State in the delivery of welfare measures in the field of health and education and protecting its citizens from cultural and social insecurities during the post-economic reform period. The constitutional obligation of the Indian state to protect its marginalised communities i.e., tribals have taken a back seat in the development discourse. The withdrawal of State from the issues of education and health has led to the growth of informalisation of health and educational services for the tribals in the district under the leadership of NGOs and COs. In this context, I am attempting to locate the issues in tribal health and education during, and after, the economic reforms to understand transitions in the social development of tribals in the district.

THE CONDITION OF TRIBAL HEALTH IN KALAHANDI DISTRICT AFTER ECONOMIC REFORMS

Different reports from the Office of the District Medical Officer at Bhawanipatna reveal that there are four particular diseases i.e. Fluorosis, Sickle Cell Anemia, Malaria and Malnutrition affecting tribals in the district, which are quite common amongst the tribal people in particular, and in the district in general[9]. Fluorosis is a water-borne disease that can disable active people. It is a product of high fluoride contents in the water coming from different perennial streams of high mountains in the district. Thus, the majority of the people in two tribal blocks, in Thuamul Rampur and Langigarh, depend on such water for their drinking requirements and become victims of Fluorosis[10]. The lack of infrastructure to provide safe drinking water in the area helps the growth of Fluorosis among tribals and is aggravated further with Sickle Cell Anemia and malnutrition. Sickle Cell Anemia is a hereditary disease, which is enhanced by malnutrition. Treatment is difficult but its prevention is possible through early diagnosis, which requires more health infrastructure, in terms of establishing Sickle Cell units in the tribal areas of the district. The food insecurity amongst tribals causes immense malnutrition among tribal people. The tribal women and children are the worst victims of all forms of malnutrition. It can be only tackled by regular food and medicine supply and this depends on the effective institutions for distribution of food and health infrastructure for medicine and health. The health problems among tribals are pervasive but confined within four major diseases, but the government has failed miserably to solve the health predicaments of the tribals due to lack of manpower, infrastructure and institutional requirements. In this way, the tribals in Kalahandi district are yet to get quality health facilities, but the policy makers and development planners have blamed the incompatibility of modern health systems with tribal culture, to hide the failures of their tribal health policy over the years. Furthermore, the health policy makers consider that geographical inaccessibility and lack of health consciousness among tribals are the cause of the dismal heath records of tribals in the district.

Reality of Geographical Inaccessibility

The first argument, based on geographical inaccessibility, to justify the dismal health condition of tribals, shows the government's failure to develop health infrastructure in the rural and tribal areas, which have remained inaccessible, even after six decades of welfare measures. The two tribal blocks of the district i.e. Langigarh and Thuamul Rampur have 471 and 294 villages respectively. Out of these, 152 villages are inaccessible and 142 villages are accessible in Thuamul Rampur block whereas in the Langigarh block, 38 villages are inaccessible and 433 villages are geographically accessible (Nayak, 2009)[11]. However, in the Langigarh block, only 23 villages with 6980 people have access to a PHC with a minimum distance of one to five kilometers from their habitation, 36 villages with 8496 people have access to a PHC with a minimum distance of five to ten kilometers and more than 216 villages with 12087 people have access to PHC with a minimum distance of more than ten kilometers. Similarly, the Thuamul Rampur block, only 16 villages with 6463 people have access to one PHC within one to five kilometers distance, 58 villages with a population of 16117 have access to a PHC with a distance of five to ten kilometers and more than 200 villages with 42311 people have only access to one PHC with a distance of more than ten kilometers Thus, in these two tribal blocks of the district more than 39 villages with a population of 13443 have access to one PHC within a distance of one to five kilometers, 94 villages with 24616 people have access to one PHC in a distance between five to ten kilometers and more than 416 villages with a population of 54,398 have access to one PHC in a distance of more than ten kilometers (Nayak, 2009)[12]. This indicates that tribal areas are not inaccessible to primary health infrastructure, which gives a gloomy picture of tribal health care facilities in the district. In terms of availability of health infrastructure, the district has one district level hospital at Bhawanipatna, one subdivisional level hospital in Dharamgarh, one major hospital in five blocks i.e. Kesinga, Karlamunda, Bhawanipatna, Langigarh and Jaipatna. Similarly, there is one community health centre and upgraded primary health centre in six blocks i.e. Bhawanipatna, Jaipatna, Koksara, Madanpur Rampur, Langigarh and Dharamgarh.

There are eight primary healthcare centres with labour rooms and the other thirty nine primary health centres do not even have a labour room. There is only one primary health centre with labour rooms in each of the two tribal blocks i.e. Thuamul Rampur and Langigarh. There are no X-Ray, ECG, incubator, cardiopulmonary resuscitation (CPR) nor ambulance facilities in any of the health centres in tribal areas of the district[13]. Further the health map of the district reveals that most of the health infrastructure is concentrated in the non-tribal urban areas of the district (Map No-6.1)[14]. A comparative study of tribal population density in the different areas in the district and coverage of health infrastructure (PHCs and SHCs) reveals that tribal areas are under less coverage of health infrastructure than the non-tribal areas. The concentration of tribal population is higher in the blocks i.e., Thuamul Rampur, Langigarh and Madanpur Rampur but the coverage of the PHCs and SHCs are lowest in these blocks. The highest coverage of PHCs and SHCs are in blocks i.e Kesinga, Dharamgarh and Junagarh where the percentage of tribal population is lowest (Nayak, 2009)[15]. It also reflects the failure of government health policies for tribals in terms of accessibility and availability of health infrastructure for tribals in the district.

Myth Regarding the Lack of Health Consciousness

The second argument based on the lack of health consciousness among tribals, which justifies their poor health condition, is an attempt to hide the failure of the health policy for tribals. It also reflects the utter ignorance of policy makers regarding tribal health practices. A recent research survey by Nayak, Behera and Misra (2004) on ethno-medico-botanical medicine and its practice by tribals in the district shows that tribals use 39 plant species under 36 genera belonging to 26 plant families as their medicine for different illness and diseases. It indicates that tribals are conscious about the nature of their illness and try to develop medicine as per the requirements. The study also reveals that such ethno-medical practice among tribals is undocumented but disseminated from one generation of family members to next generation. The families who provide medicine and treatment in tribal areas of Kalahandi are known as *Baida (a person who practices traditional medicine)* families. These families collect ethno-medical plants from the forest, use its leaf, roots, fruits and seeds to prepare medicine, name them and use them in different modes as per the diseases. Such practice is widespread in the two tribal blocks i.e., Thuamul Rampur and Langigarh, in particular and other parts of the district in general. There are only two Ayurvedic dispensaries in each tribal block of the district[16]. There is no health infrastructure to do research on the medical practices among tribals and its scientific basis as a result of which many tribals in the district are suffering from quacks. Thus, health unconsciousness among tribal argument is a fallacious propaganda of the ruling and non-ruling elites and policy makers of the district and the state. It also reflects the lack of understanding of tribal health systems and their requirements whilst making health policies for tribals.

During the post-economic reform period, the Government of Orissa has taken many initiatives to address the issues of tribal health in the district. But the National Rural Health Mission (NRHM) was the first comprehensive national health policy, and was launched in 2005. The NRHM in Orissa has promised to ensure effective healthcare through a range of interventions at individual, household, community, and most critically at health system levels. The NRHM has emphasised the idea of public and private partnerships and incorporation of NGOs and COs in the promotion of health and health infrastructure. But unfortunately the promise of the NRHM has remained just a promise for the tribal people of Kalahandi. The lack of doctors, medicine, health centres and other health infrastructures in the district have continued from the pre-economic reform period to post-economic reform period. The economic reforms have had no positive impact on the improvement of the health condition of tribals in the district, which can be discussed further while doing a comparative analysis of the gap between requirements and existing manpower, institutional and other infrastructure in the health sector in the district.

The health infrastructure in Kalahandi reveals that there is one district and one sub-divisional hospital, six other hospitals, six community hospitals, four upgraded primary health centres, forty three primary health centres, seven first referral units, eighteen Ayurvedic dispensaries, fourteen Homeopathic dispensaries, fourteen mobile health units and 226 health sub centres with one paramedical (ANM) training school. Only one private hospital cum medical college is under construction in the district. Most of these health infrastructures are based in urban and non-tribal areas of the district. There are 104 doctors and 432 hospital beds in the district for the population of 1437790. Thus, the doctor and population ratio provides a gloomy health scenario of the district in which there is one doctor for 13,825 people, whereas the hospital bed and population ratio is one hospital bed for 3328 people. In total there are 65 medical institutions, so each medical institution treats more than 22,120 people in a year and only one medical institution is available within 129sq kilometers. There are 262 paramedical staff (ANM) working in the district for a population of 1437790; thus paramedical staff and population ratio come to around one paramedical staff for 5,488. The ratio of doctor, hospital bed, paramedical staff, and availability of institutions per population ratio in the tribal areas in the district is very minimal due to the non-availability of health instrastructure in the tribal blocks[17]. Further, users' charges for medical facilities - as per the Orissa health reforms - has led to the mass deprivation and reduced accessibility to health for tribals.

Moreover, no attempt has been made to strengthen the health facilities by improving health infrastructures during the post-economic reform period. The strength of medical staff in the district is very weak due to lack of new recruitments. There are 104 medical officers in the place of 176 people and 72 medical officer posts remain vacant. A similar situation persists in the case of health workers, nurses and health supervisors. In the place of 919 medical staff, only 721 are working in the district and 198 medical staff positions remained vacant during 2001-2006 (Nayak, 2009)[18]. The post-economic reform period (2001- 2006) has had no impact on the increase of manpower. There is also a discrepancy in terms of allocation of health institutional infrastructure in tribal and non-tribal areas. In the tribal areas, 48 sub-health centres are allocated but only 34 SHCs exists in the tribal areas and 12 more SHCs are required for the tribal population of 3000 as per the government norms. In the case of non-tribal areas however, 239 SHCs are allocated but 192 SHCs are functional and 48 SHCs are still required for the population of 5000 as per the norms of the government. In a similar way, one can find, looking at the Primary Health Centres (PHCs) with one doctor in the district that there are seven PHCs and seven doctors allocated to the 20,000 tribal population and only five PHCs are functional in the tribal areas with a further requirement of two PHCs. In the case of non-tribal areas, 40 PHCs are allocated and 34 PHCs are functional with 6 further requirements for the 30,000 population (Nayak, 2009)[19]. It clearly shows how the government health infrastructure is biased regarding tribals and their areas. More health infrastructures are available in the non-tribal areas of the district than tribal ones, where 287 SHCs are required in the district but only 158 SHCs are available and 129 SHCs are further required. However, out of the existing 158 Health Sub Centre buildings, 12 buildings are completely damaged and 110 buildings are not in a usable condition. The tribal blocks of Thuamul Rampur and Langigarh, have 21 Health Sub Centre buildings in a damaged condition and in need of major repair and reconstruction work. There are 129 new medical buildings under construction, most of them in the non-tribal and urban areas of the district[20]. In this way, health for the tribals has remained unavailable and inaccessible in the district.

The non-availability, inaccessibility and non-existence of a formal health infrastructure has led to the growth of informalisation of health services in the district during the post-economic reform period. As a result, there has been a growth of mobile health units (MHUs) in the district during the post-economic reform period. There were 160864 patients treated in 2001-02 under the MHU scheme. The number of patients treated under such schemes increased to 235289 patients in 2004-05. The number of tour dates, number of village covered and the number of immunisation camps held under the MHUs Scheme increased from 2001 to 2005 (Nayak, 2009)[21]. This indicates the informalisation of health services in the district during the period of economic reforms. Further tribal areas and its peoples have received minimal benefit from such a health scheme as the MHU cars/jeeps/vans cannot go to the tribal areas, which are geographically inaccessible. The MHUs health camps are often over crowded, as a result of which the quality of treatment is quite low. At other times, few tribal people come to such MHU camps as they do not get information about the locations and times, or live too far away to make the trip. In this way, the health situation in the district in general, and the condition of tribal health in particular, are in a condition of denial, which has increased during the post-economic reform period.

The post-economic reform health policy followed after the launch of the NRHM has been able to reduce the total fertility rate to 2.4 percent but the IMR & MMR rate is 87 per 1000 lakh live births & 367 per 100000 lakh live births. Similarly, it has achieved remarkable progress in TB, Leprosy and Malaria eradication in the district as per the reports of the Chief District Medical Officer (2006) at Bhawanipatna. The achievement of reducing the rate of IMR and MMR is very low in the case of tribals in the district. However, the district health policy took a new turn after the implementation of the NRHM, which has focused on forming an alliance between public and private institutions for the promotion of tribal health in the district. This has led to the shifting the significance of the role of state led health institutions to NGOs/CO since the promotion of health. For example, Vedanta Aluminum Ltd, which is ruining the tribal environment and livelihood, has also been incorporated to promote tribal health in the district. This new alliance of NGOs/COs and different industrial houses led to the formation of the District Rural Health Mission in 2005, in compliance with the NRHM. Consequently, the promotion of health in the district, and tribal health in particular, has been left to the NGOs/COs and the Vedanta Aluminum Ltd company leading to a minimal advisory role for Government health institutions. The promotion of health especially in three blocks i.e., Thuamul Rampur, Lanjigarh and Madanpur Rampur was completely given to the NGOs and other private players. By giving a free hand to the NGOs and COs to formulate and implement policies on tribal health in the district, it appears the Government of Orissa and the Kalahandi district administration have withdrawn from the activities of promoting tribal health in the district, placing the role of state and its constitutional commitment for universal health for poor tribals to secondary position.

Education is another pillar of social development that has witnessed a similar experience during the post-economic reform period. "There is no better way of destroying a society than by undermining its educational system (Goldsmith, 1993:285)". The following section deals with the way the new economic reforms have created a gap between tribals and non-tribals in the field of education.

THE CONDITION OF TRIBAL EDUCATION IN KALAHANDI DISTRICT AFTER THE NEW ECONOMIC REFORMS

The position of tribals in the educational scenario of Kalahandi can be depicted from the 2001 Census of India. The census reveals that total literacy rate among tribals was 34.2 percent in which 51.7 percent were male and 17.2 percent were female. In the rural areas of the district, the total literacy rate among the tribals was 33.8 (51.4 percent for males and only 16.7 for females). In urban areas, the tribal literacy rate was higher, with a total of 54.2 percent (68.4 percent male and 39.6 percent female). Similarly, the majority of tribal women (82.8%) were illiterate in the district whereas tribal male illiteracy (48.3%) was lower than the total illiteracy rate of 65.8 percent among the tribals. The similar trend of illiteracy continued among the tribals in rural areas of the district making a 34.6 percent gender gap in literacy rate. The gender gap in literacy among tribals in the district is marginally lower in urban areas (28.6%). The concentration of illiteracy and the gender gap in literacy dominates the educational scenario of tribals in rural areas of the district; whereas in urban areas the literacy rate is higher and gender gap in literacy is lower (Nayak, 2009)[22]. This indicates either a failure of the education policies for tribals or lack of educational infrastructure that has led to the dismal condition of education in the district during the post-economic reform period.

Primary Education in Kalahandi

The study of primary education in the district, from 1981 to 2001, reveals that the total number of primary schools started declining during period of new economic reforms. There were 2172 primary schools with 4386 teachers in the district during 1987, which declined to 1474 schools with 3745 teachers in 2001. But the number of primary school students has increased over the years. The rate of growth in student numbers shows that the general category students have increased five times more than the tribal students in primary education. This indicates that there is a gap in the growth rate of primary students in terms of tribals and non-tribals. The gap between tribal and non-tribal students in primary education has increased from 1996 onwards (Nayak, 2009)[23]. Further, the area-wide distribution of primary schools and teachers in the different areas of the district reveals that their concentration is higher in urban and non-tribal areas of the district, i.e., Bhawanipatna, Kesinga, Narla, Junagarh, Jaipatna and Dharamgarh whereas the rural and tribal areas of the district, i.e., Thuamul Rampur, Langigarh have less of schools and teachers.

The concentration and growth rate of primary schools and teachers in urban and non-tribal areas has been at a higher rate than the tribal areas during the post-economic reform period. For example, Bhawanipatna had 530 primary school teachers in 189 primary schools during 1992 which increased to 661 teachers in 207 schools during 2001, whereas a tribal block like Langigarh had only 131 primary school teachers for 80 schools during 1992 which increased to 204 teachers in 86 schools during 2001 (Nayak, 2009)[24]. Similar trends of disparity in the growth of primary education between tribal and non-tribal areas can be found in different parts of the district. As a result of which the drop out rate of tribal students in primary education in tribal areas is higher than the other communities. The drop out rate of students of all communities was 43.42 percent in 1999 whereas the drop out rate among tribal students was 51.38 percent. The comparative analysis of drop out rate in primary education shows that the drop out rate of tribal students was higher than the other community students in the district. In 2002, the drop out rate of all community students was 44.74 percent whereas in case of tribals, it was 49.75 percent (Nayak, 2009)[25]. It shows the detrimental effect of the primary education policy and its effects on the primary education of tribals in the district. In this way the new economic reforms have had a negative impact on the primary education of tribals in the district, which has influenced middle school education as well.

Middle School Education in Kalahandi

The growth of middle school education in the district was almost stagnant from 1981 to 1984 when there were 312 middle schools with 839 teachers in the district. There were signs of marginal growth of middle school education from 1985 to 1987 and the number increased to 343 with 1082 teachers. However, the number declined to 308 with 1271 teachers during 1993 but showed an increasing trend again in 1996 when the number of middle schools increased to 375 with 1355 teachers. This period was the highest growth of middle school education in the district. But this growth trend could not be sustained during the reform period and the number of middle schools declined to 343 with 1451 teachers during 2001, which was the position of middle school education in 1987 (Nayak, 2009)[26]. In this way, post-economic reform has had a mixed impact on the middle school education in the district. Further, the area-wide concentration of middle schools and teachers reveals that there was a higher growth of middle schools and higher concentration of teachers in the non-tribal and urban areas whereas the growth rate was lower in the tribal areas. The Bhawanipatna block had 210 middle school teachers in its 44 schools during 1993, which increased to 239 teachers in 46 schools during 2001 and the Kesinga block had 120 middle school teachers in 36 schools during 1993, which increased to 196 teachers in 37 schools during 2001. But in the case of tribal blocks like Thuamul Rampur and Langigarh, there was a marginal growth of middle schools during the reform period. The Thuamul Rampur tribal block had 33 teachers in 12 middle schools during 1993, which increased to 41 teachers in 15 schools during 2001. Similarly, the Langigarh tribal block had 44 teachers in 16 middle schools during 1993 and increased to 55 teachers in 17 schools during 2001 (Nayak, 2009)[27]. This shows unequal growth of middle schools in tribal and non-tribal areas during the post-economic reform period. This unequal growth has led to the higher drop out rate in the middle school education among tribals in the district.

Secondary/High School Education in Kalahandi

The trajectory of secondary and high school education has experienced a difference in terms of its growth in the district. The district had 66 secondary and high schools with 728 teachers during 1981 and secondary high school education has shown a constant growth over the years as a result of which there were 231 schools with 1842 teachers by 2001 (Nayak, 2009)[28]. This indicates that there is a higher school to teacher ratio in secondary education in the district. Further, there is a higher concentration of secondary schools and teachers in the non-tribal areas and tribal areas have few schools with few teachers. For example; Bhawanipatna had 17 secondary schools with 188 teachers in 1992, which increased to 25 schools with 264 teachers in 2001. Thuamul Rampur had three schools with 33 teachers in 1992, which increased to nine schools with 89 teachers in 2001. Similarly, the Langigarh block had four schools with forty teachers in 1992, which increased to 11 schools with 104 teachers (Nayak, 2009)[29]. In this way the growth of secondary school education is lower while comparing the growth of secondary schools in non-tribal areas during and after the reform period.

Higher/College Education in Kalahandi

The situation of higher education is dismal in the district. Only one college offers post graduation programmes out of 28 colleges in the district. There were ten colleges in the district during 1992, which increased to 28 in 2001. There are 26 colleges which are based in the non-tribal areas of the district, whereas only two colleges in the tribal areas of Thuamul Rampur and Langigarh which provide intermediate degrees (Nayak, 2009)[30]. Further, the numbers of teaching faculties and its concentration is higher in the non-tribal areas than the tribal areas. For example; in Bhawanipatna block, there were six colleges with 115 faculty members in 1992 but the faculty strength declined to 90 by 2001. But still the college-faculty ratio is 1:15 in Bhawanipatna. The same trend can be found in other non-tribal areas of the district. There was no college or any other higher educational institution in the tribal areas like Thuamul Rampur until 1998. The Thuamul Rampur College was established during 1998 with five faculty members and the college continued with five staff members until 2002. The Langigarh block had one college with six staff members (Nayak, 2009)[31]. In this way, the ratio of higher education institutions and staff strength ratio in the tribal areas is much lower than the non-tribal areas, which makes higher education a distant dream for the tribal students in the district.

The comparative analysis of data on primary, middle, secondary and college education in Nayak(2009)[32] shows that there is a higher concentration of schools and teachers from primary education to higher education in the non-tribal areas of the district. As a result of which, tribal schools are over crowded with few teachers, leading to the decline of quality education for tribals in the district. Such a trend increased after the implementation of the new economic reforms, adding to the predicaments of education in the tribal areas of the district. The declining of state led educational institutions; lack of teaching staff and other infrastructural facilities in different sectors of education in the tribal areas has created a gap. This gap, created by the development policies, followed after the new economic reforms have given rise to informalisation of educational sector in the district.

Education is not only a source of generating consciousness but also the most important form of "critique of all forms of inequality in capitalist society – class inequality, sexism, racism, discrimination against gay and lesbian people, ageism and differential treatment of other social groups – and how all of these forms of inequality link to capital accumulation and value production (Rikowski, 2004: 567)". Any attempt to overcome the crisis arising from the above issues requires the restructuring of the educational system. After the implementation of the new economic reforms, there was a cumulative effect on different spheres of tribal life including its educational system and associated infrastructure. It has become imperative for the advocates of the new economic reforms to change the educational system systematically to suit to the needs of the economic policy[33]. Such understanding led the international financial institutions like the World Bank (1995, 2002) to consider education as a burden on the State that needs alternative sources of funding, indicating privatisation of education (Woodhall, 2007). One of the previous World Bank (1994) reports stated that education should not have much priority in the development strategy of a country. The report said that; "higher education should not have highest priority claim on incremental public resources available for education in many developing countries, especially those that have not yet achieved adequate access, equity and quality at the primary and secondary levels. This is because of the priority these countries attach to achieving universal literacy; because the social rates of return in investments in primary and secondary education usually exceed the rates of return on higher education" (World Bank, 1994:.3). It indicates a shift from universal education to literacy programmes. The same document contradicts its own prescription by stating that, "higher education is of paramount importance for social and economic development. Institutions of higher education have the main responsibility for equipping individuals with advanced knowledge and skills required for positions of responsibility....estimated social rates of return of ten percent or more in many developing countries also indicates that investments in higher education contributed to increase in labour productivity and to higher long term economic growth essential for poverty alleviation" (World Bank, 1994:1). The contradiction in the World Bank prescriptions did not deter the Government of India (1997) from defining higher education as 'non-merit service' as private rates of return are greater than social rates of return in higher education, thus there must be reduction of educational expenditure and reduction in the subsidies that go to the better sections of the society. The programme has apparently become clear with the implementation of new economic reform programmes with the intention of commercialisation and privatisation of education to reduce the financial burden of the state.

Failure of Privatisation of Health and Education in the Tribal Areas of Kalahandi District

Health and education was almost invariably afforded a central place in all tribal development plans and policies to uplift educationally and - healthwise - underprivileged tribal people for the development of their area. But during the process of the new economic reforms, the government shifted its institutional commitments to the social development of tribals by improving the condition of health and education in the tribal areas. The gap created in the field of social development with the withdrawal of state from the health and educational services during the pos-reform period has provided momentum for the growth of commercialisation and privatisation welfare services. The second generation of the new economic programmes carried out by the central government under the leadership of ex Prime Minister A.B Vajpayee gave further support to the process of privatisation of welfare services. The Prime Minister's Council on Trade and Industry (PMCTI, 2000) constituted a 'special subject group on policy framework for private investment in education, health and rural development'[34]. Unlike many other parts of the country and Orissa, privatisation could not take shape in Kalahandi as a result of state withdrawal or inefficiency in delivery of welfare services, i.e., health and education. The necessary condition of privatisation is liberalisation and reduction of state role over the economic activities of private capital. But it is not a sufficient condition for the growth of private capital in the health and education sectors. The poverty and lack of purchasing power of tribals in particular, and people in general, has discouraged the process of privatisation in the district. Only one private hospital is under construction near the Junagarh block and a few private English medium schools are there in the Kesinga, Bhawanipatna and Junagarh blocks of the district. But it is difficult to find private capital investing in the health and educational sectors in the tribal areas. Thus, privatisation of health and education in the tribal areas is a myth. The gap created by the withdrawal of the state could not be filled by the private capital, which has led to the informalisation of educational and health services. As a result, the social development of tribals in the field of education and health in Kalahandi has been left in the hands of charitable organisations, NGOs and COs. The process was legitimised by the ninth Five

Year Plan (1997-2002) and tenth Five Year Plan (2002-2007). These two development plans have given a clear direction to the NGOs to play a vital role in the field of education and health in the tribal areas of the country.

This new direction of public policy has inspired the RSS or Hindu right wing organisations to spread their network in Kalahandi district with the objective of the Hinduisation of tribals. Development and education are key vehicles through which conscription into Hindu extremism is amassed (Awaaz, 2004; Sabrang and South Asia Citizens Web, 2002; Sarkar, 1996; Sundar, 2004). The actions of Hindu right wing groups offer incriminating evidence of Hindu extremism and its project of cultural hegemony. The development programmes for tribals implemented by institutions affiliated with the Sangh Parivar lays the groundwork for social polarisation through the diffusion of Hindu right wing culture (Chatterji, 2004). The diffusion of Hindu right wing culture takes place through the NGOs and COs working in the tribal areas of the district but are directly or indirectly affiliated with the Hindu right wing organisations; *Rashtriya Swayamsevak Sangh* affiliates *Ekal Vidyālaya, Vanvasi Kalyan Parishad, Vanavasi Kalyan Samiti, Vivekananda Kendra, Shiksha Vikas Samiti, Sewa Bharati,* and many other groups. These organisations are directly and indirectly working in the tribal areas of Kalahandi.

NGO LED EDUCATION, HEALTH AND HINDUISATION IN KALAHANDI

The State-led tribal development intervention for social development has been reduced during the economic reform process. The state has increased its reliance on the NGOs and CSOs to carry out basic welfare deliveries like health and educational services. As a result, there was a massive growth of NGOs in the district during the period of economic reforms (Nayak, 2009)[35]. There were 357 NGOs during 1980-85, which increased to 802 in 1985-90. During the period of economic reforms, the number of NGOs increased to 2543 in 1990-95 and 2078 in 1995-2000. The downturn in the number of NGOs was a product of Government of Orissa control imposed on NGOs on various accounts to maintain transparency and accountability. But the government control over the NGOs could not be sustained for long time. As a result, the number of NGOs increased further to 2633 in 2000-2005 (Nayak, 2009)[36]. The study of NGOs and their nature in the district can be defined by their activities. The classification of all NGOs reveals that there is a higher growth rate of NGOs which are involved in health and education, sanitation and watershed development, tribal and rural development, micro-finance, social awareness, religious forest and environmental activities, religious and cultural. The growth rate is minimal in case of the NGOs which are involved in human rights, land, housing and food processing, agricultural, youth affairs and sports etc. There were 21 NGOs working in Kalahandi during 1980-85 which has increased to 312 in 1990-95 and 475 in 2000-2005. There were only two NGOs working on the issue of micro-finance during 198-85, increasing to 188 in 1990-95 and 333 in 2000-2005. There were 14 tribal and rural development NGOs in the district during 1980-85, increasing to 94 in 1990-95 and 303 in 2000-2005. But the NGOs working on agriculture increased from two in 1980-85 to 35 in 2000-05. Similarly, the number of industry based NGOs have increased from two in 1980-85 to 142 in 2000-05. In this way, the number and area operations of all categories of NGOs in the district increased over the period of time especially during the period of post-economic reforms (Nayak, 2009)[37].

The religious classification of NGOs in Kalahandi shows that religious affiliated (Hindu, Christian and Islamic) NGOs have increased from 12 in 1980 to 34 in 1990-95 and 95 in 2000-05 (Nayak, 2009). Further classification of religious NGOs in the district shows that the Christian affiliated NGOs increased from four in 1980-85 and six in 1985-90 to 12 in 1995-2000 and 17 in 2000-2005. Islamic NGOs related with the Muslims in the district increased from one NGO in 1980-1990 to three NGOs in 1995-2005. However, NGOs related to the Hindu right wing forces directly or indirectly increased in a massive scale in the district. There were only seven Hindu affiliated NGOs in 1980-85, thirteen in 1985-90 and 21 in 1990-95 which increased to 48 in 1995-2000 and further increased to 75 in 2000-2005 (Nayak, 2009)[38]. This indicates that the growth of NGOs affiliated to Hindu right wing forces are higher than the Christian and Islamic related NGOs in the district (Nayak, 2009)[39]. And most of these religious affiliated NGOs work in the tribal areas of the district. The time period of the growth of NGOs in the district has an unavoidable link with the shift of tribal development policies and state reliance on NGOs on tribal and rural development. Such a link has helped the Hindu right wing forces to spread their networks in the tribal areas and continue their cultural hegemony either with the state power or with the support of the tribal development policies followed after the new economic reforms.

Education and health in the district is extensively managed by the NGOs. For example; all 50 child labour schools in the district are managed by different NGOs but funded by the Government of Orissa. There are eight child labour schools in the tribal areas of Thuamul Rampur and Langigarh, out of which six child labour schools are run by NGOs directly or indirectly, linked with Hindu right wing organisations (Nayak, 2009)[40]. The Hindu right wing forces also run their own educational institutions, independent of government control and funding. The post-economic reform educational policies, which allowed private institutions in the field of education, have consequently given legitimacy to Hindu right wing-led educational institutions.

There are 27 educational institutions run by the Hindu right wing forces in the name of *Saraswati*[41] *Sishu Mandir, Vidhya Varati, Vivekananda Ashram Schools, Vanavasi Kalyan Ashram, Kanya Ashram and Ekalavya Vidyalaya.* All these organisations running educational institutions in the tribal areas have a direct link with the Hindu right wing forces known as *Sangh Paribar.* It can be said that these organisations are the root of Hindu right wing forces, i.e., RSS and VHP, entrusted with the work of Hinduisation of tribals in the district. The district has the fourth highest concentration of schools i.e Saraswati Sishu Mandir in its tribal areas, which are directly managed by Hindu right wing forces (Nayak, 2009)[42]. And the growth of educational institutions, like Saraswati Sishu Mandir, is higher in the district than the other parts of the state (ibid).

In the field of health, NGOs are playing a pivotal role in Orissa. Even supervisory work in health services is being conducted by the NGOs. The monitoring of health services in the tribals areas of Thuamul Rampur, Langigarh and Madanpur Rampur is completely left in the hands of NGOs, as per the guidelines of the National Rural Health Mission (NRHM). The NGOs are promoted to undertake different health activities, in the tribal areas in particular, and in the district in general through the Private Public Partnership (PPP)[43]. The NGOs are contracted to carry out the management of health institutions completely in the district by mobilising resources and even impose user charges for health[44]. Health programmes like; eradication of HIV/AIDS, malaria, leprosy and blindness and nutritional programmes, were handed over to the NGOs and in this way, the new economic reforms have led to the transition of state-led free and universal health policies for tribals as citizens, to NGO-managed health policies for tribals as consumers of health services in the district.

Further, as most of the NGOs working in tribal areas in the district are directly or indirectly linked with the Hindu right wing forces, they become a tool for carrying out their Hinduisation programmes among the tribals. In this way, the social development of tribals is now dependent on their activities in the district. The growth of faith-based NGOs and civil society organisations after the implementation of the new economic reforms has changed the nature of existing indigenous civil society, autonomous cultural and communitarian political organisations. The growth of external organisations in the tribal areas have shifted the base of tribal organizations, with external NGOs and COs funded by governments and many other external funding agencies having corporate, charitable or faith based interests. The proliferation of faith based or religious NGOs and COs in the tribal societies in the district has depoliticised the economic crisis inherited through the new economic policy and its negative impacts on the tribals. This depoliticisation process and the growth of religious based organisations has not only successfully diverted the failure of development policies under the regime of neo-liberal policies but also enforced the cultures of mainstream society which is market conscious and consumerist by nature.

GROWTH OF NGOS AND ITS MEANING FOR TRIBAL DEVELOPMENT IN KALAHANDI

The growth of NGOs and the weakening of state in the development process[45] of tribals during the new economic reform period has led to a decline in state legitimacy over tribals and their communities in Kalahandi, and created a gap between the tribals and the state. This gap has the potential to give rise to resistance movements to claim tribals' citizenship rights in the district. But the gap is covered up by the growth of NGOs and COs in the economic reforms. This new informal institutional trend, created with the growth of NGOs in the development process, has created volatility in culturally plural tribal societies in the district as most of NGOs and COs are directly or indirectly linked with Hindu right wing forces. In politics, it has increased the interdependence among political actors including political parties, State and mining-led industrial capital in the district. Most of NGOs are directly or indirectly linked with political parties and leaders in the district. Similarly, it is difficult to generalise all NGOs as part of a development framework sponsored either by state or by national, multinational, transnational capital. Thus, the debate on the growth of NGOs, the nature of their activities and interactions with state, society and global capitalism is so diverse that it is difficult to follow a single approach to define the troika of relationship between NGOs, State and capitalism in the district.

However, in case of the growth of NGOs, it is clear that there is a particular growth trend of NGOs as depicted in (Nayak, 2009)[46]. Most NGOs are involved in the development of tribals, children and women in the rural areas of the district. It is difficult to generalise the nature of NGOs in Kalahandi district, but the majority of NGOs working in the tribal areas have a strong link with the Hindu right wing. It is also clear from the work of Nayak (2009)[47] that the majority of Hindu right wing NGOs has increased and they have expanded their operational base. Thus, it is not adventurous to say that post-economic reform has helped the growth of Hindu right wing NGOs in the tribal areas of the district. In the process of implementing different social development programmes like health and education, these NGOs are involved in the process of Hinduisation, which is effectively a process of de-tribalisation that converts tribals to the Hindu religion.

Historically such process of assimilation of tribals into the fold of Hindu social order started with the peasantisation of tribals in the district (Pati, 1999, 2001)[48]. Though this historical process of peasantisation of tribals gave non-tribal access to land and other natural resources it did not taken away the tribal culture and identity. As in the process of peasantisation, the non-tribals have become farmers by owning land in the tribal areas and the tribals have became peasants[49] and continued their subsistence production. The extension of tribal economy from forest to subsistence agricultural production has given a new social and economic status to the tribals within their geographical range of social relationships without markets, so the tribal culture has remained integral to the nature of production in the tribal societies in the district. Thus, the peasantisation of tribals in the district was not a cultural threat to their existence in the district.

But the Hinduisation process started by Hindu right wing NGOs during the post-reform period is a threat to the tribal culture due to the very nature of Hinduisation. The basis of Hinduisation of tribals is *sanskara* (religious, cultural, moral upbringing or purification ceremony to shape perfect transformation or rectify the mistakes)[50]. The *Vishwa Hindu Parisad* (World Hindu Council) and *Ratriya Swayam Sevak Sangh* (RSS) the cultural wings of the *Bharatiya Janata Party* (BJP) conduct such purification ceremonies in tribal areas through performing a ritual called *Jagyan* (sacred burning) to convert tribals to the Hindu religion with the help of the Vanavasi Kalyan Ashrams, Saraswati Sishu Mandir and other NGOs involved in the social development activities in the tribal areas. The Hindu right wing forces consider tribals not to be unique in their religious belief. "They are not Christians but Hindus in fact, and don't call it conversion as we are just bringing them back to the fold of their ancestors' religion," argue VHP activists. (Pioneer, 30/1/07). The Hinduisation process has created violence, as the idea of religious purity and violence are inseparable twins attached with the political process (Semelin, 2005). Thus the growth of Hindu right wing NGOs and process of purification of tribals in the district for Hinduisation during the post-economic reform period has generated violence and atrocities.

ATROCITIES, VIOLENCE AND CULTURAL SUPPRESSION OF TRIBALS IN THE DISTRICT

The Article-15, 17 and 27 of the Indian Constitution provides safeguards for tribals and to give effect to these constitutional provisions, the Scheduled Castes and Scheduled Tribes (Prevention of Atrocities Act) 1989 and the Bonded Labour System (Abolition) Act, 1976 were enacted and are still in operation to protect the tribals from different forms of atrocities. Despite these constitutional and legal provisions, atrocities against tribals have grown in the Kalahandi district during each successive year since the economic reforms. The caste atrocities are an integral part of Hindu social order which has been extended to the tribal areas and have became a daily feature of tribal life, aiding in the expansion of the activities of Hindu right wing forces to carry forward their agenda of Hinduisation of tribals in the Kalahandi district. I have all ready mentioned that there is a co-relationship between economic reforms and the growth of Hindu right wing forces in the tribal areas. Now I argue that there is a correlation between atrocities against tribals, economic reforms and the Hinduisation process.

The total number of reported atrocities against tribals was confined to 52 cases in 1980-85 and increased to 57 during 1985-90. But during the post-economic reform period, reported atrocities increased on an extraordinary scale. In total, 87 cases of tribal atrocities were filed in different police stations in the district during 1991-95 and increased further to 99 in 1995-2000. The area-wise classification of tribal atrocity cases reveals that atrocities against tribals are higher in the urban and non-tribal areas, whereas they are lower in the tribal dominated areas of the district. The tribals are more vulnerable to atrocities in urban areas of Kalahandi (i.e. Bhawanipatna, Dharamgarh, Kesinga and Junagarh) than the rural areas. However, atrocities increased even in the tribal dominated areas during the post-economic reform period (Nayak, 2009)[51]. Further, the classification of the nature of atrocities reveals that there has been a constant growth of atrocities against tribals by the land owning tribal, non-tribal class and higher castes in the district. It indicates the economic and cultural basis of the atrocities. Out of 42 criminal cases during 1980-1985, most of the cases were related to forest and land. There was a very marginal increase in tribal atrocity cases during 1985-90 and, during 1990-95, all forms of tribal atrocity cases increased. The classification of different cases reported in different police stations in the district reveals the nature of atrocities. There were 12 land related, five wage related, 13 forest related, three religious related, two caste related and one culture related during 1990-95. The land, forest, religious, caste and culture related atrocity cases increased further in 1995-2000 (Nayak, 2009)[52]. The data indicates that the cultural, religious and economic nature of atrocities related with land, forest and wages increased during the post-economic reform period (ibid).

However, two inferences can be made from the above statistical figures. The inferences are as follows; the economic dependency of tribals and their growing assertiveness about their social, cultural and political identity, and refusal to submit to the Hindu/Brahminical hegemony were causes in the atrocities on tribals in the district. The economic atrocities were the result of land alienation, denials of rights over forest and related to wages as well. In this way, there was a massive growth of atrocities against tribals due to economic and cultural reasons. Cultural reasons occurred due to Hindu cultural hegemony over tribal culture, which has grown ever since the economic reform programmes (Nayak, 2009)[53]. Thus, the growth of atrocities also reveals a necessary co-relationship with the economic reform programmes of 1991. The statistics also clearly show that the economic dependency relationships and tribals' assertiveness over their land, forest and matter of wages caused atrocities in the district. These issues multiplied during the economic reform period due to the multiplication of problems related to land, forest and wages. Another interesting factor is the cultural hegemonisation of Hindu right wing forces. Villages, where tribals as landless labourers depend upon landlords or rich farmers for their livelihood, and where the traditional caste equations have a potential to yield economic surplus to the latter, provide ideal settings for atrocities. In this way, there is a new alliance between the neo-liberal capitalist economy and the feudal structure. The institutional set-ups of neo-liberalism in a feudal structure uphold feudal order to establish economic hegemony in the district. The increased number of atrocities against tribals after the 1991 economic reforms reveals that there is an unex-pressed understanding and consensus between the Hindu right wing forces, local tribal and non-tribal feudal landlords and the neo-liberal economy. The obliteration of atrocities is only possible through economic empowerment of the tribal population and waging an uncompromising and concerted struggle against its non-economic manifestations, which indicates a struggle against Hindu right wing cultural hegemony. The process of cultural hegemony moves further with the proliferation of Hindu religious symbols, statues of gods and goddesses and temples in the tribal areas of the district.

STATUES, TEMPLES, RELIGIOUS IMAGES AND MAKING OF HINDU MAINSTREAM CULTURE IN TRIBAL AREAS

The process of Hinduisation in the tribal areas can be studied with the help of social anthropologists by analysing and interpreting customary behavior, cul-ture and its symbolic representations and the ways of its manifestations in Kalahandi. While looking at ethnographic facts about tribal societies in the district, the tribal religious and cultural practices are more than a representa-tion of tribal customs and traditions – they are a 'thick description'[54]; de-scriptions of the transition and absorption of tribal culture into mainstream Hindu culture to reflect economic and cultural objectives. It is just reflection of the reality and there is no interpretation in it, unlike the work of anthropol-ogists and sociologists. Any interpretation of tribal society and culture, based on empiricists' and rationalists' models of analysis, is short sighted by na-ture, limits the wider meanings attached to symbols, place and their cultural and religious habitat, which are embodied with the materiality of economic activities. "It is an explicit attack on geographical or technological determi-nism in interpreting domestic organisation. It demands an ecological ap-proach in which structure of ideas and of society, the mode of gaining liveli-hood and the domestic architecture are interpreted as a single interacting whole in which no one element can be said to determine the other" (Douglas,

1972: 513-21). In the case of tribal societies in the Kalahandi, the ecological approach allows us to understand the ways in which the inner-cultural transition of the tribals has taken place through outside conditions and environment. It provides an analytical tool to understand the social system in which the individual and community development transpiration is the primary concern of the ecological approach that includes economy, culture and environment (Bronfenbrenner, 1986: 723-742 and Ray, 1988:9-15). It is difficult to separate tribal culture and its mode of gaining livelihood in the Kalahandi district, where culture and economy are embedded with each other. Any attempt to dismantle tribal culture through Hinduisation is nothing but an attempt to absorb the tribal economy into mainstream economy making tribal economy, culture and livelihood more vulnerable by making tribals mere consumers.

The growth of Hindu temples and religious images are higher, in comparison to the activities of Christian missionaries during the economic reform period, and serve the role of dragging tribals into the mainstream culture in the district. Temples are being built up by the Vishwa Hindu Parisad (World Hindu Council) and its sister organisations working in the tribal areas. It is a part of their agenda to bring tribals into their fold. The logical, intellectual and narrative resources which RSS uses are heavily drawn from the narratives created and circulated by *Arya Samaj, Ram Rajya Parishad, and the Hindu Mahasabha Sangathan* that attempt to spread ideas of Hindu nationalism derived from socio-religious movements initiated by high caste Hindus (Jaffrelot, 1996: 11). These higher caste Hindus are the Brahmins; perpetuating Brahminical caste hierarchy and contributing the little existing non-institutionalised caste inequality among tribals and making wider contribution to the social inequalities by the Vanavasi Kalyan Ashram (forest dweller's welfare centre) and Vanavasi Kalyan Parisad (forest dweller's welfare council) working in the tribal areas. It has caused colossal damage to the social harmony that existed earlier, even within the existing caste system among tribals. The caste system among tribals is unlike the Hindu caste structure, which is based on the so-called labour division in society to maintain social and economic hierarchy. The caste system in tribal societies in Orissa is based on tribals' food habits, marriage practices, place of living, cultural and linguistic differentiation[55]. In terms of accessibility to resources, all tribals enjoy greater equality than non-tribal Hindus. There were no untouchables in tribal society previously, which is a great marker to differentiate between the Hindu caste system and caste system in the tribal society. Now, with the growing Hinduisation process, a sense of the concept of untouchability is being shaped in tribal societies in Kalahandi. Thus the power structure that existed earlier in the tribal society, in terms of a non-exploitative caste system by nature, is now becoming more exploitative. In the process of Hinduisation, the VHP and its affiliated organisations are reinforcing the Hindu caste system and caste inequality in the tribal society. The result of Hinduisation and perpetuation of exploitative caste hierarchy can be found from the following example; there used to be a very cordial relationship among Dombs[56] and other tribal groups in Kalahandi district, but now that relationship has been lost, both for social and economic reasons. Socially, tribals consider Dombs as untouchables now and look down at them - a product of Brahminical Hindu caste order. Economically, Dombs are working as middlemen between higher caste money lenders, traders, government officials and tribals which creates a sense of abhorrence among the tribals towards Dombs.

Apart from this kind of social and cultural transition in the tribal society, the VHP and its outfits in the tribal areas of the Kalahandi are also constructing statues of tribal martyrs or leaders very close to the temples to identify them as Hindus to attract tribal masses into their fold. They also construct temples near public places like hospitals, common ponds, and public places related with tribal narratives[57]. Then they create some sort of narrative and story surrounding the temple and the statue to create a sense of fellow feeling among tribals for Hindu culture within their subconscious or unconscious mind. The next step, followed by the VHP and its sister organizations, is to paint different images of Hindu gods and goddesses on the mud walls of tribal houses or on the walls of schools and other public places, to make tribals think and change their rituals and follow the Hindu ritual cult. This is a systematic design made by the Sangha Paribar to manipulate the minds of the tribals. It reminds me of the writings of Edward Bernays who said that, "the conscious and intelligent manipulation of the organised habits and opinions of the masses is an important element in democratic society. Those who manipulate this unseen mechanism of society constitute an invisible government which is the true ruling power of our country" (Bernays, 1928: 1). The Sangha Paribar has successfully carried out the prescriptions of Edward Bernays, for post-war corporate politics in USA, in an Indian and Orissa context through the Hinduisation process of tribals in the district.

The Hinduisation of tribals by the Hindu organisations is a greater strategy than vote bank electoral politics. In recent years, there has been a greater sign towards the collapse of orthodox Brahminical social order i.e. the caste system in India which was visualised by the Hindu ideologue M.S Golwalkar (1966) who has said that "the tribals can be given yajñopavîta[58]... they should be given equal rights and footings in the matter of religious rights, in temple worship, in the study of Vedas, and in general, in all our social and religious affairs. This is the only right solution for all the problems of casteism found nowadays in our Hindu society (ibid: 479)". This is the broader philosophical and political justification the Hindu right wing forces get from their ideologue that makes the Bharatiya Janata Party and its social Hindu outfits uphold that Hindu social order by talking about greater Hindu unity by incorporating tribals into the Hindu mainstream society. This has changed the entire landscape of tribal religious practice by creating a narrative around the statues and temples near it. The narrative projects the statues of tribal martyrs or other social and cultural heroes of the locality as being somebody from mainstream Hindu society by constructing temples near to his/her statue. The entire image created by this process ends up with the celebration of local festivals along with Hindu religious festivals in the temple. Over time, the Hindu religious festivals predominate, and then overthrow tribal festivals by branding them as incorrect, unholy and unsacred.

THE CHANGING NATURE OF RELIGIOUS AND CULTURAL NARRATIVES AMONG THE TRIBALS

The dominant Hindu narrative in the tribal society, through changing religious practices, forms the oral and written tradition by the documenting work of activists, educational and social organisations of the Hindu right wing forces. In the case of Christian missionaries, they tried to document tribal culture, religious practice and social set-up in tribal languages. They respected tribal culture in order to attract them to the fold of Christianity. In a few cases tribals converted into Christian but they remained as tribals as, in the process, the tribals identity was being protected in terms of language and culture. But here the process is completely reverse, with tribals not only losing their cultural and religious identity, but also their language - which is the most defining feature inside and outside tribal society.

However, the tribal narratives reflected in the religious and cultural folklores are a collective creation by the tribal communities and disseminated through oral traditions of cultural and religious tales to many generations of tribal people (Mishra, 1995, 2007; Thompson & Robert, 1960). They have their own purposes in terms of representing realities in their life and society that carry meanings, symbols and communicate ideas and their world views in the district. In a tribal oral tradition, the narrative opens the minds of both the creator and listener to reflect on and contextualise the reality in terms of space, time and person. No tribal narrative stands outside their cultural and social realm, which makes it so natural and acceptable in tribal societies, and creates a social order based on harmony, fellow feeling and communitarian norms (Mishra, 2007). During my fieldwork, I found that tribals are being categorised on the basis of their narratives in the district. Again narratives change according to place, people and local culture. The tribal narratives in the district are based on their everyday life experiences and beliefs. "Beliefs are adopted or rejected because they are relevant or not relevant to everyday needs and concerns (Turner, 1994:10)". This indicates that the narratives are constituted according to their real life problems. If the narrator fails to reflect on reality then the listener questions the narrator and while creating the next narrative the narrator incorporates the listener's views[59]. In a sense, there is democratic space available to the tribals even in the creation and dissemination of narratives. But the Hindu organisations working in the tribal areas intend to subjugate tribal, cultural and religious narrative in content, forms, character, and performance in its social, cultural and religious context by putting narratives into written texts with a Hindu frame of social order that creates a disorder in tribal society. "The creation of disorder," says Ben Amos, "could be interpreted as a verbal creation of wishful reality, a desired state of affairs that does not exist" (Ben Amos 1978). The written Hindu narratives of life and world view of tribals have taken away the freedom of the narrator and listener. This limit on freedom of tribal narratives through written texts is a conscious act of the Hindu right wing forces to establish a different kind of reality that is far from tribal life and society. There is no space for tribals to change the written narratives and, in the process, the tribals forget their own oral narrative tradition and narratives as well. "The hegemonic text is an instrument not simply for browbeating those who demur but also for exercising a positive intellectual and moral leadership both within the educational institutions and in the other institutions that make and remake imperial formations (Inden, 2000: 31, 1986:401-6)". This process of institutionalisation of knowledge through written text, and its dissemination, reinforces the hegemony of dominant mainstream Hindu culture and ideology in the tribal society by fixing tribals and their culture as essentially inferior. "In order to understand how a dominant ideology functions, one needs to examine how ideology beliefs and perspectives operate at the everyday level of consumption, production and distribution of beliefs (Turner, 1994:17)".

The consumption, production and distribution in tribal society are different from the mainstream Hindu society. Market-led mainstream Hindu society is based on mass consumption and over production for accumulation; the primary logic of modern capitalism. Thus, the attempt to transform and incorporate tribal society into the mainstream Hindu society is nothing but an attempt to dismantle the tribal way of production, distribution and consumption, which is based on the production according to necessity, communitarian distribution and the non-accumulative consumption pattern provides a problem for the development of capitalism in the tribal society. Thus, it is important to transform tribal society through the process of Hinduisation, which will pave the way to incorporate tribals into the global market as consumers. When there is an obstacle in the process of this kind of integration, then the ruling and non-ruling elites in society blame tribal culture for being a stagnant culture that is responsible for tribal underdevelopment. This process has taken a great leap forward during the process of economic reforms, which has shifted the state-led development and responsibility to the non-govern-

mental organisations; the NGOs working in tribal areas are basically affiliated to Hindu right wing organisations.

DEVELOPMENT OF UNDERDEVELOPMENT AMONG TRIBALS IN KALAHANDI; IS CULTURE THE CULPRIT?

The Kalahandi district in Orissa is not only known for its natural resources
reservoir but also for its underdevelopment and poverty in multiple forms.
Both tribal populations in particular and non-tribal poor in general, are the
most vulnerable sections in the district. All people in the Kalahandi district
including poor and tribal people are known as Kalahandia[60], who are commonly believed to be responsible for their underdevelopment and abject poverty. The mainstream societies in Orissa, from the coastal belt, consider them
as uncivilised, unconscious, illiterate and poor people in the state. The political elites of the district and state including the tribal elites and leaders consider that the people of the Kalahandi district lack a work culture, are lazy by
nature, alcoholic and drink away all their earnings. This perception is widely
prevalent among the Oriya masses as well as among political and bureaucratic elites. This idea is accelerated by the Oriya mainstream media, which
creates a consensus among the people about the causes of tribal underdevelopment in the state and in the Kalahandi district. By creating such a consensus, the public policy making politicians and policy executing bureaucrats in
the state and in the district get away from the failures of state led tribal
development policy and necessary role politics in the development of the
people and a region. It is interesting and relevant here to share my experience
while discussing the causes of tribal underdevelopment with politicians and
district administrators in the Kalahandi.

What causes tribal underdevelopment in the district? A young tribal leader from the district who was a minister in the state replied in the following
words: "No government, no state and nobody can develop tribals unless they
develop themselves. Tribals are lazy, never work to earn more money and
spend all their money by drinking wine - whatever they earn. They never
show interest in educational programs undertaken by the different governments in the state" (Anonymous, interviewed on 19/12/2004).

Similarly, the Kalahandi district administrator (collector) who is a part of
the all India civil service has replied by asking me a reverse question in a
bureaucratic way; "Tell me, what we can do to develop tribals and Kalahandia people?" I suggested the need for creative politics and policies that are
suitable for tribals and for their development. Then he started giving a long
lecture on tribal underdevelopment. Here I quote him, to reflect the mindset
of the bureaucrats on tribal underdevelopment. He told me that; "No policy
will work for tribal development unless they learn to work hard and under-

stand the value of money. These people are illiterate, never work and always drink a lot of wine. This is not the fault of tribals as individuals, rather these are inherited in tribal culture and, whatever the government does, they (tribals) will remain underdeveloped (Anonymous, interviewed on 08/03/2005)". Similar arguments were made by the thirteen administrators of local development institutions (BDOs) in the district.

However, giving a cultural reason for the tribal underdevelopment by the politicians and bureaucrats in Orissa and Kalahandi is a part of the colonial and apolitical legacy reflected in the mindset of the actors of the post-colonial political economy of development in India. The same type of explanation was given by the Winston Churchill when the British administration failed in the management of the Bengal famine of 1943. He said famine was caused by the tendency of people there to "breed like rabbits" and said Indians were "the beastliest people in world, next to the Germans (Roberts, 1994: 213)". "The explication belongs to the general tradition of finding explanations of disasters not in the bad administration but in the culture of the subjects (Sen, 2006: 106)". In the case of tribal underdevelopment in the Kalahandi district, the non-tribals and elites (both ruling and non-ruling) think that the cause of tribal underdevelopment is their underdeveloped culture. This cultural logic of underdevelopment is, in a way, subscribed to by the coastal belt people of Orissa - along with politicians, bureaucrats and elites in the district. There is a consensus among the Oriya elites and masses on the cultural logic of tribal underdevelopment following the legacy of neo-liberal economy of development politics and policies. The politicians, public policy makers, bureaucrats, mainstream people and elite tribals view tribals as uncivilised, illiterate and unhygienic people in the district. The cultural construction of underdevelopment in the district has led to the growth of the idea of the division of development planning under 'we' developed and 'the tribal other' underdeveloped.

The division of development planning under 'we' developed and 'the tribal other' underdeveloped:

The post-colonial planning for tribal development in Kalahandi has moved forward in such a way that it has created a dividing line between tribal and non-tribal people. The people who either get priority or capitalise the development policy towards them, have become 'we developed' in the process of development in the district. The people who either got marginalized, or remain isolated from the development process, have become 'the other underdeveloped i.e. the tribals'. Such division derives its philosophical foundation from the modernist project[61] of civil society, which is an embryonic and marginal construct to represent tribals in the politics of the modern development map of the district through industrialisation and commercialisation of agriculture.

However, the issue here is to put tribals at the centre of development policies and politics to enhance the human development index of tribals i.e. health, education and income. But unfortunately the review of the condition of health and education among the tribals in the district gives a dismal picture of tribal development. The issues of education and health have become the yardstick to define somebody as developed or underdeveloped in the process of development in the district. The tribal underdevelopment in health and education sectors indicates lack of availability and accessibility of health and education facilities in the tribal areas, which puts tribals in a marginalised situation. The lack of availability and accessibility of health and educational infrastructures in the tribal areas is a product of continuous neglect of tribals and their areas in the development policy. The development policies followed after the implementation of the new economic reforms has widened the process of marginalisation of tribals in the health and education sector and thus widened the division among people i.e. 'we developed' and the tribal 'other underdeveloped'. However, there is a renewed interest in the tribal society in terms of indigenous medicines, herbs and the idea of sustainability. Even in the field of art, tribal art in the district is not considered to be modern and diversely rich to represent human life and society (Mishra, 2007).

However, the post-economic reform political economy of tribal development in the district does not take these unique aspects of tribal communities into account while making policies and programmes. The idea is to integrate the tribal economy with the mainstream market, which has a negative impact on tribals in the district. In order to avoid the criticisms of negative impacts, the policy making elite[62] give the cultural logic of tribal underdevelopment. The elites' views on tribal underdevelopment can be located in the debates within the global political economy of development where cultural explanations were given for economic underdevelopment[63]. If policy is successful in bringing tribal development then it is the result of development policy and planning. If the development policy and planning fails to bring desired tribal development then backward culture is responsible. It is a very simple logic given by the policy makers, politicians and bureaucrats. There is nothing to be critical of and no need to be accountable for the policy failure. The fallacies of cultural theorists like Lawrence E. Harrison and Samuel P. Huntington (2000), Edward Banfield (1958) and Thomas Friedman (2000) can be directly located while looking at the underdevelopment of tribals and their areas in the Kalahandi. The same cultural legacy followed by the advocates of social capital theory. The fallacies of both cultural theorists and social capital theorists are evident while looking at the development of underdevelopment in Kalahandi district.

During my fieldwork, I met many tribal men and women in the district. During my informal interaction with them, I asked the following questions directly. "What causes tribal underdevelopment? Why is your area so under-developed? Who is responsible for the underdevelopment of your area and people? Do you think your culture is responsible for the tribal underdevelopment?"

Many tribal men and women replied with a sense of discontent, which can be summarised in the words of a tribal woman[64]. The woman started talking to me on a variety of issues confronted by tribals and replied to all my questions with one answer. She put it directly in the following words;

> "All government employees including teachers and doctors, 99 percent of NGO workers, educated tribal people, contractors and politicians are respon-sible for the underdevelopment of tribals and their areas. There are few excep-tions, but their views are marginal like mine. These people are exploiting tribals and taking away all the government money to their own accounts and spreading the ideas of corruption among tribals. Any tribal or non-tribals ques-tion them, then they are bribed. I've been asked to take a bribe many times but I've declined to take one as a consequence of my culture and my own ideas. The government officials, teachers, doctors and NGO workers, those who come from outside Kalahandi, especially from the costal Orissa, they never think to leave the place and within a few years, they become rich and buy land, construct houses and stay here permanently. Tell me Babu[65]," she asked. "How come these people became rich and developed within a few years by settling down in my area and we have remained underdeveloped and poor by being the natives of this area. If the culture is responsible for underdevelop-ment and my area and people are underdeveloped then why are these people coming to this area? My area is full of natural resources and minerals and the government is allocating lots of money for our development as a part of its constitutional obligations for welfare activities and affirmative action. But everything goes into their pockets. These people are putting us in a trap of poverty and underdevelopment by which they can gain a lot from it. They can continue to exploit us in the name of development (Anonymous, interviewed on 17/04/2005)".

Thus, now cultural theorists and advocates of neo-liberal ideas, especially people like Edward Banfield, Thomas Friedman and their legacies in India, Orissa and Kalahandi must answer these questions in the context of a tribal woman's views on development led by state, its institutions and different actors. The linking of outsiders, in everything from development planning to planning implementation for the development of tribals in Kalahandi and Orissa, has caused much more harm than any good. Again the linking of modern markets with indigenous local economy through neo-liberal policies under the name of the new economic reforms has caused a lot of damage in the process of development of tribals and their area. The tribal culture, social structure and values are neither detriments to development nor responsible for underdevelopment. It is perhaps just the opposite, as they are hindrances to material progress of a market oriented capitalist economy. This is the

reason for which the neo-liberal market economy is invading the tribal culture with the help of the Hinduisation process, carried out by the right wing
Hindu fundamentalist forces and accelerated by the changing role of minimal
state and public policy in the post-economic reform period. The idea is to
incorporate tribals into the global market. When market forces have failed to
incorporate tribals into the global market, due to the culture-led economy of
tribals, it has required the help of Hindu right wing forces to dismantle the
tribal culture by which it will be easier for the global market to incorporate
tribals into its own fold.

RESISTANCE FROM THE BELOW

Resistance is a natural consequence when development becomes domination
and marginalisation in the field of economy, culture and society. The relationship between domination and resistance can be visualised in the new
social movements in the contemporary India (Sinha, 2003). Further, there is
an essentialist relationship between economic growth led development and
violence[66] (Bates, 2001), which can be in the form of resistance and counter
resistance. There is both organised and unorganised resistance from the tribals against the process of economic and cultural marginalisation in the
district. The materiality of economic activities for livelihoods of tribal communities in the Kalahandi district is embodied in their culture and natural
environment. The struggle of tribals to protect their culture and environment
is a struggle to ensure their livelihoods. The twin process of economic marginalisation and de-tribalisation by Hinduisation has one economic objective
i.e. access to tribal land and other natural and mineral resources in the tribal
areas of the district. The political output of such a process is the consolidation of Hindu right wing vote bank politics among the tribals. The resistance
by tribals to this twin process is unavoidable.

The tribal communities in the Langigarh block have strongly resisted the
establishment of the Vedanta Alumina plant and the mining of bauxite from
the nearby Niyamgiri hill (mountain of law). The organised resistance movement started with the formation of the Niyamgiri Suraksha Samiti (Save
Niyamgiri Association) on April 7, 2004, which has more than one thousand
tribal people as its members. The Prakrutik Sampad Surakshya Parisad
(PSSP-Save Natural Resources Association), based in the neighboring district of Rayagada district, has also supported and joined the struggle. The
clarion call of the struggle is 'Vendat Hatao' (Remove Vendant) and save the
lives, livelihoods, forests, water and land. The hill is a place of worshiping
Niyama raja (king of law) by the Kondh tribe.

The tribal people of two villages i.e. Kinari and Bolbhatta are at the
forefront of the resistance movement. On 22nd June, 2002, nearly one thou-

sand people submitted a memorandum to the Chief Minister of Orissa opposing the project. And 199 petitions were filed before the Revenue Inspector's office demanding cancellation of the project. On 9th April 2003, more than 170 tribals of six villages protested in front of the Langigarh police station against the proposed Alumina plant, which was said to be the first unorganised resistance to the industrial complex in the area[67]. On 11 November 2005, more than 2,000 tribal protesters under the banner of the Niyamgiri Suraksha Samiti marched towards the gate of Vedanta Alumina plant in Lanjigarh and urged the company to close the plant and leave the area. Despite adverse conditions created by the state repression and geographical remoteness, both unorganised and organised resistance movements keep resounding, even in the Bhubaneswar, the state capital of Orissa. On May 16, 2006 and March 1, 2007 similar protests were organised by the tribals of the district to save their land, environment and god. The scope of the resistance movement has expanded to London now where the Vedanta Alumina Ltd. is registered as a company. On 1st May 2008, the tribal of the Langigarh block came all the way to London with the help of the Mines and Communities, Survival International and Action Aid to protest against the company and appealed to shareholders and banks to boycott it[68].

A tribal leader and President of the Niyamgiri Suraksha Samiti Daisingh Majhi has said that the "Niyamgiri hills, popularly called Niyam Penu (God) are considered as the mother of the tribals. Such emotional issues should be kept above petty politics. The tribals are bothered about the area's forests, natural springs and wildlife resources. The parties should not indulge in politics over the nature's gift"[69]. The *Dongria Kondh* activist, Jitu Jakeskia, explains that "Niyam Raja is our supreme god. His name means Lord of Law, he made all things. Niyamgiri Mountain is the most important place for Dongria Kondh people, it is like Niyam Rajah's temple that is why our people worship nature, and they have to protect nature"[70]. In this way, the Dongria Kondh in particular, and tribals in general, have an intrinsic relationship with the Niyamgiri, which embodies their spiritual, social, cultural and economic lives. If the Vedanta bauxite mining takes place then it will have an irreversible impact on tribal people. This fear of losing lives, livelihood and culture is the basis of resistance movement in the district. But the state government, with the help of the district administration, local police and hired goons of the Vedanta company officials are trying to suppress the resistance.

However, local resistance by tribal communities is a reality in the district, which is romanticised by some NGOs and Civil Society organizations - whereas some others try to sabotage the resistance. The radical groups and communist parties[71] have joined in the local struggles whereas the district unit of the liberal Indian National Congress (INC)[72] uses populist rhetorics and supports tribal struggles. This cultural apathetic orientation of communist parties and populist politics of the INC provides space to the Hindu right wing forces to use the opportunity to Hinduise the tribal culture in the district. "The problems of adivasies are related to jal (water), jungle (forests) and jameen (land). The transfer of their resources to non-tribal areas is the question. Instead of addressing issues of political economy the Sangh Parivar and the BJP, whose social base is among upper castes and middle classes, divert the attention of adivasies to misguided targets (Lobo 2002: 4848-49)" both from economic marginalisation and de-tribalisation by Hinduisation. The struggle to save the mountain of worship i.e. the Niyamgiri hill by local tribals is a struggle to save tribal livelihood. A member of Dongria Kondh community, Rajendra Vadaka of Kajuri village says, "Niyamgiri is our God. We live in these mountains and survive. We don't have any land on which we can produce and live. We are dependent on the mountains. We won't leave Niyamgiri. We are mountain people and if we go somewhere else we will die"[73]. Similarly, Anami Dei, from Kansari village says, "we want to stay here and to keep worshipping our Mother Earth"[74].

The Hinduisation of tribals by the Hindu right wing organisations and affiliated NGOs helps the transformation of the spiritual and religious practice of tribals in the district. The non-structural form of worshiping mountain, earth and natural environment by tribals is being transformed to the structural form of worship of Hindu gods and goddesses. Once the local tribal communities stop worshiping the Niyamgiri hill, then resistance to mining and industrialisation will reduce. In this way, the process of spiritual and religious transformation helps to sabotage the struggles of local tribal communities to protect their cultural, spiritual world that embodies their land, livelihood and environment. The primitive tribal groups i.e. Dongria Kondh and other tribal communities hold customary rights over land and forest under the Indian Constitution. And mining in an area that comes under "Schedule V Area" is protected under Section 18 of the Indian Constitution. It states that land can neither be transferred to private companies nor to the non-tribal people without the consent of tribal peoples. In the case of the Vedanta Mining at Langigarh, the tribals have not given their consent yet. The process of Hinduisation of tribals by the Hindu right wing forces helps to remove these legal obstacles to the mining led industrial capital in the district. Once the tribals are Hinduised then the constitutional provisions will not be applicable. In this way, the Hinduisation of tribals serves double purposes; reduces resistance and removes legal barriers to mining led industrial capital.

CONCLUSION

In conclusion, it can be said that the Hinduisation process of tribals in the Kalahandi district, led by the Hindu right wing forces, has grown rapidly with the help of the new economic reforms, which have weakened the state-led local development institutions in the welfare delivery and development activities and shifted the role of state to market and to the NGOs. Most of the NGOs working in the tribal areas of the Kalahandi district are either directly or indirectly affiliated to Hindu right wing organisations and their politics. In the process of the Hinduisation of tribals the mainstream market has been able to spread its networks into the tribal areas. Both the Hinduisation process and the market have dismantled the tribal culture and society for the deepening of capitalism by removing their legal and constitutional protections. The deepening of capitalism has caused social, economic and cultural vulnerability in the tribal society, which has questioned tribal development planning. In reply, the present tribal development plans and the neo-liberal policy making elites give the cultural logic of tribal underdevelopment, which is an extension of global capitalist logic, for accumulation of profit through market, culture and religion. In this way the Hindu right wing forces have helped the global capitalist market to incorporate tribals and their society into its fold. The process of Hinduisation of tribals in the district has also been able to sabotage the local resistance by the tribals to protect their culture and economy.

Conclusion

Hinduisation of Tribals and the Deepening of Capitalism in the Tribal Societies of the Kalahandi District during Post Economic Reform Period

This chapter is the concluding chapter that documents the nature of the changes in the tribal societies that took place in both tribal culture and economy in the Kalahandi district as a consequence of, and in the wake of the post-1991 economic reforms. While identifying the impact of the reforms on tribals, it also illuminates the co-constitutive relationship between the economic reforms and the Hinduisation of tribals. It argues that the Hinduisation of tribals has accelerated the deepening of capitalism and its accumulation processes in the tribal areas of the district.

INTRODUCTION

There can remain no doubt that the misery inflicted by the new economic reform policies of liberalisation, globalisation and privatisation is qualitatively different and infinitely more intensive than that experienced in the tribal areas of the Kalahandi district prior to 1991. The new economic reforms have accelerated the Hinduisation process, which has supplanted existing semi-feudal societies and correspondent power relations among the tribals and their communities in Kalahandi and Orissa with mainstream power relations. This process has been accelerated by the central, state, district and local administration, through public policy and mainstream institutions, to constitute a more monstrous combination than any prior understanding of development, administration, economy, politics and culture in the tribal society.

Notably, this is not solely a distinctive feature of the new economic policy in India, but rather it is a part of the global political economy that drives people from a need based self sufficient society to a desire based consumer society. The transformation of the tribals' society and culture in the Kalahandi district is a reflection of this broader process.

The economic and cultural transformation of the tribals and their societies in Kalahandi is a result of the implementation of the new economic reforms, which accelerate mining based industrialisation, natural resource exploitation and the penetration of mainstream culture through Hinduisation. As strangely complex, rapid, and destructive as development policy in tribal areas may appear, it did not go deeper than intended by the state and its public policy making institutions. Rather, it is a result of an inner contradiction inherent to the neo-liberal new economic reforms, which prescribes economic growth with a human face, while simultaneously reducing the role of public institutions in the process of implementing structural adjustment policies. In turn, this reduces public expenditure and prescribes the progressive redundancy of public institutions by rendering them inefficient and often defunct. The new economic reforms have broken down state-led tribal development. No symptoms of reconstitution are yet apparent. In its place is a regulatory state, representing the good governance agenda of aid and donor agencies more than a welfare state. In tribal areas this process has increased vulnerability more than generating any identifiable good.

The loss of the old world and the previous orientation of public policy in India was a legacy of the Indian freedom struggle and consequently focused development policy on the welfare of its citizens with a special focus on tribals. That this previous orientation lost what had been at least a certain rhetorical gloss, without the gain of a new normative status, imparts a particular note of melancholy to the present misery of the tribals. The result for the tribals has been alienation from previous sources of livelihood in the name of economic growth and development, the suppression of tribal customs and traditions in the name of modernisation, and the effective eradication of past history, which although painful, represented a situation more preferable to present conditions. The processes scrutinised here can be further explained in terms of the capitalist and industrial transformation of agriculture, land, forest and other natural resource utilisation in the tribal areas. Again this has been extended and deepened via the Hinduisation of the tribals.

THE TRIBAL ECONOMY AND PROCESSES OF CAPITALIST ACCUMULATION THROUGH AGRICULTURE, LAND, FOREST AND OTHER NATURAL RESOURCES

After the inception of the New Economic Reforms in India, the transition in agriculture began. This involved a shift from food crop production to cash crop production. In other words, the purpose of agricultural production moved from direct consumption to the production of primary products for exchange on the market. The intrusion of the market as a result of market-dependent production has opened up the tribal economies on an unprecedented scale. This has led to the development of a novel situation where much of what tribal people consume is either imported from Andhra Pradesh or from the costal districts of Orissa. Whatever they produce is exported to these same places.

This process unfolded in the tribal district of Kalahandi via both tribal and non-tribal local elites working as intermediaries between tribal farmers and outside traders. In turn, this has generated a new class in society and amongst both the tribal, and non-tribal farmers in particular, whose power and wealth has become based on this new sector of the agricultural economy. In this process of transition, the tribal economy took on a new shape through which a new elite class formed within the tribal communities. Particularly the land-owning tribals i.e. Gantia Kandha became powerful. They are few in number, but control most of the tribal lands in the district. This class embarked upon a strategy of grabbing tribal land and so created mass landlessness among tribals. The landless tribals have become either bonded labourers or small wage labourers in their own locales. In this way, the population has been marginalised, restricted and oppressed in their own land and sometimes displaced.

The newly formed tribal land owning elites have joined with the costal elites in order to exploit tribals and their resources. The combination of newly formed tribal elites and costal belt elites in this accumulation process is important to an understanding of the way modern capitalist development proceeds on the grounds of an underdeveloped and mostly self-sustaining economy. The combined accumulation process has given rise to a class structure in which tribal elites control land, natural resources and capital and render their fellow tribals subordinate to them. It has led to a new class structure in which tribal wage labour lacks access to their property. The new agricultural production structure has invited the increasing presence of the market in the tribal areas. This increasing presence and intrusion of the market has reproduced and sustained these relations to generate more profit.

I term this as *"modern mode of accumulation in tribal areas"* represented by mining-led corporate capital'. Elizabeth Mary Rata (1997) described it as the emergence of 'tribal capitalism' in her study of tribals in New Zealand.

However, the term 'tribal capitalism'[1] can lead to fallacious conclusions. This study on tribals in the Kalahandi district of Orissa suggests that here, instead of a 'tribal capitalism', tribals are becoming marginalised and losing control over their own resources, production networks, and labour. Only a few tribal elites, in combination with costal elites, control wealth in the accumulation process unleashed under the auspices of the new economy. Rata uses Regulation Theory and Marxism to develop her thesis of 'tribal capitalism'. However, the use of regulation theory is relevant for my study. The modes of accumulation in the tribal areas of Kalahandi take place in a free market regime without the presence of a proper market structure, creating a *regime of accumulation* under the joint venture of tribal elites and non-tribal coastal elites and supported by public policy made by the state and government concomitant, with mining-led industrial capital in its local, national and international form. Regulatory laws are made by the state to protect the interests of the market. A specific regime of governance emerges; a police state to suppress resistance in the name of maintaining law, order and peace.

This transition process has fundamentally altered the entire spectrum of social relations among tribal people, as well as their location. The result is a transformed social structure in the tribal areas. This process, a derivation of wider capitalist processes, enabled the capitalisation of the traditional tribal economy and means of production and commodity production with community resources. In so doing, the meaning of communitarian social relations in the tribal society has been substantially altered. Further, through a strategy of exclusion, the tribals have lost possession of traditional sources of livelihood and the means of production. The tribal society and its social relationships have become more complex as the new economy disaggregates the tribal population as bonded labourers, wage earners, workers and tribal elites (slave shareholders of new economy). The reduced economic mobility of the tribal bonded labourers, wage earners and workers, puts them in a marginalised social position and makes them more vulnerable to crisis. In contrast, the newly formed tribal elites have moved upward, both in economic and social terms, and joined mainstream society. The Hinduisation process has incorporated tribals into mainstream society as unequal partners, while at the same time integrated the tribal economy in a global market by constituting tribals as consumers.

HINDUISATION AND THE DEEPENING OF CAPITALISM IN THE TRIBAL SOCIETIES OF THE KALAHANDI DISTRICT

The changes and transformations taking place in the tribal society, culture and economy of the Kalahandi district during the post-reform period sets many challenges for the tribal people in the district. These challenges arise directly from cultural and economic changes in the tribal societies. The tribals in Kalahandi are experiencing the deepening of capitalism in their culture and economy. The first phase of the penetration of capitalism into tribal areas took place through the market with the transformation of tribal agriculture from food production to cash crop production. The first phase of capitalist deepening in the district started with capitalist agriculture i.e. export oriented cash crop production. This has led to a contradictory situation where there is a growth of cash crop production, without a cash crop market in the district to sell, exchange and distribute these cash crops. Government marketing boards were rendered defunct under the guises of structural adjustment programmes; a package of liberal economic reform programmes. This has compelled the tribals to sell their products at low prices to local businessmen working as intermediaries between the tribals and big cash crop businesses of either the neighboring state, Andhra Pradesh, or the coastal commercial and trading elites of Orissa. This has led to the pauperisation of tribal peasantry and a situation of perpetual poverty and food crisis.

The second phase of the deepening of capitalism in the district took place in the wake of the 1991 economic reform period. In this phase, capitalism not only transformed the tribal economy, but also its society and culture. This phase illuminates the way in which Hindu right wing forces have played, and continue to play a crucial role in the deepening of capitalism in the tribal societies of the district. A change at the level of the state in the post-1991 execution of public policy has witnessed the withdrawal of the Indian state from welfare delivery. As a consequence, state and government planning for welfare and development has clearly directed Non-Governmental and Civil Society organizations to take up the function of welfare delivery. Public policy, made through the various five year plans in the post 1991 period, has made it clear that NGOs and COs would play a vital role in the development and welfare of the tribals in particular, and people in general. This new trend at the Indian state level has given a golden opportunity for Hindu right wing organisations to widen their social, cultural, and religious networks in the tribal areas of the country. Most of the NGO's and COs working in the tribal areas have their roots or affiliations (both directly and indirectly) with right wing Hindu political and cultural forces.

In the name of the development and welfare of tribals, these organisations have promoted their agenda of Hinduisation. The Hinduisation process in the tribal areas of Kalahandi district has eroded an older communitarian culture, which represented an obstacle to capitalist market integration. Thus, the Hinduisation of tribals has served the interests of the market. The promulgation of a Hindu network through NGOs in the tribal areas has served to incorporate tribals as consumers in the mainstream market, which in turn is rooted in the logic of the global capitalist market. In this way, the Hinduisation process

has created a new economic and cultural alignment between the tribal economy and culture and the global capitalist market, resulting in the commodification of all aspects of tribal life and society (i.e. tribal cosmology, forest,
tradition and culture). The commodification of tribal society and tribal way
of life has led not only towards cultural disintegration, but also more substan-
tively to cultural assassination through Hinduisation. The Hinduisation of
tribals, or de-tribalisation, has also helped remove constitutional and legal
barriers to the access of mining-led industrial capital to land and other natural
resources in tribal areas. It is impossible to access tribal land and other
natural resources in the tribal areas without dismantling tribal identity in
terms of culture, which provides them legal and constitutional protection.

Agricultural transformation in the tribal areas has caused both economic
and cultural dislocation, which, again, has been accelerated by the Hinduisation process. A market and money-led capitalist culture has found a new ally
in right wing Hindu forces in the expansion of the global market by increasing the number of consumers. The deprivation caused by this transformation
in the tribal culture and economy has bred increasing violence in the tribal
areas, both in its transformatory and regressive forms.

Transformatory violence in terms of resistance to these new developments is driven by ultra left wing political groups i.e. Naxalites Movement.
This misappropriates the language of transformation by de-politicising the
class struggle by violent means without having a class conscious organisation
and mass base. In turn, the state justifies its counter violence in the name of
law and order for peace. Thus, the 'protection of the people' is leading to a
decline in the democratic culture of the country. The retrograde form of
violence is perpetuated by the Hindu right wing forces against Christians
living and working in the tribal areas, and also occurs among tribal communities. The perpetuation of violence is innate to the capitalist system, from
the mercantile capitalism of the 16th century to the corporate or finance
capitalism of the 21st century. However, the development of the capitalist
system has proceeded by dismantling the existing communitarian social system of the tribals in Kalahandi district. Through this process of destruction, it
penetrates and establishes its institutions and the market in the tribal areas, at
the same time creating a capitalist social system. Hindu right wing forces
working in the tribal areas of the Kalahandi district are assisting the process
of creating a capitalist social system by transplanting mainstream urban Hindu culture. The process of creating a capitalist social system not only destroys communitarian social norms, but also undermines a self sufficient
economy and the culture affiliated to it. By destroying the subsistence economy and its correspondent culture, capitalism creates a culture of desire in
tribal areas where tribals can enter into the capitalist market as consumers. In
sum, a consumer culture is therefore established and provides the basis for
capitalist social relations.

The social, political, economic and cultural crisis conditions in the tribal areas have additionally created a favorable environment for the growth of transformatory politics and resistance movements. These alternative forces are yet to emerge, but are likely to play an increasing role. This transformatory resistance movement must come from the tribals if it is to sustain tribal identity, culture and economy. My thesis proposes a bottom up tribal resistance movement with twin objectives. These would be a movement against the capitalist market economy and Hinduisation and a movement against inequality and exploitation in the tribal areas, which has been reinforced by tribal and non-tribal elites. Such a movement, with these specific twin objectives, has the potential to protect tribal society and tribal identity from increasing levels of vulnerability, exploitation and underdevelopment and pave the path towards alternative radical politics. In the long run, this may influence a change in the nature of state and be augmented with a mass orientation.

POSTSCRIPT

The book examines the social, economic and cultural impact of the new economic reforms on the tribals in the Kalahandi district of Orissa. This research explores the transition in tribal economy, culture and society during and after the economic reform process. The consideration of a more coordinated impact study on social, economic and cultural transition of tribals contributes to an understanding of the development process and economic policies that have led to the negative economic and political outcomes.

Further, the research deals with the issues involved in the guided tribal development programme in the aftermath of the new economic reforms in India, which aids the growth of Hinduisation and the de-tribalisation process. I argue that the Hinduisation of tribals in the Kalahandi district is not a political process, rather it is an economic process of the capitalist market. The economic reform is the key factor that has helped the growth of economic power, political authority and thus, social legitimacy of the Hindu Right wing forces to Hinduise tribals in the Kalahandi district. The thesis is not following the idea of cumulative causation, thereby examining the causal relationship between the Hindu right wing forces with national and global capital, while analysing the conditions of social, cultural, economic and religious transition of the tribals in the Kalahandi district of Orissa. Many historians, political scientists, scholars, economists and activists argue that the Hinduisation of tribals by the Hindu right wing is a political process. My research here challenges such an assumption and argues that the Hinduisation of tribals is an economic process to integrate tribals in the mainstream market, as consumers, and at the same time control the productive resources of the tribal areas by removing constitutional protective measures for tribals. This is only possible through de-tribalising the tribals. Thus, Hinduisation is a process of de-tribalisation that has economic outcomes that marginalise tribals further in economic and cultural terms.

The relevance of this kind of study is based on its contribution to the field of public policy in terms of guiding policy makers to understand the logic of tribal society, culture, economy and their perceptions and aspirations for development. The change from a state-command welfare system to a market based non-governmental system is a radical one that is played out in the economic arena with a new set of rules and different objective functions for the government and the state in the development planning in India. The new experience of the tribals in terms of a rapid systemic change is unique. Due to the fact that unlike the other mainstream societies in India, which already had a market conscious social order before the 1991 new economic reforms, there was little experience of the market in the social order of the tribal societies in the Kalahandi of Orissa. The theoretical literature on economic transition implicitly takes for granted the existence of grassroots pressure and internal momentum for the transformation of a tribal society for development. The cultural and economic transition of the tribal society in the Kalahandi district is rather unique in that the top-down economic reform process has reinforced a crisis in a self-sufficient district where production and per capita availability of land is higher than the other districts in Orissa. Thus the impact of the new economic reforms on the tribals in Kalahandi is visible and more acute.

Empirically, the research questions the tribal development policies; an offshoot of the neo-liberal political economy development, which has aided the spread of the Hinduisation of tribals by Hindu right wing forces in the tribal areas. It also tries to explain the problems of Hinduisation and the negative consequences of transition in traditional tribal culture, economy and society, which is intertwined with each other. Theoretically, it provides the narratives delineating the relationship between the medieval, feudal and Hindu right wing forces and the intertwining of modern industrial, finance capital to accelerate the process of accumulation by expropriating natural resources in the tribal areas of the Kalahandi district in Orissa.

Notes

INTRODUCTION

1. Tribe or tribal is a contentious term in UK and elsewhere in the world but it refers to one of the primitive communities of India preferring to be called *Ādivāsīs* - literally meaning "original inhabitants". They are also known as the Atavika (forest dwellers) in Sanskrit texts and branded as Vanavasi or Girijans (forest dwellers) by the Hindu right wing forces. The colonial British administration branded tribals as Animist, hill and forest tribes, primitive tribes, criminal tribes in the Census reports of 1891 to 1941. The post-colonial Indian rulers have used the term "Schedule Tribe" for affirmative action purposes under the provisions of the Indian Constitution. The term 'tribe' and its usage are discussed in detail later in this chapter.

2. I subscribe to the ideas of case studies as it "always sought to criticise the concepts and practices of the so called development policies implemented...sketch in or explain what I believed to be the alternative to these concepts and practices (Amin, 1994:150)." The idea and objective behind taking the Kalahandi district as my case study is to reflect on the problems associated with neo-liberal economic policies which puts an affluent region and people into a trap of vulnerability (poverty, unemployment, food insecurity and underdevelopment).

3. The new institutional paradigm rejects neoclassical approach to political economy and directs interdisciplinary research to understand and explain the role of different institutions in the development and transformation of different societies.

4. For example, tribals' knowledge about ethno-medicine is both verified by natural scientists and social scientists. The work of Behera and Mishra (2005) deals with the ethno-medico-botany of the Kandha tribe and their medical practice for genito-urinary diseases in Orissa. The social anthropologists (Pramukh and Palkumar, 2006) give us the detailed idea about the value of local tribal knowledge and its scientific basis. For further debates and discussions, see; Barth (2002), Sillitoe (1998), Rajasekharan, Warren and Babu (1991).

5. By 'methodological individualism', I mean the knowledge based on and derived from methodological research is 'only scientific knowledge'. The basic argument is that the knowledge can not be scientific without a method of study. That means scientific knowledge is only methodological knowledge which is based on causality. Thus, it reduces explanation. Methodological individualism puts primacy of facts about individuals over facts about social entities; a project of post modernism. While attacking methodological individualism, I do not believe in the method of post -modernism which attack s theory and methodology. The post -modernists claim to relinquish all attempts to create new knowledge in a systematic fashion, but instead an "anti-rules" fashion. However, my argument is neither against theory nor against methodology. It is for an interdisciplinary approach towards science-knowledge and truth. There is no single

approach or methodology to acquire scientific knowledge. Any attempt to acquire knowledge through monolithic model driven methodological research makes research incomplete , produces inadequate knowledge and is reductionism by nature. In the same way, without theoretical and methodological background , the research and knowledge derived from it is fragile, limited and bias ed (For further analysis; see Audi, 1995:679, Trout, 1991). Many people like Hodgson (1988) consider methodological individualism is a neo -liberal and neo -classical economic project. Authors like Harriss-White (2006) goes further by saying that neo -liberal and neo -classical economic philosophy is asocial and ahistorical as well.

6. The most fascinating account of such trends in social science research, has given by John Holmwood who has argued that "the connection between explanation and understanding in the social sciences is not simply an issue of formal methodology, it is an urgent issue of the ethics of sociological reporting, as well as media reporting (Holmwood, 2007:88)".

7. See; Norris, C. (1979,19 97) for further understanding and a detailed study.

8. For me, political economy is more an approach than a concept. Both classical and Marxian academics tend to assume a political economy in which power is reflexive of economic relations. Engel's assertion speaks for both the classical and Marxian traditions. In his words "political economy in the widest sense is the science of laws governing the production and exchange of the material means of subsistence in human society" (Engel, 1954: 203). It indicates that the method of Marxian political economy studies the conditions that determines the production relation and helps us to understand and isolate the method of abstraction.

9. The analysis can be further extended by looking at the Theses on Feuerbach where Marx (1845) is talking about reality as sensuousness conceived only in the form of the object or of contemplation (Marx 1845: 13-15). So there is no place for subjectivity.

10. Value free research is a myth in Social Science research as social scientists deal with society where researcher is a part of it. Thus value free research can be shifted by value frank research, which has more potential to produce objective knowledge and scientific generalisations. I am trying to reflect on the reality while doing my research on public policy impact where there is no place for value judgments.

11. See the Map-3 and Map-4 for the two tribal blocks in the district i.e. Langigarh and Thuamul Rampur block respectively.

12. The tribal groups who don't stay in the schedule areas are known as dispersed tribal groups. In Kalahandi district, the tribal groups who aren't staying in the Thuamul Rampur and Langigarh block of the district are known as dispersed tribal group. The Government of Orissa formulates a different plan of action for these groups. Thus, 'dispersed tribal group' is an administrative term created for the management of development programmes.

13. This can be better explained with Karl Marx (1844). For Marx "nature is man's inorganic body-nature, that is, in so far as it is not itself the human body. Man lives on nature-means that nature is his body, with which he must remain in continuous interchange if he is not to die. That man's physical and spiritual life is linked to nature means simple that nature is linked to itself, for man is a part of nature" (Marx: 1844, translated by M. Milligan, 1967:112). This is further extended by Vernon Venable (1966:56-73), G. Petrovic (1967) and E. Fromm (1967:44). This kind of philosophical expression can be found in tribal narratives; i.e. 'the land and forest does not belongs to us, we belong to forest and land' which speaks about tribals identity and its attachment to the land, forest and environment at large. The tribals' interaction with nature transforms their natural world, activities and their existence itself which has also influenced their identity formation. And this identity formation cannot be analysed in objective terms which are "repositories of subjective activities" (Marx, 1965:86). Marx goes further to analyse human activity as "the subjectivity of objective essential powers whose action therefore, must be something objective" (Marx: 1844, translated by M. Milligan, 1967:180). This indicates that it is essential to understand the external factors and the powers that influences in the tribal identity formation that is not sufficiently analysed and explored by anthropologists, cultural studies and sociologists.

14. In 1946, there were 5000 published works on caste in India (Hutton, 1946:1). The number may have multiplied several times during five decades of studies and research on identity and caste in India.

15. Biswamoy Pati (2003) stresses the existence of caste in pre-colonial Orissa in the Varna, Jati order (Varna is a Sanskrit word means colour, *Jati* means social group, community), used to indicate caste system that can be used as race in European context. Thus the caste system is a racial idea. This idea is further elaborated in the third chapter of the book. Klass (1980) puts caste as a trans-historic institution and the continuation of old clan and tribal units, even before state formation and Gupta (1980, 1984:110-41) goes further in saying that continuous of caste system is justified "on the basis of putative biological differences". Depankar Gupta also locates the rational of natural superiority that governs the caste system; the philosophical basis of racism (Gupta, 1980: 249-71).

16. People like Peter B. Anderson (1986:8) trace the terms like 'tribe' and 'animist', applied to the Santals, in the 19th century based on the scientific theory of 'evolutionism'. Based on the evolutionary theory of categorisation, 'tribe' is a colonial construction of the 18th and 19th century which needs to abandon the term and use 'ethnic' instead of 'tribe' (Anderson, 1999). This was further replicated in the ethnographic and historical works of Damodaran (2006a, 2006b).

17. See; Jaiswal (1977, 1991, 1997, 1998), Gupta (1980, 1991) and Dumont (1972).

18. Samir Amin (1998) has called post-modernism a cultural logic of late capitalism where as David Harvey (2006:39) calls post-modernism a culture of advanced capitalist societies. But in this context, it is the cultural logic of existing capitalism that perpetuates divisive ideas to divide people based on their social and cultural systems and blames it as the cause of underdevelopment at the same time.

19. Such an argument is are invalid as it is unable to acknowledge the existing hierarchy, dependency, exploitation and inequality in the society which is maintained by higher caste and class along with the ruling elites in the name of their respective communities.

20. The Kalahandia (people of Kalahandi district) identity is based on the regional identity formation based on the territory that covers both tribals and non-tribals in the district. But tribal identity in Kalahandi district can not be categorised based on region or territory.

21. The key element in the classic statements of methodological individualism is the refusal to examine institutional and other forces which are involved in the moulding of individual (Hodgson, 1988, chapter-3) and community preferences and purpose in identity formation.

22. For example; Kondh tribe has three sub-tribes or castes based on their place of living and cultural traditions. It is discussed extensively in the fourth chapter of my thesis. Another classic example is "Purja" which indicates the caste genealogies of the Gond tribe of Orissa and they use 'Purja' meaning the depository of caste lineage of the eight Gonds of Central India.

23. The usage of the term 'tribe' dates back to the infamously the Criminal Tribes Act of 1871 that defines a tribe as criminal by birth by the British colonial rulers which has led many to argue tribe is a colonial construction (Radhakrishna; 2000, Beteille 1960, 1995; Singh; 1993, Damodaran; 2006b).

24. The analysis based on culture and the use of culture as a form of identity reflects 'a politics of nostalgia' (Pieterse, 1995) for sectarian and reactionary purposes.

25. The term Adivasi can be divided into two i.e. 'Adi' means primitive, 'Vasi' means inhabitants. Adivasi means primitive inhabitants or the original inhabitants or natives. For Hindu nationalists, Aryans are the primitive, native, indigenous and original inhabitants of India and thus Adivasies are Hindus. The idea makes an easier attempt to incorporate Adivasies into Hindu social order. But consciously they are using the term Vanavasi (forest dwellers) to keep a structural and social difference to separate mainland people from the people of the forest in terms of culture and at the same time, they can revoke the economic protection provided to the tribals in terms of tribal land right.

26. Osborne (2001)'s work on caste in India shows that caste is a cultural proposition and has remained as a useful ideological tool for political and economic interests. Though, this categorisation of caste has formed political pressure groups, it neither affects or has not been significantly affected by economic development which indicates social and economic stagnation of the caste groups and society as well. The studies of Akerlof (1976) and Scoville (1996) are reflecting on the economics of caste and its labour market underpinnings.

27. While looking at the class factor in the process of tribal development, I am not ignoring the cultural factors in the development of tribals. I do believe that there is a power of cultural

values and attitudes in tribal society. The idea of looking at tribals from class perspective is that the new economic interests of the state and mainstream Hindu society justify tribal culture and uses it for exploitation and at the same time, gives a cultural logic of tribal underdevelopment. It is used as a means for an exploitative and exclusionary social system that leads to inequality. These problems and issues can only be addressed by using class analysis for alternative development programmes of transformation in the all fields of tribal life and society that can protect their culture and promote their economic interests.

28. On the concept of tribe and its historical conceptuali sation, see; Fried (1975), Guha (1999), Beteille (1960, 1991, 1995), Damodaran (2006a, 2006b), Hardiman (1987), Vidyarthi & Rai (1985), Gregory (2003) and Bijoy (2003).

29. Interviewed on 17th December, 2004.

30. See; *Encyclopaedia of Social Sciences*, Vol. 15 for details.

31. Article 366(25) of the Constitution of India refers to scheduled tribes as those communities who are scheduled in accordance with Article 342 of the Constitution. The Article 342 of the Indian Constitution defines the Scheduled Tribes as tribes or tribal communities, or part of or groups within these tribes, and tribal communities which have been declared as such by the President through a public notification(see; Constitution of India, 2006), making Schedule Tribe an administrative term for affirmative action through several special constitutional provisions for the promotion of educational and economic interests of Scheduled Tribes and their protection from social injustice and all forms of exploitation. Though the term 'Scheduled Tribes' (ST) is not coterminous with the term 'Adivasi', Scheduled Tribes is an administrative term used for purposes of 'administering' certain specific constitutional privileges, protection and benefits for specific sections of peoples considered historically disadvantaged and 'backward'. Thus, I am using the term 'tribe' which is a more helpful term while looking at the tribal development policy as used and implemented by the governments (central, provincial and local) in India.

1. NEO-LIBERAL LINEAGES AND TRENDS IN THE POLITICAL ECONOMY OF DEVELOPMENT IN INDIA

1. I use 'political economy ' as more of an approach than a concept. Both classical and Marxian academics tend to assume a political economy in which power is reflexive of economic relations. Engel's assertion speaks for both the classical and Marxian traditions. In his words "political economy in the widest sense is the science of laws governing the production and exchange of the material means of subsistence in human society (Engel, 1954: 203)". Thus, the political economy of India is the study of determinants of production and production relations within its social and cultural contexts.

2. The explanatory interpretation of the neo-classical approach to analyse economic development and change based on assumptions that crisis led individuals to make choices and find alternatives based on desires, wants or preferences (North, 1981:4). Thus, the crisis embedded transformation in political economy of development is a product of individual choice as if there is no role of institutions; i.e. society, state, market in the creation of crisis and making of the choice.

3. The significance of historical explanations of political economy can be found in the works of Cossa (1892: 26), Lukacs (1968:27), Nisbet (1969: 302-3), Harte (1971: xvii), North and Thomas (1973), Cipolla (1976), Hall (1985), Baechler, Hall and Mann (1988) and Smith (1991), Willis (1993), Boswell and Misra (1995), Frank (1998), Wong (1978), Hausman (1981), Hicks (1979) and Dirks (2006).

4. Scarcity is either a condition of retreat from production or over production in a capitalist system which works as a means of social control (Heartfield, 2008: 6). The manufacturing of scarcity through retreat from production and over production helps the market economy to

grow and also controls power in the society and sustains authority in politics. The recent work of Klein (2008) confirms that crisis is essential for the rise of capitalist system.

5. The idea is to reflect on the difference between mainstream, neo-liberal political economy and Marxian political economy. The separation between the two competing theories of political economy does not have the intention to search for objective truth which "crucial to classic marketplace theory ... founded on selective perception (Ingber, 1984: 25)". For more debates on objectivity and truth, see; Baker (1978:974). However, the Marxian political economy tries to understand the conditions in which cause and effect (demand and supply) takes place.

6. For a detailed study, see; Harris-White (1993, 1996, 2002, 2003, 2006), Bhaduri (1993), Bardhan (1989a), Sen (1981), and Chakrabarti (2004).

7. The growth of GDP in India during 2006-07 is 9.4 %, food grain stocks are 17.73 million tonnes as on April 1, 2007, overall industrial growth is 11.5 % , 2.7 % in Agriculture and 11.0 % in Service sectors, exports increased by 23.06 % , imports increased by 40.69% and the economic growth was estimated at 9.0 % in 2005-06 which reflects growth of Indian economic development. The inflation rate is 11 % in 2008 which is highest rate of inflation in Indian economic history. Nearly 11 million children are homeless and about 300 million people are living on less than a dollar a day in India. The disparity between the poor and rich, urban and rural is growing. In recent years, the poverty, food insecurity and unemployment rate has also grown. This reflects a growth crisis and contradictions in the Indian economy.

8. For details, see; Richards (1983:22-23), Ghoshal (1930), Boserup (1965:98), Misra (1999).

9. For a detailed account of economic conditions of medieval India, see the works of Ganguli (1964:55), Habib (1963:53, 76), Moreland (1923, 1962; 1968:112), Maddison (1970: 18), Raychaudhuri (1968: 90), Sinha (1961), Foltz (1996), Richard (1990, 1997) and Bernier (1981).

10. Francisco Pelsaert has written this in a report to the *Dutch East India Company* which sums up his seven years in Agra from 1620 to 1627 (as quoted in Moreland and Geyl, 1925:60-61).

11. The political and economic interest of British colonialism in India was followed using the traditions and institutions of Mughal state (Bailey, 1971:4-5). The economy during Moghul period was controlled by the Muslim ruling and commercial elites without disturbing even the non-Muslim social structure of the pre-medieval period which helped them to continue and sustain the exploitative Moghul Empire. The same policy was followed by the European traders and subsequently by the British East India Company. In this way, the British colonialism in India maintained pre-capitalist 'moral' and ideological configurations in different spheres of social, economic and political life (Sangari, 1993: 35).

12. For a detailed study, see; Srinivas (1951).

13. Furnivall's argument can be justified in the context of commercialisation of agriculture, by focusing on cash crop production as per the demand of the external market. Thus, the new culture of trade, commerce and market creates new administrative institutions in the society that brings radical changes in the societies in rural India by the extension of administrative and commercial institutions. It has provided a source of income to the ruling class along with the revenues from land and agriculture (Bailey, 1971:9).

14. For volumes of trade transfer during colonialism in India can be found in the works of Dutt (1960), Naoroji (1962), Bagchi (1976) and Habib (1975a). The concrete example can be found in the works of Saul (1960) with a particular reference to balance payment crisis in Britain during the post-war period which was recovered by the earning from India (Saul 1960:197).

15. See; Dasgupta (1979) for a detailed study on the decline of trade and Bhargava (1934) for understanding indigenous trade and banking system during ancient and mediaeval India. In his study Bhargava (1934) outlined the social character of Banking and credit system in ancient and medieval India. Habib (1960, 1972) has also talked about banking system during Mughal India and Ray (2002) elaborates the condition of indigenous banking system during colonialism.

16. For details on indigenous banking and credit system, see; (Jain, 1929; Dale, 1994; Markowitz, 2000; Levi, 2002 and Markowitz, 2000).

17. The indigenous credit system was exploitative by nature which is documented in the works of Hardiman (1997). The Hundis were run by the collective decision but it is a mechanism of accumulation that exploits the peasantry by the landed, aristocratic, priestly Brahmin and commercial class. Still one can find Hundis in various temples today in India. It is simple a source of exploitation.

18. This argument is contested in the works of Marriot (1955) and Srinivas (1969).

19. In terms of GDP share during the 1st and 11th century India was the world's largest economy sharing 32.9 percent in 1st century and 28.9 percent in 1000CE. The position of Indian economy and its development from 1000CE to 19th century reveals that India had the largest share in World Economy in terms of its GDP share while comparing it with the GDP share of other 20 European and American countries (Maddison, 2001:261).

20. See; Maddison (1971, 2001), Misra (1999, 2003), Frank (1998), Bayly (1990), Tomlinson (1993), Stein (1992).

21. Caste hierarchy in India forms the basis of social, cultural, political and economic inequality; which denies lower caste people to exercise their rights and access resources.

22. The *German Historical School* followed a nationalistic pattern of economics, which has "emerged as a reaction against internal disunity on the one hand, and failure to face the external competition, particularly from the Great Britain on the other, the Indian nationalistic economics was fundamentally a reaction against the colonial policies of the metropolitan power (Datta, 1978:1)" under the British hegemony. The recent debates have questioned the very foundation of the *German Historical School Economics* and argue that it is neither German nor historical (Pearson, 1999). Such objections are attempts to revive the classical and neo-classical economic methods of objectivity and provide a philosophical background to the neo-liberal project devoid of history and culture.

23. See; Robertson (1999) for a detailed study on the economic and other ideas of Raja Rammohan Roy.

24. M.G. Ranade is known as the father of modern economic ideas. His economic ideas and thoughts can be found in the works of Bipan Chandra (1990).

25. The works of Pani (2002), Sharma (1997) and Narayan (1970) deal with the features of Gandhian economic ideas, its relevance and impact on Indian economic planning and development.

26. For details on Indian economic thoughts (see; Datta, 1962, 1978; Ganguli, 1977; Dasgupta, 1993 and Mukherjee, 2002). Das (2004) is a classic study which deals with ten great economists of India who have influenced and laid the foundation of post-colonial economic thoughts and development planning in India.

27. There is an artificial demarcation to differentiate Hindu religion from Hinduism. The debate concludes that 'Hindu' is a religion where as 'Hinduism' is a way of life. For details on this debate, see; Sen (2005).

28. For different ideological trends and its influences on Indian political economy, see; Dasgupta (1993).

29. For the social base and political composition party members, leaders and voters of BJP and Congress, see; Yadav (1999, 2003).

30. Connecting British colonialism with post-colonial development in India can provide us the insights to understand the contribution of the colonial modernity in establishing the relationship between the Indian industrial capitalist class in urban areas and feudal landlords in rural areas, with the post-colonial Indian state. Even though, the Indian state and its ruling class were pretending to be independent of capitalist class while upholding the interests of the capitalist class (Das, 1996). By taking the Gramscian framework, Bocock (1986) talks about the integral state shaped by the alliance of capitalism with the state which solves some of the crisis within the capitalist system by cohesive and hegemonic state power and maintains balance between different class forces and ruling class interests. This thesis can be replicated in the case of India.

31. Marx (1964) has interpreted caste in terms of a primitive form of property relations conditioned for production. The production relations emanates from this system provides a base for feudalism which is a pre capitalist social and economic formation.

32. See the debates in Thorner (1982) and Byres (1998).

33. For example; the anti-caste and other social reform movements of 14th–17th centuries were suppressed by the colonial rulers by enacting laws supporting the Hindu and the Muslim orthodoxies (Mukherjee, 1974).

34. It is remarkable to locate the continuity of uneven development or regional imbalances in development in the contemporary India which is possibly a result of the influence of local royal ruling families over post-colonial Indian politics. For example; twenty four former princes were elected to the lower house of Parliament (Lok Sabha), and princely candidates did very well in the 1967 elections (Allen & Dwivedi 1998). The influence of princely families over post-colonial Indian politics is well documented in the works of Richter (1975). This influence of the Royal family over Indian politics is declining but continues its presence today. This legacy took a new shape in the political economy of development in post-colonial India by forming an alliance of landlords, politicians and bureaucrats which constitutes the proprietary class (Bardhan, 1998).

35. The British policy of the right to intervene in the affairs of the native states was intended "to set right such serious abuses in a Native Government as may threaten any part of the country with anarchy or disturbance (Lord Canning, 1980)".

36. The idea of writing on the colonial British policy towards native states is to locate the nature of post-colonial Indian state policy towards its indigenous people. When there is a resistance movement by the indigenous or tribal people to protect their land, natural resources, environment and livelihood from the multi-national mining companies then the governments sends its police force to protect the interest of multinational companies by suppressing resistance movements in the name of maintaining law and order. The killings of tribals in Kalinganagar, Kashipur, threatening to the tribals of Kalahandi and Koraput for industrialisation and mining in Orissa are classic examples that characterise the colonial root of the capitalist nature of Indian state and its policy.

37. The policy of development is a product of 'dual economy model' derived from the Arthur Lewis's famous 'traditional-modern' formulation of development in which state was assigned a central role in coordinating, facilitating and intervening in the matters of production, distribution and consumption (Lewis, 1954). Such legacy of Arthur Lewis continued in the works of Fei and Ranis (1964). However, the structural transformation prescribed by this model did not work in India as the gradual transfer of surplus labour in agricultural sector to industrial sector did not happen. The declining of agriculture and deepening crisis in peasantry on one hand and industrial stagnation on the other has led to the crisis in the Indian economy which is reinforced by the new economic policy of liberalisation, privatisation and globalisation. For crisis in Indian agriculture, see; (Pattnaik, 1999, 2002, 2003a, 2003b & 2006) and for industrial stagnation, see; (Patnaik, 1979).

38. See; Williamson (1993) in World Bank (2000/2001:62) for details on Washington consensus.

39. Press Release No. 99/46 on the Communiqué of the Interim Committee of the Board of Governors of the International Monetary Fund, September 26, 1999, Washington, D.C.

40. See; Patnaik (2007, 2003, 1998), Chandrasekhar and Ghosh (2002), Chakravarty (1987), Chakrabarti and Cullenberg (2003). To understand the problems of capitalist transformation in India, see Chakrabarti and Cullenberg (2001, 2003).

41. See; Ruccio, Resnick and Wolff (1990), Hardt and Negri (2000), Resnick and Wolff (2001), Chakrabarti and Dhar (2002) and Chakrabarti (2001, 2003) to understand the necessity of cultural hegemony for the functioning of contemporary global capitalism.

42. The Indian capitalist class was projecting itself as anti-colonial, nationalist and anti-imperialist during Indian freedom struggle (Mukherjee, 2000; Sarkar, 1973) to consolidate its operation and create a base for an alliance formation with the post-colonial Indian state. Such an alliance was necessary to provide social legitimacy to the state-led capitalism in India (Patnaik, 2007).

43. See; Chaudhuri (1995) and Bagchi (1995) to understand the way Indian capitalist classes have successfully manipulated Indian planning in a direction to serve their interests.

44. See; Kaviraj (1998), Chatterjee (1997), Corbridge and Harriss (2000).

45. For details see; Brass, 2000; Bose, 1997; Chatterjee, 1998; Saez, 2002; Wolpert, 2000).

46. Bernard R. Bell has directed a major World Bank study in 1964-65 to study the Fourth Five Year Plan of India and prepared his fourteen volume report in 1965; the 1967 Bank report entitled "*Indian Economic Policy and the Fourth Five Year Plan*" which was a blueprint for the World Bank operations in Indian economy (see; Bernard R. Bell files, 1964-1977, Ref. Code; WB IBRD/IDA 43-02, World Bank Achieves).

47. The economic policy shift towards liberalisation during this period is branded as 'half hearted liberalisation' (Harriss, 1987), 'tried and abandoned' (Manor, 1987) and 'glass-half empty' (Datta-Chaudhuri, 1996).

48. Jawaharlal Nehru's speech at the Constituent Assembly, New Delhi, on 14th August, 1947 (as quoted from Dreze and Sen, 1995:1).

49. The policies towards foreign capital in terms of Foreign Direct Investment (FDI), its presence and role in post independent Indian economy was well documented in the work of Reddy (1978). He also established the relationship between foreign capital and national capitalist class while talking about industrial development in India.

50. The foreign debt was 0.3 percent of the National Income during 1960-61 which increased to 19 percent in 1967-68 (Reddy, 1978:60). Further, as per the report of the currency and finance for the 1965-66 by the Reserve Bank of India (RBI), the third Five Year Plan was the most difficult and crisis ridden period of the Indian economy since the beginning of the planning era. The RBI Annual Report for the 1970-71 continued to document the economic crisis due to inflation, deficit balance of payment, agricultural and industrial stagnation but reveals that the crisis was a product of under utilization of national resources (RBI, Bulletin, August, 1971).

51. The Third Five Year Plan (1961-66), Planning Commission, Government of India, New Delhi, 1961, p-8.

52. *The Hindustan Times*, September, 20, 1961, p-6.

53. The New Economic Reforms is also known as a crisis driven economic reform in the Indian economy as it was launched in July 1991. It was a crisis management response to the economic crisis that erupted in early 1991, thus known as Crisis Driven Reform. The Indian economy crisis comprised a steep fall in the foreign exchange reserve, galloping inflation, large public and current account deficits and a large amount of domestic and foreign debt. And in politics the fall of two governments in a short span of four months from November, 1990 to March, 1991, deferment of union budget, fairly long political interregnum till the election, the assassination of Rajiv Gandhi in their midst and the emergence of a minority government, reflected an unprecedented crisis which lead to the New Economic Reforms. But it neither reflected nor represented the strategic choice with a long-term vision for development of India and its people. The blueprint for economic policy reform was provided by the World Bank and the IMF, which had been adopted by many countries but not without affecting the socio-economic life of the poor. The New Economic Reforms were not a single policy package, rather a package of policies with an objective of opening and integrating the Indian economy with the global market and capital. It was a package of liberalisation, privatisation and globalisation policies with wider coverage and longer term in their objectives that included both stabilisation and structural adjustment policies. These stabilisation and structural adjustment policies took concrete shape during the 'second generation of economic reforms initiated by the centre of the NDA government under the leadership of the BJP.

54. India's current economic reforms began during Indira Gandhi's Government, but in 1985, the Rajiv Gandhi Government abolished some of the licensing regulations and other competition-inhibiting controls, currency devaluations and making currency partially convertible, reduced quantitative restrictions on imports, reduced import duties on capital goods, decreased subsidies, liberalised interest rates, abolished licenses for most industries, the sale of shares in selected public enterprises, and tax reforms as examples of the economic reforms. Apart from all these policy reforms, the Indian economy became dependent and reliance on debt and guided by the international financial institutions like International Monetary Fund and

World Bank as India borrowed heavily from these financial institutions. Increased borrowing from foreign sources in the late 1980s, which helped economic growth, but led to pressures on the balance of payments led to a balance of payment crisis. These loans frequently carried conditions that require substantial internal economic adjustments by the recipients, most of which are developing countries. India was the first Asian Country to receive a World Bank loan, on 18th April 1949, for its railway reconstruction, but it was unconditional. In the same way India got an IMF loan with conditions for the first time in 1981 during Indira Gandhi period. However, these conditionalities increased during Rajiv Gandhi's period to liberalise the Indian Economy.

55. Quoted from *Economic and Political Weekly*, March 7, 1985.

56. The Structural Adjustment Policy (SAP) indicates: "De-control of industries, privatisation of government-owned entities, structural changes in the economy aimed at export-led growth, free entry of foreign capital and technology without any let, hindrance or conditions, free entry and exit of foreign firms including financial and services industries, free cross-border movement of capital and other funds, legislative safeguards for protection of intellectual property rights, creation of legal climate for enforcement of legal contracts, private property rights, and free entry and exit of business, industrial and financial firms". Whereas stabilisation policies indicate: "Devaluation of the currency for making exchange rate more realistic, Withdrawal of restrictions on imports, reduction/ elimination of fiscal and balance of payments deficits, removal of all controls on prices, exchange and interest rate, elimination/ reduction of all subsidies, introduction of financial structure reforms and free entry of foreign financial institutions, complete autonomy of the central bank to pursue independent monetary policy" (Teltumbde, 1996). See; Desai (2001).

57. These ideas are advocated in the works of Jalan (1991), Bhagwati and Srinivasan (1993), Bhagwati (1993), Joshi and Little (1996), Ahluwalia and Little (1998), Sachs, Varshney and Bajpai (1999).

58. Government of India, Ministry of Finance, Department of Economic Affairs, 'Economic Reforms: Two Years After and the Task Ahead', Discussion Paper, New Delhi: July 1993, pp.1-2.

59. For details; see the booklet on "Budget; Measures to Revive the Economy", *Ministry of Information and Broadcasting* (1991), Government of India, New Delhi, pp-1-16.

60. The same kind of neo-liberal argument for the reform of the Indian economy can be found in the works of many economist and development professionals, for example; Pursell (1992), Virmani (1997), Desai (1999), Delong (2004), Rodrik (2004), Rodrik and Subramanian (2004), Joshi and Little (1994, 1996), Ahluwalia (2002), Ahluwalia and Little (1998), Srinivasan and Tendulkar (2003), Bhagawati (1992), Bhagawati and Srinivasan (1993) and Kaur (2007).

61. For example, national and multinational industrial corporations are setting up their industries in the rural areas of Orissa. For details, see (Nayak, 2007b).

62. See Amin (1994) to understand how industrialisation in the third world indicates capitalist expansion to non-capitalist peripheries through polarisation among regions to accumulate more and more. I have also discussed this point while talking about industrialisation in the tribal areas of Kalahandi district in Chapter 4.

63. Tenth Report (2005), Standing Committee on Agriculture (2004-2005), Fourteenth Lok Sabha, Ministry of Agriculture (Department of Agricultural Research and Education), Demands fro Grants (2005-2006), Lok Sabha Secretariat, New Delhi, p-46.

64. Ibid, p-47.

65. The new agricultural policy of the post-1991 regime advocated the abolition of input subsidies on seeds, fertilizers, irrigation, electricity and credit, removal of trade restrictions on agricultural commodities so that the domestic prices were not out of tune with world prices, unification of prices so that the current system of dual markets in food grains and other agricultural commodities would disappear, which will help for the integration Indian agriculture with global market. As a result of which Indian agriculture took a new transition from food crops to cash crops in order to meet the requirements of the global market.

66. In the post-reform period the import of agricultural products and goods has increased whereas export has declined in a massive scale (Nayak, 2009).

67. For details on debates on the food security policy during post-economic reforms, see; (Nayak, 2002). There was a decline of food consumption and per capital expenditure on food during the post reform period that indicates both poverty and food insecurity among the rural and urban consumers (Nayak, 2009).

68. Patnaik (2004)' research also shows the declining of food availability during the post-reform period.

69. See; Castells (2000), Shakow & Graham (1983) to understand the dependence of global capitalism on service sector.

70. In the Hindu religion, there are 330 million gods and goddesses registered in different religious scripts. The mythically unregistered number of gods and goddesses are growing everyday in India, which reflects the diverse religious practice in the Hindu religion. See; Fuller (1992), (Mehta (1996) and Radhakrishnan (2004) for details.

71. *The Bhagavad Gita* is one of the most important religious texts in the Hindu religion where the protagonists are from higher caste (warriors) and ruling class as well (Johnson, 1994). Thus, Johnson considers it as a non-Brahminical text in Hindu religion and thus has the tenets of more egalitarian values (ibid: X) which can be contested. It is not necessary to be a member of Brahmin caste to speak the language of Brahmins. *Brahminism* is an ideology of hegemony and hierarchical social order to control social and economic activities of the masses. It can be used by any members of the Hindu caste system as per their social and economic status. In the context of *The Bhagavad Gita,* the ruling class and higher caste warriors were speaking the language of Brahmins to continue their hegemonic control over the masses by preaching a theory which asks the masses to follow the authority without questioning its power and legitimacy.

72. The theory of *Karma* preaches about the consequences of one's own duty. No one can avoid the process of *Karma* based on *Dharma*. If you do good work then the result will be good and for bad work, there will be bad results. So one's sufferings are the product of one's work and there is nothing external to one's suffering. The problems of inequality and exploitation are the product of this cosmic causation; the *Karma and Dharma*. The logic of this infallible causation can't be questioned. Any attempt to question is considered as *Bidharma* (irreligious and evil) and the goal of *Nirvana/Moksa* can't be achieved. Good *Karma* provides the base for incarnates life.

73. Based on these ideas, Hindu religion justifies and maintains the hegemony over the social order by caste structure.

74. Kapp (1963) made similar kind of argument in the context of Hindu religion and its impact on the social and economic development in India. Myrdal (1968) and Mandelbaum (1970) explained India's economic backwardness and its relationship with Hinduism. In the context of globalisation, Huntington (1996)'s thesis assumed that the progress of globalisation would be severely constrained by religious barriers including one from Hinduism, whereas Fukuyama (1992) argues that globalisation processes have the potential to homogenize all civilizations under western modernity. But in reality, it is not the western modernity but consumer culture of the global market that hegemonise the world by forming alliance with religions. In India, it has taken the help of Hindu religion.

75. This aspect has been discussed further in chapter 5 of this thesis by giving empirical examples.

76. There is an artificial demarcation to differentiate Hindu religion from Hinduism. The debate concludes that 'Hindu' is a religion where as 'Hinduism' is a way of life. For details on this debate, see; Sen (2005).

77. The philosophy of neo-liberalism requires contradictions and collaborations for restructuring of the system which can reproduce neo-liberal policies within national, regional and local conditions (Brenner & Theodore, 2002: 351). It is central to the continual of neo-liberalism itself (ibid: 375). Such an objective of neo-liberal philosophy is only possible through aligning itself with religion, race, culture and ethnic politics (Jacobs, 1996; Appadurai, 2000) which helps embed neo-liberal values in societies. The process of embeddedness creates a totality of culture or cultural hegemony in the society. In India, neo-liberalism finds Hindu religion and culture; majoritarianism as a tool to pursue such an agenda.

78. After all the reproduction of capitalist economic relations needs ideological and political support (Peet, 1997; Sayer, 1997).The right wing forces of world's four main religions (Christianity, Islam, Hinduism and Judaism) are interested in consolidating their base for political power to boost their economic interests to serve the interests of the elites (Saldanha, 2003).

79. The neo-liberal philosophy is based on the ideas of an open market that creates poverty, generates marginalisation and increases a class of impoverished population (Marx, 1978). Many non-Marxist scholars follow the Marxian tradition while making a critique of open market systems or free market capitalism and state the cultural, religious or the ideological ethics that sustain such a system, is the root cause of economic injustice and underdevelopment (Meek, 1989; Korten, 1995).

80. For example; Berger (1986), Novak (1993), Bellah (1957), Redding (1990), Clegg and Redding (1990), Martin (1990), Caplan (1991) and Fogel (2001).

81. Religions in general serve as an instrument of mass domestication through regulatory mechanisms to control individual as well as community lives and labour. The regulatory mechanism imposed by religion helps in disciplining the labour which is a requirement for the sustenance of capitalism and its system (Grossman, 2006). "The construction of norms for the regulation of social life and individual behaviour is a compelling need of capitalism, so long as it wishes to proclaim itself as a universal form of social life (Borkenau, 1971: 96 as cited in Grossman, 2006:201)". In India, Hindus constitute 85 percent of the population and thus Hindu religion provides the base to control the labour power of the masses.

82. Berman (1983) has studies the legal history of NGOs/COs and their religious affiliation.

83. The development anthropologists consider NGOs/COs as 'non governmental sectors of development industry' (Stirrat, 1996; Ferguson, 1997:8) which creates a 'culture of consultancy' (Stirrat, 2000) and work as 'cultural consultants' (Henkel and Stirrat, 2002:169) in the field of development. As a student of political economy of public policy, I call them 'salary seeking social servants' who find NGOs/COs in tribal or rural development as a sector of employment to earn their livelihood and pursue their cultural hegemony in the rural and tribal areas of India. NGOs have achieved many things but the structures of power that control and determine the resource allocation for development at different levels (locally, nationally and globally) have remained unchanged (Nyamugasira (1998:297). Thus the structures of inequality and exploitation that emanate from these levels have continued to exist in our contemporary development discourse.

84. In the project of new development orthodoxy, "control is excercised in such a way that participants appear to be controlling themselves ; individuals attest to their conversion; sinners admit their faults before they see the light (Henkel and Stirrat, 2002:178)". It is a religious revivalist tradition followed by the advocates of neo-liberal economy of development in which they admit their failures and mistakes (for details on the World Bank's acknowledgement of its mistakes, see; *Bretton Woods Update*, No-18, August 2000).

85. For a detailed discussion on the declining of state legitimacy during the period of globalisation, see; (Lash & Urry 1994: 281).

86. See; Part-XI, XII and XIII of Indian Constitution to understand financial federalism.

2. INDIAN FEDERALISM AND THE POLITICAL ECONOMY OF NEOLIBERAL DEVELOPMENT IN ORISSA

1. See; *Orissa Reference Annual (2005)*, Information and Public Relations Department, Government of Orissa, Bhubaneswar. It provides a brief history of Orissa (ibid: 24-25) and a detailed chronological account of the Orissa history (ibid: 39-45). For details, see; Das (1949).

2. See; Nayak (2009) for detailed classification of state population.

3. Government of Orissa, Economic Survey – 2001-2002, p-1/1.

4. The state of Orissa's share of India's mineral resources reserve can be found in Nayak (2009).

5. The recent work of Deo (2001) has glorified the role of feudal kings and their contribution in the making of the Orissa state in particular and to the national freedom struggle in general. The author himself belongs to the royal family and tries to cover up the feudal exploitation. At the same time, the work exposed the historical alliance of the Congress party with kings and landlords in the state.

6. For a detailed study, see; Banerjee (1930), Behera (1993, 1999), Tripati (2002), Sethi (2002), Mahalik (2004), Bhatta & Pradhan (2005), Patra (2005).

7. See; Patel (2004) and. Patra & Patra (2004) for a detailed study. Rajesh (2001)'s study talks about the link between temple and economy in South India. The temples during C850 to 985 AD played a vital role in which agrarian and trade expansion took place. The state, temples and economy worked hand in hand during 1435-1568 AD Orissa, indicating the relationship between religion and economy in the state during ancient period (Mohanty, 2001).

8. *The Constitution of India*, Ministry of Law, Government of India, 2004, p-2.

9. There is no intention to glorify ancient and medieval India but I am just talking about the positive tenets of those days in the terms of decentralised politics and administrative structure.

10. See; Singh (2007) Santhanam (1960). and Government of India (1987, 1988), Report of the Commission on Centre-State Relations, Part-I & II to understand different administrative reforms and steps undertaken by the British colonial administration for the decentralisation of power and eventually for restoring the past federal ethos in administering India which has significant influence on the federalism in post-colonial India.

11. During the colonial period, the colonial Indian state was an obstacle in the growth of the Indian capitalist class as it was contradictory to the interests of the British capitalist ruling class (Chandra, 1992; Mukherjee, 1976, 2002). Such experiences of the Indian capitalist class have paved the way to forming an alliance with the Indian state and then with global capital. Further understanding of the relationship between state, nationalism and capital can be found in Jessop (1990) and in its Indian context, see Singh (1999).

12. See; Singh (2007) and Jenkins (1999) for a better understanding of the relationship between economic reforms and Indian centralised federalism.

13. The financial and other forms of greater autonomy of Indian provincial states are highly necessary to sustain Indian federal democracy. Because the decentralisation of power and resources helps in maintaining the multi-ethnic provincial identities in India (See, Chandhoke, 2006).

14. D.L. Sheth, 'Globalising Democracy versus Deepening of Democracy: The Post-Cold War Discourse', paper for the Lokayan seminar on 'Globalization and South Asia', Centre for the Study of Developing Societies, Delhi, 29-31 August 2001.

15. It is worth noting here that the agricultural market was regulated by the Government of Orissa during the pre-reform period which was a mechanism to control market price on consumer goods and provide incentives to both producers and consumers by giving them fair price on their production. It worked successfully in the state by protecting the consumers from market exploitation (for detail, see; Mishra, 2003). However, the regulated market and its boards were defunct after the new economic reforms due the policy changes of the government towards market. The amendment to the Orissa Agricultural Produce Market (Amendment) Act (2005) not only allowed the entry of private market into the agricultural sector (Government of Orissa, 2006) but also liberalised the entire state economy based on agriculture which is a part of internal liberalisation process.

16. It is not clearly defined which are non-essential administrative posts, giving the space for complete restructuring of government departments by giving voluntary retirement under Voluntary Retirement Scheme (VRS) and Compulsory Retirement Scheme (CRS) in the name of non-essential positions. It is followed by putting a ban on new recruitment/employment and eliminating and freezing the existing vacant posts. Such policies are vigorously pursued by different departments of the Government of Orissa from state level to local level (Source: Finance Department Letter No-32861/F, dated 03/08/2004; Letter No-Bt.V.47/04-55764 (45)/ F, dated 31/12/2004, Memo No-55765(45)/F, dated 31/12/2004, Government of Orissa, Bhubaneswar).

17. For details about the policies; see the *"Structural Adjustment Assistance Facilities Guidelines,"* Department of Economic Affairs, Ministry of Finance, Government of India,

December 2002 and World Bank (2003), *Orissa Economic Revival Credit/Loan*, Report No:-26550 – IN, Project ID:- P081882, World Bank, Washington D.C.

18. For a detailed and empirical discussion on this issue, see; Swain (2003).

19. As a part of the industrial drive, the Government of Orissa has given 607 mining leases covering an area of 101,947 hectares and out of these, 339 leases covering an area of 73,910 hectares were in operation (Report of the Government of Orissa, 2005). As per different research reports and studies (Khatua & Stanley, 2006) some 370 mining companies are active in the state of Orissa including government and private undertakings. The same report reveals that if this process of mining based industrialisation continues then Orissa's mineral reservse are conservatively expected to last as follows: Chromite; 38 years, Iron ore; 120 years, Graphite; 153 years, Manganese; 166 years, Bauxite; 310 years and Coal; 857 years as per the research (Khatua & Stanley, 2006).

20. The small scale industries in Orissa provide better employment and contribute more to the state economy which has declined over the years of new economic reforms. For details study, see; Nayak (2007b:91-93).

21. Government of Orissa (GoO), 2001, Industrial Policy Resolution-2001, Department of Industries, Government of Orissa, Bhubaneswar, p-1.

22. Ibid, p-7.

23. Ibid, p-12. Further, the Orissa Industries Facilitation Act 2004 has allowed easy routes for private investment whereas the Orissa Industrial Policy 2007 goes further to exempt tax and gives interest subsidies to the industries (Orissa Industrial Policy 2007, Department of Industries, The Orissa Gazette, No. 349, Cuttack, Friday, March 2, 2007, No.3391- XIV-HI-52/2007/I, Government of Orissa, Bhubaneswar, pp-20-23). On the contrary, fertilizer subsidies, seed subsidies and irrigation subsidies to the farmer have declined over the years and have now been abandoned by the Government of Orissa to control fiscal deficit of the state.

24. For detailed empirical data; See; Government of Orissa (2004), Annual Plan 2004-05, Vol-1, Planning and Coordination Department, Bhubaneswar.

25. *The Times of India*, 24 February, 2001

26. All the data on education is collected from the Second Report of the State Finance Commission (2004), Finance Department, Bhubaneswar, Orissa, pp-16-17.

27. The *Sarba Sikhya Abhijan* (movement for Education to all) policy is a glaring example of such new developments in which voluntary and contractual teacher were recruited for the purpose of universal education which is nothing but another form of populist public policy followed after liberalisation of economy.

28. The data on Orissa's economic development is collected from the *Orissa Human Development Report 2004*, Planning and Coordination Department, Government of Orissa, Bhubaneswar.

29. For a historical chronology and the nature of the natural calamities in the State of Orissa can be found in the works of Sarangi & Penthoi (2005:15), Das (1972), Samal (1990) and Pati (1999).

3. TRIBALS AND THE POLITICAL ECONOMY OF TRIBAL DEVELOPMENT IN INDIA

1. See; Nayak (2009) for details about tribal population in India.

2. The mainstream Indian society follows a culture which is hedonistic, acquisitive individualism based on consumer modernity which is contrasting to the collective social and cultural identities of the tribals in India. For the relationship between consumer modernity, capitalism and post modernism, See; Venkatesh (1994a, 1994b, 1995), Appadurai (1990), Featherstone, (1991), Lury (1996), Belk (1988), Slater (1997) and Panikkar (1997) for details. The mainstream Indian society considers time as money and money as power whereas tribals in India do not have a sense of time, money and power in comoditified form which creates a different space for tribal societies in India and differentiates tribals from non-tribal societies in India.

3. 'Aparigrah' is a Sanskrit word, implying the value of non-accumulation or of not keep-ing anything more than is necessary for one's minimal needs. I did not find any other word in tribal language that expresses the meaning of non-accumulation. So, I am using the word 'Aparigrah' which is a Sanskrit word and has the same expression in mainstream Oriya lan-guage as well.

4. Epistemologically, neoliberalism is based on 'assumptions' which have its root from liberal traditions.

5. The Approach to the Seventh Five Year Plan, 1985-90, Part-II, Planning Commission, Government of India, New Delhi, p-11.

6. The activities that provide the material basis for the physical survival are considered as economic activities (Majumdar and Madan, 1970:191) which need to be free from inequality and exploitation. The economic activities which constitute "economic system are designed to satisfy material wants of the people, to organise production, to control distribution and to determine the rights and claims of ownership within the community" (Piddington, 1952:18).

7. The Jajmani system is a system of labour sharing followed extensively in the tribal areas which is the basis of development of feudalism in the tribal areas. This system of labour sharing puts community as a unit of production, making the head of the community like a feudal landlord who never works but owns everything that community owns. In the process, the community head controls the land and other means of production and distribution.

8. There was a debate regarding the tribal development during the final phase of colonial rule. One group advocated for the protection of tribals from the mainstream society (Elwin, 1939) and the other group advocated for the complete assimilation of tribals within the main-stream society and national life (Ghurye, 1943; Thakkar, 1941). The debate reflects the apathet-ic attitude towards the tribals as the policy of protectionism is romantic in its ideals to keep tribals away from others and at the same time the policy of assimilation indicates the attempts to ignore the uniqueness of tribals and their culture which is different from the rest of the population in India.

9. The colonial denials of citizenship were well described by Guha (1992: 266) who has argued that "while the colonial regime, which had itself introduced among its subjects the notion of rights and liberties, went on denying these in full or in part in the principles and practice of its government, the disenfranchised subjects went on pressing the rulers to match their administration to their own ideals. Ironically, therefore, a large part of the politics of protest under the Raj, especially when initiated by the educated middle-class leadership, turned on the 'un-British' character of British rule--a theme made famous by successive generations of Indian liberals from Naoroji to Gandhi".

10. The tribal communities started facing massive exclusion after the implementation of the Indian Forest Act 1927 (IFA) which reduced tribal access to forest in the name of conservation and protection. Such an act overlooked the customary rights of tribals over forest and land which continued in the post-colonial India and Forest Conservation Act 1980 is a classic example. The Ministry of Tribal Affairs raised the question about the difficulties faced by the tribals due to this Act (28th Report, Lok Sabha, 2002:17). But the Schedule Tribes (Recogni-tion of Forest Rights) Bill, 2005 acknowledges tribals' right to access and ownership over forest land and different forest products. See; Baviskar (2003: 292) for a detailed study on the problems faced by tribals related with land and forest issues.

11. All Five Year Plans are published by the Planning Commission, Government of India, New Delhi.

12. See, the Tenth Five Year Plan (2002-2007), Planning Commission of India, Government of India, New Delhi.

13. The land and landscape of the Kalahandi district is well documented in Das, J. (1962), "Final Report of the Land Revenue Settlement in Kalahandi District; Ex-State-Khalsa-Area, 1946-56", The Board of Revenue, Indian Law Publications, Berhampur, Orissa.

14. See; Nayak (2009) for the educational and religious classification population data of the district.

15. All the data on demographic compositions, administrative division and on population is collected from the 2001 Census Report.

16. See, Economic Survey 2001-2002, Govt. of Orissa, Annexure-23, Directorate of Economics and Statistics, Bhubaneswar.

17. All the data about Kalahandi District is collected from the following sources: District Statistical Handbooks from 1989-90 to 1999, Kalahandi, Economic Survey 2001-2002, Govt. of Orissa, A Handbook on Implementation of 20-Point Programme in Orissa, Planning and Coordination Department, Govt. of Orissa. Districts at a Glance – 2002, Orissa. Statistical Outline of Orissa – 1999, Directorate of Economics and Statistics, Govt. of Orissa, Bhubaneswar, Orissa.

18. See; the summary of the Orissa Human Development Report 2004, Planning and Coordination Department, Government of Orissa, Bhubaneswar.

19. The Latin American development, underdevelopment and dependency debate can be replicated in case of the Kalahandi district. The historical conditions for which both neo-liberals, bourgeois and Marxist theories based on unilinear evolution do not provide explanations of underdevelopment and dependency (Frank, 1971:27-30). The only difference between Kalahandi and Latin America's underdevelopment is that Latin American history was shaped by international division of labor and unfavorable terms of trade (Furtado, 1970) whereas the history of Kalahandi was shaped by the circulation of regional elites both in social and economic terms. However, the current mode of cash crop production and industrialisation process in the district of Kalahandi is conditioned by international finance capital and its market which has created unfavorable trade and unequal exchange in the market. The people of the district are producing the things that are irrelevant and neither required for their instant consumption needs nor for that matter for any of their requirements in their own lives nor in the regional market. This premise again replicates Latin American experience (Dos Santos (1976:76). It is discussed in detail in the latter part of the thesis in chapter-4 & 5.

20. For details on capitalist accumulation, see; Scott (1979).

21. For details on over exploitation and capitalist accumulation, see; Banaji (1977). In the context of Kalahandi district, see; Jayal (2001).

22. For dependant development, see; Cardoso (1972).

23. Such analysis is theoretically known as "connected histories" that replaces both universal conceptualisation of history, civilisation and modernity (Subrahmanyam, 1997). By connecting histories, it is easier to locate the problems of colonialism and at the same time analyse dominant tendencies of mainstream conceptualisation associated with modernity, market, bureaucratic rationality, democratic sovereignty, civil and political rights pursued in the west and its structures are expanding in the process of globalisation. And the traditional societies (like tribal societies in India, Orissa and Kalahandi) are succumbing to this dominant process of universalisation of values and rationalisation of choices created by neo-liberal capitalist globalisation in the name of civil society (Eisenstadt, 2002; Beck, 2005; Holmwood, 2007). This is one of the agendas in the post-colonial development policies in the context of tribals.

24. Kandh is a major tribal group/community in the state of Orissa and in the district of Kalahandi as well.

25. "Karondara Raja Kandhara Beta" means "the king of Koranda is a son of a Kandh", as cited in Deo, (2000:75). Another proverb says "Kandhara Raja, Kandhara desh" means "the king belongs to Kandh as the land and kingdom belongs to the Kandhs". During my fieldwork, I heard this proverb while travelling and interacting with tribal people regarding the origin of the name of the district in the Thuamul Rampur block of Kalahandi. They proudly acclaim the past glory of making the district and ownership over the district and its formation.

26. Pati (1999, 2001) considers such tradition as the process of peasantisation and Hinduisation of tribals on one hand and on the other hand, a process of social legitimisation of Brahminical order of feudal, non-tribal and pre-colonial ruling class over the majority tribal (Kandha) population in the district. The social legitimacy gives political authority in a feudal society. Thus, the combination of social legitimacy and political authority has provided the economic power to control means of production and distribution. In the words of Pati (1999, 2001) "Hinduisation of this region was justified by the need for access to and control over its resources, as well as to absorb the consequent tensions (Pati 1999: 346; 2001:100)".

27. Elliot's Report on Kalahandi State, 28th July, 1856, Orissa Historical Research Journal, Vol-XIV, No-2, as cited in Senapati, N. & Kuanr D.C. (1980:2).

28. Hati and Tel is the name of two major rivers in Kalahandi that exist today.

29. As cited in Mishra, B. & Acharya, D. (2004), 'Ichhapur Copper Plate of the Nagavamsi King Jugsai Deo-IV', The Journal of Orissan History, Vol-XVII, p-38.

30. See; Senapati & Kuanr (1980:50-55) for details.

31. The Kalahandi region has seen a low level o capital proliferation as its society and economy was predominantly under a barter system. One rupee currency was the only currency in use during colonial British occupation (Elliot's Report on Kalahandi State, 28th July, 1856 as cited in Pati, 1999:348-57).

32. The land tax and Forest cess/tax was higher in the Kalahandi district than the other districts of Orissa under British colonialism and at the same time multiple forms of domination and channels of collecting tax have increased the vulnerability of the tribals (Das, 1962).

33. A traditional land management system existed in the district during pre-colonial time, called 'Umrao' in which tribal chiefs ruled clusters of villages, having common land based on customary laws favourable to local kings and landlords (Pati, 2003:345). The system was exploitative by nature which was comparative less than the colonial period.

34. See; Senapati & Kuanr (1980:67) for details.

35. For conceptual clarity on the term 'internal colonialism', see; Abercrombie et al. (2000:183), Calvert (2001), Casanova (1965) and for its Indian form in the context of tribals, see; Corbridge (1987, 1988, 1991; Sinha, 1973).

36. The Ganatantra Parisad and Swatantra Party formed by the royal family with the help of landlords in the district has merged with the Bharatiya Janata Party now, which gives a social and political base to the Hindu right wing forces in the district.

37. See; Orissa Reference Annual-2004, published by the Government of Orissa, Bhubaneswar to know about the details of the names of the Parliament Members elected from the royal family of Kalahandi district representing the Hindu right wing political party i.e. the Bharatiya Janata Party (BJP).

38. After lots of protests by the local tribals and other forces like the District Committee of the Communist Party of India (Marxist), the final report of the Delimitation Commission of India (2006) ensured an assembly seat (Langigarh) to the tribals in the district which is far less than the political power enjoyed by the general population in proportion to tribal population in the district. The details of the Delimitation Commission Report (2006) can be found in the An Extraordinary Issue of the Gazette of India, Part II Section 3(iii) Dated 15th December 2006 and An Extraordinary Issue of the Orissa State Gazette Dated 15th December 2006 (Delimitation Commission, Government of India, Notification No- 282/OR/2006, Order No-32, New Delhi).

39. The process of disenfranchisement has led to the failure of democracy and governance to tackle the problems of poverty and hunger in the district (Currie, 2000).

40. The passivity of tribal leaders and tribal people can be attributed to the multiple forms of exclusion, over exploitation and absence of democratic ideals (Jayal, 2001:95-96).

41. Thus, I argue that Hinduisation of tribals in the district is not a political project. It is immaterial as the BJP has its own political base among tribals and other forces in the district with the support from the royal family.

42. The poem called "The Kalahandi" is written in Oriya by Nirmal Prakash Purohit and published in the Rabibar (Sunday) special issue of the daily Oriya news paper called 'The Sambad' on 15th April 2007. I have translated into English and added 'journalists' only to the list of elites in the district as described in the poem. During my interview with five lecturers in the district, I found that they shared the same sentiment as reflected in the poem (Anonymous, date of interview in Bhawanipatna, 12/03/2005; in Kesinga, 18/03/2005).

43. See also (Stavenhagen, 1965) where Rodolfo Stavenhagen is linking ethnic social stratification, unequal development and internal colonialism with capitalist accumulation which can be applied in case of the Kalahandi district.

44. The Freudian idea of collision of individual interest with social or communitarian interest is reflected in his work 'Civilisation and its Discontents' (Freud, 1961:145) which was advanced by his nephew Edward Bernays in creation of a desired based society to expand the market through Propaganda (1928), he has also gave the same advice to the politicians and

corporate heads to sustain their power over people by creating a public relations office; an industry of advertisement to create desires among consumers to buy different products.

45. Tribals areas in India like Kalahandi district were out of the global market, so incorporating tribals areas into global market helps in the expansion of the capitalist market.

46. These formulations are based on the ideas of Soper (1981, 1990), Doyal and Gough (1991) and Slater (1993, 1996, 2004).

47. Braudel (1986: 224) as cited in Harriss-White (1996:307).

48. For the social origin of market in South Asia, see; Crow (2001).

49. See, Slater (2004:11) and Williams (1980:185) for details on the philosophical logic of post-modernism. Ewen (1976) and Marchand (1986) also talks about how consumerism is a capitalist logic and shining path to modernity.

50. These ideas about the conceptualisation of consumer society and its negative effects are derived from the works of Campbell (1989:18), Sahlins (1974:1-40), Rojek (1985) and Cunningham (1980).

51. Tribals feel everything is 'Videshi' (foreign) for them which are outside their society; their production and forest networks. For example anything from Bhawanipatna; the district capital of Kalahandi district of Orissa, India is foreign for the tribals of the Thuamulrampur block of Kalahandi district. The same feelings were being expressed in the Langigarh block and many other different parts of the Kalahandi district when I asked many tribals from different parts of the district about the availability of necessary things in the mainstream markets in Bhawanipatna, Kesinga, Madanpur Rampur and many other places. The summary of their reply can be translated as "we do not find anything interesting for us and our needs. Many things seem to be attractive but unnecessary for us as we do not know their use". It seems to me that the tribals have no for foreign goods as they do not know their use and they are not conscious about them During my interaction, I found that they are attracted to Radio, T.V, Tape Recorder, VCR, CD Player, Cosmetics and less interested in the mainstream market food and dress.

52. Toki Parab is a festival widely observed by the Kondh and Paraja tribe of Kalahandi and in other parts of the Orissa as well. When a girl or anybody's daughter in the Kondh and Paraja tribe gets her first menstruation, it becomes a community festival. The parents of the girl tell their neighbors and community people and arrange a party to celebrate it. The idea is also to tell the community members that their daughter is ready for marriage. In some places, in this festival, the girl gets married to a Mahua (the flower of this tree used as wine after boiling it with water) tree before she gets married to any person. But the right wing writers interpret this festival as the festival of female infanticide in Kalahandi (Mishra, 1995) which is not true. There is no reason for killing of girls in tribal society as women play a very significant role in the management of family's livelihood and dowry less marriage practice for girls (as per the practice men give dowry to marry in tribal society). Girls are not considered as liabilities in tribal society unlike mainstream Hindu society. So there is no question of female infanticide in tribal society, it might have taken place with the introduction of Brahminical Hindu cultural values and gender relations in the tribal society.

53. See; Bourdieu (1984)'s classic study on the consumption pattern and its impact on French society and culture and in the studies of Douglas, M. & Isherwood, B. (1978:59) gives us an anthropological account of consumption culture and its impact on society.

54. Mahua is a tropical tree found largely in plains and forests, especially in the tribal areas of India. The tree is considered as a holy tree by many tribal communities as it provides intoxicating drinks from its flowers called 'Mahuli' and oil from its seeds, which is used for cooking and many other medicinal purposes. It also provides firewood.

55. The school teacher teaches science and mathematics in a tribal residential school run by the Government of Orissa. During my interaction, I realised that he had no idea about economic reforms, liberalisation and globalisation policies. He is a tribal himself and belongs to a village near the district headquarter of Kalahandi called Bhawanipatna.

56. See, Jayal (2001) and the Kalahandi District Gazetteer (1980), Government of Orissa for details.

57. District Gazetteer, 1980, Government of Orissa, p.142.

58. There few other researches which have revealed that during crisis period in the district, food aid and relief reduced the productive capacity of the farmers as it discouraged local food

production and procurement by importing food from outside (see; Pradhan (1993:305-6) and Mallick (1974) for more details.

59. See; Das, J. (1962), Final Report of the Land Revenue Settlement in Kalahandi District Ex -State-Khalsa Area 1946-56, Published under the Authority of The Board of Revenue, Orissa, Indian Law Publication Press, Berhampur, Orissa, p-5.

4. IMPACT OF THE NEW ECONOMIC REFORMS ON TRIBALS AS A POOR ECONOMIC CLASS IN KALAHANDI

1. Bardhan (1997) and Guha (2002) considered such confrontation as a product of a fundamental cultural dualism in India which ignores the economic logic of capitalism in the making of such confrontation to rationalise and naturalise capitalist social relations. The works of Vander Pijl (2006), Bell, (1971) and Zamoshkin & Melvil (1982) have dealt with the process of naturalisation and rationalisation of capitalist social relations in detail. The characterisation of a welfare state i.e. India and projecting its failure based on efficiency and its contribution towards economic growth is nothing but a process towards naturalisation of the capitalist political and economic relationship between the state and its citizens.

2. For a general debate on mode of production, see; A.Foster-Carter, "The Mode of Production Debate", New Left Review, 1978. See Shanin (1982).

3. This is documented by the Ministry of Tribal Affairs, Government of India, New Delhi, in its report on 'Social Security and Social Insurance' (paragraph two). It can be accessed through ministry's website. http://tribal.nic.in/index1.html (accessed date; 9th July 2007).

4. Rational agriculture is conducted by the small farmers as per their own food requirements and local demands. Such mode of agricultural is incompatible with the capitalist system and thus the capitalist system works against rational agriculture (Marx & Engels, 1998: 123).

5. The details on post-economic reform agricultural policies for the Kalahandi district can be found in "An Integrated Perspective Plan on Land and Water Use for Kalahandi District, Orissa (1993-94-2002-2003)", District Planning Unit, Kalahandi, Bhawanipatna, pp-8-22.

6. The new agrarian policy in Kalahandi followed after the economic reforms were concomitant with the colonial agrarian policies for tribals. During the colonial regime, the colonial agrarian policy treated tribal agriculture in the line of the mainstream agriculture of the plains areas without taking the economic advantages and specificities of tribal agriculture into consideration. The objective of such policy was to increase revenue generation and facilitate trade and market by export based commercialisation of agriculture (For details on the impact of colonial agrarian policy, see; Stein, 1992: 17 and Saravanan, 2006). In the similar way, the new agrarian policy in Kalahandi does not take the specifics of tribal agriculture in particular and agriculture in general. Thus, the post-reform agrarian policy in the district can be regarded as a neo-colonial agrarian policy.

7. For details see; Deputy Director of Agriculture, Bhawanipatna report in the Agricultural Strategy Committee Meeting on 28/10/2002.

8. For details see; Action Plan, 2005-06 under RLTP for Development of KBK Region, Department of Agriculture, Government of Orissa, Bhubaneswar.

9. Such changes have taken place in the culture of Indian peasantry as a whole. The majority of smallholder peasants in India still think that "increase in the yields is not due to improved techniques but to our fate and karma" (Nair, Kusum. (1961: 79). I am not arguing here that the belief system is right or wrong but trying to reflect on the society and technology interface in which not the human emotion rather the market interest leads the production system. The aesthetic and cultural values attached to the production system are being separated by market values created by demand, supply and exchange, which is a source of alienation.

10. During the implementation of the new agricultural policy, (Western Orissa Sugar industries).

11. Data collected from the Office of the *Integrated Tribal Development Agency (ITDA)*, Bhawanipatna, Kalahandi.

12. Data collected from the *Deputy Director of Agriculture*, Kalahandi Range, Bhawanipatna and calculated by me.

13. Data collected from the Office of the *Assistant Director of Sericulture Cum Assistant Public Information Officer*, Bhawanipatna, Kalahandi.

14. For details on PDS, see; Swaminathan (2000).

15. Calculated from the different years of Khariff Plan-2001-2002, Food Corporation of India Report, Bhubaneswar, Orissa.

16. The *Food Corporation of India* (FCI) involved in food procurement, storage and distribution to the Fair Price Shops (FPS) working under the system of PDS.

17. The *Nanda Committee Report* (2001) on distress sale of rice in Orissa, May, 2001, unpublished Report Submitted to the Government of Orissa, Bhubaneswar.

18. The universal orientation of PDS ensures the objective of food security which can only be achieved when all people at all times have physical and economic access to sufficient, safe and nutritious food to meet their dietary needs and food preferences for an active life as per the *Rome Declaration on World Food Security, World Food Summit* (1996).

19. Report on the Activities of the Food Supplies & Consumer Welfare Department For the Year-2001-2002, Food Supplies and Consumer Welfare Department, Government of Orissa.pp-4-5.

20. For details on post-economic reform industrial policy transition in Orissa and India, see; Nayak (2007: 90-91).

21. Data on industries are collected from *District Industries Center*, Bhawanipatna, Kalahandi.

22. VAL is a UK-based mining company owned by NRI billionaire Anil Agarwal. It is a part of Sterlite Industries, which is a public limited company manufacturing aluminum and aluminum products. It is controlled and owned by Vedanta Resources Plc, a UK registered company. Other major Sterlite Group Companies operating in India include *Sterlite Optical Technologies Ltd., Bharat Aluminum Company Ltd., and Hindustan Zinc Ltd.* For details on VAL, see; *The Ravages Though India: Vedanta Resources Plc Counter Report* (2005), Mines and Communities, London.

23. However, the recommendations of the CEC is overlooked by the recent judgment of the Supreme Court bench and given its verdict in favour of the VAL (SC, Writ Petition (Civil No. 202 of 1995 and I.A. Nos. 2081-2082 @ W.P. (C) No. 549/2007).

24. The Primitive Tribal Groups (PTGs) are identified based on three factors; pre-agricultural level of technology, very low level of literacy and declining or stagnant population. Based on these factors 75 tribal communities were defined as PTGs for initiating special development programmes (Ministry of Tribal Affairs, 2002). There are 13 PTGs in Orissa and four types of PTGs i.e. Bondas, Dadai, Langia, Sauras, Kutia and Dongaria Kandhas are residing in the Kalahandi district especially in the areas of Thuamul Rampur and Langigarh area. There was a *Kutia Kondh Development Agency (KKDA)* set up in the Langigarh block during 1986-87 for the development of PTG which has become completely defunct during the post-reform period due to lack of staff in the office. The KKDA is completely closed now.

25. Industrialisation comes not only in the form of investment, capital and its industrial infrastructure. Industrialisation comes with its ideological apparatus of a modern industrial society without which it can not attain its objectives. Its ideology is aimed at harnessing all the energy of an individual in a disciplined way to achieve the full potential of the labour power for higher level of production. The ideas of punctuality, orderliness and discipline are the product of modern industrial society and carry the ideologies during the process of industrialisation (Fromm, 1949: 5-6). The idea of orderliness, punctuality and discipline is alien to the tribal society in the district of Kalahandi, for that matter for all the tribal societies in the state and in the country. The process of industrialisation reduces wider tribal meaning systems attached to time, space and production system into a mechanical understanding of a one dimensional production system based on virtues of economic output. The entire process creates a base to transform tribals as industrial labour to create capitalist social relations.

26. Data collected from the Information Sheet on the Road Works by ITDA, Bhawanipatna, Kalahandi (2005).

27. Data collected from the Revenue Section, Kalahandi District Collectorate, Bhawanipatna.

28. The very idea of economic integration is free trade and free market. For further analysis on economic integration; see; Tinbergen (1965).

29. See; *Indigenous peoples and their relationship to land*. Final working paper prepared by the Special Rapporteur, Mrs. Erica-Irene A. Daes. UN Doc. E/CN.4/Sub.2/2001/21, 11 June 2001, at para. 20.

30. During the colonial period, the Agency Tracts Interests and Land Transfer Act (ATILT Act) 1917 was implemented to protect the rights of tribals on land. During post-colonial India, the Schedule V and VI of the Indian Constitution protects the land rights of the tribals in the country. The Scheduled Tribes and Other Traditional Forest Dwellers (Recognition of Forest Rights) Act, 2006, Chapter 2, 3(a) by the Government of India is the latest protective measure to protect tribal land rights. All tribal areas in Orissa come under Schedule-V of Indian Constitution that constitutes 44.70 percent of the state land covering all tribal areas which constitutes 70 percent of forest areas in the state. In order to ensure the spirit of the Indian Constitution, the Government of Orissa has also made certain laws to protect tribal land rights in the state i.e. Land Reforms Act- 1920(1965) and the Orissa Scheduled Areas Transfer of Immovable Property (by Scheduled Tribe) Regulation 1956 (OSATIP Regulation, 1956). These laws were enacted by the state to ensure tribal land rights. For details on land laws in Orissa, see; Tripathy (1992) and Behuria (1997), for traditional tribal land ownership laws, see; (Mohanti, 1992, 1994a, 1994b, 1996), for tribal land alienation, see; Panigrahi (2001) and for transition in land laws to protect tribal right over land, see; Kumar et el (2005).

31. Land alienation is a situation which indicates separation of people from their land. Here, I am talking about tribal land alienation in Kalahandi which indicates isolating, displacing, separating and occupying tribal land from them. It also indicates denial of availability, accessibility and usability of tribal land either legally owned or customarily inherited. The industrialisation, dam building, forest protection laws and tribal poverty are some of the causes of landlessness in tribal areas in Kalahandi. The land is very vital in the social, economic and cultural life of tribals. The land alienation causes depeasantisation of tribals as a result of which tribals lose their control over their production (alienation of labour) and as consequence of which they lose their control over themselves (self-alienation). Thus, the process of land alienation in tribal areas in India is causing social, economic and cultural disintegration that enforces a sense of separateness among tribal both as individual and as the members of their community which leads to both self-alienation and alienation of tribals from their fellow beings (social alienation). For more explanations on the concept of alienation, see; Marx (1959) and Mandel (1970, pp.19-23, 49-50).

32. The Kalahandi was a princely state with no written land laws designed to protect the interests of the tenants. Only law like the Orissa States Order 1948 has offered occupancy rights but no rights were recognised for any tenants below occupancy tenants in the hierarchy of rights in land. It has created a social and legal exclusion over one's land right (Behuria, 1997). This forms the basis of denial of land access to poor in the district.

33. 'Kulthas' belong to the higher agricultural caste in the caste hierarchy in the district of Kalahandi, like the 'Brahmins' in the higher caste in the Hindu caste system. Gountias are Brahmins in the district.

34. There is a detailed discussion in Chapter-2 of the thesis, while talking about the state formation in the Kalahandi district, which deals with the genealogy of the Deo Dynasty which belongs to a family of Gangabansi Rajputs of Chotanagpur in present state of Jharkhand. It is also documented by Das (1962: 4).

35. Calculated from the *District Statistical Abstract for Kalahandi District* (1971, 1991, 2001) and District Statistical Handbook, Kalahandi (1971, 1991, 2001), Directorate of Economics and Statistics, Government of Orissa, Bhubaneswar.

36. Based on fieldwork data classification, 2005. See; Nayak (2009).

37. Unpublished data collected from Census Office, Bhubaneswar, 2005.See Nayak (2009) for details.

38. Data Collected from different reports of the Panchayat Raj Department, Government of Orissa, Bhubaneswar.

39. Fieldwork data collected from District Employment Office and District Statistical Office, Bhawanipatna, Kalahandi. The percentage is calculated by me.

40. Data compiled from the District Labour Office, Bhawanipatna, Kalahandi.

41. For all India study, see; Baviskar (2003).

42. One lakh is equal to a hundred thousand.

43. Census of BPL Families during 1992 and 1997 in KBK Districts, Panchayati Raj Department, Government of Orissa, 2001.

44. Information Sheet on Different Poverty Alleviation Programmes, BPL Survey Data Collected from the District Rural Development Agency (DRDA-1999-2000), Bhawanipatna, Kalahandi.

45. Calculated by me from the Fieldwork Sample Surveys conducted from January to March 2005.

46. There are thirteen BDOs in all thirteen blocks in Kalahandi district including two tribal blocks. All development policies basically carried out by the Block Development Offices (BDOs) in the district under the district administration in Orissa.

47. Fieldwork Data Collected from the 13 Block Headquarters of Kalahandi district and District Record Room, Bhawanipatna.

48. All data collected from the ITDA Office, Bhawanipatna, Kalahandi.

49. The *District Rural Development Agency (DRDA)*, Kalahandi has documented the process of under utilization and unspent balance of funds while presenting its report to the visiting Rajya Sabha Committee on Petitions (Information Booklet, For the visit of Honorable Rajya Sabha Committee on Petitions to Orissa from 25th to 28th May 2003, p.5). This process is even reflected in all India level i.e. the grant made under the Article 275(1) for the tribal development is underutilized which can be projected in the work of Nayak (2009).

50. Data collected from the Office of the DRDA, Bhawanipatna, Kalahandi.

51. The New Economic Reforms policy package which was l aunched during 1991 in India economy constitutes many policies as prescribed by the IMF and World Bank. One of the major policies of the package is known as the Structural Adjustment Policies (SAP) that constitutes of liberalisation and deregulation of economy, reduction of public expenditure through privatisation of public services, restructuring of the welfare delivery institutions, reduction in welfare activities, subsidies and social safety nets. The policies have coherent programme for the collapse of social and economic institutions. For details see; George and Chossudovsky et al. (1995), Chandrasekhar and Ghosh (2002).

52. Based on (Nayak, 2009).

53. Data collected from all 13 BDOs of Kalahandi.

54. ibid.

55. ibid.

56. ibid.

57. The polarisation of urban and rural areas or tribal and no n- tribal areas and people in the district is not just impact of economic policy or an accidental outcome of development policies pursued in the district during colonial and post-colonial Orissa. In such a context, Samir Amin (1994) has rightly opined that "polarisation is not an accident attributable to specific local causes in culture or demography or elsewhere. It is inseparable from actually existing capitalism and can not be avoided in the framework of the logic of the capitalist implementation (Amin, 1994: 64)". He explains further on the issues of polarisation and said that it is the basis of accumulation and pauperisation (ibid:66).

58. Samir Amin rightly put it that "underdevelopment is not a backward phase of development but a modern phenomenon of worldwide capitalist expansion initially polarising and shaping the distinction between centres and peripheries to the demands of worldwide expansion of capital which dominates the centre (Amin, 1994:68)".

59. See; Nayak (2009).

60. See; Human Development in South Asia 2001 : Globalisation and Human Development, The Mahbub ul Haq Human Development Centre for Oxford (2002), OUP, New Delhi, p-53.

61. The history and nature of natural calamities in Kalahandi district is documented in the works of Pati (2003:354-55).

62. The KBK Scheme (1996), Government of Orissa, pp.12-13.

63. Office of the Deputy Registrar of Cooperative Societies, Kalahandi Division, Bhawanipatna and Office of the Regional Marketing Officer, Kalahandi Region, Bhawanipatna.

64. Records on LAMPS, District Record Room, Bhawanipatna.

65. ibid.

5. IMPACT OF THE NEW ECONOMIC REFORMS ON TRIBALS AS SOCIALLY DISADVANTAGED GROUPS IN KALAHANDI

1. Social, cultural, educational and other organisations are known as Sangh Paribar (family of organisations) working around the *Rashtriya Swayam Sevak Sangh* (RSS) under the political wing of the Bharatiya Janata Party, known as Hindu right wing forces. Many people use many terms to describe the Hindu right wing forces; Ghosh (1999) calls it 'political Hinduism' whereas Patnaik (1993) calls it an Indian form of fascism. Teltumbde (2006) calls it Hindu fundamentalist forces having link with neo-liberalism on one hand, and American imperialism on the other hand. For many other interpretations, see; Kinnvall (2006), Zavos (2000), Jaffrelot, (1996) and Corbridge, & Harriss (2000). I prefer to use the term "Hindu right wing forces" which incorporates social, cultural, economic, political and religious understanding of right wing activities.

2. See; The Schedule-VI of Indian Constitution (2008) deals with the administration of tribal areas of the seven states in the North East region of the country whereas Schedule-V of Indian Constitution (2008) deals with the administration of other parts of the country including Orissa. Especially Article-244 (2a) prohibits the transfer of land by or among members of the Scheduled Tribes in the tribal area; (b) regulates the allotment of land to members of the Scheduled Tribes and (c) regulates the carrying on of money lending business by persons who lend money to members of the Scheduled Tribes in such area. These protective measures are essential to protect the distinct identity of tribals and their right over land and other natural resources. The spirit of the Indian Constitution is reflected in different protective laws made by both state and national governments for tribals. For example; the government of Orissa has made different laws i.e. Land Reforms Act- 1920(1965) and the Orissa Scheduled Areas Transfer of Immovable Property (by Scheduled Tribe) Regulation 1956 (OSATIP Regulation, 1956) which are concomitant with the spirit of the Indian Constitution to protect tribal right over land and other natural resources.

3. For a clear understanding of cultural contradictions of capitalism, see; Bell (1971:31-32, 1976). The way neo-liberal economy constructs economic men/women can be found in the works of Vander Pijl (2006:29).

4. The Composite Development Index (CDI) is a powerful tool to measure human development by taking different aspects (i.e. health, education and living standard) of human development into consideration. The CDI was used for the first time by UNDP in 1990 and is still using it to prepare its annual Human Development Reports.

5. Data for 1991 and 2001 from State Statistical Abstract and District Statistical Handbooks for 1991 and 2001, Directorate of Statistics and Economics, Government of Orissa, Bhubaneswar.

6. Composite variation is the total variation from all the sources or sum of those variations which has made contribution. Here different variables of health and educational sector (i.e. teacher-student ratio, doctor-patient ratio, other health and educational infrastructures, funds allocation from government etc) in the district have been taken to calculate composite variation between two periods.

7. Based on Data collected from the Orissa State Development Report (2004), Government of Orissa, Bhubaneswar.

8. Anthropologists like Padel (1995) consider remoteness as the best insurance against poverty and other forms of marginalisation. Such analysis tends to avoid the role of the forces who are working to keep the tribal and rural masses in perpetual remoteness to continue their hegemony over the tribal resources. Remoteness helps to sustain the existing inequality and exploitation in the tribal society and keep them isolated from the benefits of democratic citizenship and affirmative action of a welfare state.

9. District Action Plan for Health, Office of the Chief District Medical Officer, Kalahandi under National Rural Health Mission (2006), Government of Orissa, Bhubaneswar.

10. There are thirteen Gram Panchayats in Thuamul Rampur and only five Gram Panchayats are covered under District Water Sanitation Mission whereas out of seven Gram Panchayats in the Langigarh block only four Gram Panchayats are covered under District Water Sanitation Mission (Source: DWSM, Kalahandi, 2006).

11. Revenue Section, Kalahandi District Collectorate, Bhawanipatna.

12. Data Calculated and Collected from the District Level Data, Kalahandi Census, Census of India (Orissa-2001).

13. All data collected from the Information Booklet for the Visit of Rajya Sabha Committee on Petitions to Kalahandi, Orissa from 25th to 28th May 2003.

14. National Information Center, RGB, SOI, National Rural Health Mission (2006), Government of Orissa, India.

15. Office of the Chief District Medical Officer, Bhawanipatna, Kalahandi.

16. Data collected from the office of the Inspector of Ayurvedic, Bhawanipatna Circle, Kalahandi.

17. All data collected from Office of the Chief District Medical Officer, Bhawanipatna, Kalahandi, 2006.

18. ibid.

19. ibid.

20. All data collected from Office of the Chief District Medical Officer, Bhawanipatna, Kalahandi, 2006.

21. Ibid.

22. Census of India (2001) and the % is calculated by me.

23. Office of the District Inspector of Schools, Bhawanipatna, Kalahandi.

24. Ibid.

25. Information Booklet for the visit of Rajya Sabha Committee on Petitions to Kalahandi district, Orissa from 25th to 28th May 2003.

26. Data collected from the different issues of the District Statistical Handbook-Kalahandi (from 1981-2001), Directorate of Economics and Statistics, Government of Orissa, Bhubaneswar.

27. Ibid.

28. Ibid.

29. Ibid.

30. Ibid.

31. Ibid.

32. Ibid.

33. The origin of the contemporary relationship between education and economy can be located during the expansionary economic conditions of the post World War II era under the regime of Keynesian economic management. As a result of which the governments started spending more with an aim of economic growth (Bowen, 1981: 526). The integration of education with economy is a necessary precondition to mould the social institutions and social structures, what Harvey calls 'social infrastructures', to suit the needs of economic growth and capital accumulation (Harvey, 1982:398). The process of moulding social institutions destroys, reshapes and creates new structures or saves the old structures as per the requirement of the capitalist economy. The class relations and contradictions in social relations of production remains the same or are shifted from one place to the other (ibid: 326). Thus, the integration of educational system with the economy is a capitalist mode of education (Raduntz, 2001:317). The educational system became more utilitarian during 1960s as a part of the restructuring process of the educational systems in response to the needs of the economy (Ozga and Lawn,

1988) which paved the way for marketisation or commercialisation and thus commodification of education.

34. The committee was constituted under the leadership of two industrialist experts i.e. Mukesh Ambani as convener and Kumarmangalam Birla as member. The committee has suggested the government for the privatisation of welfare services especially in the field of education (Ambani and Birla Report (2000) on 'A Policy Framework for Reforms in Education', submitted to the PMCTI on April 24, 2000). The prescriptions of the report are concomitant with the ideas and policies of World Bank and other international financial institutions.

35. See; Nayak (2009).

36. Data collected from District Collectorate Record Room, Bhawanipatna, Kalahandi.

37. Ibid.

38. Ibid.

39. See Nayak (2009) for data on Religious Affiliated NGOs in Kalahandi district.

40. Deputy Inspector of Schools, Bhawanipatna, Kalahandi, Orissa.

41. Saraswati is known as the goddess of knowledge and education in the Hindu religion.

42. Annual Plan (2005-2006), Sikhya Vikash Samiti, Vidya Bharati, Orissa.

43. Public - Private Partnership is a partnership with the private sector, composed of Non-Governmental Organisations (NGOs), Faith Based Organisations (FBOs), Community Based Organisations (CBOs) & local self Government (PRIs) to manage the health sector of the district. (NRHM-Kalahandi, 2007: 34). The NGOs have to play a lead role in providing the health care in the tribal areas of the district as the government alone can not take responsibility for the health sector (ibid: 76).

44. For details, see; NRHM- Kalahandi, Department of Health (2007:17-18), Government of Orissa, Bhubaneswar.

45. For a detailed discussion on the declining of state legitimacy during the period of globalization, see; (Lash & Urry 1994: 281).

46. Data collected from District Collectorate Record Room, Kalahandi.

47. See; Nayak (2009) for data on Religious Affiliated NGOs in Kalahandi district.

48. The peasantisation of tribals to absorb them into Hindu social and religious order was an all India process to occupy tribal land and other natural resources. This argument has been developed and historicized by many anthropologists and historians' i.e. Kosambi (1975), Sharma (1990) and Hardiman (1995).

49. A detailed discussion on the difference between farmers and peasants can be found in the work of Wolf (1973).

50. As per the Hindu religion, everyone has to undergo sixteen compulsory purification ceremonies from birth to death which is called 'sanskaras' (refine or purify to elevate for perfection) but Sivan (2005) talks about thirteen purification ceremonies in Hindu religion for eternal liberation. There are different views about the number of 'Sanskaras' in Hindu religion as the practice differs from one place to the other and each 'sanskara' is also divided into several 'sub-sanskaras'.

51. All data on atrocities on tribals in Kalahandi district collected from the Office of the Superintendent of Police, Bhawanipatna, Kalahandi.

52. Ibid.

53. See; Nayak(2009).

54. The idea of 'thick description' is borrowed from the work of Geertz (1973: 3-30) which provides the basis for new historicism to understand contexts of time, place and people in the lens of history.

55. For example, Kandha (Kondh) is a major tribal group in Kalahandi and in the state as well. There are four groups forming the caste within Kondh tribal group based on their place of living. The Desia Kodh live on the plains, livelihood is based on agriculture and they are largely integrated into Indian Hindu society through their interaction with mainstream Hindu people via the market. The Kondh tribe who live in high up hill terrains are known as Dongaria Kondh (donger is tribal word indicates sloppy hilly area without trees, some people call it as mountain area and others call it dead mountain). Their livelihood is based on agriculture and, they cultivate donger land which might be another reason behind the naming of their group. And the third group among the Kondh tribes is known as Kutia Kondh who live in the down

hill terrains; the Government of India considers them as a primitive tribal group (PTG) for affirmative action. The Dharua tribe is one of the oldest tribe that forms the lowest caste within the Kondh community. The name of the tribe seems to be derived from 'dhur' or 'dhuli' (dust) which indicates their inferior position in tribal society. Another special feature of Kondh society is that they consider women as bejuni (spiritual medium), giving a special status to women in their society. This caste system among Kondh tribal groups is changing with the growth of Hindutva forces by bringing the practice of untouchability. The gender relationship is also changing due to both Hindu influence and massive industrialisation in the tribal area.

Dombs are the people considered to be the lower caste people in the Hindu caste order; their livelihood is based on animal skin trade, their work is to remove skin from the dead body of an animal and sell it in the market. The Government of India considers them as the Schedule Caste people for ensuring affirmative action.

56. Dombs are the people consider ed to be the lower caste people in the Hindu caste order, their livelihood is based on animal skin trade, their work is to remove skin from the dead body of an animal and sell it in the market. The Government of India considers them as the Schedule Caste people for ensuring affirmative action.

57. I found new temples in most of the tribal areas of the Kalahandi district during my fieldwork. I observed that these temples had been constructed within 5 to 10 years.

58. Yajñopavîta is a Hindu purification ceremony in which the sacred thread is given to an individual(s) in the process of Vedic initiation. It confirms that one belongs to Hindu religion.

59. The work of Mishra (2007) deals in detail about the oral epics and its social relevance among tribals in the Kalahandi district.

60. Kalahandia is an Oriya word which means people of the Kalahandi district. It is also used by the people of Kalahandi indicating their own language and culture but the people of coastal Orissa use the term in a derogatory sense indicating underdeveloped, illiterate and uncivilized people of the district. In costal Orissa, people use the term to describe naïve, unskilled, inefficient, inelegant and weak people.

61. The work of Uberoi (1996:84) provides an implicit critique of the Indian version of the ambitious modernist project that attempts to bring "religion, State and society" together, the spheres already having a strong division since medieval India. I consider the Indian modernist project as a monolithic obstinate project which is trying to hegemonise the multicultural ethos of Indian society by bringing state, religion and society together. Such integration is creating a smooth terrain for the growth and expansion of global capitalist market. The Hinduisation of tribals in Kalahandi helps such a process.

62. The policy making elites of Kalahandi include both ruling and non-ruling elites (politicians, journalists, and bureaucrats, tribal and non-tribal elites). The elites of coastal Orissa are part of the elites in the district as they have their base in the district in terms of land ownership, business network and political power.

63. Similar arguments are made by Harrison & Huntington, 2000: XII), Banfield (1958) and Friedman (2000). They argue that underdeveloped and exclusive culture is incompatible with the development of an advanced economy. In simple terms, there is no role of state, public policy and institutions of development; no one is responsible or accountable for the underdevelopment other than culture and social organisation.

64. This tribal woman left school due to her family's financial problems. Although she is a school drop out she can read and write mainstream Oriya language which is the language of the state of Orissa. She is one literate woman in the whole area who works for the distance education center in her village called Perumanji in Thuamul Rampur block of the Kalahandi district. The same kind of expression, I found while talking to many tribal men and women during my fieldwork.

65. 'Babu' is an Oriya word meaning gentleman, but it is used for the people who are at the top of the hierarchy. People in Orissa use the term for all government officials, educated people, police, lawyers, doctors, and politicians. Tribals use the term for all people from the above section along with good looking people from their area and outside their area.

66. Violence in the form of resistance provides justification for counter violence led by the state in the name of maintaining law and order for peace. Bates (2001:102) has argued that

violence has both political and economic roots and objectives that promotes the economic base and sustains prosperity of a particular class.

67. As reported in The Samaja on April 9, 2003.

68. "Save out mountains, Indian tribe urges banks", reported by Emily Dugan in The Independent, Friday, 2nd May 2008.

69. The Times of India, August 25, 2006.

70. Interviewed by Damian Grammaticas of the BBC, For details, see; 'Tribe takes on global mining firm', BBC, Thursday, 17 July 2008.

71. The mainstream communist parties like CPI and CPI(M) have supported and participated in the struggle of tribals in the district. But consider it as a deviation from the historical method of class struggle which aims at protecting culture to ensure livelihood. Culture is still considered to be the super structure and false consciousness by the local communist activists.

72. The national position of the INC is to support industrialisation in the tribal areas of the Kalahandi district. But its Kalahandi district unit and local unit at Langigarh opposes industrialization in the tribal areas of the district. They have formed an Organization called "Green Kalahandi" which is in the fore front of the struggle against the Vedanta Alumina Limited in Langigarh.

73. Interviewed by British journalist Simon Freedman, March 2007.

74. Interviewed by Indian filmmaker S. Josson, July 2007.

CONCLUSION

1. Rata, Elizabeth Mary. 1997, *Global Capitalism and the Revival of Ethnic Traditionalism in New Zealand: The Emergence of Tribal Capitalism*, Ph.D. thesis submitted to University of Auckland, 1997.

Bibliography

Abercrombie, Nicholas, Stephan Hill, Bryan S. Turner (2000), *The Penguin Dictionary of Sociology*, 4th edition, Penguin Books, London.

Abramovitz, M. & David, P. A., (1973), "Reinterpreting Economic Growth: Parables and Realities, *The American Economic Review*, Volume-63, Issue-2, Papers and proceedings of the Eighty-fifth Annual Meeting of the American Economic Association.

Adorno, T. (2001), *The Culture Industry: Selected Essays on Mass Culture*, Routledge, London.

Aglietta, M. (1979), *A Theory of Capitalist Regulation*, New Left Books, London.

Agrawal, A. (1995a), "Dismantling the Divide between Indigenous and Scientific Knowledge" *Development and Change*, 26.

———. (1995b). "Indigenous and Scientific Knowledge: Some Critical Comments." *Indigenous Knowledge and Development Monitor*, 3(3): pp. 3-33.

———. (2002), 'Indigenous knowledge and the politics of classification', *International Social Science Journal*, Volume- 54, Issue-173, Pp-287 – 97.

Ahluwalia, I.J. and I.M.D. Little, (1998), *India's Economic Reforms and Development: Essays for Manmohan Singh* (ed.), OUP, New Delhi.

Ahluwalia, M S (2002),'Economic Reforms in India since 1991: Has Gradualism Worked?' *Journal of Economic Perspective*, 16 (3).

———. (2000), 'Economic Performance and States in Post-Reforms Period', *Economic and Political Weekly* (Mumbai), 6 May.

Ahmad, A. (2000), *Lineages of the Present: Ideology and Politics in Contemporary South Asia*, Verso, London.

Akerlof, G. (1976), The Economics of Caste and of the Rat Race and Other Woeful Tales, *Quarterly Journal of Economics,* 90.

Allen, C. & Dwivedi, S. (1998), *Lives of the Indian princes*, Eeshwar, Mumbai.

Alt, J. & Sheplse, K. (1990), *Perspectives on Positive Political Economy,* University of California Press, Los Angeles.

Althusser, L. (1971), "Ideology and State Apparatuses", in L. Althusser, *Lenin and Philosophy and Other Essays,* New Left Books, London.

Altman, J.C. (1987), *Hunter-Gatherers Today: An Aboriginal Economy in North Australia*, ANU, Canberra.

Ambedkar, B.R. (1923), *The Problem of Rupee; its Origin and Solution*, P.S.King and sons Ltd., London.

Amin, S. (1994), *Re-reading the post war period; an intellectual itinerary"*, translated by Michael Wolfers, Monthly Review Press, New York.

————. (1998), *Spectres of Capitalism: A Critique of Current Intellectual Fashions*, translated by Shane Henry Mage, Monthly Review Press, New York/Rainbow Publisher, New Delhi.

Andersen, B. P. (1999), *Ethnicity, ritual integration and literature as illustrated by the Karam Ritual among the Santals.* Unpublished Ph.D.-thesis. Institute of History of Religion, University of Copenhagen.

————. (1986), Ritual Friendships as a Means of Understanding the Cultural Exchanges Between Santal and Hindu Cultures. *Temenos, 22.*

Appadurai, A. (1986), "Theory in Anthropology: Centre and Periphery", *Comparative Studies in Society and History*, 28(1).

————. (1990), 'Disjuncture and difference in the global cultural economy', in M. Featherstone (ed.), *Global culture: Nationalism, globalization and modernity*, Sage, London.

————. (1991), 'Global ethnoscapes: notes and queries for a transnational anthropology', in Fox, R. (ed), *Recapturing Anthropology: Working in the Present*, School of American Research Press, Santa Fe, New Mexico.

————. (2000), "Spectral Housing and Urban Cleansing: Notes on Millenial Mumbai," *Public Culture*, Vol. 12, No. 3.

————. (1990), "Disjuncture and Difference in the Global Cultural Economy", *Public Culture*, 2(2).

Ashton, S.R. (1982), *British Policy towards the Indian states 1905-1939*, Curzon Press, London.

Audi, R. (1995), *The Cambridge Dictionary of Philosophy* (ed), Cambridge University Press, Cambridge.

Austin, G. (2004), *The Indian Constitution: Cornerstone of a Nation.* Oxford University Press, Oxford.

Awaaz, South Asia Watch Limited (2004), *In Bad Faith: British Charity and Hindu Extremism. London: Awaaz, South Asia Watch,* http://www.awaazsaw.org/ibf/, Accessed on 19th July 2004.

Bagchi, A.K. (1972), *Private Investment in India*, Cambridge University Press, Cambridge.

————. (1976a), "Deindustrialization in India in the Nineteenth Century: Some Theoretical Implications," *Journal of Development Studies* 12 (October).

————. (1976b), 'Reflections on the pattern of regional growth in India during the period of British rule', *Bengal Past and Present*, Vol. 95, Nos. 180.181.

————. (1982), *The Political Economy of Underdevelopment*, Cambridge University Press, Cambridge.

————. (1995), 'Dialectics of Indian Planning: From Compromise to Democratic Decentralization and Threat of Disarray' in T.V. Sathyamurthy (ed.) *Industry and Agriculture in India Since Independence*, OUP, New Delhi.

Bailey, F. G. (1960), *Tribe, Caste and Nation,* Manchester University Press, Manchester.

————. (1971), *Caste and the Economic Frontier; A Village in Highland Orissa,* Manchester University Press, Manchester.

Baker, E.C (1978), 'Scope of the First Amendment Freedom of Speech', *UCLA Law Review*, 25.

Banaji. J. (1977), "Modes of Production in a Materialist Conception of History", *Capital and Class*, 3 (Autumn).

Banerjee, A., & Iyer, L. (2003), *'History, institutions and economic performance: The legacy of colonial land tenure systems in India.'* Mimeo

Banerjee, R.D. (1930), *History of Orissa*, Vol. I & II, Prabasi Press, Calcutta.

Banerji, A.K. (1963), *India's Balance of Payments: Estimates of Current and Capital Accounts from 1921-22 to 1938-39*, Asia Publishing House, Bombay.

Banfield, E.C.(1958), *The Moral Basis of a Backward Society,* The Free Press, New York.

Bardhan, P. (1989). 'A Note on Interlinked Rural Economic Arrangements', in Pranab Bardhan (ed.) *The Economic Theory of Agrarian Institutions.* Clarendon Press, Oxford.

————. (1989a*), The Economic Theory of Agrarian Institutions*, Clarendon Press, Oxford.

————. (1989b), *The Political Economy of Development in India,* Basil Blackwell, Oxford.

————. (1997), The State against Society: the great divide in Indian Social Science discourse. In *Nationalism, Democracy and Development: state and politics in India* (eds) by S. Bose & A. Jalal, OUP, New Delhi.

Bardhan, P. (1998), *The Political Economy of Development in India*, (expanded edition with an epilogue on the Political Economy of Reform in India), OUP, New Delhi.

————. (2004) *Scarcity, Conflicts and Cooperation: Essays in Political and Institutional Economics of Development*, MIT Press, Cambridge, MA.

————. (2007), 'Poverty and Inequality in China and India: Elusive Link with Globalisation', *EPW*, September 22.

Barth, F. (1969), *Ethnic Groups and Boundaries: The Social Organization of Culture Difference*, (ed), George Allen and Unwin, London.

————. (2002), "An Anthropology of Knowledge", *Current Anthropology*, 43(1).

Basu, K. (1990), *Agrarian Structure and Economic Underdevelopment*, Harwood Academic Publishers, Switzerland.

Baviskar, A. (1995), *In the Belly of the River: Tribal Conflicts over Development in the Narmada Valley*, OUP, Delhi.

Baviskar, A. (2003), 'Tribal politics and discourses of Indian environmentalism', in: P. Greenough & A. Lowenhaupt Tsing (Eds), *Nature in the Global South, Environmental Projects in South and South-East Asia*, pp. 289–318, Orient Longmans, Hyderabad.

————. (2003), "Between Violence and Desire: Space, Power and Identity in the Making of Metropolitan Delhi." *International Social Science Journal* 175.

Bayly, C.A. (1988), *The New Cambridge History of India, II.1: Indian Society and the Making of the British Empire*, Cambridge University Press, Cambridge.

Bayly, C.A. (1990), *Indian Society and the Making of the British Empire*, Cambridge University Press, Cambridge.

Bayly, S. (1999), *Caste and Society and Politics in India from the Eighteenth Century to the Modern Age* Cambridge University Press, Cambridge.

Beck, U. (2005), *Power in the global age: a new global political economy*, Polity, Cambridge.

Beckmann, A. & Cooper, C. (2004) 'Globalization', the New Managerialism and Education: rethinking the purpose of education, *Journal for Critical Education Policy Studies*, 2(1).

Behera, K.S. (1993), *Sagar O Sahitya* (Ocean and Literature), (edited in Oriya), Cuttack.

Behera, K.S. (1999), *Maritime Heritage of Orissa* (ed), Aryan Books International, New Delhi.

Behera, S.K. & Mishra, M. (2005), 'Indigenous phytotherapy for genito-urinary diseases used by the Kandha tribe of Orissa, India', *Journal of Ethno Pharmacology*, Volume-102, Issue-3.

Behuria, N.C. (1997), *Land Reforms Legislation in India* , Vikas, New Delhi.

Belk, R. W. (1988) 'Third World Consumer Culture'. In E Kumku and A.F. Firat (Eds.) *Marketing and Development: Towards Broader Dimensions, JAI*, Greenwich CT.

Bell, Daniel, (1971), "The Cultural Contradictions of Capitalism", in Daniel Bell and Irving Kristol (eds), *Capitalism Today*, New York.

Bellah, R.N. (1957), *Tokugawa Religion: The Values of Pre-industrial Japan*, Free Press, Glencoe.

Ben, A. D. (1978), *Folklore in Context. Essays,* South Asian Publishers, Delhi.

Berger, P. (1986), *The Capitalist Revolution: Fifty Propositions about Prosperity, Equality, & Liberty,* Basic Books, New York.

Berman, H. (1983), *Law and Revolution: The Formation of the Western Legal Tradition,* Harvard University Press, Cambridge.

Bernays, E. (1928), *Propaganda*, Horace Liveright, New York.

Bernier, F. (1981), *Travels in the Moghul Empire*, Irving Books, London.

Berreman, G. (1972), "Social Categories and Social Interaction in Urban India", *American Anthropologist*, Vol-74, American Anthropological Association, Washington.

Beteille, A. (1960), 'The Definition of Tribe', *Seminar* (14).

————. (1984), "Individualism and the Persistence of Collective Identities", University of Essex, Colchester.

————. (1986), "The Concept of Tribe with Special Reference to India, *Arch. Europ. Social,* Vol-XXVII, Paper prepared for seminar in the Department of Anthropology, London School of Economics and Political Science, London.

————. (1991), "The Reproduction of Inequality; Occupation, Caste and Family", *Contribution to Indian Sociology,* Vol-25.

Beteille, A. (1991), 'The concept of tribe with special reference to India', in A. Beteille, *Society and Politics in India: Essays in a Comparative* Sociology, Athlone Press, London.

————. (1995), 'Construction of Tribes', *The Times of India,* (June 19).

Bettelheim, C. (1968), *India Independent,* Macgibbon & Key, London.

Bhaduri, A. (1983). *The Economic Structure of Backward Agriculture,* Academic Press Inc. Ltd, London.

————. (1993), *The Economics of Backward Agriculture,* Academic Press, New York.

————. (1999), *On the Border of Economic Theory and History,* New Delhi: Oxford University Press.

Bhagawati, J. and Srinivasan, T. N. (1993), *India's Economic Reforms,* Ministry of Finance, Economic Division, Government of India, New Delhi.

Bhargava, B.K. (1934), *Indigenous Banking in Ancient and Medieval India,* D.B. Taraporevala, Bombay.

Bhaskar, R. (1975), *A Realist Theory of Science,* Leeds Books, Leeds.

————. (1979), *The Possibility of Naturalism: A Philosophical Critique of the Contemporary Human Sciences,* Harvester Press, Brighton.

————. (1989), *Reclaiming Reality: A Critical introduction to Contemporary Philosophy,* Verso, London.

Bhatia, B.M.(1967), *Famine in India,* Asia Publishing House, Bombay.

Bhatt, B.B. & Pradhan, P.K (2005), 'Maritime Tradition of Orissa' in *Orissa Reference Annual 2005,* Information and Public Relations Department, Government of Orissa, Bhubaneswar.

Bhattacharya, M. (1992), *The Mind of the Founding Fathers,* in N. Mukarji & B. Arora, *Federalism in India: Origin and Development*(ed), Vikas Publishing House, New Delhi.

Bijoy, C.R. (2003), "The Adivasis of India -A History of Discrimination, Conflict, and Resistance", Core Committee of the All India Coordinating Forum of Adivasis/Indigenous Peoples, *Public Union for Civil Liberties (PUCL) Bulletin,* February.

Bocock, R. (1986), *Hegemony,* Tavistock and Ellis Horwood, London.

Boserup, E. (1965), *The Conditions of Agricultural Growth,* Allen and Unwin, London.

Bosworth, B and S M Collins (2007), 'Accounting for Growth: Comparing China and India', *NBER Working Paper No 12943,* Cambridge, Mass.

Bourdieu, P. (1984), *Distinction: A Social Critique of the Judgment of Taste,* (translated by Richard Nice), Routledge and Kegan Paul, London.

Brenner, N. & Theodore, N. (2002), 'Cities and the Geographies of 'Actually Existing Neoliberalism,' *Antipode,* Vol. 34, No. 3.

Brokensha, D., D. Warren and O. Werner, (1980), Indigenous knowledge systems and development (eds), University Press of America, Lanham.

Bronfenbrenner, U. (1986). Ecology of the family as a context for human development: Research perspectives. *Developmental Psychology,* 22.

Brown, L.D. & Korten, D. (1989), 'The role of voluntary organizations in development', *IDR Working Paper,* No. 8. Boston: Institute of Development Research, Boston University, Boston.

Byres, T. (1993), 'State Class and Planning', in T. Byres, *The State and Development Planning in India (*ed.), Oxford University Press, Delhi.

————. (1998), *The Indian Economy: Major Debates since Independence* (ed.), OUP, New Delhi.

Calvert, P. (2001), "Internal colonialism, development and environment", *Third World Quarterly* 22, 51.

Cameron, J. & Ndhlovu, T.P. (2001), 'Cultural Influences on Economic Thought in India: Resistance to diffusion of neo-classical Economics and the principles of Hinduism', *Economic Issues,* Vol.6, Part 2, September.

Caplan, L. (1991), *New Religious Movements in India,* SCM Press, Madras.

Cardoso, F.H. (1972), "Dependency and Development in Latin America", *New Left Review,* 74 (July-August).

Casanova, P.G (1965), "Internal colonialism and national development", *Studies in Comparative International Development*- 1.

Castells, M. (2000), *The Rise of the Network Society; The Information Age: Economy, Society and Culture,* Volume I, Blackwell, Oxford.

Chakrabarti, A. & Cullenberg, S. (2003), *Transition and development in India,* Routledge, London.

Chakrabarti, A. (2001), 'Class and Need: Towards a Post-modern Development Economics', *Margins* (August).

Chakrabarti, A. (2003), "Aftermath of Iraq: What Should be a Radical Marxist Project?", *The Other Voice,* (May).

Chakrabarti, A. and Cullenberg, S. (2001), "Development and Class Transition in India: A New Perspective". In Kathy Gibson, Julie Graham, Stephen Resnick and Richard Wolff*(ed.), Re/ presenting Class: Essays in Postmodern Marxism,* Duke University Press, Durham.

Chakrabarti, A. and Dhar, A. (2002), 'The Nodal Possibility of Entry Point: Theorizing the End of Capitalism', *Working Paper: Department of Economics, Calcutta University,* India. Conference paper in "Subjects of Economy" held at University of Massachusetts Amherst in November.

Chakrabarti, M. (2004), *The Famine of 1896-1897 in Bengal; Availability or Entitlement Crisis?* Orient Longman, New Delhi.

Chakravarty, S. (1989), *Development Planning: The Indian Experience.* Oxford University Press, Delhi.

Chandhoke, N. (2006), 'A State of one's own: Secessionism and Federalism in India', Working Paper No-80, *Crisis of State Programme,* DCRC, DESTIN, LSE, London.

Chandra, B. (1979), 'Colonialism and Modernization', in Chandra, B. (ed), *Nationalism and Colonialism in Modern India,* Orient Longman, New Delhi.

Chandra, B. (1990), *Ranade's economic writings,* Gyan Books, New Delhi.

———. (1992), 'The Colonial Legacy', in Jalan, B. (ed), *Indian Economy; Problems and Prospects,* Penguine Books, New Delhi.

———. (1992), 'The Indian Capitalist Class and Imperialism Before 1947', in B. Berberoglu, *Class, State and Development in India (*ed.), Sage, Delhi.

———. (1999), *Essays on Colonialism,* Orient Longman, New Delhi.

Chandrasekhar, C P and Ghosh, J. (2002), *The Market That Failed: A decade of neo-liberal economic reforms in India,* LeftWord Books, New Delhi.

Chandrasekhar, C.P. (2006), 'The Progress of "Reform and the Retrogression of Agriculture', *Social Scientist,* Volume-35, No-1-2.

Chatterjee, P. (1997), 'Development planning and the Indian state' in T.J. Byres (ed.) (1997) *The State, Development Planning and Liberalisation in India,* OUP, New Delhi.

———. (1998), 'Development Planning and the Indian State', in P. Chatterjee (ed.) *State and Politics in India,* OUP, New Delhi.

Chatterjee, S., Rae, A. & Ray, R. (2006), 'Food Consumption, Trade Reforms and Trade Patterns in Contemporary India: How Do Australia and NZ Fit in?', Working Paper 2/06, Centre for Applied Economics and Policy Studies, Massey University, Palmerston North, New Zealand.

Chatterji, Angana P. (2003), Learning in Saffron: RSS Schools in Orissa*, Asian Age, Daily Newspaper,* New Delhi, November 11.

———. (2003), Orissa: A Gujurat in the Making,*Communalism Combat,* Human Rights Magazine, Mumbai, October, Issue 92.

———. (2004), Hindu Nationalism and Orissa: Minorities as Other, *Communalism Combat,* Human Rights Magazine, Mumbai, March 2004; Issue 96.

———. (2006), *Violent Gods: Hindu Nationalism in India's Present. Narratives from Orissa,* Three Essays Collective Press, New Delhi.

Chattopadhyay, P. (1970), 'State Capitalism in India', *Monthly Review,* 21 (10).

———. (1992), 'India's Capitalist Industrialisation: An Introductory Outline', *in* B. Berberoglu, *Class, State and Development in India (*ed.), Sage, Delhi.

Chaudhuri, B.C. (1969), "Rural Credit Relations in Bengal, 1859-1885", *Indian Economic and Social History Review*, Vol. VI.

———. (1970), "Growth of Commercial Agriculture and its Impact on the Peasant Economy", *Indian Economic and Social History Review*, Vol. VII.

Chaudhuri, K. N. (1978), *The Trading World of Asia and the English East India Company, 1660-1760,* Cambridge University Press, Cambridge.

———. (1985), *Trade and Civilization in the Indian Ocean* Cambridge University Press, Cambridge.

———. (1990), *Asia Before Europe; Economy and Civlisation of the Indian Ocean from the Rise of Islam to 1750*, Cambridge University Press, Cambridge.

Chaudhuri, P. (1995), 'Economic Planning in India' in T.V. Sathyamurthy (ed.) *Industry and Agriculture in India Since Independence*, OUP, New Delhi.

Chaudhuri, S and M Ravallion (2006), 'Partially Awakened Giants: Uneven Growth in China and India' in L A Winters and S Yusuf (eds), *Dancing with Giants: China, India, and the Global Economy*, World Bank, Washington DC.

Chilcote, R.H. (1974), 'Dependency: a critical synthesis of the literature', *Latin American Perspective*, 1 (Spring).

Cipolla, C. M., (1991), *Between History and Economics; An Introduction to Economic History,* Translated by Christopher Woodall, Basil Blackwell, Oxford.

Clammer, J. (1978), *The new economic anthropology* (ed.), Macmillan Press, London.

Clegg, R.S. & Redding, G.S. (1990), *Capitalism in Contrasting Cultures (*eds.), W. de Gruyter, Berlin and New York.

Clingingsmith, D. & Williamson, J.G. (2005), *India's Deindustrialization Under the British Rule; New Ideas, New Evidences* , Discussion Paper, No-5066, May, 2005, Center for Economic Policy Research, Harvard University, USA.

CMIE (2000), *Profiles of Districts*, Center for Monitoring Indian Economy (CMIE), October, Mumbai.

Cohen, A. (1985), *The Symbolic Construction of Community,* Tavistock, London.

Cohn, B. S. (1969), "Structural Change in Indian Rural Society 1596-1885", in in R. E. Frykenberg (ed.), *Land Control and Social Structure in Indian History*, WUP, Madison.

Cook, K.S, Levi M, (1990), *The Limits of Rationality* (ed), University Chicago Press, Chicago.

Corbridge, S. & Harriss, J. (2000), *Reinventing India: Liberalization, Hindu Nationalism and Popular Democracy,* Polity Press, Cambridge.

Corbridge, S., Jewitt, S. & Kumar, S. (2003), *Jharkhand: Environment, Development, Ethnicity*, OUP, New Delhi.

Corbridge, S.(1987), "Industrialisation, internal colonialism and ethno regionalism: The Jharkhand, India, 1880-1980", *Journal of Historical Geography*- 13.

———. (1988), "The ideology of tribal economy and society: Politics in the Jharkhand, 1950-80, *Modern Asian Studies* 22.

——— (1991), "Ousting Singbonga: The struggle for India's Jharkhand", in: Chris Dixon and Michael Heffernan (eds.) *Colonialism and Development in the Contemporary World,* Rutherford NJ: Mansell.

Crow, B. (2001), *Markets, Class and Social Change; Trading Networks and Poverty in Rural South Asia*, Palgrave, New York.

Cueva, A. (1976), ' A Summary of problems and perspectives of Dependency Theory', *Latin American Perspective*, III (Fall).

———. (1978), 'The Modes of Production concept in Latin America', *Two Thirds*, I (First Quarter).

Currie, B. (1998a), Public action and its limits: re-examining the politics of hunger alleviation in eastern India, *Third World Quarterly*, Vol 19, No 5, pp 873-892.

———. (1998b), `Laws for the rich and flaws for the poor; Legal action and food insecurity in the Kalahandi case', in H O' Neill & J Toye (eds), *A World Without Famine: New Approaches to Aid and Development*, Basingstoke: Macmillan.

———. (2000), *The Politics of Hunger in India: a study of democracy, governance and Kalahandi's poverty*, MacMillan, London.

Dadachanji, B.E. (1934), *History of Indian Currency and Exchange*, 3rd enlarged edition, D.B. Taraporevala Sons & Co, Bombay.

Dale, S.F. (1994), *Indian Merchants and Eurasian Trade, 1600-1750*, Cambridge University Press, Cambridge.

Dalmia, V. (1999), *The Nationalization of Hindu Traditions; Bharatendu Harischandra and Nineteenth Century Banaras*, OUP, New Delhi.

Dalton, E. (1872), *Descriptive Ethnology of Bengal*, Government Press, Calcutta.

Dalton, G. (1961), Economic Theory and Primitive Society, *American Anthropologist,* Vol-63, No-1.

———. (1971), *Economic Anthropology and Development,* Basic Books, New York.

Damodaran, V. (2006a), "The Politics of Marginality and the construction of indigeneity in Chotanagpur", *Post Colonial Studies*, Vol-9, No-2.

———. (2006b), "Colonial Construction of Tribe in India: The case of Chotanagpur" in Csaba Levai (ed), *Europe and the World in European Historiography,* Edizioni Plus-Pisa University Press, Pacinotti.

Das, B.B. (1980), "Economic upliftment of Tribals: Role of Cooperatives", *The Cooperator*, Vol-xvii, June.

Das, D.K. (2004), *Great Indian Economists: Their Creative Vision for Socio-Economic Development* (Ed.), 10 Volumes, Deep and Deep, New Delhi.

Das, J. (1962), *Final Report of the Land Revenue Settlement in Kalahandi District Ex-State-Khalsa Area 1946-56*, Published under the Authority of The Board of Revenue, Orissa, Indian Law Publication Press, Berhampur, Orissa.

Das, M.N. (1949), *Glimpses of Kalinga History*, Century Publishers, Calcutta.

Das, R. J. (2005), 'Rural Society, the State and Social Capital in Eastern India: A Critical Investigation', *Journal of Peasant Studies*, 32:1.

———. (1996), 'State Theories: A Critical Analysis', *Science and Society*, 60:1.

Dasgupta, A. (1979), *Indian Merchants and the Decline of Surat 1700-1750*, Franz Steiner Verlage, Wiesbaden.

Dasgupta, A. (1993) *A History of Indian Economic Thought,* Routledge, London.

Daspattnaik, P.S. (1984), 'Ownership Pattern, land Survey and Settlement and Its Impact on the Dongaria Kondhas of Orissa', *Adibasi Journal*, Vol. XXIII, No. 4.

Datta, B. (1962), *Evolution of Economic Thinking in India,* World Press, Calcutta.

Datta, B. (1978), *Indian Economic Thought; Twentieth Century Perspectives 1900-1950*, Tata McGraw Hill, New Delhi.

Datta-Chaudhuri, M. (1996), "Liberalisation without Reform", *Seminar*, No. 437, January.

de Cecco, M. (1984), *The International Gold Standard: Money and Empire*, St. Martin's Press, New York.

Delong, J. B. (2004): 'India since Independence: An Analytic Growth Narrative' in D Rodrik (ed), *Modern Economic Growth: Analytical Country Studies'*, Princeton University Press, Princeton.

Deo, F. (2000), A Study of State Formation in Kalahandi, *Kalajharan*: Souvenir-2000, District Council of Culture, Kalahandi, Orissa.

Deo, J.P.S. (2001), *Character Assassination in Modern History of Orissa*, R.N.Bhattacharya, Calcutta.

Deo, J.P.Singh. (2000), Hati Valley Civilization, *Kalajharan*: Souvenir-2000, District Council of Culture, Kalahandi, Orissa.

Deo, M.P.Singh (2006), A Reflection of Budhi-Garh, Madanpur (A Unique Urban Civilization of India in the District of Kalahandi, Orissa), *Orissa Review*, January, 2006.

Desai, A (1999): 'The Economics and Politics of Transition to an Open Market Economy: India', *OECD Working Paper*, Vol-11, No 100.

Desai, M. (2001), Globalization, Neither Ideology Nor Utopia, (http://www.lse. ac. uk/ collections/globalDimensions/research/globalization NeitherIdeologyNor Utopia/Default.htm), Cambridge Review of International Affairs, 14, no. 1 (2000).

Desai, A. R. (1984), *India's Path of Development: A Marxist Analysis,* Popular Prakashan, Bombay.

Desai, M. (1975), India: Contradictions of Slow Capitalist Development', *in* B. Berberoglu, *The Explosions in the Subcontinent (*ed.), Penguin, Harmondsworth.

Desai, R. (2006), 'Uneasy Negotiations: Urban Redevelopment, Neoliberal Globalization and Hindu Nationalist Politics in Ahmadabad, India', A paper presented at Breslauer Graduate Research Conference on *'The Right to the City and the Politics of Space'*, 14th April 2006. *Working Paper Series-2*, College of Environmental Design, University of California, Berkeley.

———. (2004a), *Slouching Towards Ayodhya; From Congress to Hindutva in Indian Politics*, Three Essays Collective, New Delhi.

———. (2004b), Forward March of Hindutva Halted?, *New Left Review*, 30, November-December.

Desai, R.C. (1953), *Standard of Living in India and Pakistan 1931-32 to 1940-41,* Popular Book Depot, Bombay.

Deshpande, S. (2000), "Hegemonic Spatial Strategies: The Nation Space and Hindu Communalism in 20th Century India," in Partha Chatterjee and Pradeep Jeganathan (eds), *Subaltern Studies IX*, Columbia University Press, New York.

Dev, S. M. & C. Ravi, (2007), "Poverty and Inequality: All-India and States, 1983-2005", *EPW*, 42(6).

Diamond J. (1995), Easter's end, *Discover*, 16(8).

Digby, W. (1901), *Prosperous British India*, Unwin, London.

Dirks, N. (2001), *Castes of Mind: Colonialism and the Making of Modern India,* Princeton University Press, Princeton.

———. (2006), *The Scandal of Empire: India and the Creation of Imperial Britain,* Harvard University Press, Cambridge, Massachusetts, US.

Doshi, S.L. (1997), *Emerging Tribal Image*, Rawat Publication, New Delhi.

Douglas, M. & Isherwood, B. (1978), *The World of Goods; Towards an Anthropology of Consumption*, Penguine, Harmondsworth.

Douglas, M. (1972), 'Symbolic orders in the use of domestic space' in Peter J. Ucko, Ruth Tringham and G.W. Dimbleby, *Man, Settlement and Urbanism,* Schenkman Publishing Co., Cambridge (Mass).

Dreze, J. & Sen, A. (1995), *India: Economic Development and Social Opportunity*, OUP, New Delhi.

Dube, S.C. (1977), *Tribal Heritage of India,Vol-1: Ethnicity, Identity and Interaction,* Vikas Publishing House, New Delhi.

Dumont, L. (1972), *Homo Hierarchicus*, Paladin, London.

Dutt, R.P. (1940), *India Today,* Victor Gollancz, London.

Eagleton, T. (1990), *The Ideology of the Aesthetic*, Blackwell, Oxford.

Eisenstadt, S. N. (2002), *Multiple Modernities* (ed), Transaction Books, New Brunswick, NJ.

Eldrige, P.J. (1970), *The Politics of Foreign Aid in India*, Shocken Books, New York.

Elliot, A. E. (1989), *Evaluation of the Capacity –Building*, Unpublished Doctoral Dissertation, Iowa State University, Ames.

Elwin, V. (1939), *The Baiga*. John Murray, London.

———. (1963), *A New Deal for Tribal India*. Ministry for Home Affairs, New Delhi.

Engel, F. (1954), *Anti-Dühring: Herr Eugen Dühring's Revolution in Science*, Foreign Language Publishing House, Moscow.

EPG (Environmental Protection Group, 2007), 'A Brief Report on Ecological and Biodiversity Importance of Niyamgiri Hill and Implications of Bauxite Mining', *Environmental Protection Group*, Orissa.

Epstein, A.L. (1978), *Ethos and Identity: Three Studies in Ethnicity,* Tavistock, London.

Escobar, A. (1992), 'Reflections on .development: grassroots approaches and alternative politics in the third world', *Futures*, June.

———. (1995), *Encountering Development: The Making and Unmaking of the Third.*

Featherstone, M. (1991), Consumer *Culture and Post Modernism*, Sage, Delhi.

Fei, J. C. H. & Ranis, G. (1964), *Development of the Labor Surplus Economy: Theory and Policy*. Homewood, IL: Richard A. Irwin, Inc.

Ferguson, J. (1997), *The Anti-Politics Machine: .Development, Depoliticization, and Bureaucratic Power in Lesotho,* Cambridge University Press, Cambridge.

Feyerabend, P. (1975), *Against Method,* Verso, London.

Fikkert, B. (1995) "Reforming India's Technology Policies: The impact of Liberalization on self-reliance and welfare", *Working Paper No-2,* Center for Institutional Reform and the Informal Sector (IRIS), University of Maryland, Maryland.

Firth, R. (1951), *The Elements of Social Organization,* Watts & Co., London.

Fisher, W.F. (1995), *Toward Sustainable Development? Struggling over India's Narmada River* (ed), Sharpe, Armonk, NY.

Fogel, R.W. (2001), *The Fourth Great Awakening & the Future of Egalitarianism* University of Chicago Press, Chicago.

Foltz, R. (1996), "Two Seventeenth-Century Central Asian Travellers to Mughal India," *Journal of the Royal Asiatic Society,* 3rd series.

Foster-Carter, A.(1974), "Neo Marxist Approaches to Development and Underdevelopment", in Emanuel de Kadt & Gavin Williams (eds), *Sociology and Development,* Tavistock Press, London.

————. (1978), "The Modes of Production Controversy", *NLR, 107* (January-February).

————. (1979), "Marxism Versus Dependency Theory? A Polemic", University of Leeds, Department of Sociology, Occasional Papers (8), Mimeographed.

Fowler, A. (1993), 'NGOs as agents of democratization: an African perspective', *Journal of International Development,* 5(3).

Frank, A. G. (1998), *ReOrient: The Silver Age in Asia and the World Economy* University of California Press, Berkeley.

————. (1978), *Dependent Accumulation and Underdevelopment,* London: Macmillan.

————. (1971), *Capitalism and Underdevelopment in Latin America: Historical Studies of Brazil and Chile,* Pelican, London.

————. (1996), "India in the World Economy, 1400–1750," *EPW,* 27 July.

Freud, S. (1927). *The Future of an Illusion,* New York, Norton.

Friedman, T.L. (2000), *The Lexus and the Olive Tree,* Anchor Books, New York.

Friedmann, H. (1978), "World Market, State and Family Farm", *Contemporary Studies in Society and History,* Vol-20.

Fromm, E. (1949), 'Psychoanalytic Characteriology and its Application to the Understanding of Culture', in S.S.Sargent and M.W. Smith, (eds.), *Culture and Personality,* Proceedings of Interdisciplinary Conference, Viking Fund, New York.

————. (1967), *Marx's Concept of Man,* Ungar Publishing Co., New York.

Fukuyama, F. (1992), *The End of History and the Last Man,* Free Press, New York.

Fuller, C. J. (1992): *The Camphor Flame: Popular Hinduism and Society in India,* Princeton University Press, Princeton, New Jersey.

Furer-Haimendorf, C.V. (1982), *Tribes of India; the Struggle for Survival,* University of California Press, Berkeley, USA.

Furnivall, J.S. (1948), *Colonial Policy and Practice,* Cambridge University Press, Cambridge.

Gadgil, D.R. (1924), *The Industrial Evolution of India,* OUP, London.

Ganguli, B.N. (1964), *Readings in Indian Economic History* (ed.), Asia Publishing House, London.

————. (1977), *Indian Economic Thought: Nineteenth Century Perspective,* Tata McGraw Hill, New Delhi.

————. (1977), *Indian Economic Thought: Nineteenth Century Perspective,* Tata McGraw Hill, New Delhi.

Geertz, C. (1965), 'Religion: Anthropological Study' in David L Sills (ed) *International Encyclopedia of the Social Sciences,* Collier-Macmillan Publishers, London.

————. (1973), 'Thick Description: Toward an Interpretive Theory of Culture', in Clifford Geertz, *The Interpretation of Cultures: Selected Essays by Clifford Geertz,* Basic Books Inc, New York.

Gellner, D. (1982), 'Max Weber, Capitalism and the Religion of India', *Sociology,* Vol-16, No-4, November.

George, S., Chossudovsky, M., Bournay, C., Toussaint, E & Comanne, D.(1995), *World Bank/ IMF/WTO-The Free-Market Fiasco*, IIRE Notebook for Study and Research no. 24/25, International Institute for Research and Education (IIRE), Amsterdam.

Ghosh, J. (2005), "Is India a success story of economic liberalization?" International Conference on"Acts of Resistance from the South Against Globalization", 5-7 September 2005, *The Turkish Social Science Association*, Ankara, Türkiye.

———. (2006), 'Stealing Food from the Poor', *MicroScan*, 10th January.

Ghosh, P.G. (1999), BJP and the Evolution of Hindu Nationalism, Monohar, New Delhi.

Ghoshal, U.N. (1930), *The Agrarian System in Ancient India*, Calcutta University Press, Calcutta.

Girard, L. (1965), 'Transport', in Hrothgar John Habakkur and Moisei Mikhail Postan (eds.), *The Cambridge History of Europe, Vol-VI, The Industrial Revolutions and After: Income, Population and Technological Change*, Cambridge University Press, Cambridge.

Godelier, M. (1975), 'Modes of production, kinship, and demographic structures' in M. Bloch (ed.), *Marxist analyses and social anthropology*, Malaby Press, London.

Gokhale, G.K. (1962-67), *Speeches and Writings of G.K. Gokhale*, 3 vols, Asia Publishing House, Bombay.

Goldsmith, E. (1993), *The Way: An Ecological World View*, Shambhala, Boston.

Golwalkar, M.S. (2000), *Bunch of Thoughts*, Sahitya Sindhu Prakashana, Bangalore.

Goodland, R. (1982), *Tribal People and Economic Development*, IBRD, New York.

Government of India (1971), *K.S. Bawa Committee Report on the working of cooperatives in the tribal project areas*, Government of India, New Delhi.

———. (1973), *P.S. Appu Committee Report on the Relief of Indebtedness Land Alienation and Restoration in Tribal Development Areas*, Government of India, New Delhi.

———. (1988), *Commission on Centre-State Relations: Report Part I*. Government of India, New Delhi.

———. (2003), *Economic Survey;* 2002-03, Ministry of Finance, New Delhi.

———. (2006), *The Constitution of India*, Ministry of Law, Government of India, Allahabad Law Agency, Allahabad.

———. (1987), *Commission on Centre-State Relations: Report Part II*. Government of India, New Delhi.

Government of Orissa (1999), *District Statistical Handbook Kalahandi*, District Statistical Office, Kalahandi, Directorate of Economics and Statistics, Bhubaneswar, Orissa.

———. (2002), *Statistical Abstract of Orissa*, Directorate of Economics and Statistics, Bhubaneswar, Orissa.

———. (2003), *Statistical Outline of Orissa*, Directorate of Economics, Bhubaneswar, Orissa.

———. (2004), *Report of the Second State Finance Commission*, Department of Finance, Bhubaneswar, Orissa.

———. (2006), *The Orissa Agricultural Produce Markets (Amendment) Act, 2005*, Department of Law, The Orissa Gazette, No- 660, Cuttack, 17th May, Orissa.

———. (2004), *Medium Tern Fiscal Plan 2002-03 to 2007-08 with Explanatory Note and Development Policy*, Finance Department, Government of Orissa, Bhubaneswar.

———. (2005), *Orissa Budget 2005-2006*, Finance Department, Government of Orissa, Bhubaneswar.

Grossman, H. (2006), 'The Beginnings of Capitalism and the New Mass Morality', *Journal of Classical Sociology*, Vol 6(2).

Gudeman, S. (1986), *Economics as culture: Models and metaphors of livelihood*, Routledge & Kegan Paul, London.

Guha, A. (2002) 'Participatory fieldwork and archival research: combining numbers with narratives'. Paper presented to the Combined Methods in Development Studies Conference, University of Wales Swansea, July 1-2.

Guha, R.(1992), "Dominance Without Hegemony and Its Historiography", *Subaltern Studies*, 6.

Guha, S. (1999), *Environment and Ethnicity in India, 1200-1991*, CUP, Cambridge.

Gupta, A, & Ferguson, J. (1992),"Beyond 'culture': Space, Identity, and the Politics of Difference", *Cultural Anthropology* 7(1).

Gupta, A. (1999), 'The Political Economy of Post-Independence India-A Review', in K.S. Challam (ed), *Readings in Political Economy,* Orient Longman, Hyderabad.

Gupta, A. K . (1991), 'Why Does Poverty Persist in Regions of High Biodiversity?: A Case for Indigenous Property Right System', No 938, *IIMA Working Papers* from Indian Institute of Management Ahmadabad, India.

Gupta, D. (1980), "From Varna to Jati: The Indian Caste System, from the Asiatic to the Feudal Mode of Production", *Journal of Contemporary Asia,* Vol-X.

———. (1984), "Continuous Hierarchies and Discrete Caste", *Economic and Political Weekly,* Vol-19, No-46.

———. (1991), *Social Stratification,* (Ed), OUP, New Delhi.

Habib, I. (1960), 'Banking in Mughal India', in Tapan Raychoudhury (ed), *Contributions to Indian History,* Vol-1, Firma K.L. Mukhopadhyay, Calcutta.

———. (1963), *The Agrarian System of Moghul India, 1556-1707,* Asia Publishing House, London.

———. (1963), *The Agrarian System of Moghul India, 1556-1707,* Asia Publishing House, London.

———. (1972), 'The System of Bills of Exchange in the Mughal Empire', in *Proceedings of the Indian History Congress, 33 rd Session,* Muzaffarpur, New Delhi.

———. (1975b), "Colonialization of the Indian Economy, 1757-1900," *Social Scientist* 32 (3).

———. (1985) "Studying a Colonial Economy without Perceiving Colonialism," *Modern Asian Studies* 119 (3).

———. (1995), *Essays in Indian History; Towards a Marxist Perception,* Tulika, New Delhi.

———. (2006), *Indian Economy: 1858-1914 (A People's History of India),* Tulika Books, New Delhi.

Habib, S. (1975a), 'Colonial exploitation and capital formation in the early stages of industrial revolution', *Proceedings of the Indian History Congress: Thirty-Sixth Session,* Indian History Congress, Aligarh, India.

Hall, C. (1996), "Histories, empires and the post colonial moment" in I. Chambers and L. Curti (eds), *The Post Colonial Question: Common Skies, Divided Horizons,* Routledge, London.

Hardiman, D. (1987), *The Coming of the Devi; Adivasi Assertion in Western India,* OUP, Delhi.

———. (1997) *Feeding the Baniya: Peasants and Usurers in Western India,* Oxford University Press, New York.

Hardt, M. and Negri, A. (2000), *Empire,* Harvard University Press, Cambridge.

Harrison, L. E. & Huntington, S. P. (2000), *Culture Matters: How Values Shape Human Progress,* Basic Books, New York.

Harriss, J. (1982), *Rural development: theories of peasant economy and agrarian change,* Hutchinson, London.

Harriss-White, B. (1996), *A Political Economy of Agricultural Markets in South India: Masters of the Countryside,* Sage, London.

———. (2006), 'On Understanding Markets as Social and Political Institutions in Developing Economies' in Ha-Joon Chang (ed), *Rethinking Development Economics,* Anthem Press, London.

———. (1993), 'The Collective Politics of Foodgrain Markets in South Asia', *IDS Bulletin,* Vol-24, No-3.

———. (1996), *A Political Economy of Agricultural Markets in South India,* Sage New Delhi.

———. (2002), India's Religious Pluralism and its implications for the Economy', *QEH Working Paper,* No-82, Oxford.

———. (2003), *India Working,* CUP, Cambridge.

Harte, N.B. (1971), *The Study of Economic History,* Frank Cass, London.

Harvey, D. (1982), *The Limits to Capital,* Verso, London.

———. (2006), *The Condition of Post Modernity,* Blackwell, Oxford.

Hansen, T.B (1998), The Ethics of Hindutva and the Spirit of Capitalism, in Hansen, T.B. & Jeffrelot, C. (1998), *The BJP and the Compulsions of Politics in India,* OUP, New Delhi.

Hasan, Z. (2002), 'Introduction: Conflict, Pluralism and the Competitive Party System in India', in Zoya Hasan*(ed), Parties and Party Politics in India,* OUP, New Delhi.

Hausman, D. (1981), *Capital, Profits and Prices*, Columbia University Press, New York.

Heartfield, J. (2008), Green Capitalism; Manufacturing Scarcity in the an Age of Abundance, Lightning Source UK Ltd, United Kingdom.

Henfrey, C. (1981), "Dependency, Modes of Production, and the Class Analysis of Latin America", *Latin American Perspectives*, Vol. 8, No. 3/4, *Dependency and Marxism*, (Late Summer-Autumn).

Henkel, H. & Stirrat, R. (2002), 'Participation as Spiritual Duty; Empowerment as Secular Subjection', in Cook, B. & Kothari, U. (ed), *Participation: The New Tyranny?,* Zed Books, London.

Herskovits, M.J. (1952), *Economic Anthropology,* Alfred A. Knopf, New York.

Hicks, J. (1979), *Causality in Economics,* Basil Blackwell, Oxford.

Himanshu (2007), 'Recent Trends in Poverty and Inequality: Some Preliminary Results', *EPW,* 42(6).

Hirschman, A.O. (1984). Rival interpretations of market society: civilizing, destructive, or feeble? *Journal of Economic Literature*, Vol-20.

——. (1987), *Getting Ahead Collectively: Grassroots Experiences in Latin America*, Pergamon, New York.

Hodgson, G.M. (1988), *Economics and Institutions: A Manifesto for a Modern Institutional Economics,* Polity, Cambridge.

Holloway, J. (1995). Global Capital and the National State. In W. Bonefeld & J. Holloway (eds.) *Global Capital, National State and the Politics of Money*, Macmillan, London.

Holmwood, J. (2007), 'Only connect': the challenge of globalization for the social sciences', *21st Century Society,* Vol. 2, No. 1, February 2007.

Hunter, W.W. (1872), *Orissa,* Vol-I & II, Smith, Elder & Co., London.

Hunter, W.W., Stirling, A., Beam, J., & Sahu, N.K. (2005), *A History of Orissa* (Reprint), Vol-I & II, R.N. Bhattacharya, Kolkata.

Huntington, S. P. (1996), *The Clash of Civilizations and the Remaking of World Order*, Simon & Schuster, New York.

Hutton, J.H. (1946), *Caste in India: Its Nature, Functions, Origin*, CUP, Cambridge.

IMF (1997), *World Economic Outlook*, International Monetary Fund (IMF), Washington.

Inden, R. (2000) 'Imagining India' – Introduction and Chapter 1 from *Knowledge of India and Human Agency*, 2000 and 'Orientalist Constructs of India', *Modern Asian Studies*, 20, 3.

Ingber, S. (1984), 'The Marketplace of Ideas: A Legitimizing Myth' , *Duke Law Journal*, No-1.

Inglehart, R. (1997), *Modernization and Postmodernization*, Princeton University Press, Princeton.

Iyer, L. (2004), "The Long-term Impact of Colonial Rule: Evidence from India", Harvard Business School, Boston MA.

Jacobs, J. M. (1996), *Edge of Empire: Post colonialism and the City*, Routledge, London.

Jaffrelot, C (1996), *The Hindu Nationalist Movement and Indian Politics 1920s to the 1990s*, Columbia University Press, New York.

Jain, L.C. (1929), *Indigenous Banking in India,* Macmillan, London.

Jaiswal, S. (1997), "Caste: Ideology and Context", *Social Scientist,* Vol-25, Nos.5-6, May-June.

Jayadev, A., Motiram, S. & Vakulabharanam, V. (2007), "Patterns of Wealth Disparities in India during the Liberalisation Era", *EPW*, September 22, 2007.

Jayal, N. G. (1999), *Democracy and the State: Welfare, Secularism and Development in Contemporary India*, OUP, New Delhi.

Jayal, N. G. (2001), *Democracy and the State: Welfare, Secularism and Development in Contemporary India*, OUP, New Delhi.

Jena, M.K., Pathi, P., Dash, J., Patnaik, K.K., Seeland, K., & Schmithüsen, F. (2002), *Forest Tribes of Orissa – The Dongaria Kondh*, Man and Forest Series No 2, D.K. Printworld (P) Ltd, New Delhi.

Jenkins, R. (1999), *Democratic Politics and Economic Reform in India,* Cambridge University Press, Cambridge.

Jessop, B. (1990), *State Theory: Putting Capitalist States in their Place*, Polity Press/Basil Blackwell, Cambridge/Oxford.

Jessop, B. and Sum, N-L. (2001) Pre-Disciplinary and Post-Disciplinary Perspectives, *New Political Economy*, 6 (1).

Jhamtani, H. (1992), 'The imperialism of Northern NGOs', *Earth Island Journal*, 7(June).

Johnson, P. (1984), *Marxist Aesthetics: The Foundations Within Everyday Life for an Emancipated Consciousness*, Routledge & Kegan Paul, London.

Johnson, W.J. (1994), *The Bhagavad Gita* (new English translation), OUP, Oxford.

Joshi, V and I M Little (1994): *India: Macroeconomics and Political Economy: 1961-91*, World Bank, Washington DC.

Joshi, V. (1998), *Tribal Situation in India* (ed), Rawat Publications, New Delhi.

Joshi, V. and I.M.D. Little, (1996), *India's Economic Reforms 1991-2001*, OUP, New Delhi.

Kanetkar, B.D. (1960), "Pricing of Irrigation Service in India (1854-1959)", *Artha Vijnana (The Economic Science)*, Vol. II.

Kannan, K. P. (2006), 'Interrogating Inclusive Growth: Some Reflections on Exclusionary Growth and Prospects for Inclusive Development in India', *V B Singh Memorial Lecture*, mimeo.

Kanungo, P. (2003), Hindutva's Entry into a 'Hindu Province' Early Years of RSS in Orissa, *Economic and Political Weekly*, 2, August.

Kapp, W. K. (1963), *Hindu Culture, Economic Development and Economic Planning in India*, Asia Publishing House, Bombay/ London.

Kar, N.C. (1983), *Climatological Data of Orissa 1977-1986* (Ed), Directorate of Economics and Statistics, Bhubaneswar, Orissa.

Karat, P. (1988), *Foreign Funding and the Philosophy of Voluntary Organisations: A Factor in Imperialist Strategy*, National Book Center, New Delhi.

Kaur, P. (2007), 'Growth Acceleration in India', *EPW*, April 14.

Kaviraj, S. (1998), 'A Critique of the Passive Revolution' in P. Chatterjee (ed.) *State and Politics in India*, OUP, New Delhi.

———. (1988) 'A Critique of the Passive Revolution', *Economic and Political Weekly*, Special No. 23(27), November.

———. (1997). Sociology of Political Parties, in Kaviraj, S. (ed.) *Politics in India*, OUP, Delhi.

Kay, G. (1975), *Development and Underdevelopment: a Marxist Analysis*, Macmillan, London.

Khatua, S., & Stanley, W. (2006). 'Ecological debt: A case study from Orissa, India', in Athena K. Peralta (Ed.), *Ecological debt: The people of the south are the creators: Cases from Ecuador, Mozambique, Brazil and India*, Geneva: World Council of Churches & Philippines: Troika Press.

Kindleberger, C. (2000), *Manias, Panics and Crashes; A History of Financial Crises*, John Wiley and Sons, New York.

Kinnvall, C. (2006), *Globalization and Religious Nationalism in India; The Search for ontological security*, Routledge, London.

Klass, M. (1980), *Caste: The Emergence of South Asian Social System*, Institute for the Study of Human Issues, Philadelphia.

Klein, N. (2008), *The Shock Doctrine: The Rise of Disaster Capitalism*, Penguin Books Ltd, London.

Korten, D.C. (1990), Getting to the 21st Century: Voluntary Action and the Global Agenda, Kumarian, West Hartford, CT.

———. (1995), *When Corporations Rule the World*, West Hartford, CT: Barrett-Koehler.

Kosambi, D.D. (1956), *Introduction to the Study of Indian History*, Popular Prakashan, Bombay.

———. (1965), *Culture and Civilization of Ancient India in Historical Outline*, Routledge and Kegan Paul, London.

Kothari, R. (1986), 'NGOs, the state and world capitalism', *EPW*, 21(Dec).

———. (1993), 'Masses, classes and the state', In Wignaraja P, (ed), *New Social Movements in the South: Empowering the People*, Zed, London.

Kulka, T. (1977) 'How far does anything go? Comments on Feyerabend's Epistemological Anarchism', Philosophy of the social sciences 7.

Kulke, H. (1976), 'Kshatriyaization and Social Change. A Study in Orissa Setting', in: S.D.Pillai (ed.), *Aspects of Changing India*, Bombay.

Kumar, D. (1965), *Land and Caste in South India*, CUP, Cambridge.

———. (1972), 'Economic History of Modern India', *Indian Economic Social History Review*, 9; 63.

———. (1983), *The Cambridge Economic History of India, 1757-1970 (ed.)*, vol. 2, CUP, Cambridge.

Kumar, K., Choudhary, P.R., Sarangi, S., Misra, P. & Behera, S. (2005), *A Socio-Economic and Legal Study of Schedule Tribes' Land in Orissa*, World Bank, Washington D.C.

Lash, S. & Urry, J. (1994), *Economies of Signs and Space*, Sage, New York.

Levi, S.C. (2002), *The Indian Diaspora in Central Asia and Its Trade: 1550-1900*, vol. 3, Brill, Leiden.

Levi-Strauss, C. (1963), Totemism, Beacon Press, Boston.

Levi-Strauss, C. (1966),The savage mind, University of Chicago Press, Chicago.

Lewis, W. A. (1954), "Economic Development with Unlimited Supplies of Labor." *Manchester School of Economic and Social Studies* 22.

Little, K.L. (1978), *Religious Poverty and the Profit Economy in Medieval Europe* Cornell University Press, Ithaca, N.Y.

Lord Canning, (1980), Government of India Foreign Department Despatch No. 43A to S/S, 30 April 1860, India Office, London.

Lukacs, G. (1968), 'The Marxism of Rosa Luxemburg', in *History and* Class *Consciousness*, Merlin Press, London.

Lury, C. (1996) '*Consumer Culture*', Rutgers University Press, Rutgers.

Maddison, A. (1970), *Economic Progress and Policy in Developing Countries*, Norton, New York.

———. (1971), *Class Structure and Economic Growth: India & Pakistan since the Moghuls*, George Allen & Unwin, London.

———. (2001), *The World Economy: A Millennial Perspective*, OECD Development Centre Studies, Paris.

Magdoff, H. & Magdoff, F.(2005), 'Approaching Socialism', *Monthly Review*, Volume 57, Number 3, July-August.

Mahalik, N. (2004), 'Maritime Trade of Ancient Orissa', *Orissa Review*, September.

Mahapatra, R., and R. Panda (2001). The Myth of Kalahandi: A Resources-Rich Region Reels under a Government-Induced Drought. *Down To Earth*, March 31.

Majumdar, D.N. & Madan, T.N (1970), *An Introduction to Social Anthropology*, Asia Publishing House, Bombay.

Majumdar, D.N. (1937), *A Tribe in Transition: A Study of Cultural Pattern*, Longmans, Calcutta.

———. (1961), *Races and Culture of India*, Asia Publishing House, Bombay.

Mallick, S.C. (1974), *Marketing of Rice in Orissa*, Unpublished Ph.D. Thesis, Orissa University of Agriculture and Technology (OUAT), Bhubaneswar, Orissa.

Mandel, E. (1970),The Marxist theory of alienation, *International Socialist Review*, No.31, 1970 (3).

Mandelbaum, D.C. (1970), *Society in India*, 2 Vols, University of California Press, Berkeley.

Manor, J. (1987), "Tried, then Abandoned: Economic Liberalisation in India", *IDS Bulletin*, vol. 18, no. 4.

Markovits, C. (2000), *The Global World of Indian Merchants 1750-1947: Traders of Sind from Bukhara to Panama*, CUP, Cambridge.

Martin, D. (1978). *A General Theory of Secularization*, Oxford, Basil Blackwell.

Martin, D. (1990), *Tongues of Fire: The Explosion of Protestantism in Latin America* Blackwell, Oxford.

Marx, K. & Engels, F. (1848), *The Communist Manifesto*, in *Karl Marx and Frederick Engels, Selected Works*, Lawrence & Wishart, London.

Marx, K. & Engels, F. (1998), *Capital, Volume III, Collected Works*, Volume 37, International Publishers, New York.

Marx, K. (1844), *Economic and Philosophical Manuscripts of 1844*, translated by M. Milligan and edited by D.J. Struik (1967), International Publishers, New York.

Marx, K. (1845), *Theses on Feuerbach*, in *Marx/Engels Selected Works* (1969), Volume One, Progress Publishers, Moscow, USSR.

Marx, K. (1894), *Capital*, Vol-3, International Publishers, New York.

Marx, K. (1959), *Economic and Philosophic Manuscripts of 1844*, Progress Publishers, Moscow.

Marx, K. (1965), *Pre-Capitalist Economic Formations,* translated by J. Cohen, ed. and with an intro. By E.J. Hobsbawm, International Publishers, New York.

Marx, K. (1978), "On the Jewish Question," in *The Marx-Engels Reader,* ed. Robert C. Tucker, W. W. Norton, New York.

McCleary, R.M. (2003). "Salvation, Damnation, and Economic Incentives," *Project on Religion, Political Economy, and Society working paper no. 39*, Weatherhead Center, Harvard University, November.

Meeks, D.M. (1989), *God the Economist: The Doctrine of God and Political Economy,* Fortress, Minneapolis.

Meher, R. (1999), 'Inter-state Disparities in Levels of Development and the Implications of Economic Liberalization on the Regional Economies of India', *Review of Development and Change*, 4(2).

Mehta, A.S. (1996), 'Micro politics of voluntary action: an anatomy of change in two villages', *Cultural Survival*, 20(3).

Mehta, A.S. (1996), 'Micro politics of voluntary action: an anatomy of change in two villages', *Cultural Survival*, 20(3).

Mehta, U. (1996): *Modern Godmen in India*, Popular Prakashan, Mumbai.

Metcalf, T. (1994), *Ideologies of the Raj,* Cambridge University Press, Cambridge.

Ministry of Finance, (2007), *Economic Survey 2006-07*, Government of India, New Delhi.

Ministry of Tribal Affairs (2002), *Development of Primitive Tribal Groups*, Twenty Eighth Report by the Standing Committee on Labour and Welfare, Thirteenth Lok Sabha, Lok Sabha Secretariat, Government of India, New Delhi.

Mishra, M. K. (2007), Oral Epics of Kalahandi, National Folklore Support Centre in Chennai.

———. (1995), Ethnic Identity and Oral Narratives. *Tribal Language and Culture of Orissa.* Ed. by K. Mahapatra. Bhubaneswar.

———. (1995), *Paschima Odisara Adibasi Lok Sahitya(in Oriya), The Tribal Folklore of Western Orissa*, Bhubaneswar.

———. (1995), "Toki Parab: A Kondh Paraja related to Festival related to Female infanticide", *Orissa Historical Research Journal*, Vol. XXXV, No 1&2,Dept. of Culture, Orissa, Bhubaneswar.

———. (1995), Ethnic Identity and Folk Narrative: A Study of Kamar Tribe of Orissa, 1995, *ISFNR*, Mysore session.

Mishra, R.C. (2003), *Regulated Markets in Orissa*, Nijaswa Prakashana, Puri, Orissa.

Mishra, S.K. (2001), Poverty and Economic Change in Kalahandi, Orissa: The Unfinished Agenda and New Challenges, *Journal of Social and Economic Development*, Vol-III, No-2, July - December.

Misra, B.B. (1961), *The Indian Middle Classes: Their Growth in Modern Times*, OUP, New Delhi.

Misra, M. (1999), Business, Race and Politics in British India c.1860-1960, OUP, Oxford.

Misra, M. (2003), 'Lessons of Empire: Britain and India', SAIS Review: Journal of International Affairs, Vol- XXIII (2).

———. (2004), 'The Raj and India: Lessons and Legacies', Journal of the School of Advanced International Studies (SAIS).

Mody, A. (2006), *Inclusive Growth: K N Raj on Economic Development* (ed), Orient Longman, Hyderabad.

Mohammad, S and J Whalley (1984): 'Rent Seeking in India: Its Cost and Policy Significance', *Kyklos*, 37 (3).

Mohanti, B.B. (1996), *Traditional Institutions of the Lanjia Saora of Puttasingi Area of Raya-gada District, Orissa*, Scheduled Castes and Scheduled Tribes Research and Training Institute, Government of Orissa. Bhubaneswar.

Mohanti, K.K. (1992), *Tribal Traditions and Customs: An Anthropological Study of the Kuttia Kondh of Belghar, Phulbani District*, Orissa Tribal and Harijan Research and Training Institute, Bhubaneswar.

———. (1994a), *Tribal Traditions and Customs: An Anthropological Study of the Hill Kharia of Similipal, Mayurbhanj District, Orissa*, Tribal and Harijan Research and Training Institute, Government of Orissa,, Bhubaneswar.

———. (1994b), *Tribal Traditions and Customs: An Anthropological Study of the Santhal of Mayurbhanj District, Orissa*, Tribal and Harijan Research and Training Institute, Governemnt of Orissa, Bhubaneswar.

———. (1989), 'Changing Terms of Discourse', *EPW*, Vol-XXIV, No-37, September 16.

Mohanty, M. (1989), 'Changing Terms of Discourse', *EPW*, Vol-XXIV, No-37, September 16.

———. (1990), 'Class, caste and dominance in a backward state: Orissa' In *Dominance and State Power in Modern India* (eds) F. Frankel & M.S.A. Rao, Oxford University Press, New Delhi.

Mohanty, N. (2005), *Oriya Nationalism: Quest for a United Orissa 1866-1956*, Prafulla, Calcutta.

Mohanty, P. & Mishra, B. (2000), Stone Age Cultures of Kalahandi, *Kalajharan*: Souvenir-2000, District Council of Culture, Kalahandi, Orissa.

Mohanty, P.K. (2001), 'Suryavamsi Cuttack, 1435-1568 AD', *Utkal Historical Research Journal*, Vol-XIV.

Moreland, W.H. and Geyl, P. (1925), *Jahangir's India*, Heffer, Cambridge.

Moreland, W.H. (1923), *From Akbar to Aurangzeb*, Macmillan, London.

———. (1962), *India at the Death of Akbar*, A. Ram, Delhi.

Mukherjee, A. (2002), *Imperialism, Nationalism and the Making of the Indian Capitalist Class, 1920-1947*, Sage, New Delhi.

Mukherjee, R. (1974), *The Rise and Fall of the East India Company*, Monthly Review Press, New York.

Myer, J. (1975), "A Crown of Thorns: Cardoso and the Counter Revolution", *Latin American Perspective*, II (Spring).

Myrdal, G. (1968), *Asian Drama – An Inquiry into the Poverty of Nations*, 3 Vols, Pantheon, New York.

Nagarajan, V. (2000), *Prologue to Hindu Political Sociology*, Part-II, *Kautilya and Hindu Economic State*, Aishma Publications, Nagpur, India.

NAI (National Archives of India). (1878), Forest Department, Unpublished.

Nair, Kusum. (1961), *Blossoms in the Dust*, Duckworth and Co. Ltd, London.

Naoroji, D. (1962), *Poverty and Un-British Rule in India*, 1901, reprint, Publications Division, Government of India, Delhi.

Narayan, S. (1970), *Relevance of Gandhian Economics*, Navajivan Publishing House, Ahmadabad.

Naregal, V. (2001), *Language Politics, Elites, and the Public Sphere: Western India under Colonialism*, Permanent Black, New Delhi.

Nash, M. (1965), *Economic Anthropology*, Biennial Review of Anthropology , Vol. 4.

———. (1968), Economic Anthropology, in *International Encyclopedia of Social Sciences*, Vol-IV, Macmillan & Free Press, New York.

Nayak, B.S. (2002), *The Public Distribution System and Food Security in Orissa: A Case Study of Kalahandi District*, Unpublished M. Phil thesis submitted to the Department of Political Science, University of Hyderabad, India.

———. (2007), "The History of Food Security Policy in India with reference to Orissa and Kalahandi: An Integrated and Universal Approach towards PDS" in Nayak, B.S. (2006), Nationalizing Crisis: The Political Economy of Public Policy in Contemporary India ,(ed), Atlantic Publishers & Distributors, New Delhi.

———. (2007a), *Nationalizing Crisis; The Political Economy of Public Policy in Contemporary India* (ed), Atlantic, New Delhi.

————. (2007b), 'Silenced Drums and Unquiet Woods: The Myth of Modernization and Development in Orissa', Journal of Comparative Social Welfare , Vol. 23, No. 1.

————. (2009), *Neoliberal Political Economy of Development in India The Impact of New Economic Reforms on Tribals in Kalahandi Orissa*, DPhil Thesis, Department of Development Studies, School of Global Studies, University of Sussex, UK.

Nayar, B.R. (1992), 'The Politics of Economic Restructuring: The Paradox of State Strength and Policy Weakness' *Journal of Commonwealth and Comparative Politics*, Vol. 30, No. 2.

Ndegwa, S.N. (1996), *The Two Faces of Civil Society: NGOs and Politics in Africa*, Kumarian, West Hartford, CT.

Neale, W.C. (1962), *Economic Change in Rural India*, Yale University Press, New Haven.

Nee V, Ingram P. (1997), "Embeddedness and beyond: institutions, exchange, and social structure" in *The New Institutionalism in Economic Sociology*, (ed.), V Nee, M Brinton, Russell Sage, New York.

Nee, V. & Matthews, R. (1996), Market Transition and Societal Transformation in Reforming State Socialism, *Annual Review of Sociology*, Vol. 22, August.

Nisbet, R.A. (1969), *Social Change and History,* Oxford University Press, New York.

Norris, C. (1979), *Deconstruction: Theory and Practice*, Routledge, New York.

————. (1990), *What's Wrong with Postmodernism*, Harvester Wheatsheaf, England.

————. (1997), *On the Limits of Antirealism, Manchester* University Press, Manchester.

North, D.C. (1981), *Structure and Change in Economic History*, Norton, New York.

————. (1990), Institutions, *Institutional Change and Economic Performance*, Cambridge University Press, New York.

Novak, M. (1993), *The Catholic Ethic and the Spirit of Capitalism,* Free Press, New York.

Nun, J. (1976), "Workers' Control and the problem of organization", LARU Studies, I (October).

Nyamugasira, W. (1998), 'NGOs and Advocacy: How well are the poor represented?', *Development in Practice*, Vol-8, No-3.

O'Brien, P. (1975), "A critique of Latin American Theories of Dependency", in Ivar Oxaal, Tony Barnett and David Booth (eds), *Beyond the Sociology of Development*, Routledge and Kegan Paul, London.

Orlove BS. (1997). *The Allure of the Foreign: Imported Goods in Postcolonial Latin America.* Ann Arbor: Univ. Mich. Press.

Osborn, R. (1937), *Freud and Marx*, The Camelot Press, London.

Osborne, E. (2001), Culture, development, and government: Reservations in India. *Development and Cultural Change*, 49(3).

Ozga, J. & Lawn, (1988), *Schoolwork: Approaches to the Labour Process of Teaching*, Open University Press, Milton Keynes, UK.

Padel, F. (1995), *The Sacrifice of Human Being: British Rule and the Khonds of Orissa*, Oxford University. Press, Delhi.

Panagariya, A (2004): 'Growth and Reforms during 1980s and 1990s', *EPW*, 36.

Panda, S.S. (2000), Archaeological Remains of Kalahandi in the Tel River Valley, *Kalajharan*: Souvenir-2000, District Council of Culture, Kalahandi, Orissa, *Orissa Review,* July 1999, Government of Orissa, Bhubaneswar.

————. 1993), *Some Temple Ruins of Kalahandi District, The Orissa Historical Research Journal,* Vol.XXXVIII, Nos.1-4.

Panda, T. & Padhy, N.R. (2007), 'Sustainable food habits of the hill-dwelling Kandha tribe in Kalahandi district of Orissa', *Indian Journal of Traditional Knowledge* , Vol. 6(1).

Panda, T., Panigrahi, S.K. & Padhy, R. (2005), 'A sustainable use of phytodiversity by the Kandha tribe of Orissa', *Indian Journal of Traditional Knowledge*, Vol. 4(2).

Pani, N. (2002), *Inclusive Economics; Gandhian Method and Contemporary Policy*, Sage, New Delhi.

Panigrahi. N. (2001), Impact of State Policies on management of Land Resources in Tribal Areas of Orissa, *Man & Development*, March.

Panikkar, K.V. (1997), 'Globalization and Culture', in Ajit Muricken (ed.), *Globalization and SAP: Trends and Impact - An Overview*, Vikas Adhiyayan Kendra, Mumbai.

Parkhill, T. (1995), *The Forest Setting in Hindu Epics: Princes, Sages, Demons,* The Edwin Mellen Press, Lewiston, NY.

Patel, K. (2004), 'Maritime Relation of Kalinga with Srilanka', *Orissa Historical Research Journal,* Vol. XLVII, No. 2.

Pati, B. (1993), *Resisting Domination: Peasants, Tribals and the National Movement in Orissa 1920-50,* Monohar, New Delhi.

———. (1999), 'Environment and Social History: Kalahandi, 1800-1950', *Environment and History,* 5.

———. (2001), *Situating Social History; Orissa (1800-1997),* Orient Longman, New Delhi.

———. (2002), 'Independence and After: Orissa 1946-1952', *Indian Historical Review,* Vol-XXIX, No-1-2.

———. (2003), *Identity, Hegemony, Resistance: Towards a Social History of Conversions in Orissa, 1800-2000,* Three Essays Collective, New Delhi.

———. (2006), 'Tatas and the Orissa model of capitalist development', *Social Scientist,* Vol-34, No-3-4, March-April.

Patkar, M. (1995), 'The struggle for participation and justice: a historical narrative', in Fisher, W.F. (ed), *Toward Sustainable Development? Struggling over India's Narmada River,* Sharpe, Armonk, NY.

Patnaik, A.P. (1986), "Kalinga Influence and Colonies in South-East Asia", *Orissa Review,* vol. XLII, No.9, p. 19.

———. (1992), "Kalingan Link with Countries of South-East Asia," *Orissa Review,* Vol. XL VIII, No.9.

Patnaik, P. (1972), 'Imperialism and the growth of Indian capitalism', in R. Owen and B. Sutcliffe (eds), *Studies in the theory of imperialism,* Longmans, London.

———. (1975), 'Imperialism and the Growth of Indian Capitalism', in R. Blackburn, (ed), *The Explosions in the Subcontinent,* Penguin, Harmondsworth.

———. (1979), "Industrial Development in India since Independence", Social Scientist, Vol. 7, No. 11, June.

———. (1993), The Fascism of Our Times, *Social Scientist,* Vol. 21, No. 3-4.

———. (1998), 'Some Indian Debates on Planning' in T.J. Byres (ed.) *The Indian Economy: Major Debates since Independence,* OUP, New Delhi.

———. (2003), *The Retreat to Unfreedom,* Tulika Books, New Delhi.

———. (2007), 'The State Under Neo-Liberalism', *Social Scientist,* Volume-35, No-1-2, January-February.

Patnaik, S. C. (1988), *Industrial development in a backward region: Dynamics of policy,* Ashish Publishing House, New Delhi.

Patnaik, U. (1996), 'Export-oriented agriculture and food security in developing countries and in India', *EPW,* Special Number, September.

———. (2002), 'The agrarian question and the development of capitalism in India', in A. Thorner (ed.), *Land, Labour and Rights: Daniel Thorner Memorial Lectures,* Tulika, Delhi.

———. (2003a), 'On the inverse relation between primary exports and food absorption in developing countries under liberalized trade regimes', in J. Ghosh and C.P. Chandrasekhar (eds.), *Work and Welfare in the Age of Finance,* Tulika, Delhi.

———. (2003c), 'Global Capitalism, Deflation and Agrarian Crisis in Developing Countries', *Social Policy and Development Programme,* Paper Number 15, October, 2003, *United Nations Research Institute for Social Development,* Geneva.

———. (2003b), 'Food stocks and hunger; Causes of Agrarian Distress', *Social Scientist,* Vol. 31, Nos. 7-8, July-August.

———. (1999), *The Long Transition; Essays on Political Economy,* Tulika, Delhi.

———. (2000), 'New estimates of 18th century British trade and their relation to transfers from tropical colonies', in K.N. Panikkar, T.J. Byres, and U. Patnaik (eds.), *The Making of History; Essays presented to Irfan Habib,* Tulika, Delhi.

———. (2006), 'Poverty and Neoliberalism', A paper based on Rao Bahadur Kale Memorial Lecture delivered at *Gokhale Institute of Politics and Economics,* Pune, February 03.

Patra, B. (2004), 'Kalinga in South East Asia', in *Orissa Reference Annual 2004,* Information and Public Relations Department, Government of Orissa, Bhubaneswar.

————. (2005), 'Maritime Contact of Ancient Orissa with the Western World', *Orissa Review*, January.

Patra, S.K. & Patra, B. (2004), 'Archeology and Maritime History of Orissa', *Orissa Historical Research Journal*, Vol. XLVII, No. 2.

Pearson, H. (1999), 'Was There Really a German Historical School of Economics?' *History of Political Economy* 31.3.

Peet, R. (1997), 'The Cultural Production of Economic Forms', in R. Lee and J. Wills (eds.), *Geographies of Economies*, Arnold, , London.

Petras, J. & Henry, V. (2001), *Globalisation Unmasked: Imperialism in the 21st Century*, Zed Books, London.

Petrovic, G. (1967), *Marx in Mid-Twentieth Century*, Doubleday & Co., New York.

Phillip, C.H. (1961), *Historians of India, Pakistan and Ceylon* (Ed), OUP, London.

Piddington, R. (1952), *An Introduction to Social Anthropology,* Olver & Boyd, Edinburgh.

Pieterse, J. N. (1995), 'The Cultural Turn in Development. Questions of Power', *European Journal of Development Research*, 7.1.

Planning Commission of India (2004), *'Poverty Eradication and Local Institutions: Comparative Study of Kalahandi, Chittoor and Bhojpur'*, a study conducted by Dr. G.K. Arora, Dr. G. N. Trivedi, Mr. N. Sukumar, Dr. Suranjita Ray and Prof. Manoranjan Mohanty at the Developing Countries Research Center (DCRC), Sponsored by Planning Commission and Ministry of Rural Development, Government of India, New Delhi.

————. (2005), *Review of Annual Plan 2004-05 of the Government of Orissa–Report of Adviser*, State Plans Division, Shri Chandra Pal, Planning Commission, Government of India, New Delhi.

————. (2002), *The Tenth Five Year Plan (2002-2007),* Planning Commission of India, Government of India, New Delhi.

————. (2006), *Towards Faster and More Inclusive Growth: An Approach to the 11th Five-Year Plan*, Government of India, New Delhi, June 14.

Polanyi, K. (2001), *The Great Transformation: The political and economic origins of our time,* Beacon Press, Boston.

Pradhan, J. (1993), 'The distorted Kalahandi and a strategy for its' development', *Social Action*, Vol-43, July-Sept.

Pradhan, N.B., (1979), 'Economic Backwardness and Development of Orissa', *Unpublished Ph.D.Thesis submitted to Berhampur University*, Orissa.

Pramukh, K.E.R. & Palkumar, P.D.S. (2006), 'Indigenous Knowledge: Implications in Tribal Health and Disease', *Studies of Tribes and Tribals*, 4(1).

Prasad, N. (2003), "Efficacy and Impact of a Decade of Economic Reforms on the Indian Economy'' in *Economic Reforms in India* (eds), B.N Singh, M. P. Srivastava & N. Prasad, APH Publishing Corporation, New Delhi.

Prasad, R.K. (1967), *Economic and Social Change among the Parahiya of Palamau: A Study in the Tribal Dynamics,* Unpublished thesis submitted to the Ranchi University, India.

Pursell, G (1992): 'Trade Policy in India' in Dominick Salvatore (ed), *National Trade Policies,* Greenwood Press, New York.

Quigley, D. (1988a), "Is Caste a Pure Figment, the Invention of Orientalists for their own Glorification?", *Cambridge Anthropology*, Vol-13, No-1.

Quigley, D. (1988b), "Kings and Priests: Hocart's Theory of Caste, *Pacific View Point*, New Zealand.

Quigley, D. (1993), *The Interpretation of Caste*, Clarendon Press, Oxford.

Radhakrishna, M.(2000), "Colonial Construction of a 'Criminal' Tribe; Yerukulas of Madras Presidency", *Economic and Political Weekly*, July 8-15.

Radhakrishnan, P. (2004), 'Religion under Globalisation', *EPW*, March 27, 2004.

Raduntz, H. (2001) *A contemporary Marxian critique of trends in Education and Teachers' Work in an era of major structural change*, Unpublished doctoral thesis, University of South Australia, Adelaide.

Rai, B.K. (1967), *Nature and Man: A Study of Interaction between Man and Forest in Chotanagpur,* Unpublished thesis submitted to the Ranchi University, India.

Rajasekharan, B, D. Warren & S. Babu, (1991), "Indigenous natural resource management systems for sustainable agricultural development: A global perspective", *Journal of International Development*, 3(1).

Rajesh, M.N. (2001), 'Emergence of Temple Based Economy during the Early Cola Period (C850-985)', *Utkal Historical Research Journal*, Vol-XIV.

Rao, G.R. & Misra, R.N. (2005), Industrialization in Kalahandi district: A study, *Orissa Review*, May.

Rao, V.K.R.V. (1936), *An Essay on India's National Income 1925-29*, Allen and Unwin, London.

Ray, M. P. (1988). An ecological model of the family, *Home Economics FORUM*, 22.

Ray, R.K. (2002), "Indigenous Banking and Commission Agency in India's Colonial Economy." In *Money & Credit in Indian History*, edited by A.K. Bagchi, Tulika Books, New Delhi.

Raychaudhuri, T. (1968), "A Reinterpretation of Nineteenth Century Indian Economic History", *Indian Economic and Social History Review*, March.

Redding, G.S. (1990), *The Spirit of Chinese Capitalism*, W. de Gruyter, Berlin and New York.

Reddy, T.N. (1978), *India Mortgaged; A Marxist Leninist Appraisal*, Tarimela Nagi Reddy Memorial Trust, Andhra Pradesh, India.

Reddy, Y.V. (1998), "Indian Economy: Retrospect and Prospects", *The Asian Economic Review, Journal of Indian Institute of Economics*, Hyderabad, India, Vol-XL, No-3, December.

Reilly, C. (1992), 'Foreword', in Carroll, T.F., *Intermediary NGOs: The Supporting Link in Grassroots Development*, Kumarian, West Hartford, CT.

Resnick, S. A. and Wolff, R. D. (1987), *Knowledge and Class: A Marxist Critique of Political Economy*, University of Chicago Press, Chicago.

Richard, J.F. (1990), "The Seventeenth-Century Crisis in South Asia," *Modern Asian Studies*, 24.

———. (1997), 'Early Modern India and World History', *Journal of World History*, Vol. 8, No. 2.

———. (1983), *Precious Metals in the Later Medieval and Early Modern Worlds (ed)*, Carolina Academic Press, Durham, N.C.

Richter, W. (1975), 'Electoral patterns in post-princely India' in Myron Weiner and John Osgood Field, *Electoral politics in the Indian states: Three disadvantaged sectors* (ed.), Monohar Books, Delhi.

Rikowski, G. (2004) ,Marx and the Education of the Future, *Policy Futures in Education*, Vol.2 Nos. 3 & 4.

Roberts, A. (1994), *Eminent Churchillians*, Weidenfield & Nicolson, London.

Robertson, B.C. (1999), *The Essential Writings of Raja Rammohan Ray* (Ed), OUP, India.

Robinson, W. (2005). *Theory of Global Capitalism: Production, Class and State in a Transnational World*, Johns Hopkins University Press, Baltimore.

Rodrik, D (2004): 'Institutions, Integration and Geography: In Search of the Deep Determinants of Economic Growth' in Dani Rodrick (ed), *Modern Economic Growth: Analytical Country Studies*, Princeton University Press, Princeton.

Rodrik, D (2004): 'Why India Can Grow at 7 Per Cent a Year or More, Projections and Reflections', *EPW*, April 17.

Rodrik, D and A Subramanian (2004): 'From "Hindu Growth" to Productivity Surge: The Mystery of the Indian Growth Transition', NBER Working Paper No 10376, March.

Rose, G. (1978), *The Melancholy Science: An Introduction to the Thought of Theodor Adorno*, The MacMillan Press Ltd, London.

Roy, Tirthankar. (2000), *The Economic History of India 1857-1947*, OUP, New Delhi.

Roy, Tirthankar. (2002), 'Economic history and modern India: Redefining the link.' *Journal of Economic Perspectives*, 16(3).

Ruccio, D. Resnick, S. and R. Wolff. (1990), "Class Beyond the Nation-State", *Review of Radical Political Economics*, Vol- 22, No. 1.

Rupert, M. (1995), Producing Hegemony: The Politics of Mass Production and American Global Power, Cambridge University Press, Cambridge.

Saez, L. (2002), *Federalism without a Centre: The impact of Political and Economic Reform on Indian System*, Sage, New Delhi.

Sahlins, M. (1974). *Stone Age Economics*, Tavistock Publications, London.

Sahu, B.P. (1987), 'Ancient Orissa: The Dynamics of Internal Transformation of Tribal Society', in K.M. Shrimali (ed), *Essays in Indian Art, Religion and Society*, Munshiram Manoharlal Publishers, New Delhi.

———. (1993), Aspects of Rural Economy in Early Medieval Orissa, *Social Scientist*, Vol. 21, No. 1-2, January-February.

———. (2001), 'Brahminical Ideology, Regional Identities and the Construction of Early India', *Social Scientist*, Vol. 29.

———. (2003), 'The Early State in Orissa: From the Perspective of Changing Forms of Patronage and Legitimation', in B. Pati, B. P. Sahu and T.K.Venkatasubramanian(eds), *Negotiating India's Past: Essays in Memory of Partha Sarathi Gupta*, Tulika, New Delhi.

Said, E. (1994), *Culture and Imperialism*, Vintage Book, New York.

Saldanha, V. (2003), 'Fundamentalists are not rooted in the truth of their religions', *National Catholic Reporter ; The Independent Newsweekly*, Vol. 1, No. 4, April, 23.

Samal, K.C. (1996), Features and determinants of rural non farm sector in India and Orissa: A Survey, *Occasional Paper, NCDS*, Bhubaneswar, and Orissa.

Samuelson, P.A. (1962), "Parable and Realism in Capital Theory: The Surrogate Production Function," *Review of Economic Studies*, June, 29.

Sandel, M. (1982), *Liberalism and the Limits of Justice*, Cambridge University Press, Cambridge.

Sangari, K and Vaid S. (1993), *Recasting Women: Essays Indian Colonial History* (eds), Kali for Women, New Delhi.

Sangari, Kumkum (1993), 'The 'Amenities of Domestic Life': Questions on Labour', *Social Scientist*, 21(9-11).

Sanyal, B. (1994), *Cooperative autonomy: the dialectics of state-NGO relationships in developing countries*, Research Series- 100, ILO, Geneva.

Sanyal, K. (2001), "Rethinking Development: Beyond the Narrative of Transition." *Margins*, Vol 1, No. II.

Sanyal, K. K. (1988). "Accumulation, Poverty and State in Third World Capital/Pre-Capital Complex", *Economic and Political Weekly: Review of Political Economy*, 23 (5).

———. (1993), "Capital, Primitive Accumulation, and the Third World: From Annihilation to Appropriation", *Rethinking Marxism* 3 (fall).

Saravanan, V. (2006), 'Colonial Agrarian Policies in the Tribal Areas of Madras Presidency: 1872–1947', *South Asia Research*, Vol. 26(1).

Sarkar, S. & Bhattacharya, S. (2007), *Towards Freedom; Documents on the Movement for Independence in India 1946*, Part 1, OUP, New Delhi.

Sarkar, S. (1973), *The Swadeshi Movement in Bengal, 1903-1908*, People's Publishiing House, New Delhi.

Sarkar, T. (1996), 'Educating the Children of the Hindu Rashtra', in Bidwai, P., Mukhia, M. & Vanaik, A. (eds), *Religion, Religiosity and Communalism*, Manohar, New Delhi.

Saul, S.B. (1960), *Studies in British Overseas Trade 1870-1913*, Liverpool University Press, Liverpool, UK.

Sayer, A. (1992), *Method in Social Science: A Realist Approach*, Routledge, London.

———. (1992), *Method in Social Science: A Realist Approach*, Routledge, London.

———. (1997), 'The Dialectic of Culture and Economy', in R. Lee and J. Wills (eds.), *Geographies of Economies*, Arnold, London.

———. (2000a), *Realism and Social Science*, Sage, London.

———. (2000b), 'For postdisciplinary studies: Sociology and the Curse of Disciplinary Parochialism/Imperialism', in Eldridge, J., MacInnes, J., Scott, S., Warhurst, C., and Witz, A., (eds) *Sociology: Legacies and Prospects*, Sociology Press, Durham.

———. (2005), Reductionism in Social Science, Paper for workshop on "Challenges to Dominant Modes of Knowledge: Reductionism," Dec. 16-17, 2005, Paris, France, published by Department of Sociology, Lancaster University, Lancaster, U.K.

Schudson, M. (1993), *Advertising, The Uneasy Persuasion: Its Dubious Impact on American Society*, Routledge, London.

Schufflebeam, D. L., Madaus, F. G. & Scriven, M. S. (1983), Evaluation Models: Viewpoints on Educational and Human Services Evaluation, Kluwer-Hijhof, Boston.

Scott, A.M. (1979), "Who are the Self Employed?", pp-105-132, in R.Bromley and C. Gerry (eds), *Casual Work and Poverty in Third World Cities, John Wiley,* Chichester, England.

Scoville, J. (1996), Labor Market Underpinnings of a Caste Economy: Foiling the Coase Theorem, *American Journal of Economics and Sociology*, 55.

Seers, D. (1969), 'The Meaning of Development', *International Development Review*, 11(4).

Semelin, J. (2007), *Purify and Destroy: The Political Uses of Massacre and Genocide*, Columbia University Press, New York.

Sen, A. & Himanshu, (2004a), 'Poverty and Inequality in India 1', *EPW*, September 18.

Sen, A. & Himanshu, (2004b), 'Poverty and Inequality in India 2: Widening Disparities during the 1990s', *EPW*, September 25.

Sen, A. (1981), *Poverty and Famine*, Clarendon Press, Oxford.

————. (1982). *The State, Industrialisation and Class Formations in India,* Routledge & Kegan Paul, London.

————. (2006), *Identity and Violence; The Illusion of Destiny*, Allen Lane, London.

Sen, K.M. (2005), *Hinduism*, Penguin Books India, New Delhi.

Sen, P. K., Panda, H., Mishra, H. Modi, P.J. and Choudhary, K. (2002a), '*Impact Assessment Study of Rural Development Programmes in Kalahandi District of Orissa* ', unpublished report sponsored by the Ministry of Rural Development, Government of India (Monitoring Division), Institute of Rural Management, Anand.

Sen, P. K., Panda, H., Mishra, H. Modi, P.J. and Choudhary, K. (2002b), '*Impact Assessment Study of Rural Development Programmes in Bolangir District of Orissa* ', unpublished report, sponsored by the Ministry of Rural Development, Government of India (Monitoring Division). Institute of Rural Management, Anand.

Senapati, N. & Kuanr D.C. (1980), *Orissa District Gazetteers; Kalahandi*, Gazetteers Unit, Department of Revenue, Government of Orissa, Cuttack.

Sethi, K.N. (2002), 'Maritime Commerce of Orissa in the Seventeenth Century', *Utkal Historical Research Journal*, Vol-XV.

Shakow, D.M. & Graham, J. (1983), 'The Impact of the Changing International Division of Labor on the Labor Force in Mature Industrial Regions', *Antipode*, 15 (2).

Shanin T. (1982), "Defining Peasants; Conceptualizations and De-conceptualizations; Old and New in a Marxist Debate", *The Sociological Review,* Vol.30, No.3, August.

Sharma, R. (1997), *Gandhian Economics*, Deep and Deep, New Delhi.

Sharma, R. S. (1980) *Indian Feudalism*, Macmillan, Delhi.

Sharma, R. S. (1983), *Material Culture and Social Formations in Ancient India*, Macmillan, Delhi.

Sharma, R. S. (1985), "How Feudal Was Indian Feudalism?" *The Journal of Peasant Studies* 12, no. (2&3).

Sheth, D.L (2001), 'Globalizing Democracy versus Deepening of Democracy: The Post-Cold War Discourse', paper presented in the Lokayan seminar on '*Globalization and South Asia*', Centre for the Study of Developing Societies, Delhi, 29-31 August 2001.

Shylendra H.S. and Bhirdikar, K. (2005), 'Good Governance' and Poverty Alleviation Programmes: A Critical Analysis of the Swarnjayanti Gram Swarozgar Yojana', *International Journal of Rural Management* , 2005; 1; 203.

Sillitoe, P. (1998), "The development of indigenous knowledge", *Current Anthropology*, 39.

Simmel, G. (1978), *The Philosophy of Money*, Routledge and Kegan Paul, London.

Singh, A.K. (1995), Development, Deprivation and Discontent of Tribals in India. In *Tribals in India: Development, Deprivation, Discontent* (eds) A.K. Singh & M.K. Jabbi, Har Anand, New Delhi.

Singh, K S (1993): 'The Problem' in Marginalized Tribals', *Seminar* (412).

Singh, P. (1999). Capital, State and Nation in India: Reflections with Reference to Punjab. *International Journal of Punjab Studies (IJPS)*, 6 (1), January-June.

————. (2005) Hindu Bias in India's 'Secular' Constitution: Probing Bias in the Instruments of Governance, *Third World Quarterly*, Vol-26, No-6.

————. (2007) 'Political Economy of Centralization in India: Some Critical Notes from a Decentralist Perspective', in Nayak, B. S, ed. ', *Nationalizing Crisis; Political Economy of Public Policy in Contemporary India* , Atlantic Publishers, New Delhi.

Sinha, S. (2003), 'Development Counter-Narratives: Taking Social Movements Seriously', in Sivaramakrishan, K. & Agrawal, A. (ed), *Regional Modernities; The Cultural Political of Development in India*, Stanford University Press, California.

Sinha, A. (2006), *The Regional Roots of Developmental Politics in India: A Divided Leviathan*, OUP, New Delhi.

Sinha, B.N. (1971), *Geography of Orissa*, National Book Trust, New Delhi.

Sinha, D.P. (1986), *Culture Change in an Inter Tribal Market*, Asia Publishing House, Bombay.

Sinha, N.K. (1961), *The Economic History of Bengal*, Mukhopadhyay, Calcutta.

Sinha, R. & Lakra, V. (2005), 'Wild tribal food plants of Orissa', *Indian Journal of Traditional Knowledge*, Vol. 4(3).

Sinha, R. & Lakra, V. (2007), 'Edible weeds of tribals of Jharkhand, Orissa and West Bengal', *Indian Journal of Traditional Knowledge*, Vol. 6(1).

Sinha, Sachchidanand (1973), *The Internal Colony: A Study in Regional Exploitation*, Sindhu Publications, New Delhi.

Sivan,R.P. (2005), *Hinduism for Beginners; An concise introduction to the Eternal Path to Liberation*, Simha Publications, Sydney.

Slater, D. (1997), *Consumer Culture and Modernity*, Polity Press, Cambridge.

Smelser NJ, Swedberg R. (1994), *The Handbook of Economic Sociology*, Princeton University Press, Princeton, NJ.

Smelser, NJ. & Swedberg R. (1994), *The Handbook of Economic Sociology*, Princeton University Press, Princeton, NJ.

Sofer, E.F. (1980), "Recent Trends in Latin American Labor Historiography", *Latin American Research Review*, XV (1).

Soper, Kate (1981), *On Human Needs: Open and Closed Theories in Marxist Perspective*, Atlantic Highlands, Humanities Press, NJ.

Spellman, J. W. (1964), *Political Theory of Ancient India: A Study of Kingship from the Earliest Times to circa A.D. 300*, Clarendor Press, Oxford.

Srinivas, M.N. (1969), *India's Villages* (ed.), Asia Publishing House, Bombay.

Srinivasan, T N and S Tendulkar (2003): *Reintegrating India with the World Economy*, Institute for International Economics, Washington DC.

Starn, O. (1995), 'To revolt against the revolution: war and resistance in Peru.s Andes', *Cultural Anthropology*, 10(4).

Stavenhagen, Rodolfo. (1965), "Classes, colonialism, and acculturation: Essay on a system of inter-ethnic relations in Mesoamerica," *Studies in Comparative International Development*, 1.

Stavenhagen, Rodolfo. (1996), *Ethnic Conflicts and the Nation State*, St. Martin's Press, New York.

Stcherbasky, F. T. (1962), *Buddhist Logic*, Vol-1 & 2, Dover, New York.

Stein, B. (1985), *Peasant State and Society in Medieval South India*, Oxford University Press, New Delhi.

Stein, B. (1992), *The Making of Agrarian Policy in British India 1770–1900(ed)*, OUP, Oxford.

Stigler, G. (1961), The Economics of Information, *Journal of Political Economy* 69.

Stiglitz, J. E., (2000), The Contributions of the Economics of Information to Twentieth Century Economics, *Quarterly Journal of Economics*, 115, 4.

————. (2004), 'Capital Market Liberalization, Globalization and the IMF', *Oxford Review of Economic Policy*, Vol- 20, No-1.

Stirrat, R. (1996), 'The New Orthodoxy and Old Truths: Participation, Empowerment and Other Buzzwords', in Bastian, S. & Bastian, N. (eds), *Assessing Participation: A Debate From South Asia*, Kornark Publisher, New Delhi.

Stirrat, R., (2000). "Cultures of consultancy", *Critique of Anthropology*, March Issue, Vol.20, No.1.

Subrahmanyam, S. (1997), 'Connected histories: notes towards a reconfiguration of early modern Eurasia', *Modern Asian Studies*, 31(3).

Subramanian, L. (1985), 'Capital and Crowd in a Declining Asian Port City; The Anglo-Bania Order and the Surat Riots of 1797', *Modern Asian Studies*, Vol-19, No-2.

Subramanian, L. (1987), 'Banias and the British: The Role of Indigenous Credit in the Process of Imperial Expansion in Western India in the Second Half of the Eighteenth Century', *Modern Asian Studies*, Vol. 21, No. 3.

Sundar, N. (2004), 'Teaching to Hate: RSS Pedagogical Programme', *EPW*, 17 April.

Swain, M. & Swain, M. (2005), 'Impact of Super Cyclone on Lives and Livelihood of Women; a micro level study of two coastal districts of Orissa', *Asian Economic Review*, 47 (3).

Swain, M. (2003), 'Trends in Agrarian Structure in Orissa', *Indian Journal of Regional Science*, Vol-XXXV, No-2.

Swaminathan, M. (2000), *Weakening Welfare - the Public Distribution of Food in India*, LeftWord, New Delhi.

Taradatt, Dr. (2001), *Tribal Development in India with a special reference to Orissa*, Gyan Publishing House, New Delhi.

Taylor, J.G. (1974), "Neo-Marxism and Underdevelopment: a Sociological Phantasy", *Journal of Contemporary Asian*, IV (I).

Taylor, J.G. (1979), *From Modernization to Modes of Production: A Critique of the Sociologies of Development and Underdevelopment*, Macmillan, London.

Teltumbde, A. (2006), Hindu Fundamentalism Politics in India; the alliance with the American Empire, in Hadiz, V.R., *Empire and Neoliberalism in Asia* (ed.), Routledge, London.

———. (1996), "Impact of New Economic Reforms on Dalits in India'', A Paper Presented in the Seminar on *'Economic Reforms and Dalits in India'* Organized by the University of Oxford, Oxford, UK, on November 8, 1996.

Thapar, R. (1966), *A History of India*, Vol-1, Penguine, London.

———. (1968), "Interpretation of ancient Indian history", *History and Theory*, 7 (3).

———. (1978), *Ancient Indian Social History*, Orient Longman, New Delhi.

———. (1984), *From Lineage to State, Social Formations in the Mid-First Millennium B.C. in the Ganga Valley*, Bombay, OUP, New York.

———. (1993), *Interpreting Early India*, OUP, New Delhi.

Thiongo, Ngugi wa. (1996), 'Decolonizing the Means of Imagination', in *Symphony of Freedom*, AIPRF, Hyderabad, India.

Thomson, S. & Robert, W. E. (1960), *Types of Indian Oral Tales*. FFC. Helsinki.

Thorner, A. (1982), 'Semi-feudalism or capitalism? Contemporary debate on classes and modes of production in India', *Economic and Political Weekly*, 17, 49, 50 and 51.

Tinbergen, J (1965), International *Economic Integration*, Second Revised Edition, Elservier Publishing Company, Amsterdam.

Tomlinson B.R. (1988) 'British Business in India, 1860-1970' in 1970' in Davenport, R.P., Hines, T. and Jones, G. (eds), *British Business in Asia since 1860*, Cambridge University Press, New York.

———. (1975), "India and the British Empire, 1880- 1935", *The Indian Economic and Social History Review*, 12, 4.

———. (1988), The Historical Roots of Indian Poverty: Issues in the Economic and Social History of Modern South Asia, *Modern Asian Studies*, 22.

———. (1993), *The Economy of Modern India 1860–1970*, Cambridge University Press, Cambridge.

Tordello, J. (2003), 'The Anti-Politics Machine Revisited; The Accommodation of Power and the Depoliticization of Development and Relief in Rural India', *Working Paper Series No-03-43, DESTIN*, LSE, London.

Tripathy, A.K. (1992), 'Revenue Laws and Land Administration in Orissa - A Critique', *The Administrator*, 37.

Tripati, S. & Vora, K.H. (2005), 'Maritime heritage in and around Chilika Lake, Orissa: Geological evidences for its decline', *Current Science*, Vol. 88, No. 7.

Tripati, S. (2002), 'Early Maritime Activities of Orissa on the East Coast of India: Linkages in Trade and Cultural Developments', *Man and Environment*, XXVII (1).

Trout, J.D. (1991), "Reductionism and the Unity of Science", in Boyd, Gasper and Trout (eds), *The Philosophy of Science*, MIT Press, Cambridge, MA.

Turner, B.S. (1994), *Orientalism, Postmodernism and Globalism*, Routledge, London/New York.

Uberoi, J.PS. (1996), *Religion, Civil Society and the State: A Study on Sikhism*, OUP, New Delhi.

Unnithan-Kumar, M. (1997), *Identity, Gender and Poverty: New Perspectives on Caste and Tribe in Rajasthan*, Berghahn Books, Oxford.

Vakil, C.N. (1924), *Financial Development in Modern India*, P.S.King and sons Ltd., London.

Vander Pijl, Kees. (2006), A Lockean Europe? *New Left Review*, 37, January-February, Second Series.

Varshney, A. (1995), *Democracy, development and the countryside: urban-rural struggles in India*, Cambridge University Press, New York.

Venable, V. (1966), *Human Nature: The Marxian View*, World Publishing, Cleveland.

Venkatasubbiah, H. (1961), *Indian Economy since Independence*, Asia Publishing House, London.

Venkatesh, A. & Suguna Swamy (1994), ' India as an Emerging Consumer Society: A Cultural Analysis'. In Clifford Schultz II, Russell Belk & Guliz Ger(Eds.) *Research in Consumer Behavior: Consumption in Marketing Economies, Vol. 7,*Greenwich JAI Press.

Venkatesh, A. (1994), ' India's Changing Consumer Economy: A Cultural Perspective'. In *Advances in Consumer Research Vol. 21.*

Venkatesh, A. (1995), "Ethno consumerism: A New Paradigm to Study Cultural and Cross-cultural Consumer Behavior," in J.A. Costa & G. Bamossy (eds.), *Marketing in a Multicultural World*, SAGE Publications, London.

Vidyarthi, L.P. & Rai, B.K. (1985), *The Tribal Culture of India*, Concept Publishing Company, New Delhi.

Vidyarthi, L.P. (1963), *The Maler*, Bookland, Calcutta.

Vidyarthi, L.P. (1970), *Socio-Cultural Implications of Industrialization in India: A Case Study of Tribal Bihar*, Council of Social and Cultural Research, Ranchi, India.

————. (1971), *Life and Culture in Andaman and Nicobar Islands*, MSS, Ranchi.

————. (1986), "Research on Tribal Culture in India", in Nayar, P.K.B. (1986), *Sociology in India: Retrospect and Prospect*, BR Publishing Corporation, New Delhi.

Virmani, A (1997): 'Economic Development and Transition in India', paper presented at the Tokyo dialogue on alternatives to the World Bank-IMF approach to reforms and growth, Economic Planning Agency, Tokyo, Japan, November 7.

Vyas, N.N. & Mann, R.S. (1980), *Indian Tribes in Transition*, Rawat Publications, New Delhi.

Vyas, N.N. (1980), *Bondage and Exploitation in Tribal India*, Rawat Publications, New Delhi.

Wallerstein, I. (1991), "The Construction of Peoplehood: Racism, Nationalism, Ethnicity", in Etienne Balibar & Immanuel Wallerstein (1991), *Race, Nation, Class; Ambiguous Identities,* Verso, London.

Warren, D.M. (1989), 'Linking scientific and indigenous agricultural systems', pp. 153-170 in J.L. Compton (ed), The transformation of international agricultural research and development, Lynne Rienner, Boulder.

Warren, D.M. (1990), Using indigenous knowledge in agricultural development, *World Bank Discussion Paper* 127. Washington DC: World Bank.

Warren, D.M., G.W. von Liebenstein and L. Slikkerveer (1993) 'Networking for indigenous knowledge', *Indigenous Knowledge and Development Monitor*, 1 (1).

Warriner, D.(1969), *Land Reform in Principle and Practice*, OUP, Oxford.

Weber, M. (1905), *The Protestant Ethic and The Spirit of Capitalism,* translated by Talcott Parsons (1930) and forwarded by R. H. Tawney (1958), Allen & Unwin, London.

————. (1968), *The Religion of India,* translated and edited by Hans H. Gerth and Don Martindale, Free Press, New York.

————. (1963), *The Sociology of Religion,* trans. Ephraim Fischoff, Beacon Press, Boston.

———. (2002), *The Protestant Ethic and the Spirit of Capitalism,* 3rd ed., translated by Stephen Kalberg Roxbury, Los Angeles.

Whitcombe, E.M. (1971), *Agrarian Conditions in Northern India,* Vol. I, University of California Press, Berkeley.

Williamson, O. E. (1985), *The Economic Institutions of Capitalism,* Free Press, New York.

Wolf, E. (1981), 'The mills of inequality' in G. Berreman (ed.) *Social inequality: Comparative and developmental approaches,* Academic Press, New York.

Wolf, E.R. (1973), *Peasant wars of the twentieth century,* Faber, London.

Wolpert, S. (2000), *A New History of India,* OUP, New York.

Wong, S. (1978), *The Foundations of Paul Samuelson's Revealed Preference Theory,* Routledge & Kegan Paul, London.

Woodhall, M. (2007), Funding Higher Education: The Contribution of Economic Thinking to Debate and Policy Development, *Education Working Paper Series-8,* World Bank, Washington DC.

World Bank (1997), *World Development Report; State in a Changing World,* OUP, New York.

World Bank (2003), *India: Sustaining Reform, Reducing Poverty,* World Bank, Washington DC.

World Bank (2006), 'India: Inclusive Growth and Service Delivery: Building on India's Success', *Development Policy Review,* Report No 34580-IN, Washington DC.

World Bank (2008), *Orissa in Transition: From Fiscal Turnaround to Rapid and Inclusive Growth,* May/June, 2008, Poverty Reduction and Economic Management, India Country Management Unit, South Asia Region, New Delhi.

World Bank Report (2000/2001), *Attacking Poverty (2001),* Oxford University Press for the World Bank, Oxford.

World Bank. (1986). *Financing Education in Developing Countries: An Exploration of Policy Options.* World Bank, Washington DC.

World Bank. (1988). *Education in Sub-Saharan Africa: Policies for Adjustment, Revitalization and Expansion.* World Bank, Washington DC.

World Bank. (1994). *Higher Education: The Lessons of Experience.* World Bank, Washington DC.

World Bank. (1995). *Priorities and Strategies for Education.* World Bank, Washington DC.

World Bank. (2002). *Constructing Knowledge Societies: New Challenges for Tertiary World,* Princeton University Press, Princeton, NJ.

Yadav, Y. (1999), "The BJP's New Social Bloc", Based on CSDS post-election survey analysis, *Frontline,* Volume-16, Issue 23.

———. (2003), "The Patterns and Lessons", *Frontline,* Vol- 19, Issue No. 26.

Yamin, M. (2004), 'Orissa and South East Asia: Recent Perspectives', *Orissa Historical Research Journal (OHRJ),* Vol. XLVII, No. 3.

Zamoshkin, Y. A. & Melvil, A. Y., (1982), Between Neo-Liberalism and Neo-Conservatism, In Edward D' Angelo et al, eds, *Contemporary East European Marxism,* Vol-II, p-225, Amsterdam.

Zavos, J. (2000), *The Emergence of Hindu Nationalism in India,* OUP, New Delhi.

Zivetz L. (1991), *Doing Good: The Australian NGO Community,* Allen & Unwin, North Sydney.